No Ordinary Joe

THE BIOGRAPHY OF JOE PATERNO

No Ordinary Joe

THE BIOGRAPHY OF JOE PATERNO

MICHAEL O'BRIEN

RUTLEDGE HILL PRESS®
NASHVILLE, TENNESSEE

Published in Nashville, Tennessee, by Rutledge Hill Press®, 211 Seventh Avenue North, Nashville, Tennessee 37219.

Distributed in Canada by H. B. Fenn & Company, Ltd., 34 Nixon Road, Bolton, Ontario L7E 1W2.

Distributed in Australia by The Five Mile Press Pty., Ltd., 22 Summit Road, Noble Park, Victoria 3174.

Distributed in New Zealand by Tandem Press, 2 Rugby Road, Birkenhead, Auckland 10.

Distributed in the United Kingdom by Verulam Publishing, Ltd., 152a Park Street Lane, Park Street, St. Albans, Hertfordshire AL2 2AU.

Typography by E. T. Lowe, Nashville, TN.

Library of Congress Cataloging-in-Publication Data

O'Brien, Michael, 1943–
    No ordinary joe : the biography of Joe Paterno / Michael O'Brien.
      p.   cm.
    Includes bibliographical references.
    ISBN 1–55853–668–X
    1. Paterno, Joe, 1926– .   2. Football coaches—United States--Biography.   3. Pennsylvania State University—Football—History.
I. Title.
GV939.P37037 1998
796.332'092—dc21
[B]   98-19014
                                              CIP

Printed in the United States of America

1 2 3 4 5 6 7 8 9—02 01 00 99 98

∼ Contents ∼

Acknowledgments		vii
Introduction		ix
1.	EARLY YEARS (1926–1950)	1
2.	RESTLESS AND AMBITIOUS (1950–1965)	41
3.	FOOTBALL THE PATERNO WAY (1966–1978)	64
4.	STRIVING FOR NUMBER ONE (1978–1986)	103
5.	PROFILE: THE PATERNO COACHING SYSTEM	141
6.	PROFILE: PLAYER RELATIONS AND THE GRAND EXPERIMENT	175
7.	PROFILE: PERSONALITY, VALUES, CRITICS	213
8.	PROFILE: PUBLIC SERVICE, FAMILY, LEISURE	244
9.	RECENT YEARS	263
	Endnotes	304
	Sources	321
	Interviews	325
	Index	326

To Margaret O'Brien
and
Sally O'Brien

∽ ACKNOWLEDGMENTS ∽

During the nearly ten years that this book has been in progress, I have incurred many debts and am delighted to express my deep gratitude. Judy Fenush, Shirley Irwin, and L. Budd Thalman assisted me while I studied clippings at the office of sports information at Penn State. Special thanks to former Penn State athletic director Jim Tarman. I am also grateful for the valuable assistance of librarians and archivists, including Martha Mitchell at the Brown University Library, and Leon Stout and Mildred Allen at Penn State.

Several persons graciously gave me (or lent me) valuable papers at their disposal. Among them were John Alexander, Ed Barry, Michael Bezilla, Nancy Cline, G. David Gearhart, Marie Giffone, John Hanlon, Rosemary McGinn, Veronica Perrone, Henry Sims Jr., and John Swinton. For their kindness and special assistance I want to thank Thomas Bermingham, Ron Bracken, Ron Christ, George Paterno, and Neil Rudel.

This is not an authorized study. I did not ask permission of Joe Paterno to write my book, preferring instead to write independently. Nonetheless, I appreciate the consideration and hospitality of Joe and Sue Paterno during my interviews with them.

As in my previous books I have placed a heavy burden on the staff at the University of Wisconsin–Fox Valley who have, nonetheless, responded with good humor, patience, and an extraordinary commitment of time and energy. Kathy Hosmer typed many drafts of the book, and Patricia Warmbrunn efficiently processed hundreds of interlibrary loan requests.

In the early stages of my study I received important and timely grants from the University of Wisconsin–Fox Valley and the University of

Wisconsin–Fox Cities Foundation, Inc. In addition, the University of Wisconsin awarded me a sabbatical during a critical stage of my writing.

I owe a special debt of gratitude to my volunteer typist, Reighe Nagel, who for over four years expertly and quickly typed many drafts of the manuscript.

My wife, Sally, graciously endured another book with patience, encouragement, and love. Once again, thanks to my children Tim, Sean, Jeremy, and Carey for all the love and enjoyment they bring me.

∾ INTRODUCTION ∾

To some people Joe Paterno seems complex—a "grand collection of contradictions," said one observer. Sportswriter Bill Lyon noted that Paterno has been called, at one time or another, a "modern Renaissance man, a latter-day Don Quixote, an educator, a motivator, a do-gooder, an intimidator, a hypocrite, a pious fraud, a tiresome dispenser of righteousness, a genius, and a choker." Another sportswriter, Ron Bracken of the *Centre Daily Times*, Paterno's hometown newspaper, described a different mix of traits. "Paterno can be cranky, tyrannical, dictatorial, blunt, scathing, charming, beguiling, entertaining, and witty, all in the span of thirty minutes."

No one disputes, though, that since 1966, when he became head football coach at Penn State University, Joe Paterno has been one of the nation's most successful college coaches. Through the 1997 season Joe had compiled a record of 298-77-3 in thirty-two seasons. (He came to Penn State in 1950 as an assistant coach and has never coached anywhere else.) He has guided his teams to two national championships, four national championship games, and seven undefeated regular seasons. The recipient of numerous honors, Paterno was selected by *Sports Illustrated* as its 1986 Sportsman of the Year, and his peers in the American Football Coaches Association four times have named him Coach of the Year.

Joe's "folk hero" reputation in Pennsylvania has spawned an entire line of Paterno products, including coffee mugs ("Cup of Joe"), life-size cardboard cutouts ("Standup Joe"), and golf balls with his familiar face ("like the Penn State offense, three out of four guaranteed to go up the middle"). He also has been the only college football coach ever to second the nomination of a president of the United States.

The acclaim for Joe Paterno has stemmed largely from the contrast between the high academic and moral standards he has tried to exemplify and the shameless conduct that often embarrasses and dishonors the college sport he cherishes. Intense pressure burdens coaches and athletic administrators at major schools. Because college football competes for the "entertainment dollar," it has to put on a "good performance." A good performance means not only defeating traditional rivals but also emerging with a winning record and a high ranking in the national wire-service polls. "Only those teams at the top of the polls filled stadiums, received bowl invitations, appeared regularly on network television, and generated adequate revenues to finance their expensive athletic programs," observed sports historian Benjamin Rader.

Given the high stakes involved in fielding winning teams, temptations to cheat are difficult to resist. Head coaches are especially vulnerable. Since recruiting blue-chip athletes is crucial to success, illegal inducements are sometimes offered. Alumni and booster groups, often with the tacit approval of the coaches, give athletes cash, fancy cars, new clothes, rent-free apartments, and high-paying summer jobs.

To obtain the admission of an outstanding athlete with a poor high school or junior college academic record, coaches sometimes tamper with transcripts and make up deficiencies in hours of college credits or grades by arranging for easy correspondence or extension division courses.[1]

"The fundamental illogic of sending functional illiterates into college classrooms has not yet dawned on educators and administrators," sportswriter John Underwood complained in 1979. "They would rather be liberal than right. They have consistently made it easy for the coach to bring in nonstudents as students as long as they can negotiate one hundred yards in 9.5 seconds."[2]

Under Joe's long leadership, however, Penn State's football program has never been accused of significant wrongdoing by any official investigative body. It has never been on probation and never been cited by the NCAA for major violation of its rules. Moreover, shortly after becoming head coach, Joe proclaimed his Grand Experiment, an effort to prove that academic standards and excellent football could coexist at the university. He often harped on the theme. Defensive lineman Steve Smear, whose father had died when Steve was a child, was the first member of his family to attend college. Early in his career at

Penn State in the 1960s, he skipped many classes and did poorly in his courses, sparking Joe's concern. "If you fell down academically," said Smear, "you had to go [into Joe's office], sit down, and look him in the face." Joe told Smear: "I promised your mother that you would get an education. Don't disappoint her. Don't disappoint me. Straighten it out or you'll never play here." Smear straightened out his career, served as co-captain of the team his junior and senior years, and dramatically improved his grade-point average.[3]

While proclaiming Penn State's Grand Experiment, Paterno also tried to make other athletic programs live up to his school's same high standards. "I have a tendency to get on a soapbox and preach," he concedes, and he can't help himself. Argumentative, when he sees something he thinks is wrong, he feels compelled to point it out.

As a result of his efforts and the efforts of other reformers to clean up big-time college athletics, public awareness of unethical practices has increased, college administrators have extended their vigilance, academic expectations have risen, and penalties have been stiffened.[4]

Skeptics, though, have believed that Joe has benefited from Penn State's remote location in State College, Pennsylvania, which they say isolates him from sophisticated, critical reporters from large metropolitan newspapers. Occasionally, disgruntled former players have publicly criticized him; others have grumbled privately. Detractors in the media have disliked the secrecy surrounding the Penn State program; and a few people have labeled Joe's Grand Experiment a publicity ploy. Most often, critics have accused him of being insufferably self-righteous. After one of Joe's speeches, in which he downplayed the importance of winning, saying "it is the competition that gives us pleasure," a rival coach commented, "It's enough to make us all throw up."[5]

Joe has struck most observers, though, as deeply sincere. In a sport often overwhelmed by scandal and unsavory characters, he has seemed like a breath of fresh air. A reporter for the *Boston Globe* described him as the "Voice of Ethics." Joe demonstrates how to win without compromising important principles as many of our country's "leaders" have done in their pursuit of winning. One of Joe's former high school classmates thought that America's youth "needs to see that you don't have to be a crook, or a sleaze, or a liar in order to win."[6]

~1~

EARLY YEARS (1926–1950)

JOE PATERNO'S ANCESTORS WERE AMONG THE MILLIONS OF EMIGRANTS WHO FLED SOUTHERN ITALY, ONE OF THE POOREST, MOST BACKWARD REGIONS OF EUROPE. In the last decades of the nineteenth century, the region experienced near economic collapse. Agriculture suffered a severe depression, and earthquakes, volcanic eruptions, floods, and disease intensified the despair, sapping the strength of both the people and the land, and weakening the bonds that tied peasants to their villages. The northern Italians, more educated, skilled, and wealthy, looked with disdain on the illiterate, unskilled, and seemingly shiftless southerners.

Five million Italians immigrated to the United States between 1876 and 1930, and 80 percent came from the south. Most of the southern arrivals were poor and illiterate, and more than three-quarters were farm workers or laborers with no skill of value in the urban, industrial setting of the United States. They settled in large American cities, like New York, where dozens of "Little Italys," many of them squalid slums, dotted the landscape. Congregated in neighborhoods with others from the same region, they re-created urban villages or the Italian country town in the city environment. Because these immigrants arrived in such huge numbers over a short period of time, New York and other cities had difficulty absorbing and guiding them.

The flood of southern Italians (and other emigrants from southern and eastern Europe) aroused intense opposition in the United States. "The sewer is unchoked," ranted one nativist. "Europe is vomiting. She is pouring her scum on the American shore." Bias against southern Italians could be found almost everywhere. They were abused in public, cheated of wages, pelted in the streets, cuffed at work, fined and jailed on the smallest pretense, lynched by nativist mobs, and crowded into the reeking slums. Racists lumped them together with the "brownish" races, and sometimes with the blacks. "The dagoes are just as bad as the Negroes." Nativist sentiment led to the Immigration Restriction Act of 1924, which set up a quota system that deliberately and unashamedly discriminated against southern Italians and others from southern and eastern Europe. As late as the 1940s studies of prejudice listed Italian Americans near the bottom of American preferences.

Despite all the hardship and the discrimination, the southern Italians had powerful virtues. Most were sober, frugal, and hard-working. Although the poorest immigrants in New York City, they had the lowest rates of pauperism. Only a small fraction wound up on relief. The Catholic Church, the symbol of permanence and security, upheld the deepest values of Italian life. Above all, they valued the family. The Italian family was a stronghold in a hostile land, a bastion of warmth and security for its members. Divorce, separation, and desertion were rare. Married sons and daughters tended to stay close to their parents. Relatives helped one another to immigrate, shared households, lent money, and assisted in the search for jobs. Families remained bound closely by the strongest cement—a little wine, much talk, and much laughter. No Italian who had a family was ever alone.[1]

Joe Paterno's great-grandfather, Francisco Paterno (1835–1889), lived in the Italian village of Macchia Albanese in the province of Cosenza. The villagers were an enclave of Albanians who had fled Albania in the 1830s after the Turks gained control. According to the family's history, Francisco lived better than most southern Italians. Middle class and educated, Francisco became a gentleman farmer. His wife, Nucenza Lauritto (1840–1896), may have been a woman of some stature as she was the daughter of Joseph Lauritto, secretary to Baron Campana, the brother-in-law of the first king of Italy, Victor Emmanuel II.

For unknown reasons Vincent (1869–1930), one of their three children, immigrated to the United States as a young man and became a barber because, in his words, "it was clean and honest work, and [I] didn't have to live in a ghetto." He married Rose Mascaro (1872–1952) and the couple settled in Brooklyn, raising seven children. Far more successful than most southern Italians whose ancestors had recently arrived in the United States, five of the seven children eventually became professionals: two lawyers, a language teacher, an artist-teacher, and a newspaper editor.[2]

Joe's father, Angelo, the second child, was born on September 1, 1897. At seventeen Angelo dropped out of high school to enter the U.S. Army, where he helped General John Pershing chase Pancho Villa across Mexico and then fought in several major campaigns during World War I. After the war he decided he needed an education and began attending night classes. While he finished high school, he settled into a clerical job in the appellate division of the New York State Supreme Court.

On a blind date Angelo met Florence Cafiero and the couple married on September 5, 1925. Florence's ancestors had lived near Naples, Italy. Before the turn of the century, at sixteen, her father had come to America, then returned to Italy in his thirties, found a wife, and resettled in America. The Cafieros had a brood of children, of whom ten survived. Florence's father purchased a horse-drawn wagon and later a truck and hauled wholesale goods to a distribution center, a business successful enough to feed, clothe, and house his large family in a tenement on Troy Avenue in the Bedford-Stuyvesant neighborhood of Brooklyn. Florence was born on August 21, 1896, in the middle of the ten children. She grew independent, learning to fend for herself, and after high school she worked for the telephone company in New York City.

Born on Eighteenth Street in Brooklyn four days before Christmas 1926, Joseph Paterno was the first child of Florence and Angelo. A second son, George, was born twenty-one months later; a third boy, Franklin, died at fifteen months; and when Joe was nine a baby sister, Florence, arrived.[3]

Both of Joe's parents were remarkable, and their values and example affected Joe in strikingly intense ways. While working full-time, Angelo continued an arduous program of education. After work, for twelve years he pursued his college and law degrees at Saint John's University. Often exhausted, he sometimes fell asleep while studying at home. "He got discouraged," reflected his son George, "but he never quit." Finally, when Joe was fifteen, after Angelo had failed several attempts, he passed the New York state bar exam and was admitted to the bar. Meanwhile, he had worked his way up to become a court clerk, a judge's administrative assistant. "He was well respected in the family,"

said one of Joe's cousins about Angelo's perseverance. Joe was also deeply
impressed with his dad's fortitude. "When, as a little kid, you keep hearing of how your father finished high school at night, and then you see
him come home late every night from college classes, and then at the age
of fifteen you see all your uncles and aunts and cousins and neighbors
celebrate because your father passed the bar exam, you get the feeling
that education is really important," Joe reflected in his autobiography,
Paterno: By the Book (1989).

Short and stocky, Angelo was an immaculate dresser, more so than
other fathers in the neighborhood and in the parish. Honest and kind,
modest and unassuming, the elder Paterno took seriously his responsibilities as a father. "He was very, very interested in his [children]," recalled a
neighbor, Frank Mastoloni. Occasionally, Angelo brought Joe and George
to his office and sat them in the back of the courtroom to watch the court
proceedings, stimulating Joe's interest in becoming a lawyer.

Angelo believed that one could be successful in society without
compromising one's morals, integrity, or values. He seldom cursed—
except for an occasional "hell" or "damn." "I never heard him belittle any
ethnic group, or religion, or race," said George.[4]

Angelo emphasized two important values with Joe. First, he
wanted Joe to keep athletics in a healthy perspective, advice Joe would
wrestle with for decades. After Joe returned from a game of sandlot ball,
his father's first question was, "Did you have fun?" He never initially
asked, "Did you win?" In addition, Angelo emphasized the importance of
education. Most fathers did not attend the school conferences of their
children, but Angelo accompanied his wife to the conferences. "You have
my two sons," Angelo told one of Joe's teachers at their first meeting. (He
said it with the connotation, "You have my two *treasures*.") "I want you
to know me because I want to cooperate with you in any way I can in
ensuring my boys are doing their best work."

When his children brought home a complicated school assignment, Angelo encouraged them "to *think*, think *harder*." His father's constant challenge to think, think harder, stimulated Joe to become mentally
aggressive in the same way athletic games pushed him to become physically aggressive. Joe recalled: "In both ways, I always had the feeling that
I had to compete, had to stretch; that what I'm able to do at present is not
quite enough, that there's more, always a little more."

His father's example also sparked Joe's interest in politics and the opera. An avid Democrat, Angelo enjoyed political discussions, admired President Franklin D. Roosevelt, and did legwork and wrote speeches for local Democratic politicians. On Saturday afternoons Angelo turned on the radio to listen to live broadcasts of the New York Metropolitan Opera, making sure to expose his children to the highest quality in music.

The Paternos were comfortable and secure, but because of the depression and because Angelo dispensed most of his legal assistance gratis, the family was not wealthy. Whenever a friend or a relative encountered a legal problem, they called Angelo, and he would take care of it. Some insensitively took his free assistance for granted. "I really can't thank you enough," a relative told Angelo. "It would cost me a fortune to have a *real* lawyer." In 1955, at age fifty-eight, Angelo died suddenly of a heart attack. "Dad was a warm, wonderful human being who always saw only the best in people," recalled Joe. "He was always himself. Everybody who ever met him liked him."[5]

Joe came to have more drive and intensity than Angelo, a trait he inherited from his mother. Energetic, aggressive, and opinionated, Florence Paterno seemed in perpetual motion. Gentle Angelo Paterno won few arguments with his powerful wife. "You got the impression of a father and mother of very different types," reflected Fr. Thomas Bermingham, one of Joe's high school teachers, "the father kind of even-tempered [and] steady, whose wife might have been a little impatient with him at times. She impressed me as a very ambitious woman."

Florence was a fastidious, almost obsessive, housecleaner. "In our family," George joked, "you had to wear a tie to take out the garbage. My mother would say, 'What will the neighbors think?'" A gracious hostess, she constantly entertained her sisters and brothers and friends of the family.

Florence commanded, almost demanded, attention. In a conversation with her, it was difficult getting a word in edgewise. Even her husband couldn't command the last word about family matters. "In 90 percent of the cases she had the last say," said a neighbor. "My mother [had] to have the best," George observed, adding, "She'd compete with you for it." Because of her pride and ambition, Florence wanted the Paternos to have the best of everything—food, clothes, home. "We lived better than most of the other people who were Italian," George said.[6]

Florence particularly expected her firstborn son to be exemplary. At everything he did she wanted him to be at the top. "If we had a class-room spelling bee, I was expected to win it," Joe recalled. "I had to be able to do multiplication tables faster than anyone else." In class Joe's hand shot up immediately to answer questions. Why? "Because of the image in the back of my head of my mother expecting me to defend my honor, our family honor." Partly because of his mother's example and tutelage, Joe developed a hatred of losing, of settling for number two. "I probably absorbed my shame of losing from my mother," he said.[7]

As the son of Brooklyn-born, second-generation Italian immi-grants, Joe almost thoroughly adjusted to American life. In a few ways, though, the atmosphere at home was still quite Italian. That meant the Paternos spoke with flying hands as well as competing voices, especially, said Joe, "when my mother's six sisters and three brothers all piled in to visit at the same time to eat and outshout one another." They argued about everything. "Kids from the neighborhood would walk into our kitchen, unannounced, and sit in just to listen," Joe recalled.

Fortunately, though, Joe Paterno avoided the wretched slum con-ditions that scarred earlier generations of southern Italians. Because of his close-knit family, nearby relatives, and the tolerant attitude of most of his multiethnic neighbors, Joe encountered little prejudice near his home, but he quickly learned that the world outside his neighborhood still degraded southern Italians.

Florence did not encourage her children to learn Italian, fearing that non-Italian outsiders would consider the Paternos merely a family of wops. Nonetheless, pride would never allow her to tolerate an ethnic slur. When Joe complained that someone had called him a wop, she sat him down and recited from memory all the great Italians and their exploits: Michelangelo, Leonardo, Garibaldi, Columbus, Toscanini. "Remember," she proclaimed fiercely, "every knock is a boost."[8]

Both parents were devout Catholics and insisted that their chil-dren be honest and moral. "If you got ten cents too much in change from the little grocery, you had to go back and return it," said Joe's sister Flo-rence. Joe's mother particularly stressed industriousness and self-improvement. Joe learned the work ethic early on. Every night Florence washed clothes so the children would go to school absolutely clean. Angelo Paterno set an example by showing his children what hard work

Joe's dad, Angelo Paterno, was an avid Democrat who certainly would have winced at his son's Republican ties later in life. (Copies of photos provided by Penn State Sports Information Department)

Florence Paterno, Joe's mom, always expected her firstborn son to be the best at whatever he did.

could accomplish. "My dad never sat around," Joe said. "He was either doing something in the yard, writing, helping somebody do something."

"Not to work was probably the worst sin," George reflected. "Not to work, not to try to achieve something."

Besides being a close-knit family, the Paternos were a close-knit extended family as well. With Florence's sisters and brothers living nearby, there were scores of cousins for Joe to play with. "We used to visit and go out together," Joe later said of his cousins, "not like today when you go out with your friends. Our family were our friends."

"We were all like brothers," said Joe's cousin Nicholas Dambra. "We were very close."

At family gatherings on holidays the kids played until they were exhausted, then slept five to a bed until it was time to go home. When the youngsters became rowdy at the gatherings, Uncle John, a boxing fan, would say, "If you want to fight, let's get the gloves out." Making an informal ring and offering a fifty-cent prize for the winner, Uncle John refereed as the cousins flailed away. Joe used correct form in his matches, but when bigger and stronger cousins clouted him, he backed off. Uncle John also arranged spelling contests, offering the winner a nickel, dime, or quarter, depending on the difficulty of the word.[9]

Florence insisted that the family often move, either because she found fault with their current home or because she wanted to live closer to one of her sisters. Although the Paternos moved frequently, they always stayed within the same general area in middle-class neighborhoods amid mostly hard-working Italian, Irish, and Jewish families.

Reflecting on the religious and ethnic mixture of his childhood neighborhoods, Joe expressed gratitude for having rubbed elbows with Protestants and Jews, Irish and Germans. Because of the mixture, "I had a chance to see the other guy's point of view. Today kids don't have the advantage of growing up and seeing that we're not all that different. They're asked to be sympathetic, but they never have the chance."[10]

Joe spent most of his early childhood in a home at Twenty-third Street between Avenues S and T, a middle-class section of Flatbush in Brooklyn. "It was a nice street, lots of playing room, lots of kids to play with, and we played all day in summer, all afternoon the rest of the year," Joe said. His childhood was happy, he reflected, "with no big problems."

Every day after school they played games. Among the boys Joe played with in the streets were his brother George, his cousins Nicholas Dambra and Nicholas Mangracina, and neighbors Ed Murnane and Joe Cassidy. They played stickball, punch ball, touch football (and basketball in a friend's yard). In the winter they played ice hockey and slid on sleds.

Rosemary Smith McGinn recalls Joe as being kinder than other boys to the young girls in the neighborhood. Unlike others, Joe didn't act "smart alecky" and didn't throw stones at them, pull the girls' hair, or grab their hats. "He would never be nasty," said McGinn. "He would never make fun of you. It was easy for me to talk to him." In the Smiths' home Rosemary tried to teach Joe and other boys how to dance the Lindy, but Joe didn't catch on. "I don't think Joe was really into the girls and into dancing until he was in high school," she reflected. Indeed, the boys were too busy playing games in the streets. "We never bothered much with girls," said Mangracina.

The two biggest problems with playing in the street were the cars driving by and the people who called the police when the kids were too noisy. At night the youngsters played in an empty lot. During touch football games, the passing was confined to an area near a lamppost, while fakes and running plays worked best in the darkened areas. At about age ten, Joe advanced to more sophisticated tackle games at nearby Marine Park. To ward off injuries in tackle football, Joe put towels in his knickers and sweaters and wore a woolen hat. He tried to be a "fancy-dan runner," imagining himself a contemporary college football star. ("I was anyone who had a good day the previous Saturday," he recalled.) Partly because of the poor quality of the footballs—most were balloons and some had bubbles—Joe didn't learn to pass effectively. "I wasn't much of a passer," he admitted.

Once, while running out for a pass, Joe smashed headfirst into a tree with a three-foot girth. Three teeth went to the bottom of his lip and blood spurted out. "We were losing at the time," George recalled, "and [Joe] wouldn't quit while we were behind." Finally, his buddies sent him home, still bleeding.[11]

Joe and George attended Saint Edmonds, a nearby Catholic grade school with six hundred students, run by Dominican nuns. Although exceptionally dedicated and usually kind, the stern nuns accustomed their students to rigid discipline, piled on homework, and insisted the students complete assignments. "They made sure that you learned," observed Mangracina, "and if you didn't you stayed after school." One nun was so tough she made Mangracina tremble. "She was six foot [tall] and had hands as big as a man's, and she let you have it if you didn't know your lesson."

Saint Edmonds didn't officially sponsor a football team, but seventh and eighth graders from the parish were organized unofficially by a coach who conducted practices five days a week. Players provided their own equipment, sold chances to buy jerseys, and played against other local parish squads. Joe was one of the team's best players.

Joe also tried to lead. "He always wanted to be the quarterback," said Dambra. "He always had to run things," Mangracina added. As the quarterback, Joe was always scheming, trying to figure out the opponent's defense and the most effective plays to counter it. Mangracina wasn't always happy with Joe's play selection, though, especially near the goal line. "I argued with him a lot," Mangracina said. Joe believed in power football—the offensive line should blow the opponent off the line of scrimmage. On the goal line Joe sometimes called four consecutive running plays up the middle with no success. This aggravated Mangracina. "Try something different!" he thought.

In seventh and eighth grade Joe occasionally played tackle football at Marine Park with boys who were older, bigger, and stronger. To prevent him from being injured in a smashing tackle, they directed him to play center. Still, Joe asserted himself among his older friends, aggressively suggesting plays in the huddle. "Go off tackle," he would say. "That guy is off the line!" Observed Giro Scotti, an older boy who played with him: "He would always have a play."

At school convocations all the students with the highest grades were called up to the front first for recognition. Joe was always among those called up first. "If he learned something three months before an exam, he remembered it," marveled Mangracina. "He never had to cram."

As a youth Joe loved watching movies featuring the dashing Errol Flynn or Douglas Fairbanks Jr., "dueling and jousting in the medieval courts, where clarions with colorful pennants trumpeted the call to the contests and hailed the champions and a lady awarded her handkerchief to the victor." Later he linked his love of the medieval pageant in motion pictures to his fascination for the modern football pageant with its vast stadium, colors, precision bands, cheerleaders, and football contestants.

"I did some bad stuff," Joe reflected. "I just never got caught." At about age twelve he and his buddies robbed a Chinese laundry "just for the sake of it." Friends later chuckled, though, at the notion that Joe was any kind of troublemaker. "He got along with everybody," Ed Murnane said, adding that Joe was "friendly and sociable and well liked."

"It was all kind of like a 1940s B movie," Mastoloni observed of the moral standards of his circle of young friends, including Joe. "I remember going up to one of the kids' parents' house in Massachusetts, thirty of us from the neighborhood, girls and boys, and we didn't need a chaperon—we'd divide the house in half for girls and boys. We were just good kids. We weren't as dopey as a Mickey Rooney movie, but it was close. We never got into any trouble."[12]

Joe and his brother George developed different interests and personalities. George was impulsive, feisty, full-of-the-devil, and a flashier, more gifted athlete than his older brother; Joe was more self-assured, responsible, serious, and ambitious. "[Joe] seemed always to be in control of his life," said his sister Florence. "He was always very responsible." George remembered his own deviousness before one Christmas and Joe's disapproving reaction. "We wanted bicycles," George said, "and my father hid the bicycles in the storage room. . . . I knew they were there, so I got one of my cousins to come over with a screwdriver, and I took the bicycles out before Christmas and pedaled them around the cellar. Joe thought it was awful that I would do such a thing."

Joe was a Cub Scout, a Boy Scout, and an avid reader. He read and reread *The Leatherstocking Tales*, Tom Swift, the Hardy Boys, and books by Robert Louis Stevenson that Angelo Paterno "just happened" to leave around the house. George liked to fish, but his brother would never accompany him. Instead, Joe sat home and listened to music or read. "[Joe] didn't like to kill things. When I would catch a fish, he'd throw it back in. We had fights over that," said George. "I used to think he was nuts."[13]

Restless and ambitious, Joe strove constantly to succeed and to lead. "I was constantly evaluating myself, checking to see whether I was doing enough, giving myself little progress reports," he later said. He developed a sense of humor, but most observers judged him as unusually serious. "He was a . . . serious boy," recalled Mastoloni. "We have a picture of us as kids," George later said. Joe "was about six . . . and he looks dead serious. He always looked that way." George teased him, "Joe, I think you were born with a frown on your face." Joe was even serious during street games. "He hated to lose," George recalled. "He wouldn't cheat, but he hated to lose."

George never worked as hard as his brother. "He was all business," George said. "Everything was business, business, business." Of his relationship with his ambitious older brother, George concluded: "You have to stand in his shadow because he was going to be number one."

The two brothers had their scraps. Joe threw George down a flight of stairs, and on another occasion "zonked" him with the "serious end of a rake," smashing his nose. "We fought a lot," said George. Friends called them the Katzenjammer Kids, after a comic strip about two scrappy brothers. Although the brothers had their scraps, they stuck together. "If anyone picked on either of us, we'd both go after him," said Joe. Over time the brothers developed a close relationship and mutual respect.

Joe's sister Florence sometimes resented the domineering attitude of her oldest brother. "When I got to be in my teens," she recalled, "[Joe] was a real pain because he had to comment on whether I could wear nail polish or . . . high heels." But Joe was also fun to be with. He took his sister to outdoor concerts featuring the classical music of Beethoven and Mozart. "[Joe] was always a very loving older brother," she said.[14]

When Joe finished school at Saint Edmonds, Angelo wanted him to attend a Catholic parochial high school, even though a good public school was situated only a block away. Therefore, he forked out the high tuition and enrolled his son at Brooklyn Preparatory School in February 1941.

Located at 1150 Carroll Street, Brooklyn Prep enrolled about eight hundred male students. With tuition at $210 per year by the time Joe was a senior, Brooklyn Prep was one of the most expensive high schools in the New York area. (When George also enrolled, school officials allowed the Paternos to pay only half of the second tuition.) Jesuit priests and Jesuits in training mostly staffed the school.

The Jesuits at Prep required students to attend Mass regularly and arranged special devotions and retreats. Fr. John Hooper, S. J., the headmaster, firmly believed that Catholicism must permeate the school's atmosphere. "Either we make of the boys entrusted to us real Catholic gentlemen or we might as well not run the school," he said.

Patriotism was also highly valued at Brooklyn Prep. Stories about former faculty members and students killed in World War II filled the student newspaper and the yearbook. When a former lay teacher at the school, who had fought with distinction against the Japanese in the South Pacific, spoke to a convocation in 1944, students greeted the highly decorated navy lieutenant's arrival in the auditorium with thunderous ovation, and Father Hooper granted students a half-holiday in his honor.[15]

In high school Joe encountered some prejudice, but he overcame the problem without deep scars. Some Irish-Catholic students called him a wop and a dago. "I was always ready to fight them," he later said. "But after a while, when I had proven myself, I was accepted."

Joe proved himself in athletics. Because he was a skinny kid of 125 pounds with birdlike legs, he didn't go out for football his freshman year. Although not much bigger the following year, he joined the team but was badly miscast as a guard. He did see brief action as a kickoff returner. In his junior year he started as an offensive guard, and as a defensive back he displayed exceptional ball-hawking ability, intercepting a pass almost every game. The team, though, earned only two victories.

Earl "Zev" Graham, the head football coach, was a native of Akron, Ohio, and had been the star quarterback at Fordham University in the mid-1920s. (Sportswriters judged him so swift on the gridiron that they nicknamed him "Zev," after a speedy racehorse of that era.) Graham was a kind, tough, smart little fireplug. Also a disciplinarian, while walking among the players at practice, if he spotted mistakes or goof-offs, he made the offender duck-walk around the perimeter of the football field in full uniform. "If you wanted . . . to start a game on the first string, you did what he told you to do or else you sat on the bench," said Joe's teammate Charles O'Connor. Joe and the other players respected him. "He taught me what sportsmanship was all about . . . and [kept] things simple," Joe later said.[16]

Entering his senior year, Joe weighed 170 pounds. Graham, who had grown to appreciate Joe's athletic ability, intelligence, spirit, and leadership, installed him as the team's fullback (and late in the season moved him to quarterback) and assigned him the essential task of offensive signal caller. Although quick and agile, Joe was not a good passer, but Graham's offense didn't require him to pass often (and one of the halfbacks, Dick Reilly, was an effective passer.) Graham used a double-wing formation. One halfback lined up behind the left end, and the other behind the right end; the fullback and the quarterback both lined up in back of the guards, each capable of receiving the ball from the center.

During the 1944 season Graham decided not to use a huddle and taught Joe to call all the plays and the signals audibly using a numbered code that the opponent's defense couldn't decipher. (Each week Graham changed the code.) The idea for a no-huddle offense partly stemmed from problems the Prep team had encountered the previous year (Joe's junior year) when too many players asserted themselves and argued in the huddle, creating chaos. Graham's solution was to appoint one dominant leader, devise a coded system of calling plays and signals, and dispense with the huddle. He said, in effect, "Here's my answer to the chaos. Joe knows how to run that group of people, so we'll not have a huddle."

Graham gave Joe a crash course in calling the team's plays and signals and assigned him football books to study. He insisted that Joe learn the blocking assignments of every offensive player. "How can you pick out the right play if you don't know who's blocking who?" Graham told him.[17]

During the week Graham and Joe conversed about play-calling. "Zev loved Joe and had great confidence in him," said Joe's teammate John Plunkett. "It was Joe Paterno who read the defense and called the play that he thought would work. No one else. No one spoke. . . . No one said anything." At age seventeen, Joe literally was the coach on the field. Prep didn't have a huddle during Joe's entire senior season. "I always had an immediate respect for Joe," said Plunkett. "I just respected him—totally. If Zev said Joe was going to call the plays, there was no questioning it. It was right. He should be. He was just one of those guys who you knew was going to win."

Still, Joe worried about his limitations as a passer. Maybe he would lose his job because he couldn't pass effectively. "I couldn't stand not being good enough, so at home after practice I'd throw a football against a padded wall in our cellar for hour after hour after hour. My mother thought some raging demon had possessed her oldest boy."[18]

During the 1944 season Joe inspired his teammates with his leadership. "He almost expected that he would be the leader," George Paterno

said. "He never shied away from it or stubbed his toe. He just took over."
Joe led mainly by example, by the way he acted, not by yelling. Although
he occasionally used strong language, particularly when someone made a
mistake, his demeanor primarily motivated his peers. "He was all business," said Plunkett. "Very, very serious." Lineman and co-captain Joseph
Murphy thought Joe conveyed the impression to teammates that Brooklyn Prep was indomitable, that whatever obstacles opponents placed in
front of the team, Prep would prevail. "The [primary] thing he brought to
that team," Murphy said, "was his leadership."

With his excellent instincts and reflexes, strong upper body, and
quick start, Joe was an outstanding runner. He could evade a defender
and, lowering one shoulder, use his elbow to lever up an approaching
tackler. He was particularly successful with short plunges near the goal
line. When Prep would get inside the ten-yard line, Joe would call his
own number. "No one resented it because he would get in," said Plunkett.
"He was a very determined runner." George Paterno succinctly summa-
rized Joe's attitude on the gridiron: "Fierce competitor. I mean *fierce!*"[19]

Still, Joe wouldn't swear. Foul language consisted mainly of "hell"
and "damn," but Joe didn't want to hear any swearing at all. Once he lectured the team: "Look, you guys, my kid brother is going to be out for the
team this year. He's coming tomorrow. So you better knock off all the
dirty language."

Joe was the "brains of the team," stated Prep's student newspaper,
the *Blue Jug*. He understood football better than his teammates, most of
whom were still learning the fundamentals of the game. "Right from the
very start," Murphy said, "he understood the strategy of offensive football." "[If] he could not beat you physically," added George, "he would
try to outthink you."

While maintaining a confident outward demeanor, though, Joe
had inner doubts about his athletic ability and worried about failing.
"Where I felt I had strong talent, as in running and agile footwork, I figured that was the way it was supposed to be," he later reflected. "But
where I had the slightest doubt I was tops, as in throwing, the fear of deficiency made me push myself to the limit. If you let them, the fears of
weakness and adversity can whip you down. But they can also whip you
up. And between those two choices, I already instinctively sensed, every
person has the power to choose."[20]

As this yearbook photo shows, Joe's talents at Brooklyn Prep extended beyond the football field. Here, as student council president, he speaks for the students. (Copies of photos provided by Fr. John Alexander, Fordham University)

Joe was captain and star of Brooklyn Prep's basketball team as well. He later earned three letters in basketball at Brown University.

Throughout the 1944 season Brooklyn Prep's powerful offensive line tore gaping holes in the opposition. The team relied most heavily on its running attack. (In a 46-0 rout of Poly Prep, Brooklyn Prep rushed for 403 yards and passed for zero.) George Paterno, the left halfback, who had speed, shiftiness, and pistonlike legs, was an outstanding runner, especially around end.

Joe challenged in the race for individual scoring leader among all players in New York City, a competition area newspapers extensively publicized. (Joe finished third with fifty-four points.) In Prep's 39-0 rout of Cardinal Hayes, he scored four touchdowns—on a seventy-yard run, two one-yard plunges, and a forty-yard pass interception. His exploits on the gridiron were often highlighted in the school newspaper. "Joe Paterno provided his specialty," reported the *Blue Jug* of Prep's 13-13 tie with Mount Saint Michael, "a short powerful buck through the center of the line for the touchdown after he had brought the large crowd to its feet with a fifty-yard gallop from midfield to the one-foot line." The *New York Herald Tribune*'s Leo Waldman referred to him as "little Joe Paterno, the irrepressible quarterback."[21]

On November 5, 1944, ten thousand spectators watched Saint Cecilia High School defeat Prep, 20-13. (Saint Cecilia, the New Jersey powerhouse, then in the midst of a thirty-two-game undefeated string, was exceptionally well coached by a young Vince Lombardi.) A shoulder injury prevented Joe from playing with his customary effectiveness. Joe didn't carry the ball on offense and couldn't play defense. "Joe was able to call the plays," said teammate Charles Weis, "but he had one shoulder that was almost useless." While talking to sportswriters afterwards, Coach Graham partly blamed the loss on injuries. "Considering that Joe Paterno's bad shoulder made him useless as a runner and defenseman [and that another key player was injured], I'd say we were lucky to keep it close." "[All] through the Saint Cecilia's game I had to conceal my pain," Joe later said. But he ran the offense and still acted as the coach on the field. "[Joe] played hurt and you never heard about it," Plunkett said. "He never talked about it."

In the 1944 season Prep outscored its opponents, 197 to 52, and finished with one of the best records in New York City, 6-1-1 (not 8-1 as usually reported in accounts of Joe's life). Joe was one of three Prep players named to the prestigious *New York World-Telegram*'s All-Metropolitan Prep School First Team.[22]

Joe thought he was more naturally suited to basketball than football, but his athletic career suggests the opposite. Still, he was one of Prep's best basketball players. A deliberate ball handler, ball-hawking defender, and spirited leader, he was also slightly awkward and not a good outside shooter (although occasionally he made an outside set shot).

Brooklyn Prep's basketball teams never reached the .500 mark during Joe's playing days. In his junior season (1943–1944) he played starting guard and at midseason was the team's fifth-leading scorer. Occasionally, he led the team in scoring, as he did against Bishop Loughlin, scoring twelve points in a losing effort. Brooklyn Prep finished its Catholic Conference schedule with a 6-8 record. "Paterno made his impression on the score card by his set shot and a speedy under-the-basket layup," the *Blue Jug* commented in its summary of the season.

Before Joe's senior season he was selected the team's captain. Zev Graham also coached basketball, but he was far less proficient at his basketball assignment, and his limitations placed extra burdens on the captain to direct and guide the team, a role Joe relished. "[Paterno] really knew more about the game than the coach," starting center Walter McCurdy said. "[Joe] was . . . pretty much running the team. . . . He was a natural born leader."

In Joe's senior year the team started terribly, then improved, but still concluded the season with a sub-.500 record. Joe scored 121 points, the fourth highest on the team. "The basketball season has finally come to an end," wrote a columnist for the *Blue Jug*, "and it was disappointing, to say the least. The team never lived up to the expectations of the students." The columnist thought the team "lacked spirit" and "fight" during its early-season doldrums and although it overcame those weaknesses, the team remained deficient in "chemistry." Some team members played a fast-paced game; others preferred a slower, deliberate style. "Captain Joe was a mixture of both. . . . When brewed together, these five brought nothing to the victory stomach but indigestion." The columnist didn't fault Joe, though, handing him a "bouquet" for his "excellent floor work."[23]

An incident after the regular season, while Prep played a game for third place in a postseason tournament on Long Island, provided insight into Joe's attitude toward sports. At the end of the game, Walter McCurdy was fouled and his successful free throw could tie the score, sending the game into overtime. The large screaming crowd made the situation extremely tense. As McCurdy headed to the foul line, Joe said to him, "You know [Walter], it's only a basketball game. It really doesn't mean all that very much. Just go out and do [your] best." McCurdy made the shot, but Prep lost in overtime. "[Joe] was . . . trying to manage the situation and get me untensed," McCurdy said.

Angelo and Florence Paterno loyally backed the athletic careers of their two sons. Angelo, in particular, supported his children by his presence and encouragement. "[Angelo] was always at their high school games," Mastoloni observed. On the evening of January 6, 1945, Angelo was chairman of Brooklyn Prep's first sports dinner attended by more than eleven hundred people.[24]

Away from the athletic field and the classroom, Joe was less serious, and the faculty and staff enjoyed his pleasant disposition, sense of humor, and unassuming manner. Brooklyn Prep provided few opportunities for its all-male student body to mix with young women. (However, he was among a score of students who helped organize the annual Prep football dance on Friday, November 24, 1944.) Carefully chaperoned by nuns and priests, the Brooklyn Prep students attended dances and tea parties at Saint Agnes, an all-girls school. But Joe seldom dated and had no steady girlfriend. "He wasn't a Casanova or a Romeo," said Rosemary McGinn.

To friends and observers Joe seemed emotionally healthy and confident. Fellow students respected his natural leadership and sound ideas. Joe Hurley, a classmate and football teammate, recalled, "If you took twenty guys from the high school, pulled them at random, and put them in a room to brainstorm about a theoretical recommendation for how to reshape America's foreign policy, . . . I guarantee you that Joe would be chairing the meeting within five minutes. And 95 percent of the coparticipants would think that was fine."

Very vocal among his friends, his voice was always one of the loudest and most frequently heard in any gathering. At lunch he sat with the more popular students. "Joe would be doing much more than his fraction of the group's talking," Hurley said. "He was very entertaining."

Joe was almost universally admired and liked by his fellow students. Observed Hurley: "Some like to be around a jock; some like to be around a joke teller; some like to be around a confident, positive, upbeat kind of guy. Joe was all of those things."[25]

A few acquaintances at Brooklyn Prep, though, thought Joe's leadership qualities occasionally manifested as bossiness and brashness. The football team had two popular co-captains, Joseph Murphy and Bill Snyder. "But Joe was so powerful a personality," recalled a teammate, "that you could see right away that all but a little bit of social leadership drifted from the co-captains to Joe." Occasionally, Snyder resented Joe's intrusion. "Here comes the boss," Snyder would say critically to others as Joe approached. Whatever resentment that was manifested, however, did not noticeably disturb the team.

When a teammate asked Joe to autograph the cardboard matting of the football team's photo, Joe said, "Sure. Give me that!" He then signed his name six inches long, taking up half the room on the matting of the precious photo. "Where am I going to put everyone else?" said the dismayed teammate. "You don't need anyone else!" Joe responded. (Afterward the teammate located some ink eradicater and eliminated Joe's entire signature.) Overall, however, the teammate had a favorable impression of Joe: "Ninety-nine percent of the time Joe was engaging."[26]

The librarian at Brooklyn Prep encouraged Joe to read extensively, and when he worked a summer job, he spent his lunch hour at the New York Public Library. Joe took part in a book discussion club and for four years attended meetings of Sodality, a religious discussion group at Prep which encouraged students to work with the poor in the neighborhood. (He was secretary of the organization in his senior year.) The yearbook described Sodality as the "very heart of . . . spiritual life and development at school," where members learned a "sense of true values to put in practice every day." Joe seemed to soak up religious instruction like a sponge. "When you would give him religious instruction, . . . he was devouring it," one of his teachers said. "He was buying it in the good sense." Joe seemed to be saying, "Yes, this is true!"

Joe's fellow students elected him to leadership posts. Athletic prowess appeared to be the most attractive quality when students selected him vice president of the student council in his junior year. The election took place in midterm, on January 14, 1944, and was a one-sided contest. Joe outpolled his opponent, 451-105. The *Blue Jug* almost exclusively praised the athletic ability of the newly elected president and then described Vice President Paterno as an "honor student" who was "popular and aggressive," but "the quality which most truly characterizes him is his spirit and burning determination to win . . . to win for Prep. His 'hustle' and alertness were displayed when he intercepted his 'weekly' pass and turned them into tallies for the Blue and White. An 'iron-man note' was introduced as Joe played a full sixty minutes of nearly every contest." In fall 1944, Joe's senior year, students elected him president of the student council. In both elections Joe's friends stumped for him, and he gave several speeches. (He was a "good" public speaker, said a classmate, who thought his addresses were "natural" and not "canned.")[27]

The headmaster, Father Hooper, selected Joe and four other young students to meet with him periodically to talk about the priest's special interest, leadership. For about two hours every other week Father Hooper probed the five students about how they would manage specific problems at the school. "What are your ideas?" the priest asked. "Why would you do it that way?" "[Father Hooper] was a very farsighted guy," Joe reflected.

Although Joe loved football and basketball and enjoyed student government, he focused on his primary responsibility. Mindful that his mother and father were making a financial sacrifice putting him through a private Catholic school stimulated him to be diligent in his academic work. "What school was really about, and I never had a moment's confusion about this, was getting an education," he later said.[28]

The Jesuits insisted students be on time for classes and complete all homework assignments. "They laid the homework on you," said one student, "and if you didn't have it done, [they gave you] verbal abuse and more homework."

Some of the teachers at Brooklyn Prep were scholastics—young men in training to become Jesuit priests—and Joe admired them. "All of them burned with idealism, and that made them marvelous teachers," Joe said. In the fall of 1943, his junior year, he enrolled in a literature class taught by Thomas Bermingham, a twenty-five-year-old scholastic (who later became a Jesuit priest.) The first time the class met, Bermingham asked his thirty students to compose a list of all the books they had read. Their grade for the assignment would depend on the honesty of their effort. That evening, as Bermingham studied the responses of the students (most of whom had listed mundane reading), he was most impressed by the list prepared by Joe Paterno because it contained works by John Steinbeck, Ernest Hemingway, and F. Scott Fitzgerald. The next day Bermingham asked Joe if he would be willing to engage in extra work—special reading in addition to his normal class load. Joe leaped at the offer. "He just glowed when I told him," Father Bermingham recalled. The young scholastic thought to himself, "Here is someone with a strong intellectual appetite!" Later, after Bermingham learned that Joe played football and basketball, he worried that the extra assignment would be too burdensome for a seventeen-year-old. But Joe didn't complain. "I was impressionable, eager, proud of my mind, probably overly so, simmering with intellectual curiosity," Joe reflected. For two or three afternoons a week, therefore, the pair spent forty minutes together discussing Joe's extra reading. "Anything I suggested he would just devour," said Father Bermingham. Joe's intellectual drive was so intense that Bermingham advised him to be patient. "Joe, don't feel that you have to read everything at once," he told his protégé.[29]

In his senior year Joe took another course from Bermingham, this time Latin, and again the scholastic singled him out for extra self-education. He suggested that Joe translate Virgil's epic, the *Aeneid*. Challenging Joe's pride, Bermingham told him, "You've got to do more than anyone else in this class because you [have the ability]."

The *Aeneid* lay on Bermingham's desk, more than four hundred pages thick. Joe later observed: "I always had the attitude about any challenge, 'Hey, if it's difficult, let's do it.' That made it more fun."

"But if it's in Latin," Joe asked Bermingham uncertainly, "will we be able to cover all that?"

"What's important," Bermingham responded, "is not how much we cover. I don't like that word *cover*. It's not how much we do, but the excellence of what we do." The word *excellence* excited Joe. "The way he pronounced that word made it shine with a golden light," Joe said.

In the fall of 1944, therefore, Bermingham and Joe met three afternoons a week to translate the *Aeneid*. Joe would read ten lines; Bermingham would read twenty. Joe's exceptional diligence impressed Bermingham: "Here was this fellow, . . . at the end of a heavy class day and having to face football practice, begging to fill in the time with Virgil's *Aeneid*."

Joe never forgot the majestic ring of the opening lines of the poem:

Arma virumque cano, Troiae qui primus ab oris . . .
Of arms and the man I sing.

He heard cymbals and trumpets. "I envisioned a procession of gallant gladiators. At their head, on a huge horse, rode the most gallant of all, a king or a prince or some kind of general. It rang in my ears":

Of arms and the man I sing.
And then:
From the seacoast of Troy in the early days
He came to Italy by destiny . . .

"I still feel the spell of that young robed cleric's eyes searing into me, reminding me that I was special and that this was important," Joe said in his autobiography.[30]

Written in 29–19 B.C., the *Aeneid* is one of the finest epic poems of world literature, infused with mythology, history, patriotism, religious feeling, pathos, adventure, and romance. It describes the wanderings of Aeneas and a band of Trojans after the capture of Troy by the Greeks. With great difficulty they journey westward to Sicily, to Africa, and finally to Italy. Courageous, determined, and persevering, Aeneas struggles and fights for a better civilization and is constantly tested along the way. (He is also overbearing and humorless.) The characters in Virgil's story have "freedom of will," observed Princeton University scholar George Duckworth, and "make their own decisions and suffer the consequences." There are many tragic deaths and characters "fail in part because they stand for the irrational forces of darkness and disorder as opposed to world order and justice," symbolized on the human level by Aeneas.

Then and later Joe was intrigued by Virgil's use of the word *fatum* to explain Aeneas's destiny. Joe interpreted *fatum* to mean a divine word, the inner voice, destiny. Exhausted and discouraged, Aeneas had to struggle within himself to renew any faith in the voices of his destiny. The *fatum*, Joe thought, tells a person what he is destined to do, but it doesn't tell him how to do it. Instead, Joe observed, "Aeneas has to struggle and suffer—and make his own decisions. How he *acts* is not determined by fate. He listens, he considers. But then he must act out of free will."

Bermingham stressed Virgil's portrayal of the ideal leader. Joe learned that Aeneas had to suppress his own individual feelings of fear, self-doubt, and disappointment, never showing his feelings to his men. "Joe was so struck by . . . the idea of being supremely tested by defeat," recalled Father Bermingham.[31]

Aeneas was a totally new kind of epic hero, one who had a duty to others. The "worst storm," Joe thought, was the one that raged within the hero himself. "[Aeneas] yearns to be free of his tormenting duty, but he knows that his duty is to others, to his men." Joe later said of Aeneas: "Destiny has stuck him with being a leader, and he can't escape it."

Angelo had wanted Joe to view sports as fun, but in the *Aeneid* Joe picked up a different message. In his autobiography Joe used the words *struggle*, *torment*, *suffering*, and *tears* when he referred to Aeneas. No one is guaranteed victory or reward for suffering. "The best man, the best team, isn't automatically entitled to win," Joe came to believe. "The winds of fate can turn you around, run you aground, sink you, and sometimes you can't do a thing about it. You can commit yourself to accomplishing a goal, doing something good, winning a game. Just to make that commitment to something you believe in *is* winning—even if you lose the game. But for committing yourself to winning the game, whether you win it or not, you always pay in tears and blood."

Many years later, Joe reflected on the benefits he gained by reading Virgil and the classics: "The problems of the ancient Greeks, we let our kids decide, have little 'relevance' to life today. Latin? It's dead and anything written in Latin has meaning only for ancients. What bearing can Plato and *The Republic* have on modern civilization today? The Romans and the Greeks had no television, no computers, no widespread affluence and mobility in any modern sense. What's the point of paying attention to *them*? So, abandoning the deep roots of our culture, including morality, today's kid has to make daily decisions based on [rootlessness], a here-and-now existence."

Aeneas, therefore, entered Joe's life. "More than entered it," he later said. "The adventures of Aeneas seeped into far corners of my mind, into my feelings about what is true and honorable and important. They

helped shape everything I have since become. I don't think anybody can
get a handle on what makes me tick as a person, and certainly can't get
at the roots of how I coach football, without understanding what I
learned from the deep relationship I formed with Virgil during those
afternoons and later in my life." Once a person experienced a genuine
masterpiece, "the size and scope of it last as a memory forever."

Father Bermingham, who remained Joe's longtime friend, also
believes the *Aeneid* helped to shape Joe. "What we did together," the
priest said, "acted as a confirmation and a clarification for much that was
going on in himself and helped confirm what he already in some sense
wanted to be—deep down." Father Bermingham concluded: "If Joe had
never had that experience of coping with himself as a young fellow
when I first came to know him, I don't think [he would have been able
to lead others]."[32]

To help pay his own way through school, Joe worked every summer—once as a baggage checker at Penn Station, another time as a mail
clerk. He also worked as a counselor at a sports camp in the Catskills. During the summer of 1944, he ushered at Ebbets Field and watched the
Dodgers play.

On January 25, 1945, Joe graduated with his small midterm class
in the auditorium of Bishop McDonnel Memorial High School. (He could
have taken an accelerated course in summer 1944, graduated, and then
entered military service and served in World War II, but he and some
other athletes elected to stay for the fall semester of 1944 to play football.)
The combined academic, athletic, and leadership qualities Joe displayed
in his senior year were exceptional. Besides being president of the student
council, treasurer of the senior class, secretary of Sodality, captain of the
basketball team, and an award-winning football player, he also delivered
two major public speeches before large crowds—at the sports dinner and
at commencement. To top it off he was salutatorian, ranking second in
his class of forty-two students.[33]

Joe had several opportunities to continue his athletic career in
college. Holy Cross showed interest in having him play football, and
Fordham offered him a partial scholarship to play basketball. Angelo
hoped to secure him a commission to West Point, but after visiting the
campus on a cold, bleak January day, Joe lost interest. The Ivy League
hadn't attracted Joe because the tuition was excessive, but that difficulty

vanished when Joe was offered major financial assistance to attend Brown University in Providence, Rhode Island.

Coach Zev Graham had become friends with Everett M. "Busy" Arnold, an alumnus of Brown and a wealthy publisher of comic books. An avid booster of Brown's athletic programs, Arnold helped recruit athletes for his alma mater and provided them with substantial financial aid. When Graham suggested that Arnold recruit Joe, the businessman invited Angelo and Joe to visit Brown where they met the head football coach, Charles A. "Rip" Engle. Both Joe and Angelo liked Brown and Engle; Arnold offered to pay for Joe's tuition, books, room, and board.

Like many Catholic parents, however, Angelo Paterno felt pressure not to send his son to a secular college, fearing that Joe might lose his Catholic faith. Angelo asked for Bermingham's guidance, and the scholastic reassured him. "I think I know [Joe] well enough [to say that] you'll have no worry about that boy's faith, much less his moral integrity," Bermingham said. The advice seemed to tip the scales, convincing Angelo and Florence to accept Arnold's offer and let Joe enroll at Brown. (Subsequently, George Paterno also received Arnold's financial assistance and attended Brown.)

Later it became strictly illegal for an individual like Arnold to pay an athlete's college expenses, but his aid was still within NCAA guidelines at the time Joe entered Brown. Some close observers of Brown's athletic program, however, viewed Arnold as an unsavory character. John Hanlon, sportswriter for the *Providence Journal*, thought Arnold was "despicable." Hanlon said he witnessed Arnold arrange female sexual contacts for two prospective Brown basketball players in a penthouse on Fifth Avenue in New York. For many years Paul Mackesey, Brown's athletic director, was unaware of Arnold's recruiting methods and financial support. When he learned the extent of Arnold's gambits, he was shocked. "[Arnold] was scum. He was a bum. He was the archetype of the affluent, football-crazy alumnus." Mackesey learned that Arnold would arrive in Providence on the night before a game and rent a suite at a hotel. "Then he'd invite these high school kids [from New York] and have them in the suite and there would be an open bar and drinking and carousing. It was just disgusting—terrible." In the early 1950s, after Joe had graduated, Mackesey informed Brown's president of Arnold's actions, an investigation followed, and eventually the kind of financial assistance Arnold provided was stopped. Neither George nor Joe Paterno personally witnessed the seedy side of Arnold, but they later learned about his reputation. "A lot of people thought he was an angel," George said, "an amoral angel." The Paterno brothers were just grateful for Arnold's assistance.[34]

After graduation Joe worked for several months at Brooklyn Prep, handing out basketballs and picking up attendance sheets, waiting until he was drafted. To get an early start at college, he enrolled in summer school at Brown, but then his draft notice arrived, and he entered the army. When the Japanese surrendered in August 1945, Joe was in training at Fort Dix, New Jersey. In January 1946, the army shipped him to Korea and assigned him to operate a radio. With his tour of duty uneventful, Joe read extensively to ward off boredom. Discharged from the army, he returned home in August 1946, in time to enroll at Brown for the fall term.[35]

After Labor Day 1946, Joe and friends waited at New York's Grand Central Station for the train that would take them to Providence. While the group walked fifty yards away to buy Cokes, someone stole Joe's new suitcase containing all of his clothes. "[Joe] went to Brown with the clothes on his back," a friend recalled. "He was distraught, to say the least."

Founded in 1764, Brown University was the seventh-oldest college in the country. Dotted with elm trees, the sixty-three-acre Brown campus sat on top of a hill in the city of Providence and enrolled about twenty-eight hundred undergraduate male students. By the time Joe enrolled, the university was private and nonsectarian, and its progressive president, Henry Merritt Wriston, was regarded as one of the best college presidents of his era. Brown's brush with football greatness lay in the past—its 1915 Rose Bowl squad and the immortal "Iron Men" team of 1926.

While Joe served in the army, George Paterno had caught up with his brother in school and entered Brown as a freshman on the same day as Joe. For a while the brothers roomed together, but it didn't work out. "[Joe] was always telling me what to do," George recalled. "I used to fool around, play a little cards. He was trying to make me stay in and study every night. He was very dedicated to excelling in sports and studies."[36]

Joe's football coach, Rip Engle, was a native of Pennsylvania, where he had been a highly successful coach at Waynesboro High School

With Joe having served in the army, younger brother George caught up with Joe as freshman teammates at Brown University. Here, Joe hands off to George. (Photo courtesy of Penn State Sports Information Department)

in the 1930s. He moved to Brown University as an assistant in 1942 and became head coach in 1944. Over a period of six years Engle would coach Brown to a record of 28-20-4 (and a glittering 15-3 during his last two years). Some players poked fun at Engle because of his peculiar personality, mannerisms, and expressions. Nervous and shy, he often dug his toe into the ground as he talked to players. Straightforward and moralistic, he didn't drink, smoke, or swear. Everything was "Gee," "That's swell!" "My goodness!" "Heck!" The opposite of Notre Dame's fiery Knute Rockne, Engle gave less-than-inspiring halftime talks. Normally a gentleman, he became nervous and frenzied during some games. "Nothing ever disturbed that gentlemanly image," Joe deadpanned in his autobiography, "except his sudden sideline outbursts of fretting, shouting, yelling, grunting, moaning, and flailing his fists in the air." Despite his eccentricities, Engle was a fine football coach—bright, innovative, and organized. He taught fundamental football—the double-team block, the off-tackle play, the counter play. Patient and a good teacher, he explained to a lineman *why* he missed a block on a play. Brown seldom passed. "If you threw twelve, thirteen times a game, that was a lot," said quarterback Walt Pastuszak. Engle enforced consistent discipline as well. "Everyone knew he meant business," said assistant coach Bill Doolittle. Because he was affable and self-effacing, kind and gentle, Engle commanded the respect and affection of his players and the media.[37]

As a football player at Brown, Joe was a classic overachiever. At five-foot-eleven, 170 pounds, he was a halfback in his freshman year (1946), played infrequently, and was always on the verge of not making the traveling squad. The following year Engle moved him to quarterback. Against Colgate in 1947, Joe replaced the injured starting quarterback, Ed Finn, and led Brown to two touchdowns. Although Joe played infrequently on offense, he did play safety on defense and occasionally returned punts and kickoffs.

In Joe's junior year (1948) Brown emerged as an Ivy League power, winning seven and losing only two. Sportswriters noticed Joe playing defense with reckless abandon, smashing into ballcarriers, ball-hawking, and intercepting passes with regularity. Four games into the 1948 season Brown led the nation in pass defense, giving up only 32.3 yards per game, partly because of Joe's sparkling play. While displaying a photograph of Joe running an interception back for thirty yards during Brown's 33-0 victory over Rhode Island, the *Pawtucket Times* described him as an "outstanding defensive back." Another Rhode Island newspaper thought he was "blossoming into stardom" on defense and "tackling like he's mad at everybody." Highlighting Joe's effort against Holy Cross, Norm Sadler, sportswriter for the *Brown Daily Herald*, said, "Paterno nearly cut Don Davis, Crusader back, in two with a vicious tackle on the opening kickoff in the second half."[38]

The Princeton game in 1948 dramatically illustrated Joe's ability to think on his feet. With less than a minute to play, the score was tied, 20-20, and Brown had used all its time-outs. As Princeton was about to punt, Joe, the punt receiver, realized that a fair catch would give Brown an automatic time-out and a chance to score. As the Princeton punt sailed through the air, therefore, Joe raised his hand signaling the fair catch. "That little piece of brilliance," observed Mervin Hyman and Gordon White in *Joe Paterno: "Football My Way"* (1971), "gave Brown time to move the ball within field-goal range on a couple of passes." With nine seconds to play, Joe Condon kicked a thirty-nine-yard field goal that beat Princeton, 23-20. (Joe's play was not always outstanding. Against Yale in 1948, he fumbled the opening kickoff, Yale recovered, and quickly scored a touchdown.)

Besides being a starting defensive halfback, in his junior year Joe also backed up senior quarterback Ed Finn. Although Finn was an exceptional passer, Engle periodically replaced him with Joe in order to inspire the team. Finn couldn't lead the team as well as Joe. "Finn was a good athlete," said assistant coach Bob Priestley, "but he didn't quite have the flair that Joe had for getting along with people." "Joe would inspire the team a lot more when he was in the huddle," agreed a teammate. "Finn just didn't have the zip." In the 1948 season Joe rushed for sixty-three yards and passed for 127, but he didn't score any touchdowns.[39]

During the week, Joe studied film with the coaches, critiquing previous games and learning the tendencies of the upcoming opponent. "As quarterbacks we were expected to know what *every* guy would do on every play," Pastuszak observed. The coaches tested them. "What does the left tackle do on 14X?"

At quarterback meetings Joe politely questioned some of Engle's ideas. Engle told the quarterbacks, "You never want to run the same pass pattern twice in a row." Joe disagreed. "At defensive safety," Joe pointed out, "we don't *expect* the [quarterback] to run the same thing twice in a row. If [our offense] could do the same thing in a row now and then, we might fool the [defense]."

During the summer before his senior year, Joe worked diligently to stay in shape and to improve his quarterbacking skills. He practiced his passing, threw a medicine ball in the basement of his home to strengthen his arm, and squeezed a small ball to strengthen his hand and fingers. "He would go out there and work at each phase of his quarterbacking," end Frank Mahoney recalled. "He was very serious about trying to improve himself," added teammate Gerard Walters.

On December 2, 1948, at Brown's football banquet, athletic director Paul Mackesey had put forward the team's 1949 goal: "Nine-for-Nine-in-49." With a nucleus of twenty-one lettermen from the 1948 team and fine talent coming up from the freshman squad, Brown's prospects for 1949 looked excellent. Grantland Rice, the dean of American sportswriters, tabbed Brown one of the best teams in the East.

Early in the fall of 1949, John Hanlon interviewed Joe and asked him how many games Brown would win. "We'll win 'em all," Joe confidently predicted. Recalling the interview, Hanlon commented: "[Paterno] didn't hedge at all. I'll bet he believed it, too." There was something special about Brown's 1949 team. "With the possible exception of the famous 1926 Iron Men," said an observer of Brown's football history, "it's extremely doubtful if Brown ever had such a rough, tough, talented collection of football players."

"After a couple of games," recalled Hanlon, who covered Brown's football teams for many years, "you realized that these guys could really play the game and that was so un-Brown it was unusual."[40]

Before the 1949 season the players elected Joe co-captain of the team. In Brown's first game, a 28-6 victory over Holy Cross, Joe scored his first collegiate touchdown on a sixty-eight-yard punt return. "In addition," wrote the *Providence Journal*, "Paterno did a workmanlike job of directing the Bruins' attack. Not brilliant, but more important, adequate."

Princeton's 27-14 victory over Brown in the third game of the season dashed the goal of "Nine-for-Nine-in-49." Overall, though, Brown played well and so did Joe. After Joe's outstanding performance in Brown's 28-14 victory over Harvard, Stanley Woodward, the prominent New York sportswriter, allegedly wrote, "Paterno, the Brown quarterback, can't run. He can't pass. All he can do is think—and win." (The Woodward statement, the most frequently quoted description of Joe's college football career, may have been apocryphal. No one has documented it. Joe doubted its existence. "I don't think that was ever written of me," Joe later said. "I think somebody made that up a long time ago and it [became] the truth.")

No one confused Joe with Arnold Galiffa or Babe Parilli, the nation's leading college passers of the time. Joe's passes fluttered, wobbled, and seldom spiraled. One of Brown's offensive drives stalled, a sportswriter wrote, because "[Frank] Mahoney went hither for a Joe Paterno pass that was going yon." He had the most difficulty throwing the long pass. Describing a "spectacular" twenty-eight-yard pass play from Joe to Marty Gresh, the *Brown Daily Herald* said, "Joe threw a long high pass that Gresh had to backtrack in order to make a brilliant catch." ("Joe invented the 'come-back pass,'" kidded George Paterno. "Joe couldn't throw that far. You had to 'come back' to catch it.") By necessity Brown's passing game was usually restricted to short passes that Joe often successfully completed. "He didn't throw the hard spiral," said Bill Doolittle, "but he could get the ball to the receiver."[41]

During the game Joe remained composed and focused. "He made decisions that we talked about earlier in the week," Doolittle said. "He then would do a good job of executing." Joe liked to probe a defense, looking for weaknesses and setting plays up that he could come back to later in the game. Indeed, one of Joe's strongest assets was his play selection. "He was an excellent play caller," said Priestley. He effectively kept the defense guessing. He would fake the draw play, then hit the pass; or he would fake the pass and run the draw.

On offense Joe was totally in charge, the commander in chief. "If anyone said anything, unless it was constructive, Joe would stop him in his tracks," teammate Fred Kozak said. Joe was not a loud-mouthed leader on the field, but he occasionally snarled at a player who missed an assignment. To a lineman who missed a key block, he said sharply, "Hey! What are you doing? You're a better football player than that!" Joe used controlled anger to prod players in the huddle: "This play has got to work!" or "Shake your asses on this thing and move the ball!" He'd say sharply to a lineman, "Now *this time* there's going to be a hole there!" "[Joe] would be the first to kick [the] ass of his own men just to get everybody going," said Walters. Mahoney, the team's leading receiver, described Joe as "two steps ahead of everybody else" and an excellent motivator. "Joe was a needler and made great efforts to get under your skin. It worked to a great degree, and he was usually successful."

Against Harvard, while Brown was driving for a touchdown, halfback George Paterno injured his ribs. "I'd taken some real licks," George remembered. George thought he had broken ribs and was about to leave the field, but Joe wouldn't let him leave. "You're not going out!" Joe ordered. George stayed in the game; Brown scored and won the contest. (George later learned he hadn't broken any ribs.)

Engle usually let Joe direct the team because Joe acted like a coach on the field. "I've coached better runners and better passers," Engle later said, but "I've never coached a more heady quarterback. Joe was a real strategist. In addition, he was an inspirational player, the type who can carry a team."

Even as a senior quarterback at Brown, Joe was starting to assert his authority in questioning some of head coach Rip Engle's ideas. (Photo courtesy of Penn State Sports Information Department)

"We felt he was right for the job of co-captain," said teammate Arnie Green. "He always seemed to know the right thing to do."

"Joe probably knew the whole game of football better than anyone else on the team," said the other co-captain, John Scott.[42]

One of the most thrilling games in Brown's history was the final game in 1949, and the Paterno brothers played starring roles. Expected to run roughshod over weak Colgate (1-7) in their traditional Thanksgiving Day game before eighteen thousand shivering fans at Brown's field, Joe and his teammates played sluggishly in the first half. (One of Joe's passes was intercepted, leading directly to a Colgate touchdown.) Early in the third quarter, Colgate led, 26-7. From all indications the underdog had locked up a victory; Coach Engle morosely paced the sidelines, apparently reconciled to defeat.

But Joe wasn't ready to concede defeat. "We're going to win this game!" he insisted. During a time-out he yelled at his teammates. "He cajoled, threatened, berated, shouted, implored, begged, even called on long-forgotten ancestors," Hyman and White reported, exaggerating, "and within minutes had roused his team to a fighting pitch."

In the last seventeen minutes of the game Brown scored thirty-four points, including three touchdowns in two minutes and fifty-five seconds. The Paterno brothers, both playing their final college game, were the heroes. Joe slithered off tackle for a forty-two-yard gain and threw a four-yard pass for the touchdown; then he intercepted a Colgate pass, returned it twenty-five yards, setting up another touchdown. He expertly exploited a weak Colgate defensive lineman, calling the same quick, straight-ahead running play against him. "[Joe] just kept at it," said Arnie Green. "It was unbelievable!" George Paterno scored twice and gained 162 yards—120 of them in the dramatic second half. In all, the Paternos accounted for more than two-thirds of Brown's total rushing yardage, 222 of 321. The final score: Brown 41, Colgate 26. When the whistle sounded ending the game, Brown's players carried Rip Engle off the field on their shoulders. The team's 8-1 record was one of the best seasons in Brown's history.[43]

In the 1949 season Joe had led Brown in scoring (seven touchdowns, forty-two points), punt returns (158 yards), kickoff returns (204 yards), and was second in pass interceptions (six). He finished his career with a total of fourteen interceptions for 290 yards returned, both Brown career records. Yet his senior season was not sterling enough to earn him postseason honors. Four of Brown's players made the second squad of the All-Ivy League Team, but Joe was not among them (and he did not make honorable mention either.)[44]

Joe also played basketball and earned three varsity letters. Fred Kozak, a starting guard, thought Joe's strengths were hustle and ball handling, not shooting. During his freshman year Joe played sparingly and after sixteen games still hadn't scored a point. "He was the type of athlete you love to coach," reflected Weeb Ewbank, the basketball coach in Joe's freshman year. "He was an intelligent and industrious player." (Ewbank later coached the New York Jets football team.) In Joe's sophomore year (1947–1948) new coach Bob Morris, impressed with Joe's zeal, used him to liven up the team. "We used to weave a lot in those days," Joe recalled, "and any time we were in a jam, when the game seemed to slow down, Bob would send me in with instructions 'to get that damned team fired up.' I'd get in there, yell a lot, and run around like a crazy man, and the team really began to move. We'd never score much, but at least I would get them juiced up and out I'd come."

Late in his sophomore year, Joe broke into the starting lineup, and the team won three of its last four games. "His steadying influence was a key spark to the . . . late season successes," said the *Brown Daily Herald*. He concluded the season having scored seventy-three points, sixth highest on the team.

Several times Joe played against Bob Cousy, the Holy Cross All-American guard and subsequent professional star. "I psyched myself up for days about covering him," Joe remembered. "Then he scores twelve points off of me in the first two minutes." In Joe's junior year an influx of new, talented players sent Joe to the bench again, and he played sparingly. He didn't go out for basketball in his senior year.[45]

Joe was awed by Brown. "He was a little Italian kid from Brooklyn," observed Gerard Walters, "and he [was] going to an Ivy League school." In his autobiography Joe dwelled on the stimulating intellectual worlds suddenly opened to him, the "worlds of art, history, literature, music, politics, all-night arguments about the way society is, the way it ought to be, how to change it." Surrounded by this "intellectual feast," he didn't want to limit himself to athletics. He "loved" football, but the game "wasn't my life."

Older veterans, like Joe, were more responsible and mature in their academic work than their young nonveteran classmates, and less interested in partying. "When you had to do the [academic] work, you did the work," observed Walters. "Then you partied." "A lot of guys . . . screwed around," recalled George Paterno. "They would get kegs of beer and get all drunk up. [Joe] never did that. He was a very dedicated student."

In letters home Joe tried awkwardly to impress his father with his new knowledge, especially with the fancy words he thought he had learned. But Angelo chuckled at Joe's prose. "[Joe] would use words with as many syllables as he could find to say the simplest things," recalled Joe's sister Florence.[46]

Because an uncle had advised him that diesels were the engines of the future, Joe had decided to major in engineering in college. Soon he abandoned his engineering goal, having discovered that while he was good at math, he was a "mechanical moron." He switched to economics and finally settled happily on a major in English literature. "I . . . never regretted it for a moment," he said. The Romantic period captivated him. "I'm a romantic," he later said. "I dreamed then, and do now, about gladiators and knights winning battles." In an English literature class he sat in the back row with the athletes, but when the professor asked a question, he answered in his scratchy voice.

In the fall of 1948, Joe was among five candidates vying for vice president of the junior class, the class of 1950. He campaigned with two friends (who were running for president and secretary) on a slate that claimed to be independent. "We represent no fraternity and are backed by no block," said their campaign statement printed in the school's newspaper. The three campaigned on the vague theme of friendship. "During our past two years on the Brown campus, we have seen the spirit of friendship—the integration of diverse interests—spread throughout the student body. We believe that we can enhance this atmosphere of unity; for we, ourselves, are close friends and would work in closest cooperation." Joe lost the election.

He enjoyed arguing, sometimes until three in the morning, with his Protestant friends about birth control and the infallibility of the Pope. He often researched in the John Carter Brown Library to bolster his arguments because "I hated to be intimidated intellectually." "Those debates

. . . were a form of *competition*," he added, "and I was not about to lose an argument, whether I was right or wrong." Catholic doctrine was not the primary issue. "I just wasn't about to let a Protestant think he was smarter than I was."[47]

An acquaintance described Joe as a skinny kid with olive skin who slouched across the Brown campus, "tilted left," with his hands jammed into the pockets of his army fatigue jacket. Friends enjoyed his company and respected his character. "He was serious in the sense that he always seemed to have a mission," Walters said. "Joe had good manners," said fellow football teammate Arnie Green. "He was a gentleman." Friends also enjoyed his sense of humor. "He was not afraid to laugh at himself," said Walters. "He could see the humor in situations." "Everybody liked Joe," added Priestley. "He was always very cheerful and had a lot of self-confidence."

Joe dated occasionally, usually a young woman back in Brooklyn, but he didn't have a steady girlfriend. One reason was a lack of money. "We didn't have a lot of money," said George. "We couldn't really socialize with the other guys." Some friends thought Joe was ill at ease in his relations with women. "He was not a lady's man," Walters said. The young women at nearby Pembroke intimidated him. "I didn't think the girls over at Pembroke were interested in a poor little guy from Brooklyn," Joe later said.

Joe seldom drank and stopped drinking entirely during the football season. "When we were playing football in the fall, we always went on the wagon," said Walters. "You were sacrificing [drinking and] that made the game seem that much more important." They were sacrificing for the good of the team. Even in the off-season Joe was not much of a drinker. Walters classified him as a "shitty drinker." He didn't drink that much "because he couldn't handle that much. He'd never go really overboard."[48]

Fraternities were the main source of social activity at Brown, and Joe's introduction to the world of fraternities proved unpleasant. After receiving an invitation to a cocktail party at a fraternity, he dressed in a shirt and sweater, but on entering the party he immediately sensed he was out of place. "I walked into a calm sea of blue blazers, sharkskin suits, and Harris tweeds. I knew I had blown something when all those cool-eyed faces turned toward me and my sweater, slowly, so as not to tip and spill their stemmed glasses that seemed to hold nothing but clear water, except for an olive in each. I heard somebody whisper, 'How did that dago get invited?' My clothes scratched at my skin, and a chill surged down my insides." They never invited him back, and the rejection angered him. "At home, if I ever felt I was better than another kid, it was because I could play better or think better—not because I *was* better. This time I caught a whiff of people who put themselves in a higher echelon for starters, without a contest."

Initially, when Joe attempted to pledge at the Delta Kappa Epsilon fraternity, he was also turned down. In October 1946, after Gerard Walters and Joe had visited the fraternity, Walters received an invitation to pledge but not Joe. The main objection was Joe's Italian background. "He's just a little Italian kid," some seemed to think. "We don't need this guy." Later, when Joe again attempted to pledge the fraternity, he was blackballed by two or three members. However, most members of the fraternity liked him and wanted to accept him. "The feeling was strong for Joe," Walters said. Finally, the fraternity accepted him.[49]

After his junior year, Joe moved from his dormitory into the fraternity house and roomed with two others. Life in the fraternity was carefree. The house had a bar in the basement and the members hosted cocktail parties after football games and a dance once a semester.

The Dekes included a wide variety of different students, but athletes comprised the largest block of members. Of the seventeen fraternities at Brown, Delta Kappa Epsilon ranked among the highest in members and pledges (about sixty-five); among the lowest in the cost of initiation fees and annual dues; and near the bottom in grade-point average. In Semester I, 1948–49, the average grade for all fraternities was 2.13; Delta Kappa Epsilon had the lowest average, 1.86.

Eventually, Joe became a leader in Delta Kappa Epsilon and its vice president. During the rushing period, when members pushed their favorite candidates, Joe objected strenuously if the discussion displayed prejudice against Jews or any ethnic group. At one meeting Joe took the floor and raised hell. "You . . . are opposed to this guy because his name ends in a vowel!" he charged. "[Joe] was always really correct on a moral position," recalled his friend Pat Flynn. "He was always the voice of reason . . . and a hell of an adversary." Indeed, during rushing, Joe paced back and forth in front of the room like a lawyer, making declarations and expressing his strong opinions. "He always wanted to stand up and be counted," said another friend. Sometimes Joe angrily made his point. "In those cases, where he felt there was a moral issue [involved], he was very volatile [and] outspoken," said Flynn.[50]

Joe was accepted into Boston University Law School and planned to enroll there in the fall of 1950. Before spring football practice in 1950, Engle asked Joe to assist him in coaching a young freshman quarterback, and Joe agreed. Earlier Joe had given some consideration to becoming a coach, and although he now intended to go to law school, the part-time job gave him something fun to do in the spring. To prepare himself he read every book he could find about quarterbacking.

But Engle never finished coaching spring practice. In recent years he had turned down several opportunities to leave Brown (having been mentioned for head coaching jobs at Yale, Wisconsin, and Pittsburgh). But in the spring of 1950, when Pennsylvania State College offered him a position, he accepted. Penn State enticed him with a full professorship and lifetime tenure, and the new position allowed him to be nearer his Pennsylvania home and his elderly parents. (That Engle would leave in the middle of Brown's spring practice, however, greatly irritated officials at Brown.)

Penn State had been using the single-wing formation, and because Engle intended to install his own tricky wing-T, he desperately needed an assistant who knew his system. Athletic officials at Brown didn't want him to raid Brown's staff (and the staff members he quietly asked anyway didn't want to leave). "I was somewhat over a barrel," Engle recalled. "Brown didn't want me to take any of my staff. . . . But Penn State had all single-wing coaches. I needed Joe as sort of a 'go-between.' He was very intelligent and crazy about football."[51]

Partly in desperation, therefore, Engle asked Joe if he was interested. "Would you like to go to Penn State with me to be one of my assistant coaches?" Engle asked. Joe was astonished, flattered—and intrigued. Now he wasn't sure what he wanted to do. Maybe he should give coaching a try for a few years and if he didn't like it go on to law school as he originally intended. He told Engle that he needed time to consult with his family. Angelo made Joe's decision easier. As much as Angelo wanted Joe to enter law school, he told his son, "You know what you want to do. I can't live your life for you." Joe later reflected, "If he had in any way pressured me, I probably would have gone to law school." Florence took a different stance. "A *coach*? You didn't have to go to college to be a coach!"

Joe decided to postpone law school and join Engle in the boondocks of Pennsylvania. Asked to comment on Joe's hiring, Barney Madden of the *Providence Journal* told the *Daily Collegian*, Penn State's student newspaper, that Joe was the "smartest quarterback Brown had in the last five or six years." Joe "was the guy who made Brown go," Madden said. "You'll like Paterno."[52]

~2~

RESTLESS AND AMBITIOUS (1950–1965)

IN 1950 PENNSYLVANIA STATE COLLEGE (CHANGED IN 1953 TO PENNSYLVANIA
STATE UNIVERSITY) HAD AN ENROLLMENT OF 12,600 STUDENTS. An early land-
grant college, Penn State was situated in State College, a small community that journalists joked was equally inaccessible from all parts of
Pennsylvania—80 miles from the capital at Harrisburg, 140 miles from
Pittsburgh, and 190 miles from Philadelphia. The town seemed isolated,
cut off from the congestion, noise, clamor, and crime of big-city living.
"Citizens took pride in the neatness and cleanliness of their community,
whose well-maintained properties and quiet, tree-lined avenues seemed
to represent the epitome of the American college town," said Michael
Bezilla in his history of Penn State. "Not without some justification did
both residents and outsiders refer to State College and Penn State as being
located in 'Happy Valley.'"

Penn State, though, still had the image, shared with other
land-grant schools, of being a cow college with an inferior academic
program and intellectual climate. Its pastoral, isolated location contributed to its hick image, and its puny library holdings hardly suggested serious academic intent. When compared to other eastern
schools, particularly with the prestigious Ivy League, Penn State
seemed nothing more than a vocational school. The cow-college image
was unconsciously adopted by some of its own faculty. "Too many
members of the Penn State community," observed Bezilla, "considered
their school worthy of competing on the gridiron . . . with the likes of
Penn or Syracuse or Ohio State but inferior to those institutions by
almost every academic standard."

41

In the late 1940s the death or retirement of many Penn State administrators allowed new blood into the college and a new self-image. So did the hiring in 1950 of a progressive new president, fifty-one-year-old Milton Eisenhower, the younger brother of World War II hero and future U.S. president Dwight D. Eisenhower.[1]

Despite its academic deficiencies, an enlightened attitude toward athletics had evolved at Penn State, a belief that athletics was simply another form of instruction and expression. The primary role of the faculty was to teach and the primary role of the coach was to teach. Coaches held academic rank and, unlike other universities, where coaches remained isolated from faculty, at Penn State coaches and faculty mingled. Coaches were expected to attend faculty meetings. "We used to tease about the fact that our coaches couldn't even go to the john without running into a faculty member who was apt to criticize him if [coaches] were bending the rules," said Penn State administrator Robert Scannell.

President Milton Eisenhower insisted on strict academic standards for athletes and strict rules to be followed by the athletic department. To enforce his views, in 1952 he hired Ernest McCoy as the new dean of the school of physical education and director of athletics. A strong leader, McCoy had been assistant athletic director at the University of Michigan, which had policies similar to those of Penn State: Administrators controlled athletics, the coaching staff held academic rank, and student-athletic assistance was aboveboard and subordinate to academic regulations.

Backed by Eisenhower and his successor as president, Eric Walker, McCoy was determined to keep Penn State's athletics squeaky-clean. He firmly endorsed the NCAA regulations governing athletics and zealously insisted that all the Penn State coaches follow the rules and be honest in recruiting athletes. Reasoning that if Penn State intended to become a major football power, it ought to have less provincial opponents, McCoy upgraded the football schedule, arranging games with Illinois, Wisconsin, Missouri, North Carolina State, and other highly ranked teams. In addition, because he wanted all students to take part in athletic competition, McCoy greatly expanded athletic programs, intramurals, and physical facilities.[2]

In the 1950s intercollegiate football reigned supreme at Penn State. The Nittany Lion Shrine, a concrete statue of a lion, was the symbol of the football team. (Mountain lions supposedly had roamed nearby Mount Nittany at one time.) Generating the largest following year after year, football was the most profitable athletic enterprise. The large surpluses garnered from the football program compensated for deficits elsewhere in the athletic budget and assured the survival of other varsity sports that could never hope to pay their own way. Thanks to football, moreover, millions of people were becoming acquainted with Penn State. In 1958 the team made its first appearance on national television; four bowl appearances in the late 1950s and early 1960s received national television and press coverage.[3]

At first Joe lived with his new boss in a home Engle purchased for his family. After a few weeks Joe moved in with Steve Suhey, a former Penn State All-American guard, and his wife, Ginger, the daughter of Bob Higgins, the former Penn State football coach.

Joe initially disliked State College. He had never been in central Pennsylvania, and when friends teased him about moving to a cow college in the middle of nowhere, he agreed. Too sleepy and slow moving for his taste, State College had inferior roads and parks, not nearly as good as those in Brooklyn. "I'm gonna go nuts in this hick town!" he thought during the first few months. In the fall of 1950, he informed Engle he was unhappy and didn't expect to stay a second season. "You better start looking around for another coach because I am getting out of here," he told his boss.[4]

Engle had inherited a chaotic football program at Penn State, but he handled the difficult situation admirably. After nineteen years as head coach, Bob Higgins had retired following a successful 1948 season. Two of Higgins's assistants, Joe Bedenk and Earl Edwards, both sought to replace him. When Bedenk won the job, his appointment alienated Edwards's supporters, who included most of the other assistant coaches. Edwards left, but the resentments smoldered throughout 1949 as Bedenk struggled through an unhappy season, winning five and losing four. Bedenk resigned after the 1949 season but elected to remain as an assistant coach. Complicating the awkward situation, Engle had been told that one condition of his new job was that he must retain the entire Penn State coaching staff, including Bedenk. "That was very unusual," Engle later said, "because usually a new coach is permitted to bring in his own staff. But I thought we could somehow make things work." Recruiting had suffered badly since 1948 with the chaos caused by having three head coaches in three years. Most of the offensive players on the 1950 team were non-scholarship walk-ons.

Engle's offensive system, the wing-T, was an adaptation of the T formation, the dynamic new offensive system that had become the rage in college and professional football in the early 1940s. The T formation had many advantages over the traditional single wing, including a balanced attack, deception, speed, and more effective blocking. In the wing-T, a back was placed on the wing, outside the offensive end, and could effectively be used for reverse plays. Because neither the Penn State players nor the holdover coaches understood Engle's system, Engle relied heavily on Joe as his primary assistant.[5]

"[Joe] had more leeway than anybody," said Ed Sulkowski, a team trainer, "because he was Rip's boy." With the other coaches uneasy, Engle used Joe as his sounding board. Joe argued with Engle, but Rip didn't mind because he knew Joe was loyal. Engle appreciated Joe's willingness to challenge the other coaches. "That had to be done," Joe said, "but it just wasn't Rip's nature to do it, especially when he was trying to develop their loyalty. I had the advantage of knowing how Rip Engle thought, felt, and acted about most things. They didn't, so they felt insecure, or at least watchful, until they got a handle on how to work with their new boss."

Assigned to coach the quarterbacks, Joe dived headlong into his new challenge. Since he knew little about coaching or Penn State's players or its opponents, he spent many hours in the office every night with a movie projector. "I was trying to find out what kind of players Penn State had, what Pitt had, what kind of play would win, how good you had to be, trying to evaluate. Then, I had pads and pads of plays. . . . [Every] time I'd see something I'd draw it. I'd want the whole play right across the field—all twenty-two guys."

Players reacted differently to the new young assistant. In the early 1950s many football players at Penn State were military veterans. (A few were older than Joe and married.) Some were far less intense than Joe about playing football. Joe's strenuous practices and late-night bouts working in his office led players to wish he would find a hobby—anything to take his mind off football. "It would be nice if he'd get married," players joked.

Joe insistently barked orders to his players, which increasingly included the entire offense.

"You do it this way!"

"There is only one way to do it!"

"It has got to be this way!"

Some veteran players resented his manner, complaining privately, "Lighten up, for Christ's sake!" "A lot of guys were bitching," said quarterback Don Bailey, who played at Penn State from 1951 to 1954. (On reflection Bailey supported Joe's approach. "I think he did what he had to do in handling older players.")[6]

After a slow start Penn State finished the 1950 season with four consecutive victories and an overall 5-3-1 record. Meanwhile, Joe had become energized and stimulated by his coaching and was growing more comfortable in State College. The Suheys introduced him to their young friends, and Joe met other people in town. He was starting to appreciate the kind of students who attended Penn State. "They were friendlier and more serious about getting an education," he said, and "there was a much more wholesome attitude." Coming from poor or middle-class homes, the students weren't "snooty" like so many people Joe had met at Brown. They were strivers. "They liked people for the way they shaped their thoughts and for the things they chose to do, not for who they 'were.'"[7]

By the end of the 1950 season, Joe wanted to make coaching his career. Almost every waking moment he found himself thinking about football, always trying to improve himself and the team. For hours every night he watched game films, analyzing the mistakes of both teams. "Soon I knew the strengths and weaknesses of every member of our squad."

During Christmas break, he again talked with his father about his future.

"What do you really want to do?" Angelo asked.

"I think I like coaching," Joe replied, "but there's no money in it. I'm only making thirty-six hundred dollars a year."

"Well," said Angelo, "I've never made any real money, but I'm doing what I want to do and I think that's more important than money. If you like coaching, Joe, stay with it." That was the encouragement Joe wanted, bolstering his inclination to make coaching his career.[8]

In 1952 Jim O'Hora, one of Joe's friends and a fellow assistant, asked if Joe wanted to live with the O'Hora family in their small, new home. Joe accepted and in June moved in with the O'Horas. Since the O'Horas could provide him with almost no furniture, Joe started out with a chest of drawers, an old iron bed, and an orange crate from an A&P grocery store for his night stand. Nonetheless, said Bets O'Hora, Jim's wife, "[Joe] was so happy." At first he lived downstairs, but after the birth of the O'Horas' second child, he moved to the unfinished upstairs. For the early part of each summer Joe returned to his family's home in Brooklyn; then he moved back with the O'Horas in time for preseason practice to begin, a routine he followed for the next decade. When the O'Horas moved to a larger home, Joe moved with them.

Early on a rainy morning in 1955, Joe stuck his razor into the bathroom sink at the same moment a bolt of lightning slashed through the roof and struck his bed, creating a wall of flame, and smashing Joe against the bathroom wall. The fire burned his upstairs room, destroying his clothing and personal belongings, including his treasured set of opera records. He was lucky he wasn't killed. "Had he been in his bed," Bets O'Hora speculated, "he may not have been with us now." While the O'Hora family moved in with neighbors, Joe continued to live in the downstairs of the smelly, badly burned home.[9]

Joe cherished his life with the O'Horas because it re-created a family environment like his own family in Brooklyn. Not a boarder, Joe actually lived with the family, sharing their meals and many of their activities. He wrestled with the children, took them for rides in his car, went on the family's picnics, joked, and told stories. He washed and dried the dishes while belting out his favorite songs. ("Joe was a lousy singer," said Jim O'Hora.) On Thursday evenings, when the coaches and their wives took turns hosting a cocktail party before dinner at a restaurant, Joe took his turn as well, hosting the party in his bedroom with the guests sitting on his bed.

They shared sorrow as well, particularly the sudden death of Angelo Paterno in 1955. Joe had often talked proudly about his father, especially about Angelo's persevering struggle to gain his law degree. Angelo's death was a "terrible shock," recalled Bets. "It was a very trying moment for Joe," added Jim. "[Joe] is a very soft individual underneath, although he has armor that perhaps speaks differently."

Jim and Joe contrasted sharply in mood and temperament. Ten years older, Jim was easygoing, usually passive, and more inclined to conciliation than combat; Joe was impetuous, impatient, and critical, with a short fuse that ignited with the slightest provocation. The two discussed athletic policies and recruiting, replayed football games, evaluated players, and argued the merits of offensive and defensive strategies. Because Jim coached on defense and Joe worked with the offense, they learned from each other.

Sometimes the two friends argued until 2:00 A.M. "Many times I would take the opposite [side] just to egg Joe on," said Jim.

"They would be livid," Bets recalled, "pounding on the [table], hollering. You'd think the neighbors would hear." Moments later, though, after the two had settled into bed, Bets would hear, "Good night, Jim." Then, "Good night, Joe."[10]

At first Joe's personality antagonized some colleagues at Penn State. Cocky and inexperienced with adult relationships, he thought he knew more because, unlike his peers, he had graduated from an Ivy League university. He had an opinion on everything—politics, football, religion, Shakespeare, music. "In his first three years [Joe] was pretty much a bastard," a Penn State athletic official bluntly stated. "He was a brazen young man," said fellow assistant Frank Patrick, whom Joe initially offended. "He knew it all. . . . He would tell you off." Joe often argued with former head coach Joe Bedenk. Bedenk usually ended up calling Joe a "young whippersnapper." In the late 1950s and early 1960s, Joe also had angry confrontations on the practice field with the offensive line coach, Sever Toretti. "They were two pretty volatile and fiery Italians," quarterback Pete Liske said. "At times you could sense they were competing against each other for influence on the offensive game plan." Quarterback Al Jacks agreed: "Sever Toretti and Joe Paterno didn't see eye to eye at all. They butted heads more than a few times."

When Dr. Al Griess, the team physician, wanted to pull an injured player out of a game at halftime, Joe strenuously objected. "We needed him and I thought he was well enough to keep playing," Joe later said. While walking by the training room and overhearing the argument, Ed Sulkowski interjected, supporting Dr. Griess. Joe reacted by swearing at Sulkowski, who immediately took a swing at Joe, but missed. Joe later expressed regret for his impulsive behavior. "Obviously, I had no business either taking the position I did with the doctor or provoking the trainer with a personal insult."

Occasionally at social gatherings Joe inadvertently insulted the wives of the assistant coaches and Sunny Engle, Rip's wife. He became irate, for example, when someone suggested that a woman be allowed on the team's plane. "No way!" said Joe. "Over my dead body will a woman get on an airplane with my team!"[11]

Impatient for progress, Joe blamed administrators, like Ernest McCoy, for not immediately solving problems. "No way could he wait till next year," observed Bets O'Hora of Joe's attitude. Because the practice field near the stadium was in poor condition, Engle speculated that perhaps the field could be aerated, ventilating the soil. Joe vociferously agreed. "Yeah, that's what they ought to do, aerate it!" Joe blamed the athletic department officials for not performing the work. "It must be done *now!*" he insisted. While McCoy strived to keep the athletic program in the black, Joe disagreed with some of the economies McCoy had adopted to keep the budget in line. Why didn't the football team have a training table for meals? Why didn't the team travel first class?

While out to dinner at a restaurant with the coaches and their wives, Joe occasionally pounded a table as he engaged in heated arguments with McCoy. In 1956 the two argued at a social gathering at McCoy's home. "The discussion raged hot and heavy and there was some name-calling," said one account. "Cooler heads tried to calm down both men. Paterno concluded his tirade by brandishing his finger under McCoy's nose and shouting, 'McCoy, we're going to win in spite of you!'"

Joe's fellow coaches respected his courage for speaking his mind with McCoy, even while they winced at his intemperance. "Sometimes [McCoy] and Joe would get into the damnedest arguments you could ever imagine!" said Sever Toretti. "And Joe was only an assistant coach!" McCoy could have fired Joe, but he didn't. Why? "Because McCoy saw something in Joe," Toretti said. "He saw a guy who was willing to speak his mind. Whether it was right or wrong—he spoke his mind." Others agreed. "Ernie [McCoy] took it in stride because he knew Joe would be somebody someday," said Bets O'Hora.[12]

Engle's reticence bothered Joe. Diplomatic and cautious, Engle seldom asserted himself and always went through proper administrative channels at the university. "This disturbed Joe greatly," said Jim O'Hora.

When problems emerged, Joe wanted Engle to circumvent bureaucratic barriers and march directly to the university president. "Damn!" Joe would say. "Rip ought to do this!" After one of Joe's tantrums at a social gathering, Jim O'Hora scolded him when they arrived back home. "Joe, you can't do that! You'll never get ahead! You must learn to control [yourself]!"

Later, Joe conceded that he had often been rude. "In those days, I was frustrated because . . . I wanted to move faster, to get rid of people, to change things," he said. "I was impatient for success and always moaning and complaining. . . . I thought I was smarter than everybody else and I had no patience for anyone who disagreed with me. I thought I had all the answers." Feeling regretful after he insulted someone, Joe often phoned the victim the next day to apologize. "The apology [was effective]," Bets O'Hora said.

Although Joe was sometimes irritating and abrasive, other qualities endeared him to people. He was bright and intelligent and a stimulating conversationalist. He spent a good portion of his meager salary buying gifts for others. In fact, he was overly generous, often running out of money late in the month. He was funny. Asked solemnly, "Mr. Paterno, you have quite a reputation for turning out quality quarterbacks. How do you do it?" Joe replied, "I recruit." "Whenever he entered the room, the atmosphere changed," said Bets O'Hora. "It became electric. People were waiting for him to say something." He argued, joked, and laughed. "He got your attention," she added. "He had charisma."[13]

Although Joe was occasionally impatient with Engle, Joe and his boss were usually congenial and their traits complemented each other. Engle was the organizer; Joe was the strategist. Engle was gentle and compassionate; Joe was fiery and compassionate.

Engle served as Joe's mentor, teaching Joe to be more patient. "Rip taught him that you can't bowl everybody over," George Paterno observed. "You've got to take a step back, take an oblique step . . . I often thank God he got under the influence of Rip."

Coaching under Engle was fun, Joe said, because Engle wasn't "a slave driver" and the coaches didn't have to sit "hour after hour" looking at blackboards and movies. Rip allowed them to experiment, to have ideas of their own.

Sometimes Joe gently corrected Engle on the practice field. "Hey Coach," Joe would say, "remember, we changed that." Engle responded,

"That's right, Joe. That's right. You do it." Joe always spoke respectfully about Engle and deferred to him. On Friday evening before a game, if reporters wanted a quote, Joe made absolutely certain that his statement was something Engle would say.

Engle advised Joe never to give up on anybody who wanted to be a football player. "Never cut a kid unless he's a problem, unless he's lazy," Engle said. "And understand that there's a tremendous difference in the ability of these youngsters year in and year out."

Joe admired Engle's moral character and easygoing manner, and he spoke in highly complimentary terms about his boss. "Rip did a fantastic job of getting that staff to work together," Joe later said. "He never imposed himself on anybody. He always let everybody have his say until, after awhile, they all discovered they were agreeing with him and with each other. I learned a great deal from Rip about how to handle people."[14]

Engle worried that football could dehumanize young men and convey immoral values. He deplored television commercials that glamorized the violence of the game. Instead of telling a defensive lineman to "cheat" by moving sideways to get a better angle against opposing linemen, Engle would tell him to "fudge" the maneuver.

Some teams devised special names for defensive positions—a "blood end," a "monster back." But Engle couldn't bring himself to use the savage terms. "I don't want to hear that word 'monster,'" he said. "It doesn't belong in football." Instead of the "monster" back (the secondary back playing to the open field), Penn State had a "hero" back. "To this day at Penn State," Joe wrote in his autobiography, "even in our technical discussions in coaches' meetings, that roving back is 'the hero.'"[15]

In early November 1964, during the week of practice before a tense confrontation with Ohio State, Engle became overly excited and hollered, "Son of a bitch!" "It was like a lightning bolt hit the field," recalled Warren Hartenstine, who had never heard Engle swear. At a team meeting the following evening, Engle profusely apologized.

Joe was a driver, unrelenting in his approach to his coaching. "In those days, things had to be done yesterday," he reflected. Whether Penn State won or lost, on the plane after the game he busily worked in his seat preparing for the next opponent. "He was restless—all the time," said Bets O'Hora, "and very, very ambitious."

Joe devised new offensive and defensive variations, and Engle listened carefully to him because he appreciated his assistant's keen mind. Unlike the married assistants, who were busy with their families, bachelor Joe spent extra time at the office, including many weekends. "He worked hard," Frank Patrick said. "[Success] was not put on a silver platter for him."

He was constantly scribbling notes. While eating breakfast at the kitchen table, he scribbled his notes, writing on anything—even the tablecloth. "All over the room—notes," said Bets O'Hora. "In his bed, on his dresser, in his drawers. Notes. Notes. Notes. Everywhere. . . . In his shoes." Once a month she would leave him a message saying, "Get this cleaned up or leave." Soon the room was cleaned up.[16]

Joe was a major asset for Penn State's football program. "It was very obvious when Joe Paterno first came here that he was going to be very successful. . . because of his drive, his desire, his work habits, his intensity, and his competitiveness," head trainer Chuck Medlar said. "He lived and he slept football. If he had to, he'd work twenty-four hours a day."

Although the youngest coach, Joe tutored his older peers. When the assistants were confused about the wing-T, Joe enlightened them. Jesse Arnelle, a star receiver at Penn State from 1951 to 1954, believed Joe was clearly a leader even as a young coach. "You could see that in some ways the older coaches would defer to Joe. There was something about Joe's creative energies [that allowed] him to come up with the answer for the play you needed." Joe tried to absorb ideas from his peers as well. "Little by little he started to learn [from the other coaches]," said Frank Patrick. To comprehend every facet of the game, Joe made a habit of quizzing an associate about his area of expertise. He asked Toretti about line play and Patrick about the defensive secondary. "He wanted to find out everything," said Patrick. "That's when we knew that eventually this young man was going to be a head coach someplace."[17]

He attended clinics, where he was engrossed by presentations from the finest coaches of the 1950s. While others chatted or roamed the halls, he concentrated on the clinician and asked questions. After driving for two days, he and three others arrived at a clinic in Dallas at midnight, delighted to find Woody Hayes, a rising coaching star, fielding questions in the hotel lobby. Joe was mesmerized. "I completely forgot my sleeplessness and stood there till 4:00 A.M., lapping up every precious word."

At another clinic in Saint Louis, Joe stepped into an elevator and was followed by Bud Wilkinson of Oklahoma, Frank Leahy of Notre Dame, and Wally Butts of Georgia. "I couldn't believe my awesome luck," he later said. "How I hoped they wouldn't know my destination was the third floor. One of them pushed the button for the eighth. I nervously hit nine and hung back, ready to record in my head every word they said to repeat to my roommates." Although they uttered nothing memorable, Joe still savored the experience.

In the late 1950s Joe received his first invitation to speak about coaching—to a football clinic in Pittsburgh. He outlined his talk, purchased a tape recorder, and rehearsed his speech. He wrote effectively and clearly conveyed his thoughts, but he fretted about his diction. Friends teased him about his asphalt-thick Brooklyn accent. He said "coib" (curb), "idears" (ideas) and "toidy-toid" (thirty-third). Determined to improve his diction, he practiced constantly on the tape recorder while the O'Horas listened and critiqued. He also took greater care of his appearance. As his salary increased, so did the quality of his clothes. He asked Bets O'Hora's advice on his wardrobe, seeking the proper tie for his shirt.[18]

By the mid-1950s no one doubted who actually controlled the team, particularly the offense. "It didn't take very long for all of us to realize that [Joe] was running the whole offensive show," said quarterback Al Jacks, who played from 1956 to 1958. Joe designed the offense, called most of the plays, and hollered more than the other coaches. When there was confusion among all the coaches on the practice field, Joe dominated. He seemed to know exactly what needed to be done. "If he saw something not going right, he took charge, even though he wasn't the head coach," said an observer.

During games Joe usually stayed in the press box, relaying plays and information by phone to Engle on the sideline. But when he became impatient with Engle's cautious coaching or thought the team needed to be fired up, he rushed down to the field and coached from the sideline. He had a fire in him that Engle lacked. "Joe was right," said Jim O'Hora of Joe's decision to leave the press box. "He got everybody on the bench into the game because *he* was fired up." Once Joe charged out of the press box, ran down the steps of Beaver Stadium, and inserted a Penn State player into the game without consulting Engle or even looking at him. "It was the craziest thing I have ever seen," said a scout who observed the scene.

As halftime approached, Joe rushed from the press box to the locker room, ready to instruct at the blackboard. After players arrived, Engle announced, "Go get your oranges and go to the bathroom." Then Joe took over. With one arm flapping, he conducted the entire halftime strategy session. At the end Engle said, "OK. Let's go get 'em."

Jim O'Hora understood the unbridled, noisy approach Joe sometimes displayed. "He would lose himself in his coaching," O'Hora observed. Winning and losing football games was serious business and affected Joe's future career. If the team succeeded, his chances of becoming a head coach increased. "I was very ambitious," Joe said, "and I wanted to make sure I would get to the top. I thought the only way I would get ahead was by the success of the team."

Joe helped develop excellent quarterbacks—Galen Hall, Dick Hoak, Pete Liske, Milt Plum, Al Jacks, Jack White, Tony Rados, and All-American Richie Lucas. He worked extensively on coaching the mechanics of being a quarterback. On a running play he insisted that each step by the quarterback be precise. "On a rollout," said Jack White, "you had to be in a certain position at a certain time to be able to throw the ball, and he would make sure it was exact." Persistent and deliberate, Joe became upset when Vince O'Bara, the team's quarterback in 1950, quickly fled the pocket on pass plays. To counteract O'Bara's tendency, Joe drew a ring on the practice field, indicating where O'Bara was supposed to stay. "When you drop back for that pass, *this* is where I want you to be! Don't you leave that circle!" Overall, O'Bara was "very comfortable" with his quarterback coach. "[Joe] was very understanding," O'Bara said.

Because the quarterbacks called their own plays, Joe had to prepare them expertly. "We had to know it well," said Pete Liske. To assist his quarterbacks, Joe printed a special manual. (He gave tests to make sure they grasped it.) The manual described precisely the correct way to take the ball from the center, the number of steps needed to drop back for a pass, and which plays to call for a variety of different situations. When inside the opponent's forty-yard line, Joe wanted his quarterback to realize that the offense was in a four-down area, unlike three-down territory on Penn State's own thirty-yard line. In meetings with his quarterbacks during the week, Joe placed them in hypothetical situations to improve their judgment during Saturday's game. Penn State was winning the game and had the ball at midfield, he instructed them. Rain had made the ball slippery, but Penn State needed to maintain ball control because only seven minutes remained in the fourth quarter. "Here's what we ought to do," he taught. "He would cite situation after situation after situation," said Don Bailey, who eventually absorbed his coach's thinking. "After a couple of years, you became very familiar with what the hell he wanted called." Joe's teaching proved effective, Bailey reflected. "We didn't beat ourselves that often."

Quarterbacks found it difficult to escape from Joe. As Jacks was on his way to lunch, Joe spotted him. "Come over here," Joe said. "We'll sit together." Jacks thought to himself, *Oh brother! We're going to talk offense and strategy!* Sure enough, during the lunch Joe discussed offense and strategy.

When interviewed, Joe expressed modesty about the high quality of the quarterbacks he coached. "I don't make great quarterbacks," he said. "They have to do it themselves."[19]

At practice Joe would place himself in front of a group of offensive players and say, "Look, this play will work if everybody does exactly as it's designed and everyone puts out 110 percent effort."

"He made sure that you understood perfectly what you were to do," said Jesse Arnelle.

Joe impatiently criticized players who didn't quickly absorb the mental portion of the game. "If somebody had trouble mastering a physical technique, that was a little different, because I had always had trouble mastering techniques. But I never had any problem learning the mental part quickly, so I had no patience with anybody else who had trouble."

Sometimes Joe was overly harsh. "In Joe's world there [was] no room for error," observed Warren Hartenstine, who played for Penn State from 1963 to 1966. "He considered a penalty a mistake akin to a fumble because it compromised the team. . . . He absolutely [would] go to the film and just destroy the player—punish him verbally in front of the team for having made such an error."

Occasionally, he reacted insensitively to an injured player. Hartenstine recalled one awful instance:

I remember him, frustrated with our [lack of] success during a practice, ordering a quarterback with pulled hamstrings to remove the "red cross" jersey that only the omnipresent doctors were to order removed, and putting him into "Nine on Nine," one of our most physically punishing drills. The play was "busted" when the fullback went the wrong way, leaving the quarterback to run the ball. He was hit in the area of the injury several times on his way to the end zone and fumbled the ball. Coach Paterno was beside himself with anger and would not allow the downed and reinjured player, a real team leader and favorite, to receive immediate medical attention. As I recall, he sent us to the showers. The downed player had to crawl to the locker room.

The victim, Jack White, confirms some of the details described by Hartenstine. "Paterno went crazy," White said. "He thought I wasn't giving a full effort." But White does not recall being so badly hurt that he had to crawl to the locker room.

The incident related by Hartenstine and White was not typical. Still, Joe later conceded that he wasn't always sensitive enough to the players' feelings. "That was my personality. I was the same way at Brown. I felt things should go right all the time. We weren't in the business of making excuses." But he thought the players put up with his haranguing. "They realized I was trying to make them as good as they wanted to be."[20]

Many players effusively praised Joe and his coaching. "The thing I appreciate more than anything else is the fact that Joe never criticized me in front of the other players," Richie Lucas said. "We had a conversational relationship. If he disagreed with a play I called, he'd tell me about it privately and then he would hear out my reasons for it." Joe's approach gave Lucas confidence. "If you sat down with Joe for five minutes, he could make you feel good, like you were walking on air after you left the office," Lucas said. "He had a burning desire to have you succeed, have you reach your potential."[21]

Starting immediately in 1950, Joe began supervising the academic progress of the players he coached. Before the 1950 season O'Bara had met with a coach about once per month concerning his academic progress; Joe met with O'Bara once per week. Before 1950 the team was quartered at an off-campus site on the Friday evening before a home game, making it necessary for players to skip their Saturday morning classes. Joe altered the routine. If one of his players had a Saturday morning class, the player didn't join the team off campus on Friday night but remained on campus. That player would attend his Saturday morning class and then join the team in the locker room before the game.

If a laboratory class was scheduled for 3:00–5:00 P.M. on Tuesday and Thursday, conflicting with football practice, the player was supposed to attend the class. Nor were players to alter their fall course schedule to accommodate football. In his normal progression toward fulfilling requirements in his major, a player took a difficult class even though it might interfere with football. "You just stayed with the normal progress of your education," said Pete Liske.

Joe constantly talked to Jesse Arnelle about his classes.

"How are your classes going?"

"Who are your professors?"

"Do you need a tutor?"

"How are your grades?"

"Consider taking this course in English literature."

"He would jump down your throat in a second about your [poor] grades," Don Bailey recalled. "What are you doing to solve this [academic] problem?" Joe asked O'Bara. "Joe was really concerned with our academic progress," O'Bara reflected. "To me that was impressive."

After Liske started playing professional football, he was shocked to learn that many fellow players had been allowed to place less emphasis on academics than he had experienced at Penn State. They had lived in athletic dorms, taken light class loads, scheduled classes around practices, and in other ways placed football far ahead of their college classes.

Occasionally, Joe wondered if he had made a mistake by not going to law school. Was he evading his destiny? "Then I'd come across some student who was serious about his schooling and his life, serious about how he approached the game, and that made it feel okay."[22]

Players often praised the integrity of the program at Penn State and the values Engle and Joe conveyed. "I was proud of the fact that they always kept the program in perspective," said Glenn Ressler, an All-American middle guard who played from 1962 to 1964. "They kept reminding you that academics was the reason for being in school and that sports were secondary."

Assistant coach Earl Bruce often recruited with Joe in western Pennsylvania where they energetically competed for prospects with archrival University of Pittsburgh. Bruce, who was twenty years older than Joe, provided the father figure for the recruit; Joe had the knack for buddying up to the prospect. Bets O'Hora watched Joe talk with prospects and their parents at the O'Horas' home. "He [had] the wonderful gift of making you feel at ease immediately," she said. "He is just Joe, and he means what he says."

Many of the ideals Joe later espoused had been Engle's ideals in the 1950s. "When [Engle] came into my living room my senior year in high school, he emphasized academics over athletics," said a former Penn State player. "He came off as a perfect gentleman." Engle sought athletes who would retain their eligibility and graduate. He wanted them to be able to have a career after football; besides, every time a player dropped out of school, all the effort coaching him was wasted. When Engle and his staff recruited high school players, they first checked with the guidance counselor to inspect the student's academic transcript. "We lose a lot of kids that way," acknowledged Dean McCoy, "but we'd rather lose them before they get here than after."[23]

Earl Bruce described Joe as "very honest" in recruiting. So did Jesse Arnelle. Joe did not sound like a college coach, said Arnelle. "He talked to me about the kind of college education I was looking for. Then he talked about Penn State University and the advantages it had for students." Other players agreed. "You learned from Rip Engle and from Joe Paterno that football was important, but that being a student and a person [was] more important," said Robert Mitinger, who played at Penn State from 1959 to 1961 and later opened his own law firm in State College.

Recruiting rules in the 1950s were lenient, encouraging some underhanded, freewheeling tactics. Joe was less concerned with the niceties of recruiting than he would be later. "Sometimes, Bruce and I drove a kid around for hours tickling his ears with great football stories," Joe related in his autobiography. "We'd do that not to impress the kid, but because we heard a competing coach was in town looking for the recruit and we didn't want any rivals to get their hands on him."[24]

One spring Joe and Bruce spent considerable time recruiting Emil Caprara from Turtle Creek, Pennsylvania, and Ron Markowitz, a youngster who played at nearby Braddock High. Because both players were leaning toward enrolling at the University of Maryland, Joe and Bruce decided late in the summer to try to "steal" the two athletes away from Maryland. They drove to Turtle Creek, picked up Caprara, and set out for Markowitz's home twelve miles away. Hyman and White explained what happened next: As they were driving along, another car approached from the opposite direction and Caprara suddenly ducked his head and hit the floor. "Gee," he yelled, "that was Jack Hannameyer, the Maryland assistant coach. I bet he's up here to see Markowitz and me."

"We took off like a shot," recalled Paterno. "We raced over to Markowitz's house, bundled him into the car, and then spent the next five or six hours driving all over the area. We rode past Ronnie's house a couple of times and, sure enough, Hannameyer's car was parked outside. We had lunch, ice cream sodas, hamburgers, dinner, anything to kill time until Hannameyer got tired of waiting for Ronnie."

Finally, the coast was clear and the party returned to Markowitz's house. Paterno and Bruce got permission from Ronnie's parents for him to spend the weekend at Penn State. The cloak-and-dagger ploy worked. Caprara and Markowitz enrolled at Penn State and they both had respectable football careers.[25]

Although Bets and Jim O'Hora loved Joe and enjoyed his company, after ten years they privately agreed that Joe should move on. With the O'Hora children growing older and needing more attention, Bets worried that her children were being shut out. In 1961 Jim O'Hora tactfully began explaining to Joe that their arrangement needed to change. He started to tell the story of how his Irish father had explained to visiting relatives that it was time to leave the home and be on their own. Joe took the hint immediately. "Jim, you don't have to go any further," he said. "I understand." In June 1961 Joe moved out and rented an apartment three blocks away.

Joe hadn't moved earlier because he had been so content and didn't want to be alone. "He could not be without people," said Jim O'Hora, who laughs at the memory of having to kick Joe out of his home. "It became apparent he'd never leave." On reflection Joe knew that leaving was a decision he should have made much earlier, "but the O'Horas were like my own family and I liked living with them." He remained grateful to Bets and Jim for their kindness and understanding. "They got me over a lot of rough spots."[26]

During his leisure Joe listened to classical music, read books, studied poetry, and attended concerts and lectures on campus. On weekends he dined at the Elks or the American Legion. "There were not many places to eat in town during the mid-1950s," said Charles Mann, who would see Joe at the American Legion. "We would go there often to watch the television news, eat, and mingle." Joe was also a highly competitive handball player. A friend who played handball with him liked singles better. "When we played doubles, and Joe and I were on the same side, I never got much of a workout. He'd take the whole court."

Outside of his activities with the O'Hora family, Joe didn't have much social life because he worked constantly. "Joe was so busy thinking, discussing, and coaching football, recruiting players, and being Rip Engle's alter ego," Hyman and White observed, "that he really didn't have much time for socializing, except with other members of the coaching staff and a few close friends." He seldom dated. "I never saw him with a girl all those years," recalled assistant coach J. T. White.[27]

Unbeknownst to most of his friends, however, in the winter of 1959 Joe met a young woman who attracted him. One of his duties was to run the study hall in the library for football players, and every day, when the study period ended, Suzanne Pohland was waiting for her boyfriend. Attractive, bright, and humorous, Sue was a freshman from Latrobe, Pennsylvania. Joe asked her to keep tabs on her athlete friend, who was having academic problems. "If he cut a class or got a poor grade, I wanted her to tell me so we could help him by applying an ounce of prevention," Joe later said. As their paths kept crossing, Joe and Sue discovered a mutual interest in English literature. After Sue's boyfriend transferred to another school, she still kept running into Joe, and they were attracted to each other.

One evening Joe listened to a lecture by Leslie Fiedler, the provocative literary critic, and Sue also attended. Joe and Sue left together. "One of us got a little book of Fiedler lectures, and we lent it back and forth, reading one essay after another, and discovered we both enjoyed the competition of disagreement," Joe reflected in his autobiography. "She was very bubbly and would say whatever came into her head, which I liked. I could see her smarts, especially when I went out to her house and saw what kind of leader she was among her roommates. In all our discussions, I don't think football or athletics ever came up once."

Joe became Sue's father confessor. "I thought of him as a friend, advisor, and confidant," Sue recalled. Their relationship continued as they shared ideas, books, and thoughts about life.

In the summer of 1961, Sue took a job on the New Jersey shore; Joe rented a house with his sister and her family in a nearby town to be near Sue. They sat on the beach reading aloud from Albert Camus's *The Stranger* and discussing Camus, Nietzsche, Hemingway, and Faulkner. Near the end of the summer, Joe asked her to marry him and she agreed. Sue was twenty-two; Joe was almost thirty-five. Most of Joe's friends and fellow assistants didn't even know he was dating Sue until they announced their engagement. On May 12, 1962, they were married in Latrobe.

Of their postwedding plans, Joe reflected: "At first we planned a two-month honeymoon in Europe until I realized I couldn't afford it—I told her I couldn't take that much time—so we backtracked to a few weeks in Bermuda, which soon shrank to two weeks in the Virgin Islands, which shortened to ten days in Florida, until I proposed a week at Sea Isle, Georgia. The bottom line was we had a wonderful five days at Virginia Beach. On the way down, I stopped off to see a recruit at Somerset, Pennsylvania, while Sue waited in the car. We lost him to Miami."

"He went in; I read," Sue recalled of Joe's recruiting on their honeymoon. "And it hasn't changed. At that time, there were few restrictions on recruiting. So on our honeymoon we bought saltwater taffy for his recruits' mothers, sent postcards to his recruits. It was fine. It had better be fine. You have to roll with the punches. When we got home from the honeymoon, he left two days later with Earl Bruce to go recruiting. I thought he was married to Earl Bruce for the first two months of our marriage."[28]

With few exceptions Engle's staff remained intact throughout his sixteen years at Penn State. A close-knit group, they worked effectively together with infrequent backbiting or maneuvering for credit or for position in the hierarchy. Engle was careful to be liberal with his praise of his assistants and allowed each man his opportunity to be heard. "It was more a partnership than a boss-assistant relationship," said Hyman and White.

During those years Engle and his staff built solid teams that Joe believed were slighted by the national media. From 1950 to 1965 Penn State compiled a 104-48-4 record, including victories in three of four bowl games. The Lions peaked in the early 1960s while winning consecutive bowl victories over Alabama, Oregon, and Georgia Tech. "We had awfully good football teams," Joe mused, "but we didn't get the recognition."

Joe loved Penn State, but the lure of the big city and a more prestigious coaching opportunity also captivated him. An excellent opportunity came along in 1958 when the University of Southern California offered Engle its head-coaching position. Engle seriously considered the offer and traveled to Los Angeles to discuss the position. Joe feverishly tried to convince Engle and the other assistants of the advantages of coaching at a major football power in a large city. "Joe was gung ho and viewed this job as a great step forward for his coaching career," Jim O'Hora said. But the O'Horas had three children and didn't want to pull up roots, and the other assistants didn't want to leave Penn State either. So when Engle polled his assistants to see if they wanted to go, Joe found himself a minority of one in favor of leaving. Engle rejected the job. "Joe was furious!" J. T. White recalled. "He wanted to go to Southern Cal with Rip."[29]

Joe was itching for a head-coaching position. Aware of Joe's frustration, Engle hoped nonetheless his young assistant would be patient. "[Engle] was always reluctant for me to take some jobs that were offered to me because I think he really felt that I'd be better off [at Penn State], that I'd probably get [the Penn State] job, and that this job was as good as there was in the country," Joe later said. "Joe never asked me to commit myself under any circumstances," Engle said of the prospect of Joe succeeding him as head coach, "although he knew how much I thought of him." All the assistant coaches assumed that Joe would be Engle's successor. "I think we all felt that Joe was very capable and would do a great job," said Earl Bruce.

In 1959 Weeb Ewbank, head coach of the professional Baltimore Colts (and a coach at Brown when Joe was a freshman), asked Joe to become his offensive backfield coach. "I would have been pleased to have him on my staff," Ewbank recalled. "He impressed me." Joe mulled over Ewbank's offer, but he was unwilling to leave Penn State for a job as an assistant coach. "Something told me I should stay there," Joe later said. Subsequently, when he was offered jobs as an assistant with the Philadelphia Eagles and the Oakland Raiders, he rejected them as well. In 1962 he interviewed for the head-coaching vacancy at Yale, but the Ivy League school selected John Pont.[30]

Meanwhile, weary physically and mentally, Rip Engle had started considering retirement after the 1962 season and decided to remain in coaching for only a few more years. When he thought about his successor, Joe was the logical choice. In June 1964 Penn State named Joe associate football coach, a promotion that established him officially as Engle's primary assistant and heir apparent.

After the 1964 season, John Pont left Yale to become head coach at Indiana University, and this time Yale extended the coaching position to Joe. The offer was a crucial turning point in Joe's career because many considered the position at Yale one of the plums of the profession and hard to turn down.

Holding the Yale offer, Joe approached Penn State officials with his high hand. He talked to Engle and McCoy about his future at Penn State. If he turned down Yale, would he eventually have an opportunity to get the Penn State position? "I dreamed about nothing other than becoming head coach [at Penn State]," he said. Nobody promised him anything, but Joe knew Engle would retire shortly and McCoy and Engle assured him that, as far as they were concerned, he would have the job.[31]

Still, Joe sought additional assurance from Eric Walker, Penn State's president. Engle secured him the appointment with Walker and accompanied him to the meeting. In his autobiography, Joe recalled their discussion:

> The president's cordial greeting was memorable: "What do you want to talk about?"
>
> "I've been offered the head-coaching job at Yale. Before I decide, I want to know what my chances are for Rip's job when he retires."
>
> Dr. Walker looked me straight in the eye, both sternly and warmly. "If you're good enough, you'll get the job. That's the only thing that's going to count."
>
> I understood him perfectly. There was no doubt in my mind that over the years I had become good enough. I turned down Yale.

After the final game of the 1965 season, Engle informed Joe that he was going to retire. "He told me he wanted me to get [the job]," said

Joe. Shortly after Engle announced his retirement, Dean McCoy offered the position to Joe. "I'll pay you twenty thousand dollars a year," said McCoy. "Holy smokes, that's super," Joe replied, and he accepted the position. At thirty-eight, after sixteen years as an assistant, Joe was the new head coach at Penn State.[32]

~3~

FOOTBALL THE PATERNO WAY
(1966–1978)

As Joe assumed his head-coaching duties, the entire Penn State family expressed confidence in his ability. Said President Walker: "I know of no one as well qualified to carry on Penn State's football tradition. Joe Paterno is an outstanding leader of young men, both on and off the field." Ernest McCoy added his endorsement: "He is what we are always looking for—an excellent teacher—and his teaching skills have been proven by the fine quarterbacks and backs he's turned out." Engle praised Joe's "intelligence, dedication, [and] loyalty."

In turn Joe declared that he would continue most of Engle's approach, but he also signaled his independence. Not wanting to be a "carbon copy," he indicated that he would replace his predecessor's wing-T with the I formation and that he expected to "gamble a bit more than Rip."

Joe inherited a wise and veteran staff of assistants: Jim O'Hora (interior defensive line), Earl Bruce (freshman coach), Frank Patrick (defensive backs), J. T. White (defensive ends), and Dan Radakovich (linebackers). Others on the staff were George Welsh (offensive backs) and Joe McMullen (interior offensive line). Bob Phillips, a successful head coach at Montour High School, was recruited to help with the offensive ends. His staff, Joe bragged, was the "best in the country."[1]

Joe was finally where he wanted to be. Ironically, though, his first year as head coach turned out to be confusing and frustrating. What should have been a happy year turned out to be one of Joe's most distressing.

Penn State lost three of its first five games, including a 42-8 rout by Michigan State and a 49-11 drubbing by UCLA. Joe imagined that the entire burden of success had fallen on him, and that he was leading Penn State toward mediocrity or worse. He witnessed for the first time the ugly wrath of fans. "Hate mail and vile, abusive phone calls invaded my home daily, startling and bewildering Sue more than me."

Part of the problem was the quality of the senior players. While the underclassmen displayed outstanding potential, the senior class was weak in leadership and football talent. Senior players particularly had trouble adjusting to Joe's new role and expressed unhappiness with his coaching. Some thought that he played favorites among the players. He issued rules, they said, but then allowed certain players to escape punishment when the rules were violated.

"He gave his word, but wasn't honoring it," said Warren Hartenstine. "So there was a loss of faith."

"During my senior year [1966]," co-captain Mike Irwin observed, "there were a couple of situations in which he thought the team should be involved in the decision-making process." Joe asked the players to vote on a discipline problem, a convenient method of avoiding the imposition of punishment. When star defensive lineman Dave Rowe broke curfew early in the season, Joe asked senior players to vote on whether Rowe should play in the next game. Naturally, the group voted to allow Rowe to play. "I don't think [Joe] would have done that the next year," said Irwin.

At halftime Joe usually discussed strategy and tactics. But at the half of the second-to-last game against Georgia Tech, he verbally and personally attacked two players. "I was taken aback," said Irwin, "because it was uncharacteristic for Joe to get that personal with people. . . . Some of the frustrations were coming through. He sort of lost it at halftime."

"He didn't seem decisive," quarterback Jack White added. "He didn't seem to have the same persona that he had as an assistant coach." Some players predicted he wouldn't succeed; he seemed too young and immature. "He is a good assistant coach," the critics mumbled, "but there is no way that he is going to make it as a head coach."

A loss to Pittsburgh in the last game would have assured Penn State of a losing season, its first since 1938. But the Lions prevailed, defeating a weak Pittsburgh team, 48-24, giving Joe a .500 record (5-5) for his first season, but not much satisfaction. "I was not sure I was a good head coach, and I was not sure of my future when that year ended," he later said.[2]

Joe had started off headstrong and insecure. Because of his burning desire to succeed, he didn't see why he had to share the number-one spot with "Bear Bryant or Vince Lombardi or anybody else." He hated losing and hated the idea of settling for number two. "I think I was kind of overreacting," he later said of his first year as coach. "I wanted to make sure that people didn't think I was going to be exactly like Rip Engle. I wanted to let them know I would do things my way."

Twice during the 1966 season Joe inserted a new maneuver late in the practice week, too late to practice thoroughly, thereby confusing his players. "When you practice something new on Friday, you're out of business." He learned to put innovations into his game plan early in the week. Joe also thought he had made his players too nervous, too afraid to make mistakes. "I learned that a young man must feel comfortable at his position in order to play well," he said, "and this takes time."[3]

During the transition year Joe had problems adjusting to his assistant coaches. A year earlier he had been working with them as an equal, as another assistant coach; now he was their boss. In some cases he was too reluctant to overrule them when he thought his instinct was right; more often, he made decisions on his own when he should have listened to the advice of his assistants who understood the situation.

"I think Joe was trying to do it all by himself," said Frank Patrick, "until he found out he couldn't. Then he started to delegate [and] we started to move." Jim O'Hora thought Joe made a mistake in his peremptory approach to evaluating personnel. "He had his opinion and went with his opinion, irregardless [sic] of the opposite opinion."

In the fifth game, the 49-11 slaughter by UCLA, Joe learned another valuable lesson. Disgusted with the performance of his defense, he said to assistant Dan Radakovich, "Never again [do I] want that scoreboard lighting up like . . . a pinball machine!" He resolved to get better athletes on defense. The following year, therefore, Joe gave first priority to defense, and all the players were tried out at defensive positions. "The goal was to put the best players on defense," Radakovich said. "*Everybody* was tried on defense. . . . That decision was probably the most important decision he ever made."[4]

In the summer of 1967, Joe devised a new defensive system different from anything then existing, using ideas that had been percolating in his mind for several years. He wanted to confuse and disarm opponents, not with a gimmick or a trick that might work for a few plays but with a new system that might take years for other coaches to figure out.

He closed the door to his office at home, isolating himself from intruders. He was the first to admit that his family suffered during the summer, but Sue understood and cooperated. "He hadn't quite done it in 1966," she pointed out. "He felt he let the school down and that he would have to do a better job. He felt he let the team down. Joe is stubborn that way." Sue woke the children (by now, they had three), fed them, explained that their father was working, and then took the family swimming for four or five hours.

When there were moments of success, Joe shared the joy with the family. "[He'd] hit upon something," Sue recalled, "and for about two days we'd have a human being with us again. He was relieved that all of a sudden things fit together. Then he'd try to figure out names for his plays on defense, and we'd play these games of naming them. He'd try to explain these plays related to something we both knew. We tried to think up names and, really, that was the most fun we had all that summer."[5]

After studying the entire summer, Joe came up with innovative ideas for pass coverage and stunting that confused opponents for almost four years. In his autobiography he explained the innovations. To prevent opponents from getting outside Penn State's defensive perimeter, he added one man to the defensive line (making a total of four players on the line of scrimmage). He positioned the player wide enough to absolutely contain the quarterback. The heavy cost of making the change was that he now had only three instead of four defensive backs. Joe had another concern: "When I position a man to cover outside, I have to ask, How am I up the middle?"

To solve the weakness up the middle Joe devised an intricate system of "stunting," lining up one way to tempt the opponent to a hole, then shifting at the snap of the ball. "Okay, their quarterback is not going to get outside my defensive end. He's not going to run the option. I've got enough stunts and blitzes so they won't run inside." So far, though, Joe had used eight players to accomplish what other teams tried to do with seven.

Joe and Sue enjoy a family moment with daughters Diane Lynne and Mary Kathryn after Joe was introduced as Penn State's new head football coach in February 1966. (AP/Wide World Photo)

Because he was going to use only three defensive backs, Joe designed a system of "rotate coverage." The three backs spread out and watched the quarterback. "If [the quarterback] tried coming to our left on a sprint-out or option, our outside guy on that side would immediately come in to handle him. The middle man of the three, the safety, would shift to the left to back him. Then the third guy, from the far side, would shift over and play safety."

To add variety to the system he also developed "half coverage." As soon as the center snapped the ball, the defensive back on the wide side of the field rushed toward the line on the assumption the play was coming to him. The center safety sprinted to back him up and played a zone. The third defensive back played man-to-man, covering the one receiver usually assigned to get back there. "What is not ideally covered is the zone up forward," Joe said. "So we're announcing to them, 'You want to pass? Go ahead and try. But you'll have to make it a short pass. If it's good, you'll get eight yards, no more.'" The best part was that the defense required exactly the same formation as the rotate coverage, confusing opposing coaches trying to figure out what Penn State was doing. Still another coverage had the linebackers fall back into the short zones to watch for a pass, depending on how they read the offensive formation and the quarterback's eyes.

All the defensive formations looked exactly the same until the snap of the ball. There were other changes and adjustments as well: He harmonized the stunts with the coverage and developed a new technique to play man-to-man defense. He studied the lengths of hypotenuses between sides of triangles to determine the mathematical rules for playing men in the secondary. Then he devised new terminology for all the possible action and, finally, taught and sold the innovations to his skeptical staff of assistants. "Every day required a pep talk. Then they began to see, I think, how much work, thought, and figuring had gone into this." When an assistant asked a question, Joe had the answer. "Supposing they do this?" Joe pulled out his ledger sheets and responded. "It was all written down," Joe reflected, "the rules, the terminology—all thought through and laid out."[6]

Opponents had difficulty interpreting the defense because they usually had only one week to prepare for Penn State and had to change their blocking rules. "When they played against us, they had to make a lot of adjustments," Robert Phillips said.

Fortunately, Joe also had excellent players to carry out his new schemes. (Fate "took care of me," he said). The result? His 1968 and 1969 teams were among the greatest defensive teams in college football history. Many college coaches visited Penn State to study Joe's innovative concepts.

The summer of work in his hideaway "made a living for me for four good years, at least," Joe later said. It took that long for opposing coaches to decipher and understand Penn State's new defensive schemes. Joe loved being referred to as an "unorthodox" coach because then opposing coaches had to worry about his team. When the opposition fretted about all the unexpected things Penn State might do, they wouldn't be properly prepared for what Penn State did do. Besides, experimenting with new concepts stimulated Joe's mind and warded off boredom.[7]

In the first game of 1967 Penn State lost to Navy, 23-22, "in about as poorly a played and coached game as I ever was involved in," Joe said. His team's shabby performance had allowed Navy to gain an incredible 489 yards. "The players just went through [the] motions," Joe reflected. "No commitment, no intensity, just flat."

For the first time Joe seriously wondered about his future as a coach. "I wondered whether I really had it," he later said. "I had coached eleven games at Penn State as the head coach and I was five and six. It just had never dawned on me prior to that game that I wasn't going to be a real good football coach. . . . But now, out of a clear blue sky, I'm in trouble." For the next game, against Miami, he decided to go with his younger players. "I needed to develop my own way of coaching, and I had to do it with a fresh squad that I could make my own."[8]

Against Miami he took a chance by inserting several sophomores, among them future stars Dennis Onkotz, Pete Johnson, Steve Smear, and Jim Kates. The lively Penn State team played with vigor in the Florida humidity and outclassed their hosts, winning in the end, 17-8. "Nothing like this should have happened from a team out of the unproductive East," commented the *Miami Herald*. The game turned Joe's career around. After losing the next contest to UCLA, 17-15, Penn State embarked on one of the longest nonlosing streaks in college football's history, extending over four seasons.

Penn State easily defeated Ohio University and Pittsburgh to conclude the 1967 schedule with an 8-2 record. As the season was drawing to a close, speculation had mounted about a bowl appearance. To forestall any daydreaming by his players and coaches, Joe promulgated rules for bowl preparation that he followed for many years: no talk about a bowl game until after the final regular season game, no interviews, no mention of a bowl at any time in Joe's presence or that of his players. The team must concentrate on the job at hand, winning the remaining games.[9]

Penn State accepted an invitation to face Florida State in the Gator Bowl on December 30, 1967. Joe made major adjustments in his offense and defense in preparation for the contest. "If you don't try something new in the two weeks of practice before a bowl game, the team gets bored and then goes stale," he explained privately to a few sportswriters. "If you stay with the old, the players say, 'We know these things, so why do we practice so long?'" This way he gave them something novel to learn and made them want to practice. "And then, of course, anything new will temporarily upset the other team," he said, "at least at first."

The crucial play of the game occurred in the second half when Joe elected to try for a first down on fourth-and-one at his *own* fifteen-yard line while Penn State led, 17-0. The play failed, Florida State rallied to score two touchdowns, then kicked a field goal, sending the disappointed Nittany Lions home with a 17-17 tie.

Sports Illustrated dubbed Joe's fourth-and-one decision as the "bonehead play" of all the postseason bowl games that year. The call aroused muttering and criticism from Penn State's fans and alumni as well. Joe admitted his gamble was unorthodox and had undoubtedly cost Penn State the game. "I had told our kids to be reckless in the second half," he explained, "not to worry about sitting on that lead. So, the first time we had a chance to gamble, I just had to go for it."

On the postseason banquet circuit Joe justified his play calling but also poked fun at himself for his "fourth-and-one" decision. In similar circumstances he might call the play again, he boldly stated. "You'd better get used to it, because that's how we're going to be at Penn State. We're going to be reckless, we're going to take chances. I made up my mind when I got this job I was not going to be a stereotyped coach. Lousy maybe, but not stereotyped." (Actually, Joe didn't take similar chances in future contests.)[10]

Only two years after his mediocre start, in 1968, Joe directed Penn State to an undefeated (10-0) regular season and faced Kansas in the Orange Bowl. With about one minute left to play and Kansas ahead, 14-7, Penn State quarterback Chuck Burkhart passed to halfback Bobby Campbell who lugged the ball to the three-yard line. Kansas stopped two running plays, but on third down on a broken play, Burkhart ran around left end for the score. Nobody noticed, but Kansas had twelve men on the field for all three plays. "Our coaches in the press box were going nuts," Joe later said. "They knew something was wrong because every hole we tried was plugged. But nobody did any counting." On Penn State's failed attempt for a two-point conversion, an official spotted the extra Kansas defender and stepped off a yard-and-a-half penalty, and on the second effort Campbell scored, giving Penn State a dramatic 15-14 victory. Joe seemed like a gambler against Kansas when he successfully tried the two-point conversion, risking defeat, his winning streak, and the team's national ranking. "If we don't win, we lose," was his simple postgame explanation after his team's one-point victory.

A crowd of five thousand jammed Penn State's Recreation Building to welcome the team home after its triumph over Kansas. Joe received a thunderous standing ovation as he walked to the stage with president Eric Walker. Three bands increased the decibel level. "Every dream I have ever had has been fulfilled this season," Joe told the crowd. "We have the greatest staff in America, bar none. Our players are all great young men, gentlemen with fine character. They have made me feel very humble and inadequate at times." In the final polls Penn State was voted number three by the UPI and number two by the AP, and the American College Football Coaches' Association named Joe as Coach of the Year.[11]

Meanwhile, trying to win for winning's sake was leaving Joe with an empty feeling. Slowly, he was developing a philosophy he labeled the "Grand Experiment." Something made him itch for a different kind of goal, "not football that puts winning first, but first-class football played by students who put first-class lives first." He said he wanted "to re-create at this more-or-less ordinary state university, for these kids of more-or-less ordinary farm and working-class family backgrounds, something like the excitement that made most days at Brown University wonderful for me— the books, the bull sessions, the sense of wonder and anticipation, all that and football, too."

Rip Engle and Ernest McCoy had both believed that academics and athletics could coexist. McCoy and president Eric Walker particularly deserved credit for demanding the strict adherence of athletics to university policy and NCAA rules. Joe agreed with Penn State's athletic philosophy, but after becoming head coach, he added his own innovations and, most importantly, vigorously promoted his reformist ideas, winning heaps of praise from adherents who were disgusted with the corruption pervading college football, plus the disapproval of a few critics who thought he was being self-righteous.[12]

Joe publicly expressed his personal philosophy for the first time as a guest columnist for the local newspaper, the *Centre Daily Times*, on July 28, 1966. He noted that recently the president of Hamline College

Quarterback Chuck Burkhart soaks up some of Paterno's wisdom, evident early on when Penn State cruised to an 11-0 season behind Burkhart in only Paterno's third season at the Penn State helm. (Photo courtesy of Penn State Sports Information Department)

had lashed out at intercollegiate athletics, indicting the "cheating, bribery, and dishonesty" in college sports, and condemning the "double standards of grades and admission policies" that favored athletes.

The criticism accurately described some universities, Joe thought, but not all of them, and certainly not Penn State. At too many universities, Joe argued, neither the faculty nor the administration controlled athletics. Instead, "the power to determine goals and policies and to make decisions rests in the hands of alumni, booster clubs, friends of the 'establishment,' or perhaps business entrepreneurs." Too often these groups overemphasized aspects of athletics extrinsic to the world of university life.

Penn State officials had eliminated "extraneous pressures," Joe contended, and reaffirmed the administration's and the faculty's proper jurisdiction over athletics. He explained that various faculty committees at Penn State controlled the rules for the admission of students, the academic standards of eligibility, and the faculty exercised complete autonomy in grading the students. (Joe cited statistics indicating that the grades of football lettermen compared favorably with those of the university as a whole.) Penn State held up to student-athletes the ideal of the ancient Greeks and the salient qualities this ideal encompassed: "excellence in all fields; energy and moderation; keeping their bodies as fit as their minds; living in harmony with fellow citizens." Anything less than 100 percent commitment to excellence, Joe contended, was "self-defacing and intolerable. We ask of them only their very best in every arena: the classroom, the football stadium, and the 'stage of seven ages.'"

Athletics was not an end in itself and not necessarily for everyone, Joe argued, but for those who participated there were important rewards in personal development. Moreover, sports enriched and seasoned college life and established moorings on which alumni and friends could anchor their enthusiasm and their loyalty. "True there can be abuses, but isn't this true of every activity which is allowed to go unfettered by the people directly responsible for its well-being?"[13]

In early March 1967, with ideas still percolating in his mind, Joe spoke to fifty Penn State alumni at a country club on the subject of football and academics. He proudly pointed out that one-third of his most recent team had ranked as B students or better, and he speculated that the dropout rate of football players at Penn State over a four-year span was "perhaps the lowest in the nation." He wanted to do away with freshman games (Penn State played two) because the first-year players should concentrate on their studies. Penn State assigned assistant coaches to meet once a week with individual players to go over each player's academic program.

"We want the good football players," Joe told the alumni. "I'm not kidding about that. But we want the students. My pitch when I go out and recruit is that Penn State can offer you a top education and a chance to play big-time football. We think we have the best of both worlds. . . . We don't go all over the country recruiting boys, we won't take in a lot of marginal kids, expecting to hold on to a few of them, letting the rest of them flunk out. We want them for four years." Yes, he wanted to have the best team in the country, he said, "and one of these days we're going to have that big winner, but we'll do it within university policy."

When Joe finished, a sportswriter looked through his notes of the speech and observed that it seemed "a little stuffy here on paper, but coming from Joe it sounded just right."[14]

In a column on October 19, 1967, sportswriter Bill Conlin of the *Philadelphia Daily News* first reported Joe's concept of the Grand Experiment. After an interview, Conlin wrote that Joe wanted to make Penn State a perennial national football power. The "screwy thing," reported Conlin, was Joe's innovative and high-minded approach to going about it. "No under-the-table recruiting. No promises of medical school or Cadillacs. No redshirting or lowering of admission standards for athletes." Conlin thought Joe's method "wouldn't be enough to recruit a big-league band at a lot of places."

"We're talking about the idea of having a great football team," Joe had told Conlin the previous day. "I'm thinking in terms of a Grand Experiment. It sounds a little corny, I know. . . . Everybody assumes if you have a great football team, there have been some sacrifices made in the area of standards. People tell me it can't be done without sacrificing standards; they tell me I'm daydreaming."[15]

Subsequently, Joe expanded on his approach. "We want our players to enjoy football," he repeatedly said. "We want them to enjoy college. We want them to learn about art and literature and music and all the other things college has to offer. College should be a great time. It is the only time a person is really free. We don't want them just tied to a football program." Joe conveyed the impression that it would thrill him more to produce a Nobel Prize winner than a Heisman Trophy winner from among his Penn State players.

A few years after Joe initially described his Grand Experiment, a reporter for the *Los Angeles Times* asked him to explain an apparent contradiction in his views about winning. Joe had said he would like to win every game and be ranked number one, but he added that the world wouldn't roll to a stop if Penn State didn't achieve those goals. Winning wasn't everything. "On the one hand you sound determined to win them all, and on the other hand you say it doesn't matter," said the reporter. Wasn't there a conflict in this view?

"Some people have the wrong idea about us," Joe responded. "We're drivers here. We work hard to win them all. If we didn't try, it would be an insult to our opponents and, besides, we like to win.

Winning is the most important thing, but it isn't everything. In football or anything else, there's often a difference between aspiration and achievement. If you're licked, you're licked. The idea then is to learn something from losing."

What can you learn?

"The most important thing is that a man doesn't have to be a loser in life forever just because he's lost a football game. . . . If you're licked by a better man, you're still a winner. Our definition of a loser is a guy who doesn't do the best he can. . . . The idea is to keep football in perspective."

Joe seemed to have a strong opinion on every subject. He praised college students (except for leftist radicals) for criticizing our "hypocritical society, with its corruption, scandals, and smooth-talking politicians." College administrators were not much better than the politicians. "I blame college administrators for a great deal of the trouble," he charged. He also blasted some college professors for being "terrible teachers," interested primarily in "making a reputation for themselves in research or in writing a book or in becoming the so-called star of a department."[16]

After Joe became head coach he embarked on a plan to cultivate the media. He visited the offices of small newspapers and radio stations in Pennsylvania, urging more extensive coverage of Penn State's football team. Within a few years he was widely known and admired. Joe's prominence in the media in the late 1960s emerged because of his personality, Penn State's success on the gridiron, the appeal of the Grand Experiment, and changes in the sports media. Sports journalists were beginning to relate sports to the nation's social problems, and because Joe was becoming the most prominent and successful coach in the East, major media markets in New York, Pittsburgh, and Philadelphia gave him a forum for his views. "With Joe being the [most] visible coach in the East," observed Dave Baker, one-time sports information director at Penn State, "a coach who was very intelligent and had opinions, he became a natural person for writers and broadcasters to want to interview about . . . the issues that affected sports."

In the late 1960s, while Joe's teams were piling up victories, a cadre of reporters descended on Penn State on Friday evenings before the Saturday home games. There were sportswriters from Pittsburgh, usually Roy McHugh or Phil Musick. From Philadelphia came Frank Bilovsky

(*Evening Bulletin*), Bill Lyon (the *Inquirer*), and Bill Conlin (the *Daily News*). Also present were Ralph Bernstein representing the Associated Press, Gordon S. White of the *New York Times*, and Merv Hyman of *Sports Illustrated*. (Others drove in on Saturday, the day of the game.) The Friday night press party consisted of cocktails and hors d'oeuvres, usually at the home of the sports information director; a large crowd was a dozen reporters. "We came early and stayed late," recalled Conlin. Joe stayed until about 10:00 P.M., when he would join his athletes sequestered at a hotel on the eve of home games.[17]

At the Friday sessions Joe was relaxed and charming, bantering with his guests, enjoying the give-and-take. Because he did not expect to be quoted, discussion was intense, irreverent, and informative. "We would shoot the bull about everything," Bernstein recalled, "from politics to science to sports to sex. We'd tell jokes. It was really a friendly thing."

On New Year's Day 1970, before the Orange Bowl contest with Missouri, Joe gathered ten sportswriters who normally covered Penn State. "I'm giving you the game plan," Joe told them. "I'm begging you to keep this in this room. I am going to trust you." He added that he wanted the writers to have the advanced knowledge so they could more effectively report on the game. The sportswriters were stunned. During the game Joe did exactly what he said he would do. "Once he did that and trusted them," observed Ernie Accorsi, assistant sports information director at Penn State at the time, "they totally believed in him." For a while Joe continued to explain innovations he planned for the upcoming game, confident his guests would maintain his trust. "We wouldn't print it," said Bernstein. "We would use it as a guide to covering the game and write about it afterward."

Because Joe was frank, honest, and quotable, the reporters gave him a forum that boosted his national reputation. That Penn State was successful on the football field magnified the value of his opinions. (If Penn State had won only two games per year, few would have been interested in Joe Paterno's opinion.) "We spread the gospel," said Bernstein, whose Associated Press reports put Joe on front pages all over the country.

The sportswriters enjoyed Joe's personality, intellect, sharp sense of humor, and funny stories. "Paterno is one of the great storytellers," said Frank Bilovsky. While describing one of Joe's stories, a reporter interjected, "He's a ham, just like Woody [Hayes]." Some of Joe's stories, Penn

State's football chronicler Ridge Riley said affectionately, were "a fabrication of Paterno's inventive after-dinner-speaking brain."[18]

When Joe delivered a forty-minute speech to a Penn State alumni group, he was cool and cocky, funny and serious. "[You] Ivy League guys who think you own all of the smooth, class guys, move over and make room for Joe Paterno," observed a sportswriter after listening to one of Joe's speeches. "People who have been hearing and meeting Joe Paterno for the past year are smitten. This is the new breed. This is not [a] bombastic, win-'em-all-for-old-State rabble-rouser; this is an astute, erudite, witty, personable fellow, and . . . a winning football coach."

Most sportswriters found his ideas unique. It was refreshing to hear a college coach say, "Football can be an important part of a young man's overall makeup, but it isn't the only part, and sometimes people make it too important." One should gamble in life, but football should still be kept in perspective. "You've got to gamble with ideals, with principles; and when something seems right, you take a chance," he said. "I do not think a licking is the worst thing in the world. Look, think back when you were nineteen or twenty with all the frustrations, doubts of the future, you had then. You can't tell these kids a football loss is a great tragedy. It's not."

In 1968 Joe sharply attacked the NCAA Football Rules Committee for approving a new punt-return rule one year but wiping it off the books the next. "It seems ludicrous," he said, "to change a rule that has been in effect only one year. Why can't the NCAA make up its mind and let us play the same game two years in a row?" Commenting on Joe's stand, *Sports Illustrated* added, "Why not, indeed!"[19]

Because Penn State played most of its games in the East, the rest of the country had difficulty identifying the university. "Are you from the University of Pennsylvania or Penn State?" people often asked. "Good luck in the Ivy League," others stated. To counter the prevalent view, Joe promoted eastern football and lobbied for a new eastern conference featuring the two service academies, Syracuse, Pittsburgh, Boston College, Temple, and West Virginia; but several problems thwarted creation of the conference. Gene Collier of the *Pittsburgh Post-Gazette* observed: "To noted headknockers in other regions—notably the South, Southwest and Midwest—Eastern Football was not only a dubious notion, but a flat-out, . . . oxymoron, like jumbo shrimp or military intelligence.

Paterno never thought it beneath himself to do something like taking off his glasses to give a practice demonstration, such as proper contact with a blocking sled. (Photo courtesy of Penn State Sports Information Department)

"And yet at every public forum as a young head coach, Paterno preached the Eastern homily, the one about the challenges facing Penn State as it made its way through the flourishing black forest of programs like Pitt and Syracuse and Rutgers and Temple and Boston College and West Virginia."

Following the 1967 season, the first rumor circulated that Joe was being courted by professional teams. In late December 1967 the media speculated that Joe would replace Weeb Ewbank as coach of the New York Jets in the American Football League, but Joe denied that anyone had spoken to him about the position.

After the 1968 season, the Pittsburgh Steelers tried to dazzle Joe with a lucrative long-term contract. Joe was fond of Art Rooney, president of the Steelers, liked the city of Pittsburgh, and was tempted by the challenge of coaching professional football. Rooney kept raising the ante to induce Joe to give up college football and coach the Steelers, finally producing an exceptional package. If Joe accepted Rooney's offer, it probably would have meant no more financial problems for the Paternos and their children for the rest of their lives. The length of the contract and the money and fringe benefits would have ensured financial security.

Word spread that Joe might leave Penn State. "I've been under terrible pressure all week with calls coming in at all hours of the day and night," said president Eric Walker. "Almost all of the calls have said the same thing: 'Tell Joe not to go.'"

"Joe kept giving the Steelers impossible things that they couldn't come up with," Sue Paterno recalled. "But then they came up with everything, which unnerved us both." Joe sensed, though, that Sue didn't want her husband to take the Pittsburgh position.

On January 8, 1969, after a week of discussions with the Steelers, Joe rejected the offer. "I have a good job where I am," he told a reporter. "The time wasn't right to leave Penn State. I like working with kids. It's stimulating."[20]

Some thought it was inevitable that Joe would leave for a better position. "He'll make the move one of these years," speculated the *Cleveland Plain Dealer*, "and it will be a fortunate pro club that finally does land friendly, astute Joe Paterno."

Although Joe received a modest raise after the 1968 season, he did not use the Pittsburgh offer to extort an exorbitant salary from Dean McCoy. Joe did receive tenure at the university, however, and insisted on some changes in the football program at Penn State—some personnel changes, assurances of a beefed-up football schedule, and a new, attractive coaches' office, a show-spot through which to usher recruits.[21]

At the banquet honoring him as Coach of the Year for 1968, Joe sat next to coach Bear Bryant of Alabama, the closest thing college football had to a god. Wasting no time, Bryant took charge between the fruit cup and the salad, offering his advice to the successful neophyte. In his autobiography Joe described their conversation:

> "I hope you're going to renegotiate your contract."
> I said I didn't have any contract.
> "Why not?"
> "Well, I just got tenure."
> He peered queerly at me. "Tenure?"

"Yeah. The Pittsburgh Steelers just offered me their coaching job. I turned it down. But I went to our president, Eric Walker, and told him I was the only head coach he'd ever had that didn't have tenure. So he gave me tenure and made me a full professor."

"Full professor?" His peculiar glare was hard to read. Getting back on track, he said, "Now here's what you ought to get in your contract." He named a sum of money that was so incredible I don't remember it.

I had started as head coach two years earlier at twenty thousand dollars, so I guess my routine raises had brought me to a shade more. But I didn't tell him that.

"Your contract should be for five years, and you ought to be able to roll it over."

I had no idea what rolling it over meant. Although I felt a little naive and foolish, I appreciated his interest in me, a newcomer, and he didn't let up.

"You ought to have a car and you ought to have the country club."

"I don't play golf." I don't think he heard me, because he was preparing to drop the big one.

"You ought to have two hundred tickets—season tickets."

"What would I do with them?"

"The way you're going, you're going to have good football up there. I know enough about Penn State to know that people are going to be fighting to get into that stadium. You've got to have two hundred good tickets. That's going to give you the power to do whatever you want with your program and with yourself."

Not naive, Joe understood what Bryant was suggesting: Take advantage of your new success and accumulate favors and power. But Joe felt uncomfortable with Bryant's approach. "The discomfort was not from difference in scruples," Joe said, "only style." Bryant's approach was the style of an old-time southern politician: doing favors and then turning them into power. For example, if Bryant gave football tickets to a dentist or a doctor, he never received a doctor's bill.

"I have tried to develop a different way of gathering power to protect Penn State football," Joe reflected. "I try to win football games. Doing so has given me power and I work it for all it's worth. Without it, we'd have no chance of continuing a first-class program and a winning team.

"Make no mistake. I don't claim that my way is morally superior. There's nothing necessarily unscrupulous about making important friends for the football team through supplying good tickets. I just feel more at home with my way."[22]

Every opponent was keying on Penn State as the 1969 season began. "We'll need momentum sustained week after week," Joe said, summing up the challenge, "preparation styled for each opponent, and toughness to take each game as it comes." Meeting the challenge, Penn State plowed through its second consecutive 10-0 regular season, bringing more national prestige, recognition, individual honors, and a third consecutive Lambert Trophy that honored supremacy in eastern football. Still, Joe and Penn State's fans couldn't make a strong enough case for the highest honor.

Paterno could have taken his team to the Cotton Bowl and played Texas for the national championship, but when invitations were issued, Ohio State was leading in the polls. Paterno wrongly concluded that the Buckeyes would probably remain undefeated. Therefore, he allowed his players to make the bowl decision. Since they had enjoyed the Orange Bowl trip to Miami the year before, they voted to return. Awaiting their Orange Bowl game against Missouri on January 1, 1970, with a powerful team featuring offensive backs Franco Harris and Lydell Mitchell and linebacker Jack Ham, undefeated in 1969, and possessing a twenty-nine-game unbeaten streak, Joe and Penn State's supporters thought they could lay claim to being number one.

But President Richard Nixon, a self-styled football expert, attended the Texas-Arkansas showdown in Fayetteville, Arkansas, and after the Longhorns defeated Arkansas in an exciting contest, 15-14, Nixon blessed the Texas team. In a hot, noisy dressing room, he gave a number-one plaque to Darrell Royal, coach of Texas, before millions of viewers on national television. To placate Penn State and its fans, Nixon said that at an appropriate time he would present a special plaque to Penn State for its long unbeaten streak.

However, Penn State's fans were livid and so was Joe. To them Penn State seemed as deserving of the top ranking as Texas. Within a few hours of Nixon's statement, Joe and Jim Tarman, then Penn State's sports information director, wrote a polite rejoinder firmly rejecting Nixon's consolation prize. In his statement Joe congratulated Texas for its victory but said that before accepting the president's plaque, he would have to confer with his squad. "I'm sure they would be disappointed at this time, as would the Missouri squad, to receive anything other than a plaque for the number-one team. And the number-one team following the bowl games could be Penn State or Missouri."

To accept any other plaque before the bowl games would be a disservice to his squad, to Pennsylvania, to the East, and even to Missouri, which might be the best team in the country. It would seem a waste of Nixon's valuable time, Joe said, "to present Penn State with a plaque for something we already have undisputed possession of—the nation's longest winning and unbeaten streaks."[23]

One of Penn State's problems with the polls was the reputation of eastern football. "Eastern teams don't play as tough a schedule as those conferences," went the view. Penn State played teams from the "weak" East. "The polls have become an end in themselves," Joe said. "It's no longer a question of winning. Now it's a question of how big a margin you win by." He thought that some teams had rolled up scores in order to impress the coaches and writers on the rating boards. In Joe's estimation, this sometimes put the wrong emphasis on the way a team played its games.

In the Orange Bowl, Penn State had one of the nation's greatest defenses, Missouri one of the nation's finest offenses. In the contest Penn State emerged victorious, 10-3, intercepting seven Missouri passes. Following the game Terry McMillan, Missouri's star quarterback, said, "I've never seen a defense like Penn State's. . . . [They] always rushed four men and forced me to throw before I was ready. Seven men were in their pass coverage. . . . [They] covered my men like blankets. . . . I threw a few passes away to avoid interceptions at first, but when we got behind I had to try to hit, but heck, the receivers were always covered."

After viewing films of the game, Missouri's coach, Dan Devine, labeled Penn State "the best defensive team I've seen in twenty years of college football. It may not have been obvious at times, but our staff put more time and effort into this bowl game than in any of our five previous bowl trips."

Penn State players give Joe his due, a celebratory shower after the Nittany Lions held off Missouri in the 1970 Orange Bowl. (AP/Wide World Photo)

After the contest exuberant players carried Joe into the shower fully clothed. He emerged dripping wet to meet the media. "I don't like to keep pushing this thing," Joe said calmly, "but I still think we have as much right to be number one as Texas or anybody else. Why should I sit back and let the president of the United States say that so-and-so is number one when I've got fifty kids who've worked their tails off for me for three years. People can say it's sour grapes, but I'd be a lousy coach if I didn't argue for my team."

Nineteen years later, in his autobiography, Joe was far less diplomatic. "The blood-curdling nerve! In his Solomon-like presidential wisdom, Nixon *favored* us with an honor that any idiot consulting a record book could see that we had taken for ourselves, thank you, without his help."[24]

Despite Penn State's problems with the national polls, Joe credited the back-to-back Orange Bowl victories over Kansas and Missouri as crucial for establishing the credibility of Penn State's program. Until then respect had come only grudgingly. "After our 15-14 win over Kansas in 1969," he observed, "there was a lot of comment that it was a one-time thing. They kept saying it wouldn't last." But the victory over powerful Missouri the following year convinced many skeptics. His ability to recruit head-on with Michigan and Notre Dame dramatically improved after the 1970 triumph. "Those two Orange Bowls made our program," Joe later said.

Shrewdly and diplomatically, Joe avoided problems associated with the Vietnam War and with rebellious athletes in the late 1960s. "The storm of protest and dissent that overtook many college campuses shook the foundation of athletics, particularly football," observed Dennis Booher, whose Ph.D. dissertation focused on Joe's career at Penn State. "Many coaches fought the rise of the free-thinking and free-speaking athletes with ever greater rigidity, and refused to recognize a changing society." Joe was more perceptive and tolerant than most of his peers, helping him overcome problems at Penn State. He consulted with his players and clearly and frankly discussed problems and the reasons for specific rules, thereby alleviating most conflict within the football team.

Joe expressed little public interest in the protests against the Vietnam War, but he was concerned about the protests by blacks. He didn't discourage players from participating in campus demonstrations, but he never wanted them to embarrass themselves or the university. "The black activists were fighting for what most of us felt was a just cause," Joe recalled. "We did not have a lot of black players, but with the ones we had, I spent a lot of time talking with them."

Black activists at Penn State asked two prominent black players, Charlie Pittman and Jim Kates, to "walk out" on the team in protest against alleged racism at the university. "It was an awful lot of pressure," recalled Pittman, who worried that if he didn't support the black activists, he would encounter problems with blacks on campus. "Your loyalty was really being tested." Joe pulled Pittman aside and said, "I know you have a tough decision to make and I am going to leave it up to you to make it. But the team is a family . . . and I think you can make a greater impact for your race by not doing that. . . . But the decision is yours. I'm going to respect whatever decision you make." Both Pittman and Kates decided to stay with the team.[25]

Editors dedicated Penn State's 1969 yearbook to Joe with a brief message: "Usually yearbooks aren't dedicated to coaches, but he's an exception." Johnny Bach, Penn State's basketball coach, thought Joe's success had rubbed off on other sports at the university. "At some schools the football coach selfishly looks out for football and isn't interested in the other sports. Joe is not only the football coach at Penn State but he is the leader of our entire athletic program. He is a steadying influence on all the other coaches. It's stimulating to work with him."

Some Penn State alumni and fans were spoiled by the team's success. Although the Nittany Lions had lost many star players—Mike Reid, Dennis Onkotz, Steve Smear, John Ebersole, Charlie Pittman, Neal Smith, Jim Kates, Paul Johnson, Pete Johnson, Don Abbey, Tom Jackson, and Chuck Burkhart—who had made Penn State the talk of the nation, fans expected that Joe, the miracle worker, "would pull players out of a hat, wind them up, and presto, produce a third-straight unbeaten team."[26]

On September 26, 1970, in the second game of the season, Colorado finally ended Penn State's thirty-one-game nonlosing streak, 41-13, in Boulder, Colorado. Afterward, amid the silence in Penn State's locker room, broken only by the tumultuous celebration of the nearby Colorado team, Joe told his players, "Listen to them—let them have their glory. We've had our share."

He dropped by the Colorado locker room, congratulated the players on their victory, and wished them luck over the rest of the season. After he left, two Colorado linemen looked at each other in astonishment. "Can you believe that?" said one. "Can you believe that after what just happened out there that he could come over and say that?"

Later Joe sat down and chatted amiably with the media. Offering an occasional joke, he didn't seem bereaved. Only when a reporter suggested that he might be relieved to get out from under the long streak did Joe bristle slightly. He never worried that much about winning streaks, he said.

Joe told Jack Newcombe, an old friend and a reporter for *Life*, "There's an elation to winning. . . . And when you get beaten too often you get angry. But when you haven't lost in a long time you find out just how ignominious it is. But look at me," he added, whacking Newcombe on the back, the idea for the joke he was about to produce forcing a grin under his wide nose, "I've finally acquired character. That feels good."

For many years, Joe had a comfortable, trusting relationship with members of the press. Here, Paterno meets the media in December 1971 leading up to that season's Cotton Bowl game against Texas. (AP/Wide World Photo)

Most Penn State fans took the loss in stride. About two thousand stood in the rain to greet the team at 3:00 A.M. on Sunday when they returned to the university. Joe addressed the crowd: "We've won a lot of games during the past few seasons and we've always tried to be gracious winners. Now I hope we can be gracious losers. We've shared many moments of glory, and I'm sure we'll share more such moments in the future. But right now we must regenerate ourselves—and we'll need your support—the kind of support you've shown us this morning."

Other fans phoned the Paterno home to complain, sometimes viciously, about Joe Paterno, giving Joe a refresher course in what it meant to lose. Sue took incessant calls from anonymous fans who demanded to talk to Joe and called her a liar when she said Joe wasn't home. "[They] wanted me to know I had lost my touch," Joe later said, and "demanded that I listen to their prescriptions for getting back on the road to winning now that we had that disgraceful losing streak of one."[27]

In 1970 Penn State struggled through the first half of the season with a 2-3 record until Joe successfully juggled his lineup and adjusted his offense. He inserted sophomore John Hufnagel at quarterback, simplified the offense, and relied heavily on his powerful running game. The strategy paid off. Over the last half of the season, the Lions averaged almost 337 yards rushing and 36.2 points per game. "We were making a lot of mistakes early in the season," Joe said. "I felt it was time to make a change. We went back to the things that we do best." The 7-3 season boosted Joe's five-year record at Penn State to forty-two wins, ten losses, and a tie.

In 1971, *Joe Paterno: "Football My Way"*, a book about Joe's life and beliefs, was published by Macmillan. In 270 pages the book described Joe's background at Brooklyn Prep and Brown, his coaching career at Penn State, plus the people, events, and ideas that had shaped him. He came through as far more open to dissent than most coaches, and he expressed distress with the evils of the college recruiting system.

The book was assembled and written by Mervin Hyman, chief of research for *Sports Illustrated*, and Gordon White, veteran sportswriter for the *New York Times*. Joe said that at first he didn't want to support the book project because he was reluctant to get into "controversial" subjects. "But the more I saw of what was going on in college football the more I decided, what the hell. If you believe in something, you might as well go ahead and shoot your mouth off." Of the book, Joe said: "Actually, I had very little to do with it. I talked into microphones, making tapes, for perhaps twenty hours in all. I am very happy with the result."

Most reviewers praised the book. "Excellent reading," said the *Pittsburgh Post-Gazette*. "One of the most satisfying reading experiences any football fan could wish for, largely because of its subject," said the review in *Library Journal*. In *Saturday Review*, Cleveland Amory wrote that Joe was "more than just an outspoken man. He is also a well-spoken one."

Although informative and often insightful, the co-authors exaggerated Joe's virtues and promoted a saintly image. The critical review in the *New Republic* labeled the book "hagiography." "This, then, is Joe Paterno," said Hyman and White. "Football coach, intellectual, maverick, philosopher, social worker, leader, gambler, idealist, romanticist, humanist, activist." Some sections were so laudatory they could have been written by Penn State's sports information department. "[Paterno] doesn't talk loudly about pride, patriotism, perfectionism, dedication, loyalty, or character building. That doesn't necessarily mean that Paterno doesn't believe in those ideals, but he is more interested in relating to the sophisticated and intellectually eager football players of the present and to contributing to the broadening of their horizons."[28]

As Penn State continued to produce excellent teams (11-1 in 1971, 10-2 in 1972), speculation mounted about Joe's future. Would he remain indefinitely at Penn State? Would he jump to another university? Or would he move to the greener pastures of professional football? Officials at Penn State preferred not to discuss the possibility of ever losing Joe. Early in 1971 the Green Bay Packers talked to him before hiring Dan Devine of Missouri. By late December 1972, though, there was constant speculation that Joe would join the pros—specifically the New England Patriots.[29]

William H. Sullivan Jr., president of the Patriots, initially extended an offer to Joe after Penn State had defeated Boston College, 45-26, in Boston on November 18, 1972, in the next-to-last regular season game. "Coach, I'm ready to make you an arrangement that would ensure your family's well-being," Sullivan told Joe. "You'd never have to worry about them again."

Shortly after Penn State defeated Pittsburgh on November 25, Joe flew to New York and discussed the Patriots' offer in detail with Sullivan. At the time the deal was one of the most lucrative ever offered to a coach by a

Joe perhaps signaling yet another Nittany Lion touchdown? (Photo courtesy of Penn State Sports Information Department)

professional team. Besides extending total control of the football operation (both coach and general manager), Sullivan offered him a $200,000 home, a two-car garage, two cars, and a salary of $200,000 the first year, rising to $275,000 the fourth year. The financial prize came to about $1.4 million. In addition, Sullivan was prepared to offer Joe about 5 percent ownership in the valuable Patriots' franchise. Everything about the Patriots' deal made Joe "dizzy." (He was then earning about $35,000 per year at Penn State.)

Joe insisted that subsequent conversations be postponed until after Penn State played Oklahoma in the Sugar Bowl in New Orleans on December 31, 1972. However, during preparation for the game, reporters got wind of the story and pestered Joe about his negotiations. Penn State's fans put plaintive stickers on their cars saying, "Say It Ain't So, Joe." Penn State's players were upset. "We were all panicked," said Greg Buttle, who had just completed his freshman season. Buttle thought, "Joe Paterno is leaving. What did I come here for?"[30]

Back in Pennsylvania after the Sugar Bowl (which Penn State lost, 14-0), Joe took a few days to contemplate the offer. Sue was noncommittal (but secretly didn't want to leave Penn State). Joe and Sue made lists of the advantages of going to New England or staying at Penn State. All the lists kept coming up "go." Joe felt he couldn't refuse Sullivan's deal. "It gave me everything I'd ever dreamed of: the summer house on Cape Cod that every rich Yankee kid I'd met at Brown assumed was coming to him, the same as inheriting his dad's club membership. It meant bringing up my kids around Boston, a lively place that had always appealed to me. Pro football would mean more time to spend with Sue and the kids. No more week after week on the road, recruiting high school players from the end of the playing season till spring. Fans and alumni don't understand the wear and tear and drudgery of that part of college coaching." There seemed to be no choice except to say yes.

After a few days, Joe said to Sue, "I have to take the job." Sue replied, "Joe, whatever you want to do is fine with me. If you want to go, we'll go." ("I could tell she wasn't crazy about it," Joe later said.)

Joe told his brother George, "I think I'm going to take it." On Thursday, January 4, 1973, Joe informed Sullivan that he would take the position. "In principle, I had accepted," Joe later said.

On Thursday evening the Paternos and the Tarmans celebrated the decision over dinner at the Paternos'. Unfortunately, no one had

much positive to say about the move. Sue said she would miss the family's doctor; son David, six, cried about leaving his friend; they worried if
Joe's successor would continue to employ Penn State's longtime assistants. "This was turning out to be the most cheerless celebration party
I'd ever been at," Joe later said. "Sue says she can't remember anybody
saying a jubilant, or even a positive, thing all evening." Still, they were
curious and excited about getting on with their new life.[31]

Later that evening Joe began rethinking his decision. "I started
wondering what the hell I had done. I began to realize that all I'd prove
at New England was that I can coach a good football team both with college kids and with pros. What's that prove?" He didn't want his children
merely to say about their father, "He was a good football coach, he won
a lot of games." He wanted to be remembered for more than winning
games. Thinking of himself primarily as a teacher, he thought it would be
difficult to "teach" professionals, some of whom had played for many
years. Working at Penn State and living in State College felt comfortable.
It took him only ten minutes to walk to work. He had a nice house with
a park in the backyard for his children.

He lay awake thinking: *When is it right for a guy to say good-bye to
a place he loves, the place he found his wife, where his kids lived all of their
days? And my other kids—those young, tough, thick-necked, fragile-hearted
football players—the ones who grow and ripen before your eyes before they go
off to cut their own pathways in the world?*

He continued wrestling with his thoughts:

*Hey, what the hell was going on in my head? Why did I keep bat-
ting this back and forth as though I couldn't make up my mind? I'd made
up my mind. Why was this thing tossing and turning around, keeping me
awake, nagging me, chattering in my brain? It was time to get logical
about this.*

*No, not logical. If something was my destiny, no logic in the world was
going to get me out of it.*

Was going to Boston my destiny?

Was staying at Penn State my destiny?

What to do? Go or stay?

*Destiny is a trick bag. How's a guy to know? God gives each of us a
destiny, then confuses us with the power of free will. We're still stuck with
having to decide every step of the way.*

It wasn't the challenge of coaching the Patriots that mostly attracted him, he finally concluded. It was something else:

Come on, face it. I knew damn well what it was. The money. The house on Cape Cod. Hobnobbing with the hottest shots in a big-time town, in high-tone bars, being their hero. Not having to worry, for once, about the example I have to set in a small college town, being watched by kids. It was the only chance at a million dollars I'd ever have.

Early Friday morning Joe phoned Sullivan and rejected the Patriots' offer. At 10:00 A.M. on Saturday morning, January 6, 1973, Joe held a news conference to explain he was staying at Penn State.[32]

Joe's announcement at the morning news conference shocked many people. "I've decided to remain at Penn State," he said. He admitted that he was almost hypnotized by the glitter of the gold. "I realized that I was merely flattered by the amount of money, and I got back to what I really wanted to do. I realized that I wouldn't be happy just being a football coach in which winning and losing is everything."

Joe said he still faced a challenge at Penn State—a national championship. "I still have a dream that Penn State could be the greatest in everything, whether it be a library or the soccer team." He felt he could make a contribution to some of those goals. Those challenges are "what kept me at Penn State."

Subsequently, Joe told reporters he was through playing Russian roulette with professional teams every winter. By rejecting the Patriots, he had made a commitment to Penn State. "I'm here for at least five years," he said a month after his decision. "We've got a challenge here."

"I've got a little more humility about myself now because I accepted that job," Joe also said. "I was disappointed with myself for doing it—and a little surprised. Now I know it's possible to buy me for a million bucks."[33]

Actually, what impressed most people was that Joe's final decision showed that he could *not* be bought for a million dollars. "So many people have asked us what kind of an offer Penn State made to Paterno to get him to stay," said a Penn State official. "Did you have to buy him a car? This kind of thing. No, the answer is that Paterno just has a commitment to education and to young people. If you turn down the kind of money that the New England Patriots offered, you must really have a commitment to your beliefs."

Rich Allocco, a prized high school running back, was being recruited by Penn State when Joe rejected the Patriots' offer. Allocco was deluged with laudatory tributes to Joe on his visit to Penn State. "That's all they talked about there, how a guy could be so dedicated," he recalled. People said to Allocco, "How can you turn down a man with such values?"

Rejecting the dazzling bauble turned Joe into a national folk hero. Faraway newspapers wrote laudatory editorials, like the Honolulu *Star-Bulletin* ("There's more to life than one million dollars.") and the Terra Bella, California, *News* ("Money Isn't Everything!"). "In the long run it came down to lots of money vs. lots of idealism," said an Associated Press report, "and for a change idealism won. Joe Paterno walked away from more than one million dollars to remain with his life's work—kids."

After learning of Joe's decision, Penn State halfback John Cappelletti said: "If ever there was a man who would turn down a million dollars, he is the guy. You take one look at him driving around in his '65 Mustang, and you know he would rather stick to his principles than take the money."

Sports Illustrated embarrassed Joe by asking him if he was an "authentic folk hero." Joe leaned forward intently and said, "Look, I'm reluctant for people to read too much into me. I get letters from people who seem to think that if only Joe Paterno can spend twenty minutes with a kid then his troubles will all be over. Nuts! People want to give me too much credit. I'm a football coach who has won a few games—remember? Now what the hell does that mean? If I were an accountant no one would pay that much attention to me, right?"

In the *Sports Illustrated* article, writer William Johnson said that the admiration for Joe sprang mostly from the fact that he was a man who seemed "to speak truthfully and with candor and who does not believe that money is the root of all the fruits of life. It is that simple. In these days when feet of clay and souls of brass seem to be the identifying marks of so many leaders, the mere fact that Joe Paterno expresses himself with an unforked tongue is apparently enough to warrant standing ovations and hero worship." Johnson concluded by labeling Joe an "authentic folk hero in a society desperately hungry for integrity."[34]

A group of Penn State's fans, led by Rev. Elton P. Richards of Reading, gratified with Joe's decision to remain at Penn State rather than accept the offer from the Patriots, arranged a testimonial dinner in Joe's honor at the Penn Harris Motor Inn near Harrisburg on March 31, 1973. (Governor Milton Shapp proclaimed the day as "Joe Paterno Day" throughout the state.)

"A number of us felt that Joe's decision to stay at Penn State reflected a loyalty to his vocation in working with young people and a deep feeling for Pennsylvania and Pennsylvanians," said Reverend Richards. "Joe has made strong and worthwhile statements about values in our society, and we just wanted to create the opportunity for Pennsylvanians to say 'thanks' to him for his leadership and positive influence."

Seven hundred persons honored Joe at the dinner. Nearly everyone who touched Joe's life was there—relatives, Zev Graham and friends from Brooklyn Prep, teammates and fraternity brothers from Brown, new Penn State president John Oswald and other university officials, state government leaders, former Lions players, and fans. Lieutenant Governor Ernest Kline and first lady Mrs. Milton Shapp presented a proclamation to Joe as part of the night's tribute. The event collected enough money to purchase a new Dodge Charger for the Paternos and to send them on vacation to Italy, which they took more than a year later.

Mrs. Florence Paterno beamed with pride during the testimonial for her son. "No one could be more deserving," she said. "Joe was always considerate. Even as a little boy, he was that way. He always thought of his family and his friends before he thought of himself."

"When I think of Joe, I think of my dad," said George Paterno. "Joe took my dad's philosophy that 'You could be a success with energy and dedication and correct values and then come back and help others.' I'm proud to be his brother."

Joe was overwhelmed. "You people have done more for me than I can ever do in return," he said. "I would like you to know this is not a retirement. We've got much to accomplish. I still want Penn State to be number one—not just in football but in everything."[35]

Another outgrowth of Joe's rejection of the offer by the Patriots, and a highlight of Joe's career, was the invitation extended to him by a student committee to deliver the commencement address on June 16, 1973, at ceremonies honoring 4,650 graduates. He was the first athletic coach at Penn State ever chosen to be the speaker.

Joe opened his address by telling the graduates he had been reluctant to accept the offer to speak because he doubted that an "unlettered

individual" such as himself should "represent its academic community."
Some in the audience, he said, "have every right to feel let down that after
four years of hard work you have to listen to a coach at your graduation."

Still, he understood that the invitation stemmed from his rejection of the financial offer by the Patriots. "I accepted because I realize that
in a day when materialism is rampant, many of you felt that my interest
in doing other things besides making money has in some way helped you
to reaffirm your ideal of a life of service, of dignity, and a life of meaning
which goes beyond financial success."

Interspersing his remarks with quotes from the nineteenth-
century English poet Robert Browning, the journalist Walter Lippmann,
the Swedish scholar Gunnar Myrdal, the poet W. H. Auden, and the
novelist John Steinbeck, Joe alluded to football, to Watergate, and to society's complex problems.

He thought he was probably one of the few commencement
speakers in 1973 who was not going to focus directly on Watergate,
the current national scandal. Still, he couldn't resist a humorous dig at
President Nixon. "I'd like to know, how could the president know so little about Watergate in 1973, and so much about college football in 1969."
(Joe later said, "I was just trying to get a laugh, but some people took
me seriously. There sure are a lot of serious people in the world.")[36]

In the main focus of his address he urged the graduates to strive
vigorously to change the "system." "I chuckle at people who blame the
'system' for our problems," he said, "just as I laugh at those who claim
that we should have blind faith in our government and our institutions."
What was this notorious system? The system included the new graduates.

> The system, the organization, the method, the govern-
> ment—is you. If each of us is easily seduced by expediency, by
> selfishness, by ambition regardless of cost to our principles,
> then the spectacle of Watergate will surely mark the end of this
> grand experiment in democracy. One of the tragedies of Water-
> gate is to see so many bright young men barely over thirty, who
> have so quickly prostituted their honor and decency in order to
> get ahead, to be admired, to stay on the "team." These same
> young people within the short period of the last ten years sat in
> convocations such as this. They were ready to change the world.

They didn't trust the over-thirty generation. I warn you—
don't underestimate the world—it can corrupt quickly and
completely.

He hoped the graduates would strive to improve themselves and
the system in the same way Joe's football players strived to win.

We strive to be number one. We work hard to achieve our
goals and when Saturday comes and we walk on the grass in this
stadium, we stand as a team. We tighten up our belts. We look
across at our opponents. We say, come on, let's go, let's see how
good you are, let's play. We are ready. We play with enthusiasm
and recklessness. We aren't afraid to lose. If we win, great, wonderful—and the alumni are happy for another week. But win or
lose, it is the competition which gives us pleasure.

It is being involved in a common cause which brings us joy
and memories which endure in teammates.

It is making our very best effort, that we have stretched to
the very limit of our ability, which makes us bigger men and
more able to stretch again; to reach even higher as we undertake
new challenges.

Strive to make at least small changes and don't be discouraged. So you may not make our society perfect, but you can
make it better, and I guess it follows that first you must get better before you can get perfect. We like to tell our football team,
do the little things right and the big things will take care of
themselves. Don't look for the touchdown run all the time;
think about hitting in there tough play after play and then,
boom, all of a sudden a big play will present itself. . . . W. H.
Auden said it beautifully when he wrote on the death of Sigmund Freud: "Every day there dies among us those who were
doing us some good and knew it was never enough but hoped
to improve a little by living." Live your life so that by some
little thing you will improve our world just by living. But be
realistic enough as you continue your adventure in life to
understand that regardless of how strong you are and how
smart you are, you will at times become discouraged.

The problems we face are agonizingly complex because they ultimately deal with people and their institutions.

Individuals cannot escape their moral responsibility but the nation can never again do what is right just for America. We will never again have a supreme confidence that everything we do is right—not after Vietnam and Kent State. Not after the assassinations of Martin Luther King and John Kennedy, not after the death of Bobby Kennedy, and not after Watergate. But this doesn't mean we can be less decisive than our forefathers. We must always act, but when we are wrong, we must be mature enough to realize it and act accordingly. This is where greatness lies and national frustrations end. We must be mature enough to admit we didn't win in Vietnam, that we don't really have peace with honor, that we can't force all of our citizens to love each other— then we can stop tearing ourselves apart. We shall act, and we shall act with good intentions. Hopefully we will often be right but at times will be wrong. When we are, let us admit it and immediately try to right the situation. Our country right or wrong. Yes, but love her enough, respect her enough that when she is wrong we stand bigger for admitting it.

He concluded by urging the graduates to love each other because a "little bit of you is inside one another." Love each other like Penn State's football team did. "[To] be in a locker room before a big game and to gather a team around and to look at grown men with tears in their eyes, huddling close to each [other] . . . reaching out to be a part of each other . . . to look into strong faces which say 'if we can only do it today'. . . . To be with aggressive, ambitious people who have lost themselves in something bigger than they are—this is what living is all about."

The offer to speak at commencement had been one of his "biggest thrills," Joe later said. "I'm really pleased that I've been received that way."[37]

In its 1973 season, with a team featuring Heisman Trophy winner John Cappelletti, Penn State won all twelve games, yet was still ranked only fifth in both major polls. Angered by the slight, Joe unilaterally declared that his team was the national champion, and he bought each player a national championship ring. "We were so happy . . . that our coach cared about us that much that he would take a stand," said Greg Buttle.

Until Penn State finally was officially voted a national title in the early 1980s, Paterno and the Nittany Lions had to be content with the occasional undefeated regular season and the familiar Lambert Trophy, symbolic of Eastern supremacy. Paterno here is joined by Robert Scannell, Penn State's dean of the College of Health, Physical Education, and Recreation; and athletic director Edward Czekaj as they admire the 1973 Lambert Trophy. (AP/Wide World Photo)

By 1973 those who knew Joe best thought he had developed some equanimity and had lost some of his irritating, abrasive cocksureness. "He didn't used to be able to handle losing," reflected Sue Paterno. "He'd shut the door and not come out. He was a real SOB. But he's matured now, he's not so tough." Joe credited Jim O'Hora and Rip Engle for tempering his fiery impatience. "I don't think he's getting mellow," O'Hora explained in 1974. "That's the wrong word. If anything, he developed more patience. Where in earlier years he would move brusquely to conclusions, he's softened his touch."

Until his death in the mid-1970s, Ridge Riley wrote a weekly football newsletter each season keeping alumni abreast of Penn State's football developments. He spent an hour interviewing Joe each Sunday morning during the season and was drawn to one unmistakable quality. "I'm always so conscious of the guy's brain," Riley said. "He's made mistakes, but I think Joe has that confidence that nobody is going to outcoach him during a game."

In 1974 there were twenty-seven Penn Staters on the roster of professional teams, two more than Southern California, seven more than Notre Dame, and nine more than Nebraska. Many great players had played for Joe, including running backs Franco Harris, Lydell Mitchell, and Cappelletti; linebackers Jack Ham, John Skorupan, Doug Allen, Jim Laslavic, Ed O'Neil, John Ebersole, and Bruce Bannon, as well as other stars such as tight end Ted Kwalick and defensive tackle Mike Reid.[38]

At the midseason of 1977, on the Friday before the sixth game against Syracuse, Joe's life was jarred into perspective by a family tragedy. His son David, a sixth grader, fell from a trampoline atop a stage at Our Lady of Victory School in State College and fractured his skull. After receiving the emergency phone call at home, Joe rushed to the school and found David lying, as though lifeless, on the concrete floor at the school. An ambulance took David and Joe to the Centre Community Hospital and then transferred the boy to Geisinger, a large modern hospital about a hundred miles from State College. "Again I climbed into the ambulance to ride with Dave, who was still unconscious," Joe later said. "It was the longest ride of my life. Every mile, I concentrated on prayers, simply begging God to keep my son alive." At Geisinger, Dr. Henry Hood, a neurosurgeon, provided almost round-the-clock care for David, earning Joe's lasting gratitude.

There was a point on Saturday night when it looked like David wasn't going to live. Only sophisticated life support systems sustained his life. His brain had begun to swell and several medications failed to stop the swelling. At a critical point, with David apparently slipping away, Joe called his brother George. "He was crying," George recalled. "There was nothing more the doctors could do for David. Joe said it looked like David wasn't gonna make it." Later Joe told Fr. Thomas Bermingham that he and Sue were kneeling before their son, who was in a coma, and Joe said to himself, "Nothing else in this world means anything to me like my son. . . . Everything else fell away. Nothing else mattered."[39]

It wasn't until several hours after Saturday's game that Joe learned that his team had defeated Syracuse. Earlier he hadn't cared. "At times like that," he said, "you start to reevaluate your life and put your priorities in order." Following the tough loss, the Syracuse players knelt in prayer for David. The Paterno family was deluged with sympathy messages.

By Tuesday David had regained consciousness and brain scans revealed no permanent damage. The same day Joe showed up for practice, haggard but smiling. Expressing his appreciation to all the well-wishers, Joe said, "I want to thank all of you who prayed for [David], and tell you how much my wife and I were moved by the outpouring of concern you showed."[40]

Joe continued to pile up honors and awards, among them the Pennsylvania Award for excellence in athletics and three honorary degrees—a doctor of laws from Brown University, a doctor of humane letters from Gettysburg College, and a doctor of laws from Allegheny College. The citation from his alma mater said: "You advocate and exemplify integrity in athletics. . . . You treasure the magnificence of teaching and learning."

There were more feelers for jobs with professional teams. In November 1978 columnist Dave Anderson wrote in the New York Times that the professional Giants should make Joe an offer he couldn't refuse. "I'm not sure there is such an offer," commented John Morris, Penn State's sports information director. Would any professional job have pried him away from Penn State? Joe was later asked. "I'm a New Yorker," he responded. "If the timing was right, I might have been interested in an arrangement with the Giants. But it would have to have been on my terms. We talked at one time, just to feel each other out, but I was never offered the job."

Subsequently, Joe received feelers from the New England Patriots again, in 1982, and from Donald Trump and his New Jersey Generals of the U.S. Football League. "I don't even look into them anymore," Joe said. "I hate to waste their time."[41]

From 1973 to 1977 Joe continued to turn out excellent teams, earning top-ten ratings in four of the five years. In his thirteen years as coach through 1978, Penn State had been ranked eleven times among the top ten teams in the nation and had gone to bowl games eleven times. Still, they had never achieved a number-one ranking in the final year-end polls.

Joe was asked in 1975 what would happen if Penn State was ever voted number one. Would that be the end of the road? No, Joe responded; it would only be a new beginning. Anticipation, dedication, and striving were what really counted. "The quest is the thing," he said. "And once you reach your goal, you set new goals. When you reach the top, the quest then becomes staying on top with new kids. We owe it to our people and our fans to become the best and stay the best."[42]

~4~

STRIVING FOR NUMBER ONE (1978–1986)

EARLY IN THE 1978 SEASON, AFTER TWO PLUG-ALONG VICTORIES OVER TEMPLE (10-7) AND RUTGERS (26-10), PENN STATE FACED POWERFUL OHIO STATE IN COLUMBUS. "Last week I yelled at them a lot, because they weren't practicing well and they weren't playing up to their capabilities," Joe said following the game with Rutgers. "Now we've got Ohio State, and I shouldn't have to yell. This is the fun game. This is the kind of game you win if you want to be number one. This is eighty-eight thousand people, and Woody Hayes, and the strategy and the preparation. I love it. I'm anxious to play it."

Penn State won a stunning 19-0 triumph, one "gorged with promise and performance," wrote John Underwood in *Sports Illustrated*. When the team arrived back at State College, thousands of fans welcomed them.

Winning the national championship had become a crusade at Penn State. After defeating North Carolina State in the tenth game on November 11, the Lions remained undefeated and finally ranked number one, earning the right to play number two, Bear Bryant's Alabama, in the Sugar Bowl. Consequently, the media descended on Joe for interviews. "All of a sudden you go from two to one, and people want to know what kind of a guy Joe Paterno is," Joe laughed. "You can be number two eight years in a row, and nobody cares. Be number one, and everybody wants to know about you."

Joe looked a sportswriter in the eye and told him that being ranked number one was not very important to the coach. "It's important to seniors and alumni and fans more than to me. If we get it, we'll have a big party and everybody will be happy, . . . but we don't have to

103

have it. . . . Let's be as prepared as we possibly can. And if we win, we win; and if we lose, we lose. But either way, let's enjoy it."

Then Joe lurched forward toward the reporter. He wanted his statement clearly understood. "But even with that statement, paradoxically, I must tell you my pride is such that I want terribly—desperately—to win." Then he grinned. "Although, I am reminded of Aquinas. Didn't he say, 'Anticipation was the greater joy'?"

The night before the game, Joe dined with friends at Antoine's, the famous French Quarter restaurant in New Orleans.

"It's been a great season," somebody there told him. "Win or lose tomorrow."

"It has been a great season," Joe agreed, "but we're not going to lose."[1]

But Penn State did lose. In the fourth quarter, from inside the one-yard line, the Nittany Lions twice tried to plunge the ball up the middle but were repulsed by Alabama. The Crimson Tide held on to win, 14-7, dashing Penn State's dreams of its first national championship.

The loss to Alabama was one of the most frustrating in Joe's coaching career. After the defeat, Pennsylvania governor Milton Shapp tried awkwardly to offer condolences to Joe as the coach headed for a television interview. "I know what it's like to lose," the lame-duck governor said, putting his arm around the coach. Joe didn't respond. Before the Alabama game Joe seemed to have a swagger about him. Penn State's former assistant sports information director, Ernie Accorsi, had "always been around this cocksure man who was full of self-confidence."

After the game Accorsi saw a Paterno who was filled with self-doubt and who criticized himself. "I just got outcoached," Joe said. "I just didn't prepare properly." Concluded Accorsi: "I saw a vulnerability in him." In the locker room Joe told his players not to dwell on the loss, to remember that they had a great season and not to go into "hibernation" because of an 11-1 record. Nonetheless, many people associated with the Penn State football program, including Joe, hibernated for many months afterward.

Joe's ego had been badly hammered. When he stood toe to toe with the legendary Bear Bryant, the Alabama coach had outcoached him. Writers and fans said, for all to hear, that Joe couldn't win the big one at the critical moment. Even former players said openly, "He should have won that one."[2]

"The crafty old Bryant coached rings around Joe," wrote Pete Axthelm in *Newsweek*. "Stuck in the craws of the fans was not so much that Penn State had lost, it was *how* it had lost," observed sportswriter Bill Lyon. "Those two plays [up-the-middle runs] seemed to embody what had infuriated the Lions' backers; they were the manifestation of all that was wrong with Joe Paterno as a coach: He had grown too conservative, too stodgy. He had no imagination."

Joe had his defenders as well. "I can't criticize the calls," reflected Chuck Fusina, Penn State's quarterback in the Sugar Bowl. "We only had six inches to go. We had a big offensive line, we had two tough backs in [Mike] Guman and [Matt] Suhey. The play worked for us all year; there was no reason to assume it wouldn't work again. . . . I know people say we should've run wide, or we should've passed, or I should've rolled out," Fusina said. "That's easy to say now. If we had tried that and failed, the same people would've said, 'You only had six inches to go. Why didn't you just dive over?'"

Even so, Penn State still had a chance to win until it was penalized for having twelve players on the field when Alabama squibbed a punt. The penalty allowed Alabama to maintain possession of the ball until time expired.

"The kid didn't come out when he should have," Joe explained afterward.

"Which kid was responsible for the penalty?" the coach was asked.

"What's the difference," Joe said. "It's not his fault."

Joe meant that the mistake had been his own fault, the coach's fault.[3]

The game was so close and would have validated the success of the Grand Experiment. (Penn State dropped to fourth place in the final polls.) Joe didn't get over the loss until the middle of the next season, and that was only after Sue Paterno chided him. "Joe, the Alabama game is over!" she said. "It's just another game you lost."

Usually, Joe was optimistic and energized, but he remained dispirited for most of 1979. He told colleagues that he had let the team down. "I was really discouraged," he later said. "I was really depressed. I thought that maybe I should give it up. It was affecting my family as well as me." He thought about quitting coaching and starting a different career. Sue told him to do what he wanted to do.

Throughout the spring of 1979, John Morris, Penn State's sports information director, thought that Penn State hadn't gotten over the defeat. "The coaches hadn't gotten over it; the players hadn't gotten over it. People were still dwelling on the loss."

As the 1979 season approached, Joe hoped his excellent defense would hold up while his offense matured. Then everything unraveled. In his fourteenth year as head coach, he confronted an avalanche of problems and a mediocre 8-4 season. During the year some Penn State players uncharacteristically flunked out of school, others were arrested for a variety of offenses, and still others disobeyed Joe's orders. One was even shot at.[4]

Trouble began before the season even started. Todd Hodne, a former Penn State player, was arrested on a series of rape charges. University police caught two linemen violating the on-campus drinking rule; Joe was informed, and the players were demoted. On the first day of fall practice, Joe announced that defensive backs Karl McCoy and Pete Harris and defensive lineman Frank Case were academically ineligible for the season. Harris, the brother of professional star Franco Harris and an All-American who had led the nation in 1978 with ten interceptions, was a stunning loss. (Joe later bluntly told *Sports Illustrated*: "He was a goof-off in high school and he was a goof-off here. What could I do about it? I don't care whose brother he is.") The following day Joe said, "I'm obviously upset about our situation, but we've made a commitment to play with student-athletes. We want to play with people who put forth their best effort—a legitimate effort—to get a degree. If the only way to win is to give up on that principle, then I don't want to coach."[5]

At an early practice defensive tackle Matt Millen, one of the nation's top linemen and a co-captain, quit in the middle of the mandatory mile run. Consequently, Joe stripped him of his co-captaincy. Millen had come into camp in poor physical condition, setting a damaging example for the rest of the squad. "As one of the captains he should have been the first guy out there wanting to run," said a Penn State official. Normally an aggressive, enthusiastic team leader, Millen had disappointed Penn State's coaching staff.

Two days later Millen made the required run, but his co-captaincy was not restored. Said Joe, "Matt will be very careful the rest of his life before he says, 'I can't.'" Joe added, "I so miscalculated the role of continuing leadership on the squad."

Many players felt that the season went sour after Joe's encounter with Millen. "What a battler," observed one player of Millen. "You could cut Matt's legs off and he'd still come at you. When Joe took his captaincy, it took a lot out of Matt and it took a lot out of the team."

"When I think back on it," said Millen, three years later while he was a linebacker with the Los Angeles Raiders, "I really screwed up. . . . I not only messed up myself, but I messed up a lot of other guys. As a captain, I should have shown more responsibility."[6]

The problems continued. An unhappy tailback, Leo McClelland, quit the team because he wasn't playing enough. In midseason, star tailback Booker Moore, only hours after his biggest game ever—166 yards and three touchdowns—was arrested by campus police for drunken driving. Reserve fullback Dave Paffenroth got into a fight with another student when he was told he couldn't attend a dorm party. Both players were suspended for one game. More disruption.

There was active sniping at Joe and even some booing during home games. Penn State was too conservative and predictable. The Nittany Lions didn't beat you, some critics said, "as much as they bore you to death." Fans booed, observed Douglas Looney in *Sports Illustrated*, "because they didn't like [Joe's] quarterback Dayle Tate; they booed because after fourteen years they had become tired of watching Penn State run off tackle; they booed because they don't like losing—even four games." George Paterno conceded, "Joe's going to have to open up the offense. They've got to be less predictable."

Joe tried to take the booing in stride. "It would be nice if everyone would say, 'Joe, don't worry about it. You can have a bad season this year and maybe lose five next year.' But that's never gonna happen." The booing was to be expected, he thought. "There's a whole generation around here who don't know what it took to build the program up, don't know what's gone into it, who've never seen us really have bad seasons." Still, Joe felt the harsh glare of the public eye. On November 3, after losing to the University of Miami, 26-10, he told reporters, "I'm going off by myself for a while and think."

"Every time something would start to go good," Joe later said, "something bad would happen." Always on edge, he worried when the next disruption would occur. When the phone rang at night, he would say, "Here we go [again]."[7]

In Memphis for the postseason Liberty Bowl, Joe reminded his players to be on time for the first team meeting. Two players were late, and Joe sent them home. Subsequently, reserve tight end William LeBlanc was found wandering around in a private house. A shot was fired, narrowly missing him. Initially accused of first-degree burglary, his charge was later reduced to malicious mischief and officials placed him on probation. After the arrest of LeBlanc, a weary Penn State official said, "Suddenly, it seemed like we were all a bunch of felons."

All in all it had been an embarrassing year for a school that prided itself on its lofty standards of conduct and academic integrity. "[The] papers really went after me," Joe said of media criticism. A few anonymous coaching peers came out of the woodwork to criticize him in the *New York Times* after the series of mishaps. Some of them originated from rival University of Pittsburgh. A Panther coach said, "Now they know what it is like living in a glass house and throwing those stones. They've learned that boys will be boys, even when they are men playing Penn State football." Pitt coach Jackie Sherrill publicly praised Penn State's program but was quoted saying privately of Joe, "He's told too many people too long how to run their programs. Now look." The *Times* quoted another coach, who had been criticized by Joe in the past, saying chillingly: "If a transfusion would have helped them, I don't think there would have been many donors."[8]

Joe won sympathy and praise as well. Notre Dame's coach Dan Devine said, "Any good program has a family feeling. Joe reacted to his troubles like all of us do with our own kids, whom we love very dearly. It hurts and it makes you mad." Although Penn State and Notre Dame sought many of the same athletes, Devine said, "The main thing about recruiting against Joe is you know he won't break the rules."

"We are a victim of our own image," stated Milton Bergstein, a Penn State professor and an admirer of Joe. "Nothing ever goes wrong here. Suddenly, we're falling apart. Well, I guess we were due for a little bad luck." "He will straighten everything out and we'll be good," said Penn State's basketball coach, Dick Harter. "Having Joe here is one of the charms of Happy Valley." After a long article in *Sports Illustrated* analyzing Joe's troubles in 1979, Douglas Looney concluded: "Here ye, then, that Joe Paterno is not a saint. But he'll do till one comes along."

On reflection, Joe thought there had been a slippage in discipline. "There wasn't that fear—which is a terrible word to use—but there wasn't

Joe Paterno and Jackie Sherrill have never been two coaching peers you want to leave alone in a room together. Sherrill had long been privately critical of Paterno prior to Joe's famous remark about leaving "college coaching to the [Barry] Switzers and [Jackie] Sherrills." Paterno later apologized to Switzer, but Sherrill is still waiting. (AP/Wide World Photo)

that fear of Paterno." He also worried about the character of his recruits. Values had changed; players were a little more selfish. "They have to understand that giving themselves to a group means getting more in return."

As usual Joe blamed himself for much that went wrong. In December 1979 he held a series of meetings with players to find out what had gone awry and what should change in the future. Some of the players told him that he always seemed too busy to consult with them and that when they did visit him, he seemed abrupt, abrasive, and unsympathetic. One player told him, "We're not as bad as you think we are. We're good kids." Touched by their comments, a few months afterward he reflected, "I probably didn't like them for a while and it showed. . . . I admit I got to thinking of that bunch as a group of jackasses."

The season had been the low point in his career. He later said, "Football always had been fun for me up to that point. Kids had responded to what I told them. But all that fell flat on me that year. I couldn't communicate like I had." After the season ended, Joe spent a few days in his native Brooklyn, meditating and consulting with old friends, trying to get his bearings again. Friends told him, "Don't let one bad experience drive you from a profession you love. Reevaluate things and give it another shot." Joe returned home fortified, more determined to "stick with it."[9]

That the media publicized all the problems his team faced during the 1979 season upset him. "Why humiliate a kid?" he said. Moreover, Joe experienced his most unpleasant and embarrassing incident with the media during the year.

Jackie Sherrill, a linebacker at Alabama under Bear Bryant in the 1960s, was the prominent coach at the University of Pittsburgh. The hard-driving Sherrill had three consecutive 11-1 seasons at Pittsburgh and a gaudy overall record there of 50-9-1. In December Sherrill accepted the Lambert Trophy, recognizing his team's supremacy as the best in the East in 1979.

"[Sherrill] is the only person [Joe] really doesn't like," observed George Paterno. Joe was convinced that Sherrill cheated and treated many of his players like chattel, yet hypocritically made solemn public statements.[10]

At one of the cozy Friday evening sessions with sportswriters, someone asked Joe if he had any plans to enter politics. Confident he was speaking off the record, Joe stiffened and said, "What . . . and leave college coaching to the [Barry] Switzers and [Jackie] Sherrills?" (Switzer was the coach at Oklahoma.) To Joe's horror his remark leaked out. After the comment appeared in the *New York Times*, it flashed across the country, making quick time to Pittsburgh and to Norman, Oklahoma. Joe was mortified. His remark had indirectly reaffirmed his commitment to the ideals of the Grand Experiment, that excellent football and academic integrity can and should work together. "What I said, I said in a flippant, smart-aleck way," Joe reflected, "but it has its point." Nonetheless, feeling that the media had violated his confidence, Joe grew more withdrawn and no longer held his Friday night gathering with the media. "Fool me once, shame on you," Joe said. "Fool me twice, shame on me."

Although Joe never sought to apologize to Sherrill, he was sorry about his reference to Switzer. The Oklahoma coach recalled in his memoir: "A real gentleman and a stand-up guy, Paterno phoned me when the quote hit the papers and apologized. Joe didn't apologize to Jackie, because there was some true bad blood there. But Joe knew Jackie was a friend of mine, and for years Joe had been hearing Darrell Royal [head coach of Texas] telling the establishment coaches that I was a crook and so Joe said it flippantly and without really even thinking about it." (Sherrill later coached at Texas A&M until he left under a cloud in 1988 after his program was slapped with a NCAA probation for twenty-five rules violations, nine of which the NCAA termed "significant.")[11]

Meanwhile, Joe added burdensome new duties to his already overloaded schedule. When Dean McCoy retired, Edward Czekaj had taken over as athletic director in 1969. But on January 14, 1980, President Oswald announced an administrative reorganization, naming Joe athletic director as well as coach. Czekaj would be reassigned as a special assistant to the senior vice president for finance and operations, Robert Patterson. Under the new alignment, Joe would report to Patterson on budgetary, contractual, fiscal, and nonacademic personnel matters; on matters relating to academic programs, such as admissions and eligibility, Joe was responsible to Dr. Robert Scannell, dean of the College of Health, Physical Education, and Recreation. The reorganization was to be effective on March 1, 1980.

Oswald stated that the primary purpose of the reorganization was to focus the strength of the central administration—specifically the senior vice president for finance and operations—on the budgetary and fiscal matters of the Department of Intercollegiate Athletics, while at the same time the department was to remain an integral part of the College of Health, Physical Education, and Recreation.[12]

That Joe would accept the position of athletic director while remaining football coach was inconsistent with what he had said throughout the troubled 1979 season. While things went sour on and off the field, Joe maintained that he had become too involved in areas outside of coaching (worrying about where funds were going to come from to support women's golf was an example he gave). He was constantly being pulled away from his team, he said, and therefore couldn't get a handle on the players' personalities. He said he needed to spend more time with the team. Now, as athletic director, in charge of everything from football to women's field hockey, Joe's attention would presumably be more fragmented.

"How does a man who is the head football coach at a major university find time to administer an entire athletic department?" asked Bob Smizik in the *Pittsburgh Press*. "Being a head football coach is a full-time job." Indeed, why did Joe accept the time-consuming additional duties?[13]

From the media's perspective the mysterious part of the realignment was Penn State's cloak-and-dagger approach to the announcement. No press conference. No questions asked. No returned phone calls. Such an approach fueled rumors and speculation, particularly from sportswriters in Pittsburgh. Some contended that Joe was power hungry and had privately conspired for the new role; others maintained it had been offered to prevent him from jumping to the pros.

Assuming there had been a three-way power struggle in the athletic program at the university, a sportswriter for the *Pittsburgh Post-Gazette* thought Joe had made the "niftiest end run of his career." He had "swept" by Czekaj and "outflanked" Dean Robert Scannell. "Scannell used to be in charge of intercollegiate athletics, with Czekaj under him and Paterno under Czekaj, on paper," said the writer. "Now Paterno is in charge of all intercollegiate athletics, on paper and off." Another report claimed that Joe had presented President Oswald with an "ultimatum"— that he be made athletic director or he would leave. Rumor circulated that the Baltimore Colts had dangled an attractive job offer in front of Joe. "Maybe Paterno told the powers at Penn State that if he didn't get the AD job he'd be off to the pros," went the speculation.[14]

None of these explanations was correct. "It was a mutual agreement between President Oswald, Mr. Paterno, and myself," said Robert Patterson. "Plus Joe was highly [respected] by the board of trustees." Why was the announcement made so quietly? "It happened over the holidays," said Patterson. "The institution was shut down."

Oswald's primary concern, shared by Joe, was the spiraling costs of athletic programs and the way in which the budget was managed. Inflation, costly national recruiting, new athletic facilities, stadium expansion, the growth of nonrevenue sports, the expansion of women's athletics, all contributed to spiraling costs at Penn State and elsewhere. In the 1960s and 1970s forty-two colleges dropped football. Patterson also pointed to serious fiscal problems as the primary reason for Joe's appointment. "The entire intercollegiate program was becoming much more expensive," Patterson said, and deficits were mounting.

Oswald did not have faith in Czekaj's ability to manage the budget, later saying that "[Czekaj's] strength was not in the financial area." Joe also worried about the way money was being spent. "Joe was [most] concerned . . . that football was underwriting all of intercollegiate athletics to the point of 95 percent of the budget," said Karl Stoedefalke, associate dean of the College of Health, Physical Education, and Recreation.

President Oswald had to twist the arm of his reluctant football coach to accept the dual role. In December 1979 Joe and Oswald held a closed-door session for almost an entire day to discuss problems and solutions. "Why not go out and get somebody else to be athletic director?" Joe asked. Oswald explained that he believed Joe was the best person for the position and could adjust effectively to the dual reporting role within the organization. They agreed to talk again. Meanwhile, Joe took his team to the Liberty Bowl and defeated Tulane. When he returned, he learned that the reorganization was a *fait accompli* and that the only question was whether a new athletic director should be brought in from outside the university or selected from within. Oswald took another stab at convincing Joe to take the additional responsibility, apparently pointing out that Joe had been with Penn State for years, understood the entire athletic program, knew the mistakes that had been made, and could take quick positive action. Oswald preferred someone from within the university rather than an outsider who would have to learn the university's philosophy and personnel.

Joe had not coveted the new position. "I've repeatedly told people no when they brought up the subject," he said. Robert Patterson, with whom Joe would work closely, believed that Joe never wanted the new assignment but became convinced that it would take time to find a new athletic director, and it would be difficult to find someone from outside the university who would carry on the athletic philosophy started by Ernest McCoy.[15]

Gradually, Joe came to believe that if he delegated responsibility effectively, he could perform both tasks. "If I thought it would hurt football," he stated on January 14, 1980, "I wouldn't have taken it." Once he made up his mind to accept the new job, though, he was excited to begin.

Sue supported his decision. "We hope this ends the uncertainty [in other people's minds] that I might leave Penn State or get out of coaching," said the coach. "Sue is happy because now I do have a little more control over what I do. I'm real excited about it, but two weeks ago if you mentioned [being athletic director], I'd have said you were nuts."

One of Joe's first administrative moves was to help formulate a five-year plan for athletics, the first time long-range financial planning was conducted within the athletic program. One of the most prosperous football programs in the country, in 1980 Penn State grossed about $5.5 million from football; expenses totaled roughly $3.1 million. That left about $2.4 million, but from that amount Penn State had to support financially about thirty other men's and women's varsity sports. (Except for football, all the other sports operated in the red.)

The cost of fielding teams was rising rapidly. "Equipment costs have quadrupled in the last five years," Joe observed in 1981. "Motel room rates have doubled and tripled. A few years ago, we paid twenty-six dollars a night per room. . . . Now, it's over fifty dollars. . . . A couple of years ago, we could buy a helmet for twenty-six dollars. Now, one costs fifty-one dollars."

There were only two ways to improve the bottom line—reduce expenses or bring in more money. Now that he had responsibility for thirty sports besides football, Paterno the coach had to bend to the demands of Paterno the athletic director. "We've canceled two [football] flights this season," he said in September 1980, "because the money we'll save [by bus] will keep our bowling team going." He said the football flights equaled the yearly budget for bowling.[16]

Joe tightened the athletic budget by cutting expenses and eliminating three minor sports. Coaches whose programs received less support were upset. "Despite the frustration," observed Dennis Booher, "many coaches believed that Paterno was not afraid to make decisions, and at least the coaches knew where they stood in the overall athletic program."

All the budget projections were based on 99 percent occupancy of Penn State's eighty-four-thousand-seat stadium. That was "scary," said Joe. "That's a lot of pressure to put on a football program, knowing that you *have* to win because if you don't have one sellout after another, pretty soon you're going to have to start dropping sports. And all of this comes at a time when there is pressure to add more sports."

During Joe's tenure as athletic director, several offices and locker rooms were remodeled, the Indoor Sports Complex was completed, and the athletic department's administration was restructured. He promoted the men's and women's basketball programs, trying to turn them into national championship teams. "I'd like very much to have people consider Penn State the basketball capital of the East," he said in June 1980.

Joe was dealt a setback in trying to organize an all-sports eastern conference. Difficult negotiations with Syracuse, Boston College, and Pittsburgh fell through as each school opted for what they perceived was their self-interest. "There was a lot of time spent working on that league without anything being accomplished," Joe said sadly.[17]

On January 18, 1982, after two years in the dual role, Joe resigned his position as athletic director. President Oswald immediately named associate athletic director Jim Tarman as Joe's successor (effective March 1, 1982). Although Joe tried, it had been difficult for him to keep football in the front of his mind. To do both jobs he had to sacrifice time with his family. "I've got teenagers I need to spend more time with," he said as he announced his resignation. "It was impossible to do that trying to handle both jobs." Nor had he been exercising like he wanted. "I don't do the walking I used to do because I've been so busy I'm always in a hurry." While admiring the job Joe did as athletic director, athletic department administrator Richie Lucas endorsed Joe's resignation. "It was too hard for him," said Lucas. "It was too difficult."

Joe enjoyed coaching and didn't want to remain in administration. "I want to coach," he said, "and any free time I have I don't want to spend it on five-year budgets."

That Penn State named Tarman as Joe's successor was no surprise. Tarman had joined the Penn State staff in 1958 and had been associate athletic director since 1973. The two had become close friends and Tarman was a trusted aide, confidant, and protégé. Particularly during the football season, Tarman had actually been handling the day-to-day operations of athletic director since Joe had assumed the position. "Jim [Tarman] has really run the athletic department for two years," Joe said, "He's ready to take over."[18]

Regaining their morale, Penn State's football teams rebounded, going 10-2 in 1980 and 10-1 in 1981. In 1982 Joe successfully adjusted his offense, de-emphasizing the grinding, methodical style designed to wear down the opponent. "[We] are going to try to make big plays happen," he said as the season was about to start, "rather than physically [wearing] people down. . . . We may depend more on the pass than we did in previous years. . . . We're going to try to do some cute things."

He gave Todd Blackledge, his six-foot-three, 225-pound quarterback, carte blanche to throw the football. Blackledge was one of the most talented quarterbacks ever to play for Penn State. During the 1982 season, for the first time in Joe's head-coaching career, the Nittany Lions averaged more yards passing than rushing and even scored one more touchdown by throwing the ball than by running.

Although Penn State had lost one game (to Alabama), when the Lions played Georgia in the Sugar Bowl on January 1, 1983, the national championship was at stake. A man dressed in Penn State blue and white told the TV camera before the game: "We'll win this one because we're gonna lock Joe in a closet before kickoff. He always chokes in the big ones."

Joe didn't deliver a fiery pep talk to his team in the locker room before the game, except to stress that they were there to win. "He had done all his talking in the three or four weeks before the game," said tailback Curt Warner. "He was really on us, more so than usual. I had never seen him get so angry or so emotional at practice."[19]

The Sugar Bowl was a tense, savagely fought contest. A 20-3 Penn State lead was sliced to 20-17; then a 27-17 margin was pared to 27-23. "A couple of times," Joe admitted, "I thought I could feel it slipping away. But that is what has made this team so special. They have poise, courage. They have been able to handle adversity." Those were traits he had always admired.

Near the end of the game, with Penn State in control of the ball, third down and three yards to go, and needing to run out the clock to win, Joe was seized by the similarities to four years earlier, the loss to Alabama. "Same stadium, same event, the Sugar Bowl, another Southeastern Conference team, and forced to gamble the whole year's marbles, a national championship, in a single short-yardage play."

The assistant coaches urged a running play, but young Blackledge wanted to throw it. Joe agreed with his quarterback. The resulting six-yard pass gained the first down, allowing Penn State to run down the clock.

"That moment's crucial decision had come easier for me than on New Year's Day 1979," Joe later said, "because I was not the same person I was then. Facing Bear Bryant four years earlier on this very spot, I wasn't big enough, strong enough, grown enough to face the ridicule if we had thrown the ball and the pass had been intercepted. The scare of it faced me down, and I lost. This time I didn't care about the ridicule. I cared about the first down, the pass, and the thrill of the risk. I knew this time that I was not afraid to lose. And I knew this time that listening to your heart and going with it is a winning principle."

Using a variety of defensive configurations, anchored by defensive end Walker Lee Ashley and safety Mark Robinson, Penn State had kept outstanding Herschel Walker in check. Georgia's Heisman Trophy winner gained 103 yards in twenty-eight carries, but his longest run was only twelve yards. Penn State's Curt Warner carried eighteen times for 117 yards and two touchdowns, outplaying Walker.[20]

Pandemonium broke out after the game. Fans, photographers, and players swarmed around Joe, knocking his glasses off. When Joe saw his brother, he gave George a big hug and said, "We did it!" George reflected: "I knew [then] what it really meant to him. Even though he said it didn't mean a lot, it did. It was due."

The final polls named Penn State number one. "There simply cannot be another coach in America who deserves a national championship more than [Paterno]," declared *Sports Illustrated* after the victory. An editorial in the *Centre Daily Times* praised Joe for adding the number-one honor to his long list of accomplishments. "The achievement affirms the correctness of Mr. Paterno's emphasis on scholar-athletes, and should quiet criticism of that approach from some skeptics."

Indeed, it seemed to Joe's admirers that Penn State's Grand Experiment had triumphed. As Bill Lyon observed: "Penn State didn't buy athletes, didn't phony up academic transcripts, didn't falsify test scores, didn't give credits for nonexistent classes, didn't pay for abortions for some player's girlfriend, didn't buy some hotshot recruit a car."[21]

Joe expressed sympathy to disappointed Southern Methodist, which had lost out to Penn State in the wire-service polls, and he took the opportunity to reemphasize his support for a national championship play-off system. "I've been in that position. Those are the circumstances involved when you have a poll to determine a national champion and

After all those bittersweet seasons of great success with no national championship to show for it, the Nittany Lions celebrated by carrying Paterno off the field after Penn State's momentous victory over Georgia in the 1983 Sugar Bowl. (AP/Wide World Photo)

not a play-off. If we were going to play SMU next week, things would be different. But there's also no question, with our schedule and the results, that we should be number one."

At a victory party celebration after the game, Joe excused himself about 2:00 A.M. and went to bed. "I didn't sleep," he later said. "I just wanted to be alone." Earlier in the evening he had to keep his emotions in check. "I was getting nostalgic," he said. "I wanted to get off in a corner for a while and remember all the players, the coaches before, who weren't around for this moment."[22]

At the Harrisburg, Pennsylvania, airport, the team was met by Governor Richard Thornburgh, and from there traveled a short distance to a rally at the university's Capital Campus, where about five thousand people cheered them. At the ten-minute rally Thornburgh led the crowd in chanting, "We're Number One! Joe's Number One." From there buses took the entourage through Dauphin, Speeceville, Clarks Ferry, Burnham, Lewistown, Milroy, and Boalsburg. All along the route thousands turned out with homemade signs celebrating the national championship.

"With emergency lights circling, each town's fire engines escorted us up the highway to deliver us to the care of the next town's engines in a hundred-mile relay of joy and pride," Joe said in his autobiography. "I never saw such love between people who didn't know each other. And never in one place at one time have I sensed so many football players in their private darkness sneaking so many silent, exultant tears."

The buses led a caravan to the Indoor Sports Complex on the Penn State campus where four thousand students waited. "We've got the greatest fans and the greatest team," Joe told the throng. "Three cheers for everyone." The next day, January 3, fifteen thousand Penn State fans stood shoulder to shoulder on the Old Main Lawn and listened as Joe talked about his pride in being part of Penn State. Although everyone should be proud of the team, there were many other things at Penn State about which to be proud. While feelings of unity remained, he urged everyone to translate the sense of togetherness into pride and commitment to the university as a whole.[23]

Joe and Sue Paterno continue the post-Sugar Bowl victory celebration during a snowy parade back home in State College, Pennsylvania. (AP/Wide World Photo)

During the year after the national championship, Joe seemed to be everywhere. The prestige of the championship amplified his voice as a longtime crusader against abuses in college football. On the lecture circuit and in interviews he spoke about the moral conflicts coaches faced and the problems of student-athletes. A few weeks after the Sugar Bowl, Penn State's board of trustees invited Joe to address them.

Joe had long been upset with Penn State's unwillingness to engage in systematic fund-raising. "Nobody lowered themselves to utter a single word about money," Joe observed in his autobiography, and "nobody was taking leadership." Joe took the lead, hoping that his speech would ignite a fire, stimulating a major fund-raising drive. "I seized the opportunity to cough up some things long stuck in my craw," he later said.

On January 27, 1983, at the trustees' meeting he received a proclamation praising the achievements of the football team. Instead of giving an innocuous speech, Joe electrified the gathering with a stunning vision for the university. Later, commentators misconstrued Joe's remarks, contending erroneously that the main thrust of his address had abrasively lashed out at the trustees, administration, and faculty. Actually, except for a few pointed comments, his speech was tactful and diplomatic and was primarily designed to inspire.[24]

Referring to a recent study that rated doctoral programs nation-wide, Joe expressed displeasure that some of "our academic departments are not rated very high." Some departments were "lousy" and some professors were "lazy" and "only concerned with tenure and only concerned with getting tenure for some of their mediocre colleagues." He also criticized the trustees for being too "reactionary" and "conservative." He thought Penn State needed "more controversy, . . . more freedom . . . more people that come with different ideas . . . [and] more minorities." But he also commended the "excellent departments" at the university and praised president John Oswald for cooperating with the athletic program and for doing a "magnificent job" during difficult times.

For the most part, Joe tried to inspire. Winning the national championship provided a "magic moment" for Penn State, he thought. The university needed a major fund-raising campaign to take advantage of the moment:

> We need chairs. We need money so that we can get some stars. We need scholarship money. We need scholarship money to get scholars who can be with the stars so that the stars will come in and have some people around them that can stimulate them and they can be stimulated by the stars.
>
> We need a better library—better libraries would be a better way to put it so that the stars and the scholars have the tools to realize their potential. We need an environment of dissent and freedom of speech and freedom to express new and controversial ideas. . . .
>
> I think we're literally looking for a soul. . . . We need to find our soul. We need vibrant, aggressive, brilliant teachers and scholars. We have some of them. We don't have enough of them; that's why we need chairs.

The endowed chairs Joe referred to moved a professor's salary from general operating expenses to a special account funded by the benefactor.

"I think you know how much I love this institution," he concluded, "and how much I appreciate what it has meant to me and my family through thirty-three glorious years, thirty-three years of a great love affair I've had with this place and this town."[25]

Both before and after his speech the trustees gave him a standing ovation. "It may go down as the only time in history that a coach yearned for a school its football team could be proud of," joked Rick Reilly in *Sports Illustrated*.

The *Daily Collegian*, Penn State's student newspaper, thought his "game plan" for his meeting with the trustees was one of his "most courageous." When the Coach of the Year strode to the podium to acknowledge a trustees' resolution in honor of his national championship team, the trustees settled back for the usual "We're Number One" rhetoric. What they heard was something no one but Joe Paterno could have told them, something no one but Paterno could say without fearing for his career, his job.

Joe's remarks apparently bruised the egos of some members of the faculty, but no one complained in public. Those who did comment agreed with Joe's assessment and praised his address. "He makes a pretty accurate assessment," trustee Kenneth L. Holderman said. "I would say the same thing."

Trustee Jay B. Claster said that it "was one of the best talks Joe ever gave, and he's given a lot of great ones. It was clear-eyed and very fair," he said, adding that the board "has a lot of homework to do to react" to the speech.

"I thought it was quite unusual for a football coach to say those things," said Henry P. Sims, a professor in Penn State's College of Business Administration. "Paterno just really challenged the academic community here. He said that we should think of ourselves as a university that should have national championships in terms of academic excellence. There was a certain amount of rhetoric involved in that, but it struck a chord. As a teacher, I can appreciate that very much."

On April 5, 1983, Joe delivered a similar speech to the University Faculty Senate, after the faculty body had commended Joe and his team for their athletic and academic performances. "I hope [my observations] will create discussion and generate a stir in people who are the ones who can literally move our university upward," he said.[26]

Two separate incidents after the 1982 championship brought Joe under scrutiny for his racial views, and in both cases his thoughts and feelings were misconstrued. His situation was laced with irony. As the *Pittsburgh Press* observed after the 1982 season: "Penn State Coach Joe Paterno has finally won the national football championship with his blackest team ever. Yet now people are calling him a racist."

Joe used his new notoriety to advance his favorite causes. "He has always been outspoken," observed Ira Berkow in the *New York Times*, "but his voice now is heard more loudly than ever." Joe relished his opportunity. "I can get people's ears because my team was ranked number one in the polls. What is number one? It's just some subjective determination. But people are impressed with it. Fine."

In January 1983, in a speech at the annual convention of the National Collegiate Athletic Association in San Diego, Joe embroiled himself in what turned out to be a bitter controversy concerning Proposition 48. Many college presidents were in San Diego to try to curb the abuses in college athletics. The NCAA Presidents Commission, established to push reforms, eventually convinced the NCAA to restrict the activities of boosters, cut athletic scholarships, curb the size of coaching staffs, shorten the recruiting season, and cut back the number of visits coaches could make to potential recruits. But at the 1983 convention the most explosive issue was Proposition 48.

Most colleges seemed more interested in keeping their varsity athletes eligible than whether they graduated. Although basketball star Chris Washburn was unable to answer a single question correctly on the verbal portion of the Scholastic Assessment Test (SAT) in 1983, more than 150 colleges recruited him (he finally chose North Carolina State). "Only one-third of the NFL players and even fewer NBA players ever earned college degrees," noted sports historian Benjamin Rader. Black athletes suffered severe problems in their academic programs. "A survey of 1,359 black athletes who entered colleges in 1977 revealed that only 31 percent graduated in six years," Rader observed. "Fifty-three percent of the whites obtained degrees." Unconcern for the academic success of athletes damaged the moral credibility of colleges. Columnist George Will glumly concluded that American colleges were "our schools for scandal."

Athletic exploitation had always disgusted Joe, and he took the lead among his peers in condemning the practices. Proposition 48 stated that in order to compete as a freshman in college sports, a high school senior had to earn a combined 700 on the Scholastic Aptitude Test *or* 15 on the American College Testing (ACT) program, *plus* graduate from high school with a grade-point average of 2.0 out of a possible 4.0. In addition, the athlete's high school curriculum had to include eleven designated core subjects, including three years of English, two of math, two of social science, and two of natural or physical science. A special committee of the American Council on Education had suggested the reform legislation for consideration by the NCAA. Proposition 48 was to take effect in the 1986–87 academic year.[27]

Disturbed about awarding scholarships to athletes not academically qualified, presidents and faculty representatives from some of the nation's largest universities spoke in favor of the measure. Dr. James Zumberge, president of the University of Southern California, called the proposal the first step "toward reestablishing the integrity in our institutions of higher education."

While speaking in favor of the measure, Joe used strong language, making him a lightning rod for all its opponents. The system had "raped" black athletes for the last fifteen years, Joe contended in his speech. "We can't afford to do that to another generation. I'm really surprised that so many black educators have gotten up and sold their students down the river. I think you're underestimating their pride and competitiveness." The talents of such black stars as Magic Johnson and Herschel Walker had made college sports exciting, Joe said. "But I don't want to bring kids into our programs and tell them they can do something they can't do." More and more black athletes were frustrated later in life because they had never received the education promised them while in college. "If number forty-eight is passed, they'll take up the challenge."

Moments after approving Proposition 48, NCAA delegates also endorsed Proposition 49B, which specified that athletes who didn't meet academic standards could still receive scholarships, but could not play or practice their sport for one year. They would have three years of eligibility if they met academic requirements of all freshmen students. Joe strongly endorsed Proposition 49B as well. "I've always been opposed to freshman eligibility for varsity sports, anyway," he said. "I think a student needs his first year as a period of adjustment into college life. With Proposition 49B, the student who doesn't reach the academic standards before entering college, can, with diligence, get his grades up so that he can be eligible for sports during his following year in school."[28]

Outspoken in his support for the NCAA's academics-toughening legislation, such as Proposition 48, Paterno many times was forced to explain and justify his views. (AP/Wide World Photo)

The passage of Proposition 48 enraged the presidents of mostly black universities, who thought the changes would damage their institutions. The black presidents had three main objections: that representatives of historically black institutions were not included on the committee which formulated the new measure; that historically black institutions would be most adversely affected; and that biased standardized test scores should not be used as an academic requirement for eligibility.

Several of the black presidents threatened to bolt from the NCAA because of the new rule. Joe was a special target of their wrath. "Condescending," some charged. "Joe Paterno insulted all blacks," said Dr. Joseph Johnson, president of Grambling State. "He does not know anything about black athletes." Chancellor Charles Lyons Jr., of Fayetteville (North Carolina) State University, probably expressed the feelings of many black leaders at predominately black universities when he wrote to Joe: "I deeply resent your statement about 'black leaders selling their black students down the river.' [Some of these leaders] have spent their entire professional careers giving opportunity to low-income and deprived black youngsters, but for [these leaders] and institutions which they head, these youngsters would forever languish and perish on the scrap heap of humanity."

Touched by Lyons's letter, Joe cooled his comments about "selling black students down the river," but he remained adamant in his insistence on better education for blacks.[29]

Fewer than 50 percent of black high school students scored 700 or higher on the SAT, compared to 75 percent of white students, leading critics to charge that the test had a built-in bias. Joe realized that Proposition 48 might have some initial negative consequences, but in the long run he thought it would benefit blacks. If the NCAA raised standards, blacks eventually would work harder and meet the standards. "It is difficult to oppose that [view]," said Donald Sheffield, a black member of Joe's staff. "Joe is one of the few persons within the 'System' [who] is literally trying to hit some of these issues head-on."[30]

Supporters of Proposition 48 came to Joe's defense and reemphasized their concerns. Dr. Charles Young, chancellor of UCLA, said he was "surprised" at the charges of racism. "I can't believe they meant it. Those of us who supported No. 48 probably have more black athletes than they do. This was done to protect academically marginal athletes, black [and] white."

Powerful support for Joe's position came from black leader Harry Edwards, a sociology professor at the University of California at Berkeley. "You cannot tell me that Vietnamese kids who never spoke English before they came here can outdo our kids. I have faith in black kids. Rule 48 is a blessing in disguise—it gives blacks a chance to hit the books." Edwards added: "Rule 48 communicates to young athletes, beginning with those who are sophomores in high school, that we expect them to develop academically as well as athletically. If we do not support this rule, we are saying to black youth that we do not believe that you have the capacity to score 700 on a test that you have three years to prepare for, a test that gives you. . . a total of 460 [points] by random marking of the test."[31]

After the San Diego convention, Joe addressed Proposition 48 and the corruption in college athletics on television and on the lecture circuit. "We have got to have some meaningful way to determine whether a youngster can be put into an institution where he has to read, has to be able to write," Joe commented on Phil Donahue's television show. "We have got to put the burden back on the high school in some way. . . . I had kids who get into a classroom and they get embarrassed. They are absolutely embarrassed and because they are competitors, they don't want to get embarrassed."

Despite his busy schedule, Joe often explained his views to black groups. At a forum at Penn State, black faculty and staff members reacted favorably to his speech. "He was wonderful," said Sheffield. "He knows that we have to do something about the exploitation of the athletes—particularly Afro-American athletes."

Ron Dickerson, a black assistant coach at Penn State, invited Joe to present his views to a convention of black coaches. "He did an outstanding job," recalled Dickerson, who agreed with Joe's argument. "Joe was just a pioneer in doing something that is demanded now of every other institution."

Joe's friends and associates admired his "courageous" stand on Proposition 48. Despite public criticism from black college administrators that could have damaged Joe's ability to recruit black players, he had spoken his mind. "He [wanted] to challenge black athletes to be better than they were," insisted Donald Ferrell, a black staff member in Penn State's athletic department.

Still, the criticism stung. "I expressed my opinion," Joe told Dickerson. "I sincerely feel as though the ruling is going to help blacks, and I'm sorry that other people don't feel that way."

"He felt strongly that [his] was the right approach," added John Coyle, Penn State's NCAA faculty representative. "He accepted the criticism, but I think he felt bad about it."[32]

Another incident that misconstrued Joe's attitude about race occurred simultaneously with the dispute over Proposition 48. In January 1983 black halfback Lenny Moore, who played at Penn State from 1953 to 1955 before starring with the Baltimore Colts, issued a vague but widely publicized charge about racial problems at Penn State. In an interview Moore was quoted as saying, "I know they are having problems up there with race, constantly. . . . If you put a yardstick of where it is today and where it was when I was there, it would not be much different."

Moore focused his attention on the fact that Penn State had only one assistant coach at the time who was black—the coach of receivers, Booker Brooks. (Before the 1982 season Joe had apparently offered a job to another black coach, but the person rejected the offer. "I don't want to say I'm going to hire a black coach," Joe said; "that's so condescending and insulting. We're looking for a good coach and I'm hoping he's black.")

If Moore's charges weren't so serious, Penn State's administrators might have laughed. In 1982 Joe was doing much better at recruiting blacks than the rest of the university, thought Bill Asbury, the university's affirmative action officer. "If we had the same results in the rest of the university as we have had in athletics, we'd be pretty happy," Asbury said. "The university's real problem is not enough black students in general."

Jesse Arnelle, Moore's black roommate at one time, thought Moore was "out of touch" with the situation at Penn State. "Lenny's reported statement about Joe Paterno having bad relationships with black athletes is dead wrong," Arnelle said. "That Joe Paterno has been a dedicated educator and recruiter of black athletes is well established." Joe also retorted that Moore was out of touch with Penn State's effort to improve its racial climate. "I'm not sure Lenny is in a position to tell," Joe said.

After Moore's charges received national publicity, Moore claimed he had been misquoted and misunderstood. He had directed his comments generally at Penn State, which he thought had dragged its feet in efforts to integrate. He had not aimed his remarks at the football team or at Joe Paterno. ("The next thing I knew," Moore later said of the news reports, "I was being accused of calling Joe Paterno a racist.")[33]

Despite Moore's subsequent clarification, the damage had been done. The media throughout the country had seized on his remarks and their stories implied that Penn State's coach might be a racist. "Moore Accuses Paterno of Racism," "Paterno Criticized for Handling of Black Athletes" screamed news captions. There were reports that some black high school players being recruited by Penn State received copies of Moore's original comments in the mail from competing recruiters.

Because of Moore's charges and Joe's support of Proposition 48, some blacks thought he didn't care about them. "Blacks, in general, have a misconception of Joe Paterno," Ron Dickerson believed. "In my community back home [near Pittsburgh], everybody believes Joe is a racist," Don Ferrell said sadly. "Contrary to popular belief, Joe Paterno is not a prejudiced person." Nonetheless, to gain advantage in recruiting blacks, some schools painted Penn State as a hotbed of rampant bigotry.[34]

Amid all the speeches and controversy, Joe coached his football team. Unprepared for its opening game in 1983, the newly sanctioned Kickoff Classic, Penn State was drubbed by an outstanding Nebraska team, 44-6—the widest margin of defeat suffered by one of Joe's teams since his first year as coach. The Nittany Lions lost their next two games as well, before regrouping and finishing the regular season with a 7-4-1 record, followed by victory over the University of Washington in the Aloha Bowl in Hawaii.

In 1984, when his team was 6-3 after defeating Boston College, Joe thought the season looked promising. Not wanting his players to burn out, he eased up on them, conducted shorter practices, permitted less contact, and barked at them less often. He backed away from pushing them because he didn't think they could sustain the intensity of consecutive games against West Virginia, Boston College, Notre Dame, and Pitt.

But in the next-to-last game Notre Dame slaughtered Penn State, 44-7. Then Pittsburgh wobbled into Beaver Stadium with a 2-7-1 record but nonetheless whacked the Lions, 31-11. After losing to Pittsburgh, Joe walked away from the field in a mist of doubt and confusion. "I'm more puzzled than anybody," he said. The collapses to Notre Dame and Pittsburgh marked the first time in Joe's career that his team finished the regular season with back-to-back defeats. Penn State's 6-5 record was the worst since the 5-5 record in 1966, Joe's first year as head coach. "Most teams are satisfied with 6-5," observed a sportswriter, "but at Penn State it was met with shock and embarrassment." (During 1983–1984, his two-year record had been 14-9-1, the worst for the Paterno era.)[35]

The late-season collapse haunted Joe, and once again he speculated about what had gone wrong. While his young team struggled in 1984, he slept less and less. "I was getting up, going to the office at 4:30 in the morning," he said. "By midafternoon, I was tired. And maybe I was making some bad decisions as a result." As customary, he took the blame for the mediocre season. He hadn't pushed his players hard enough, he concluded, hadn't expected enough from them. He had "babied" them. As a result, they babied themselves.

After the season, with his fifty-eighth birthday stalking him, Joe conducted a personal inventory. "I assessed the situation," he recalled. "I looked at the kind of football programs that are being built in the East at places like Boston College and Syracuse and West Virginia. I had to decide whether I wanted to get back in the fight."

He asked himself probing questions. Had he pitched his command tent too far from the front lines? Had he lost the all-consuming hunger to meet the challenge? Was his best still good enough? Was he willing to make the sacrifices necessary to succeed?

Some thought Joe was over the hill. "Is it true that Joe Paterno plans to retire at the end of this year?" a fan from Harrisburg wrote hopefully to his local newspaper. Sportswriter Ron Christ thought Penn State's 1984 team had just gone through the motions—"a team that played with little or no discipline, emotion and toughness, all those things that usually characterize a Penn State team." Fans expected more from Paterno, and "they usually get it," said Christ. "Paterno expects more from his players, and you can bet your last dollar he's going to find out why he's not getting it."[36]

After the disappointing 1984 season, Joe and defensive coordinator Jerry Sandusky reevaluated their defensive concepts and sought fresh ideas. Joe brought in defensive specialists from the Chicago Bears and the Denver Broncos to discuss their ideas at Penn State before the 1985 spring practice. Sandusky incorporated some of their concepts into Penn State's system. For Joe the additional expert advice was like management bringing in a consultant.

In 1985 Penn State rose from the ashes. In the off-season Joe had told his players about letters people had written him, telling him he was over the hill. "He had a lot to prove to people [that] it wasn't time for him to leave," said cornerback Duffy Cobbs. Cobbs and other players noticed a difference in Joe on the first day of spring practice in 1985. "Joe was *determined*," Cobbs said. "He instilled that in us from the beginning."

During the season Penn State escaped with one close victory after another. Through six games they were undefeated, but they trailed in every important statistical category except the most important one—points scored. They completed the season undefeated, 11-0, and could be the clear national champion if they beat Oklahoma in the Orange Bowl. But Oklahoma defeated the Nittany Lions, 25-10, snatching away the right to number one.[37]

Following the Orange Bowl loss, Joe showed up for the media interview looking as "grim-visaged as a Puritan preacher." He hunched over a thicket of microphones and squinted through his tinted glasses into the glare of the TV lights. "You don't come this close and not be disappointed about not getting the national championship," he said. More than anything "I'm disappointed for them," referring to the players. At one point Joe was interrupted in midsentence by a Penn State fan who shouted, "We'll get 'em next year, Joe." For the first time during the media conference, Joe looked up and smiled.

Of the forty-four players on the depth chart in 1985, thirty-seven were returning in 1986, including fifteen talented and experienced fifth-year seniors, their last crack at a national championship. At spring practice Joe shocked everyone by giving the fifth-year players time off from full contact, an unprecedented approach. "I think there ought to be at least one spring in college where you're not out for spring football," he said. "Spring is a pretty nice time of the year here. Play a little golf, tennis, take a look at the girls—those kinds of things I never did."[38]

Penn State started the 1986 season with six wins against creampuff opponents, then established credibility by blowing away Alabama (23-3), endured scares against Maryland (17-15) and Notre Dame (24-19), and finished undefeated (11-0) by blasting Pittsburgh, 34-14.

Partly because the 1986 team had excellent leadership and experience, Joe didn't have to ride them. He seemed mellower. "He *is* cool,"
said linebacker extraordinaire Shane Conlan, grinning broadly. "He's
cooler to be around. He's funny, you know. . . . I think he's changed a lot.
He was really bad that one year; the year we didn't go to a bowl [1984].
He was tough, but he should've been. We played terrible."

Joe developed special affection for his outstanding 1986 team.
"I'm going to really, really miss these guys," he said. "This has been a
great team to coach. They're mature; they know me. They give me the
business; you know, make references to my pug nose, that kind of thing.
They're a good bunch of kids. They know when to back off, and they
know when to have fun."

The pot at the end of the rainbow was Penn State's second consecutive attempt at a national championship. The location and opponent
were different. Instead of meeting Oklahoma at the Orange Bowl in
Miami, the second-ranked Nittany Lions were facing undefeated and top-
ranked Miami at Tempe, Arizona, in the Sunkist Fiesta Bowl. This "Dream
Game" was deemed so important it was moved from New Year's Day to
January 2.

"He wants to win this game very much," George Paterno said of
his brother. "Not so much for his ego. There's not much more of a mountain [for him] to climb. But I really do think he loves these kids. . . . This
one, he wants for the kids."

On December 26 one thousand cold but jubilant Penn State fans
formed a river of blue and white jackets and hats to show their loyalty as
the football team boarded a charter flight at the Harrisburg airport. "This
club has done everything anybody could ask it to do," Joe said. "It's been
a football team that's been committed to one thing, and it's got one game
to do what they committed themselves to do—and that's to go out and
beat Miami and to come home national champions."[39]

During 1986 there had not been much uplifting news on the
sports pages. Maryland's basketball star Len Bias died after using cocaine;
baseball star pitcher Dwight Gooden brawled with police in Tampa,
Florida; former WBA heavyweight boxing champion Tim Witherspoon
had allegedly failed urinalysis twice and seemed to have a drug problem;
and James Lofton of the Green Bay Packers was arrested and booked on
suspicion of sexually assaulting a woman. "But, alas, all is not ugly in the

world of sports," wrote a New Jersey sportswriter. "It took some searching, but there is some upbeat news to report." The upbeat news, arriving in mid-December, was that Joe Paterno had been selected Sportsman of the Year by *Sports Illustrated.*

The honor had been accorded to only one other coach (UCLA's John Wooden) in the thirty-year history of the magazine's prestigious award. Steve Robinson, senior editor of college football at *Sports Illustrated,* stated that Joe's selection was based on his consistent, enthusiastic, and phenomenal ability to balance athletics and academics. "Paterno has set a tremendous example by producing a winning team year after year while remaining true to the values of a major state university," Robinson said. "We thought that kind of achievement deserved to be honored."

A small newspaper in New Jersey expressed a common theme when it praised Joe for receiving the *Sports Illustrated* award: "Paterno is what college athletics are all about—or should be. In an age where cheating has corrupted so many schools, he stands as a paragon who will not cheat—and still succeeds. And when so many colleges with big-time programs seem little more than sports factories for the athletes they recruit, he has never lost sight of what his players come to Penn State for—an education."[40]

A few days after receiving the *Sports Illustrated* honor, Joe was named recipient of the Bear Bryant Award, presented by the Football Writers Association of America to college football's coach of the year. When notified of the Bryant award, Joe responded modestly. "I've been a very fortunate person," he said. "You've got to attribute this [award] to all the good people around me at Penn State. In my time there I've been fortunate to have been surrounded by quality players, coaches, and administrators. I know this sounds a little trite, but this is a Penn State award—not just a Paterno award." In 1986 Joe also became the first four-time winner of the Kodak Division I-A Coach-of-the-Year citation presented by the American Football Coaches Association (passing up three-time-award recipients Bear Bryant of Alabama and Darrell Royal of Texas).[41]

Miami, the team Penn State was about to face, was probably the most talented team in the country, and the least disciplined. Miami's trump card was quarterback and Heisman Trophy winner Vinny Testaverde, projected as an exceptional professional prospect, who had thrown twenty-six touchdown passes and only nine interceptions during ten regular season games. Miami also had Outland Trophy nominee Jerome Brown and several other future high draft choices. By game time Penn State would be a six-point underdog.

Like Penn State, Miami was inspired because the year before Tennessee had swamped the heavily favored Hurricanes, 35-7, in the Sugar Bowl. Had Miami won, they might have been voted national champs. "It will be a game between two teams desperate to atone for letting all the marbles roll off the table a year ago," observed sportswriter Ray Parrillo in the *Philadelphia Inquirer*. It was also a contest between two starkly contrasting styles, images, and values.

Because of numerous brushes with the law in 1986, Miami had gained the national reputation as an outlaw team. Police charged defensive end Daniel Stubbs with resisting arrest and petty theft for siphoning gasoline; a handgun belonging to tackle Jerome Brown had been found in a shopping cart outside his dormitory room; former All-American tight end Willie Smith was arrested on cocaine and weapons charges; halfback Melvin Bratton was arrested for shoplifting; linebacker George Mira Jr. engaged in a brawl with campus police; receiver Michael Irvin drove over the feet of two university law students; forty-seven current and former players were among a large number of Miami students who used other people's credit cards to charge hundreds of long-distance calls; and fourteen police cars arrived at the dorm where a gathering of Miami players grew loud and disturbing. The joke circulated that Miami was number one in the AP, UPI, and FBI.[42]

Some contended that the incidents should be no surprise in a teeming melting pot like Miami, where the drug trade thrived, a party atmosphere pervaded, temptations abounded, and "where the city's sleazy underbelly is glamorized weekly in a television series."

Far from admitting shame over the incidents, Miami players adopted a bunker approach of "Us Against the World." They flaunted differences with their staid opponent. Penn State arrived wearing blazers and ties while many Miami players walked off the plane wearing battle fatigues, like mercenaries headed to Nicaragua. (Commenting on his players' combat fatigues, Miami's coach Jimmy Johnson laughed. "I had a smile from ear to ear," he said. "It showed a little individuality on their part. I loved it.")

Surrounded by the Nittany Lion faithful, Joe seems to really be enjoying this pep rally leading up to the 1987 Fiesta Bowl Classic that would decide the national championship. The look of genuine laughter on Paterno's face seems to be saying "I know something you don't" to Paterno's absent counterpart, Miami coach Jimmy Johnson. (AP/Wide World Photo)

Miami players refused to sign autographs for eager youngsters at Fiesta Bowl functions (and before the game would refuse to shake hands with Penn State's captains). Some Miami players petulantly walked out of a steak fry sponsored by the Fiesta Bowl. Jerome Brown asked his teammates, "Did the Japanese sit down and eat with Pearl Harbor before they bombed 'em?" When the reply was no, he led his teammates out of the affair and boarded the team's bus for the hotel. Avoiding controversy, Joe brushed the incident off as kids being kids, joking, "There are a couple of our guys I wouldn't eat with, either. I've been trying to get their table manners cleaned up for years."[43]

In nearly twenty years of covering college football, Ron Christ of the Harrisburg *Patriot-News* thought he had never seen a team that brought so much disgrace to a university. "I don't remember ever seeing so many players who went out of their way to be rude and crude," Christ wrote. Many seemed to regard the Fiesta Bowl as football's version of a morality play. "Not since Ronald Reagan bombed Gadhafi has there been such a clear-cut, good guy-bad guy confrontation," said a story in the *Dallas Morning News*.

At the time Joe commented diplomatically about the actions of the Miami players, as did officials of the Fiesta Bowl. (Privately, though, the officials expressed their disgust for the way the Miami team behaved.) Later, in his autobiography, Joe was more frank. "Where's the character building," he said, "when a team is encouraged to climb off a plane for a national championship bowl game wearing combat fatigues? Why not hang bayonets and hand grenades on their belts, too, and lead them in the infantry cry 'Kill or be killed'?" He blamed Johnson for not raising a finger when Penn State was disembarking from the bus for the locker room and Miami's players "just about blocked our path, waving and taunting and yelling, 'We'll get you, you mothers.' (I'm only using half their word.) The Penn Staters were so shocked I placed myself between the two teams and ordered my guys, 'Just keep going.'"[44]

With his players Joe was upbeat and enthusiastic the entire week before the Miami game. He instilled confidence in the team. "He had us so motivated, so mentally ready, that we knew we weren't going to lose," said reserve quarterback Matt Knizner. All week Joe was loose and confident during the unprecedented pregame hype and the Fiesta Bowl press conferences and functions. He carefully avoided saying anything to upset Miami. "He simply has been around too long to say anything that may rile the opposition," noted Neil Rudel.

Joe did deliver clever one-liners. When a reporter asked the Miami coach about petitioning the NCAA for overtime if the contest for the national championship ended in a tie, Johnson sarcastically replied, "It wouldn't have the same clout that it would if Saint Joe did it." A little while later Joe opened a news conference by saying, "I left my halo at the house, but I wore this outfit because it's saintly looking."

Joe laughed when a reporter asked if he was enjoying himself. "For a guy who is used to going to bed at eleven o'clock and getting up at five in the morning, I'm having a little trouble adjusting to being such a social gadabout. But other than that it's kind of fun." Actually, it had been one of Joe's busiest years. "When we get to January 3," he said, "I'm going to find a pool some place and just go float on my back for a while."

On the eve of the contest an editorial in the *Herald* of Sharon, Pennsylvania, praised Joe's values. "If he wins tonight, Paterno will let his players share the limelight. If he loses, he'll take most of the blame and get ready for next season. But after the game stories are read, re-read, and filed, Paterno will stay in the forefront as a testimonial to all the right stuff in amateur athletics."[45]

The game was expected to be viewed by seventy million people, the largest audience ever to watch a college football game. More than six hundred reporters, broadcasters, and photographers covered the contest. With the possible exception of Testaverde, the person garnering the most pregame attention was Joe. The *Sports Illustrated* award and the coaching honors had assured him of extraordinary attention. NBC opened its prime-time Fiesta Bowl coverage with a fifteen-minute pregame show. The featured subjects were Testaverde and Joe Paterno. "They're the two people with marquee value," explained host Bob Costas.

Joe told his players before the game, "We're a better football team, just remember that, it's our football game, it's our national championship, let's go get 'em." Penn State had devised a game plan to befuddle and frustrate Testaverde and his receivers. "We set as our main target not Testaverde but his receivers," Joe explained. "Instead of concentrating on sacking and shutting down the quarterback, we said we'd let him throw—but change our coverage so frequently we'd confound his receivers." The coaches spent many hours trying to read some of Miami's key routes.

Jerry Sandusky's defensive scheme used a variety of zone coverage, some man-to-man, a blitz package, and a nickel defense. Penn State disguised each defense to keep Testaverde guessing. And he often guessed wrong.[46]

During the game the Lions, mostly ineffective on offense, relied on their defense. Defenders knocked Miami's receivers off course. "Testaverde likes to drop back nine steps and zip it," said Penn State assistant coach Ron Dickerson. "But because [the receivers] were knocked off stride, his receivers weren't where he expected them to be." Penn State's linebackers and defensive backs dished out punishment to the Hurricane's receivers, forcing them to drop several passes. Punter John Bruno pinned Miami deep in its own territory, forcing the Hurricanes to start with poor field position.

To ensure victory Penn State had to withstand a late Miami drive that ended when Penn State linebacker Pete Giftopoulos intercepted a Testaverde pass at his own one-yard line with nine seconds to play. "It all came down to one play," Joe later said of the dramatic contest. "We made it and they didn't. That's what competition is all about."

Penn State grabbed five interceptions and two fumbles, keying its 14-10 victory and guaranteeing its second number-one ranking in five years. Most of the important statistics favored Miami. The Hurricanes had more first downs (22-8); more total yards (445-162); and ran thirty-four more offensive plays (93-59). Joe, though, downplayed the importance of the statistics. "Are we going to play for statistics or are we going to play to win games?" he said. "I've been in that boat before—many times we've won football games and people have had better statistics."[47]

When it came time to meet the hundreds of media in the tent outside Sun Devil Stadium, Joe praised his players. "It's a national championship, and we won it on the field," he said. "I'm happy for that. It was good for college football, but I'm more happy for these kids." He had one more thing to say before departing: "We're happy to win it, but my hat is off to a great Miami team." Then Joe walked off the podium, hugged Sue, and shook hands with athletic director Jim Tarman.

Why had Penn State won? "The answer is simple," declared a sportswriter for the *Pittsburgh Press*. "Joe Paterno. . . . He is a football genius. . . . Give him six weeks to plan and plot and you know he will come up with something that will work. He came up with a national championship this time." Said Neil Rudel in the *Altoona Mirror*, "If ever there were a team of destiny, this was it. And if ever there were a team that knew how to win and was a reflection of its head coach, this was it."[48]

Joe later thought that Penn State had claimed its second national title partly by force of will. "I'm a great believer in self-fulfilled destiny," he said. "These guys literally made up their minds they were going to win a national championship."

Twelve hours after the Miami victory Joe faced the inevitable question: When would his team be ready to deliver still another number-one team? The question during a packed media conference in Tempe came from one of Joe's favorite members of the media, veteran Associated

Still basking in the glow of Penn State's victory over Miami in yet another Game of the Century, Joe escorts Sue to a January 1987 White House State Dinner honoring the French prime minister and his wife. (AP/Wide World Photo)

Press reporter Ralph Bernstein. Given its huge graduating class, Bernstein asked Joe, "What is the future of Penn State football?" Joe couldn't fight back a smile. "Hey, Bernstein, what are you looking for, another trip?" he said with a crooked grin. "Geez. Give me at least one day to enjoy this baby, will you? I love you, Ralph, but talk to me a month from now."

Following the game there were more special honors and tributes—from Pennsylvania state legislators and from President Ronald Reagan ("he's never forgotten that, first and foremost, he's a teacher who's preparing his students not just for the season but for life. . . .").

While celebrating its one-hundredth year of football, Penn State had gone undefeated, won the national championship, and its veteran coach had been voted Coach of the Year and *Sports Illustrated*'s Sportsman of the Year. "It's a script even the most imaginative of Hollywood writers would have dismissed as unrealistic," said a Penn State observer.

On January 6, 1987, Joe delivered a fifty-minute speech to one thousand coaches at a convention in San Diego. "You could have heard a pin drop in that ballroom filled with mostly eager young coaches," said an observer. "They applauded enthusiastically, then mobbed him when he left the ballroom. He was a winner in a business loaded with losers, and they wanted to see him, to hear him, to stand close to him."[49]

∼5∽

PROFILE: THE PATERNO COACHING SYSTEM

BECAUSE FOOTBALL HAS BECOME STAGGERINGLY COMPLEX AND REQUIRES CAREFUL PLANNING AND PREPARATION, THE SUCCESSFUL COACH HAS TO BE MULTITALENTED. Besides a master tactician and strategist, the coach has to be a supersalesman to compete successfully in recruiting blue-chip athletes and to sell his program to the university's administration, the players, faculty, students, and alumni; he must be a master psychologist to handle all the diverse individual problems with his players and coaching staff. He also needs to relate with people and with the media, to be an expert in public relations, to project a radio and television personality, and to be a stimulating public speaker. "He lives in a glass house, his every word and action subject to critical scrutiny," said one authority. "He is a father confessor, hero and scapegoat."[1]

Joe Paterno thought he had a vocation—a calling—to coach. First and foremost he believed the coach must be a teacher. He saw little difference between a coach and a teacher. They both prepare, urge, and motivate. Because they influence people, both must serve as a role model. "He uses the playing field like a laboratory," George Paterno perceptively observed of his brother.

Joe has believed that many coaches were so concerned about winning that they neglected the teaching aspects of their vocation. He has been an educator in charge of an area of responsibility in the university, just like the chair of the English department. "I am supposed to be developing certain character qualities and teaching the young people who come under my influence some values in life."

Coaches had the same obligations as all teachers, he said, "except that we may have more moral and life-shaping influence over our players than anyone else outside of their families." At the heart of the football curriculum, as important as teaching skills and tactics, were the purposeful uses of emotion, commitment, discipline, loyalty, and pride. By facing competition, the athlete learned the meaning of excellence and professionalism plus the will and the determination to rebound from disheartening defeat.[2]

Sometimes he has explicitly taught his players values. "I cannot look at you and just evaluate you on your football ability," Joe told a player. "I look at you and I know your grade-point average, I know your living habits . . . and I know your abilities as a football player. I may be wrong in making judgments about your character. I may be wrong in going to your parents and saying that you've got to do better academically. Maybe I ought to just sit here and say how good a football player you are . . . but I can't."

A coach establishes a code of conduct and accepts the rules and plays by them. "Success without honor is an unseasoned dish," he said. If the team succeeded, while playing the game with the idealism of sportsmanlike conduct, that was success with honor.

Joe hasn't wanted his players to "hate" arch rivals such as Pittsburgh or Syracuse. Yes, the game must be played with intensity, but not with hate. Feelings of hatred diminish the "humanity" of the player. Competition is related to compassion. "The more you pit yourself against the other guy and he pits himself against you, the better you understand each other because you're both struggling for the same thing in the same way."[3]

Periodically, Joe has felt he has grown too distant from his team and his coaching staff and has allowed the distractions of speeches, banquets, and public service to divert him from his primary role. He has mistakenly thought he could handle more outside diversions than he actually could. Asked to speak at a fund-raising banquet for inner-city youth and told his presence as speaker would generate a huge turnout and thousands of dollars in proceeds for a worthwhile cause, Joe has found it hard to refuse. "Why does he say yes?" observed assistant coach Tom Bradley. "How can you say no?" Joe has enjoyed attending banquets, delivering speeches, and raising funds for Penn State, but he has felt guilty when he returned to his office. "He'll come into [the office] and he'll be mad at himself because he has been away so much," said Bradley.

Joe has publicly given credit to others for the team's success. To his players—"We've had good athletes." To his assistant coaches—"I've always had great people around me." Exceptionally responsible and dedicated, he has blamed himself for the poor performance of his team. "I'm hard on myself." He has often said, "I could have done better." He has never shifted the blame for failure on to his assistants; he has always shouldered it. "When we lose a football game, it's his fault," offensive coordinator Fran Ganter observed of Joe's attitude. Ganter approached Joe after a defeat and said, "I don't think I've done—" Not letting him finish the sentence, Joe cut him off. "Get out of here," Joe told him. "That wasn't your fault." Then Joe cited his own failures and mistakes. Was Joe inaccurate in accepting blame? "Absolutely," Ganter reflected. "It was not [his fault]."[4]

Full of energy, zest, and vigor, Joe has seemed to work nonstop. Beginning with training camp in August, he has often labored sixteen hours a day until the final game of the season. Because Penn State usually has gone to a bowl game, the end of the season has stretched to the New Year; then the time-consuming recruiting season moves into high gear. "I've never seen him not work," said Joe's daughter Mary Kay. "Even on vacation he is always working."

"Joe doesn't sleep a lot," deadpanned Joe's one-time boss, Dean Robert Scannell. "The button [on the alarm clock] goes off about 5:30 A.M.," said George Paterno, "and he goes and goes and goes until it is time to go to bed." Worried that Joe was a workaholic, George wished that his brother would take time to smell the roses. "I don't think he can stop," George said. "Some people have got it in their genes—they can't stop."

"Every day Joe gets up and thinks about what he is going to do today to make himself better than yesterday," said staff member John Bove. He has his things-to-do list. At meetings he has focused on the business at hand; at practice he has concentrated on the drills. During fundraising for Penn State, Bove observed, "When those two hours appear on his schedule, he's going to take that coaching hat off and put that fundraising hat on and he is going . . . to give you the best two hours he can give you. . . . He gives everything he has—mentally and physically—to the effort and without distraction."

Joe has seemed to program himself for hard work. He has come home in the afternoon, done some work, then stretched out on the La-Z-Boy. Sue Paterno observed: "It will be twenty to the hour, and he'll say. 'Wake me at ten to.' In twenty years I've had to wake him once. He says it's all a matter of mental discipline."[5]

Joe has motivated his assistants and his staff by his exceptional dedication. "Joe works so damn hard to get things done that he inspires the rest of us," said one-time athletic director Ed Czekaj. "He motivated you just by the way he worked," agreed assistant coach Ron Dickerson.

"Joe demands so much of himself, he drives himself at a terrible pace," Sue Paterno said in 1971. "He thinks he can be a good coach as long as he works hard at his job, as long as he pays attention to details. . . . He blames himself when we lose, that he didn't work hard enough, that he could have done something different if he had paid attention to one more little detail. I think his biggest fear in life is overlooking a detail."

"If you take care of the little things," Joe stressed of his organizational philosophy, "the big things will take care of themselves." Always looking for a better method, another way to defeat an opponent, he has constantly taken notes. "He's a doodler," said assistant coach Booker Brooks. "He usually is writing something down, some new scheme, some new approach—always trying to find something a little bit better."

"I've got a checklist for everything," Joe said. "I've got a checklist for a checklist." On Saturday evening, flying home from a game out of town, Joe has busily taken notes for the following week's game. Especially during the football season, he hasn't wasted time. "When you get him on the phone, you don't visit for an hour," said William Schreyer, a prominent Penn State trustee and fund-raiser. "What we talk about, we get done and hang up." Only rarely has he been late for a meeting. Studying film in his office at home one morning, he forgot about a 7:15 A.M. breakfast meeting with some players. "He had a hemorrhage," said Sue. After Joe apologized, the players teased him that he would have to run laps.

Sue has teased him about his sleeping habits. "You're going to give me lead poisoning from the sheets," she has told him. The bed has always been full of pencils, and he falls asleep with a pencil and pad in his hand. "He'll catnap for a couple of hours, then wake up at three in the morning and jot something down," said Sue. Then he'll fall back asleep.

On the Friday before Saturday's game, Joe has often taken a walk by himself. "He didn't want anyone with him," said assistant coach Frank Patrick. "You could see he was starting to play the ball game in his mind." For games out of town, Joe has been up and at his hotel room desk early on the morning of the game preparing notes. After a game, even a major victory, he has usually been subdued, probably exhausted emotionally from his long hours of preparation and the drama of the game itself.[6]

Meetings with assistant coaches have been more frequent, intense, and productive than those conducted by Rip Engle. The common thread for all meetings has been finding ways to get better and not becoming complacent with the victory the previous Saturday. Amid Coke bottles and coffee cups, the coaches have planned practices and strategy. As for their common enemy, time, the coaches have carefully spent it— "like a band of misers in a common counting house"—with Joe allotting the final disbursement. Businesslike, purposeful, and organized, the coaches have wasted little time on small talk or extraneous issues. If the discussion has drifted, Joe has quickly brought it back on track. He has welcomed the opinions of his assistants. Although Jim Weaver was an inexperienced assistant and didn't say much, "I felt I was able to say what I wanted to say."

He has tried to be fair with all his players. He has often asked his assistants, "Did I do that the right way?" At meetings he has inquired whether the weakest player on the team was getting an opportunity to display his ability. "Do I have him in the right position? Maybe if we move him over to tight end." (Meanwhile, an assistant coach was thinking privately, "This kid doesn't have a chance.")

Joe has been demanding. When a problem has arisen or failure occurred, he has examined himself first. "After he examines himself," Jerry Sandusky said, "he is going to examine us." Even after Penn State has enjoyed a successful season, Joe has insisted upon an ongoing process of reexamination. He might alter his approach to the next spring practice. His constant drive for improvement has forced his assistants to seek innovations. "He guards so much against complacency," said Sandusky. "He is constantly trying to get better [and] wants to do things differently."

Joe has continually refocused his goals. After a mediocre season, when things have gone wrong or he has become distracted, he has brought himself back to the basics, the fundamentals of what it took for him to be successful: excellent coaching, attention to detail, and a closer relationship with his players and assistants.

He has enjoyed the stimulation and creative benefits from discussion and debate, and if he has judged them lacking, he has prompted them. "Football can be an intellectual exercise," he said, "and I want people who will think about what we can do and not be content to rubberstamp my thoughts or be satisfied with what has worked in the past."

"We don't call them arguments," Tom Bradley said, "we call them discussions. We have good discussions." Joe has often played the devil's advocate to challenge the depth and firmness of an assistant's suggestion. If the assistant has strongly believed in his idea, he has been more likely to coach it with zeal and effectiveness. "An assistant coach who is allowed to present an idea and have it accepted will work twice as hard to make that idea work on the practice field than if he walks out of a meeting turned down all the time," Joe said. "Your assistant coaches will only grow if you allow them to try new things."

"I wanted to change the punt coverage," Bradley reflected. "We'd been doing the same thing for ten years. He fought me on it the whole way through it. I think he liked my idea, but he wanted to find out how much I really believed in it. Obviously, if I backed down right away once he challenges me, then I don't have a firm conviction in my idea."[7]

Joe has sometimes encouraged even boisterous disagreement. Young Gregg Ducatte vividly recalled a heated argument with Joe that occurred in the spring of 1975. Joe wanted Ducatte, who coached the defensive secondary, to install a new coverage for the defensive backs. Ducatte resisted, contending the proposed changes put too much pressure on the defensive halfbacks when Penn State didn't have enough talented players to handle the new coverage. "I didn't believe it could be done," Ducatte later said.

Joe rose from his chair and began diagramming his concepts at the blackboard on his side of the room; Ducatte did the same at a blackboard on the other side. They began yelling at each other.

"God—— it. You're so stubborn," Joe said, temporarily ignoring his rule against swearing.

"I'll be a son of a bitch if I'm going to teach this!" responded Ducatte.

Each drew pass patterns on the board to illustrate their points.

Banging his chalk on the board, Joe said, "Well, this is the way I want it done, God—— it! Why the hell can't they do this?"

"Because, Joe," replied Ducatte, making his point on the blackboard, "how in the hell are we gonna cover that? You're asking the impossible of these kids."

Joe smashed his chalk on the blackboard; so did Ducatte. Each threw pieces of chalk at the other's blackboard.

Finally, Ducatte simply said, "I cannot do this. I cannot teach this. . . . If you make me do it, it is not going to work. . . . I don't think I'm the man for the job if you want me to coach it this way."

"Okay," Joe said, conceding the point to his assistant. "If that's what you believe." Joe calmly sat down and resumed the staff meeting. Still emotionally upset, Ducatte also sat down. "[Joe] was as cool as a cucumber," Ducatte recalled. "I was still shaking."

Later, Ducatte praised the way Joe had handled their five-minute encounter. Ducatte had been forced to think and to defend his position. "I always admired him for that. He was a manager of people. . . . I disagreed with him and said I didn't believe. He wanted to know what I believed."

Joe has been so skilled at reasoning and arguing that inexperienced assistants, like Ducatte, have occasionally felt intimidated. "It was intimidating because he makes you know what you're talking about," said Ducatte. "You cannot just say you don't agree without being able to back it up. If you are not skilled at argumentation, you're going to lose."[8]

Despite differences of opinions during meetings, afterward the coaches have loyally supported the final decisions. Assistant coach Dan Radakovich enjoyed the vigorous give-and-take. "If you had an argument—and we [coaches] had a lot of them, probably more than most places—when it was over, it was forgotten," said Radakovich. Even after the most heated argument, the next day Joe acted like the incident never happened. No bitterness or resentment lingered. "[Joe] does not carry a grudge," said Fran Ganter. "Ever."

Joe has handed out compliments, but not often and not lavishly. He has said, "Nice job," "I appreciate what you have done," "I like the way you analyzed this." If Joe didn't like the way assistant Tom Bradley handled a drill, he told him, "Tom, I didn't like the drill you did with those guys. It could be done better." Or he praised Bradley: "I liked what

Assistant coach Fran Ganter (right) makes a point during a sideline conference with Paterno and Penn State quarterback Mike McQueary during a 1997 game against Illinois. (AP/Wide World Photo)

you did. Maybe you should do more of that." Some head coaches have verbally abused their assistants, thrown film projectors at them, or fired them in the locker room. "[Joe] is by no means anything like that," Ganter said. "I can't think of a better guy to work for."

The assistant coaches have been intensely loyal to Joe and to Penn State, and Joe has been loyal to his assistants. They have all been part of Joe's Penn State family. "The loyalty [of his staff] has been very important to him," said Sandusky. Joe has cared about the people who have worked for him. When an assistant coach was receiving improper medical treatment for a blood clot, Joe intervened, contacted medical experts, and made sure the man received the finest care.[9]

By loyally remaining with Joe for so many years, the coaching staff created exceptional stability. Sandusky declined offers of head-coaching jobs in order to stay at Penn State. Nor did Ganter actively seek a head-coaching position. "I really have not gone out and tried to pursue another job," Ganter has said. "It is just an ideal situation [at Penn State]. I like the job."

There has been too much stability for some. Young, ambitious assistants have found their path to advancement blocked. After fifteen years on Joe's staff, Booker Brooks was still only fifth in seniority, and consequently, although he admired Joe and liked Penn State, he left for a position with more coaching responsibilities. "There wasn't a lot of room for growth [on the Penn State staff]," he reflected.

There have been some drawbacks to working for Joe. He was "too impatient," Sandusky thought. "He is impatient," agreed Booker Brooks, "and that is tough on an assistant coach. He would want a player to develop faster than is humanly possible."

The assistants also would have preferred that he delegate more responsibility. For most of his head-coaching career, Joe has been totally and completely involved in decisions made during the week. He has been the chief administrator, public relations director, and recruiter, as well as the dominant force molding the offense, defense, and special teams. Although he has allowed ample discussion and input on decisions, he has still presented *his* plans.[10]

As college football became more complicated, he began to turn over major responsibilities to coordinators, the first being defensive coordinator Jerry Sandusky. Still, the problem remained. "If I had a criticism of Joe," said Ducatte, who coached in the mid-1970s, it was that Joe "tried to keep his finger in all the pies too long. He just couldn't do it all. It got to be too specialized."

Booker Brooks didn't think Joe effectively delegated either. "He [had] his finger on the pulse of just about everything that went on," Brooks said, which was another reason Brooks left Penn State. In cold-weather games Brooks wanted his receivers to wear catching gloves, but Joe refused Brooks's request, convincing Brooks that Joe was inflexible and wouldn't delegate a simple responsibility. Brooks told Joe, "You want some leadership, yet you won't allow [a] coach to make this simple decision!"

Joe had to learn to deal with his dilemma. "When I was forty-five, I had all kinds of energy," he said. "There wasn't a thing going into the offense, defense, [or] kicking game that I didn't have a direct bearing on. It was fun for me."

Starting about 1984 Joe began to delegate more effectively, wait-ing for his offensive and defensive coordinators to present their ideas to him. Then he offered his input and suggestions. "I'm not the man I used to be," he admitted in 1986. "You are stupid if, at sixty, you think you can do what you did at forty-five. It used to be that four or five hours' sleep was fine. But then I got a little older. I was forced to [back off]."[11]

Penn State business professor Henry Sims studied Joe for a chap-ter in a book Sims co-authored, *SuperLeadership: Leading Others to Lead Themselves* (1989). Sims thought Joe was a perfectionist who wanted to control everything, but as coaching became more complex and his responsibilities increased, he was forced to delegate. Joe had to wrestle with the classic dilemma of any leader, Sims thought, a conflict between his emotional or "natural" self, which had a strong desire to control—in Joe's case perhaps overcontrol—the situation, and his "intellectual" self, which realized the necessity and benefit of providing more opportunity for his assistant coaches. "From what I can see," concluded Sims, "Paterno has made that adjustment. It appears he's delegated more of his author-ity and is in more of a symbolic role."

Joe improved his ability to delegate, but he didn't master it. Sometimes he discouraged creativity among his assistants because he seemed too intimidating. "Because he is such a strong leader and highly competitive," said Sandusky, "sometimes he may not get the most out of some people because he will not delegate enough. He may have more cre-ative people than he realizes. He can sometimes stifle that [creativity] because of his own involvement."[12]

Shortly after Joe appointed Ganter offensive coordinator in 1984, he explained one reason he hadn't delegated more earlier. He admitted to Ganter that as his head-coaching duties became more complex, he could no longer spend as much time on both sides of the ball. But he wanted to remain involved, primarily with the offense. "I don't want you to ever think that I lack confidence in you," Joe told him. "I just want you to understand one thing: I don't want to be an administrator. I don't want to be a guy who shows up on Saturday, folds his arms and argues with the officials, and doesn't know what play is going in on offense. . . . The only reason I've stayed in [coaching] is because I love to coach."

"It touched me the way he said it," Ganter recalled. "I even admired him more." After about 1984, therefore, Joe arranged to spend about 30 percent of his coaching time with the defense, enough to under-stand what the defense was doing and to offer general advice. About 70 percent of the time he worked with Ganter and the offense.[13]

Like other great coaches, Joe has had the extraordinary ability to analyze opponents and figure out ways to beat them. The more time he has had to prepare a game plan, the more likely he has been to defeat any opponent. If Penn State's style has been unsuited for an upcoming chal-lenger, he has adjusted. While viewing films of opponents, he and his assistants have looked for tendencies, coverages, formations, and other intricate details that gave Penn State an edge.

He has wanted to know everything about the opponent, offen-sively and defensively. He has wanted his scouts to chart every play by the opponent in the previous game. "Get every play charted," he said in 1983. "Put all the inside plays together and chart them. Put the outside plays together and chart them. Put the pass plays together and chart those. This is important so that when you go into practice, you can do specific breakdown work, in which you practice the plays you'll need to play that particular team."

He has prepared to stop the opponent's best player and best plays. He has wanted to know the starting count and the type of huddle they used. He has looked for line splits and patterns in the play calling. Do they like to run on first down? What is their pattern of substitution? Was there a reason they wanted to get a player out of a certain situation? How do they cover first and ten? How do they handle third-down situa-tions? What have other teams done well against the opponent? Why? What plays were successful? Did the opponent have clutch plays? What do they do on the goal line, both offensively and defensively?

Joe has meticulously instructed his quarterback to watch for "keys" in reading the defense. "When they're going to blitz," he instructed quarterback Chuck Burkhart during a film session, "this guy comes up and waves his arms." Prepared thoroughly, Burkhart said, "We always knew what we wanted to do going into a game." Linebacker Dennis Onkotz thought he was prepared so well by excellent coaching that he often knew the upcoming play before the opponent ran it.

Joe has stressed defense, then the kicking game, and, finally, the offense. He has hated to stand on the sideline knowing he couldn't stop the opponent. Penn State has used quick, smart, aggressive linebackers to blitz, stunt, and fall back into pass coverage, creating innovative schemes opponents have had difficulty deciphering.[14]

Joe has wanted to wear down the opponent through his own team's persistence. Cause attrition. Keep hitting the opponent until he got tired of being hit. "You just hit him so many times and so hard that he quits," Joe explained. Joe has wanted each player to play each down as hard as possible instead of pacing himself.

Joe's first principle of offensive football has been to maintain possession of the ball. Don't make mistakes in key situations; never put the defense in a poor position. In considering his next offensive play, Joe has usually thought: What is the chance of fumbling? What is the chance the opponent will intercept? If the risk has been high, he has been likely to choose an alternative. "Hang onto the football," Joe said. "That rule is not very fancy, and it doesn't always excite the customers, but it's a winner."

Normally, the passing game has complemented the running game. He has never had an exceptional team that didn't have an exceptional running attack. Nonetheless, he has effectively adjusted his offense to his players' special talents. With an outstanding passing quarterback and excellent receivers, Penn State passed more.[15]

Some critics have judged his offense as too conservative. "He [took] a lot more chances [on offense] in the early days than he seems to now," Ron Christ observed in 1988. "I guess this will be the thirty-second straight game in which the opening [play] will be a tailback off tackle," teased a sportswriter.

Ducatte thought that Joe sometimes designed plays that were essentially the same and used them in the same series. Because they were blocked differently, Joe saw them as two different plays; Ducatte thought the opposition's defense saw the same play. Joe needed a better mix of plays, Ducatte thought. "His series . . . didn't always make sense."

Jack Bicknell, then the Boston College coach, had played against Penn State for five years when he observed in 1986 that despite changes in personnel, Joe's teams remained fundamentally the same. "They don't change much," he said. "They run the ball first, then try to get some balance. They have a good kicking game. Their defense is very physical and more or less geared to stop the run."[16]

Joe doesn't want a player to feign serious injury as an excuse to get out of practice. He has wanted the nature of injuries fully explained

Head down and hands in pocket, Joe walks across the field before a 1988 game. (Allsport USA Photo by Rick Stewart)

to him by his medical staff and trainers. Sometimes he has been upset if an injured player couldn't perform, but when the medical staff made its decision, he has accepted it. "He puts great pressure on you to get things evaluated and get a decision made," observed team physician Dr. Harry Weller, "and he will question your decision." He didn't just accept the doctor's opinion at face value. If the doctor said a player could return to action in a week, Joe would say, "Do you really mean seven days and not six days?"

"He never played a young man whom I said couldn't play," said Dr. James Whiteside, Penn State's team physician from 1974 to 1987. Still, "he always made sure the medical staff was very thorough in their physical examinations and firmly believed their decisions." Dr. Whiteside provided objective tests—strength tests, for example—to back up his judgment. "Once he understood the medical side was firm and had proof of the situation," Dr. Whiteside said, "he abided by it."

Occasionally, Joe has read an account in the newspaper of a football player who made a "miraculous" recovery from a serious injury. Noting that a player on Penn State seemed to have a similar injury, he grilled Dr. Weller as to why it took the player in the newspaper account only three days to recover. "How come you're saying three weeks?" Scurrying to find an explanation, Dr. Weller's research disclosed that the two injuries actually were *not* similar, that the Penn State player's injury was more serious. Joe accepted the doctor's conclusion.

Joe has expedited the diagnosis and treatment of injured players. When a premier wide receiver was thought to have an irregular heartbeat, Joe and Dr. Weller flew with the player to Hershey Medical Center on a Thursday for a full cardiac evaluation. When the tests showed no serious heart problem, the wide receiver played on Saturday and scored a dramatic touchdown. Dr. Weller observed that Joe could "push the right buttons to get things done rapidly."

An injured player has been instructed not to talk about his injury lest the next opponent learn of it and adjust plans. When linebacker Pete Giftopoulos broke his hand on October 10, 1987, and couldn't play in the upcoming game against Syracuse, the coaches told him not to mention his injury to anyone. "Everything [was] a secret," Giftopoulos said later. "Come game time, as far as Syracuse knew, I was starting. Nobody knew that I had a broken hand." Syracuse had prepared to play against Giftopoulos as an inside linebacker, but when the game started he wasn't there. "It's such a big business," Giftopoulos said, "that every advantage you have you try to use it."[17]

Penn State's teams have been quick-thinking, superbly trained, organized, and motivated. Joe has repeatedly told his players, "You either get better or worse every day. You never stay the same." At practice he has energetically pushed them to get better every day. He has compared his job to rehearsing a symphony orchestra. "You work hard with the various parts during the week and hope it all fits together on Saturday."

Football should be fun, but practice has been work, something the young men have had to put up with in order to get the enjoyment out of football games. In *For the Glory* (1994), a book about the difficult regimen endured by Penn State players, author Ken Denlinger observed that in preseason drills, morning meetings were "followed by morning

Like most highly successful coaches, Paterno long has been driven, consistently drilling his players in practice, as he is doing here in 1974 heading into a nationally televised game against Stanford. (AP/Wide World Photo)

practice followed by lunch followed by some rest followed by more meetings, more practice, dinner, and, of course, more meetings."

Because of the heavy demands on the student-athlete, practices and team meetings have had to be exceptionally efficient. Before every practice Joe has gone over the schedule with his assistants—budgeting five minutes for one drill, eight minutes for another. The drills have been timed and when Joe has blown the whistle, the players have immediately moved to the next drill. "Time is our enemy," Joe said.

If practice was scheduled for two hours and eight minutes, usually that was exactly how long it turned out to be. In his book *Coaching Winning Football* (1983), Joe provided a sample practice period for the defense:

> 1—Kicking Improvement—10 min.
> 2—Individual Pass Defense and Option Work—14 min.
> 3—Flexibility Exercises—6 min.
> 4—Individual Improvement vs. the Run—10 min.
> 5—Pursuit—5 min.
> 6—Alignment and Plugging—5 min.
> 7—Teach vs. the Run (Inside, Outside, Perimeter)—16 min.
> 8—Teach vs. the Pass and Adjustment Period—16 min.
> 9—Goal Line and Special Emphasis Work (Options and Play-action Passes)—14 min.
> 10—Thud (Situations)—18 min.
> 11—Punt Blocks and Returns—8 min.
> 12—Punt Coverage—8 min.

The practice field has been one place where he has had complete control of the players, and he has tried to make the most of it. He has insisted his players concentrate and not become distracted. He has drawn a blue line next to the practice field, and when the player has crossed the line, that player has understood that for the next hour and forty-five minutes he was to devote himself completely to improving his ability at football, not to worrying about his girlfriend or academic work. "Look, there is nothing you can do about your studies or your personal problems now," Joe has told them. "You are on the practice field, so you better concentrate on one thing, and that is busting your butt to get better." Through habit, players have become used to his approach; when they have arrived on the practice field, they have been ready to work.[18]

Joe has pressured the players at practice so they could effectively handle any pressure that arose during Saturday's game before eighty-five thousand people. "We do everything faster at practice than it happens in a game, work harder and longer," linebacker Trey Bauer said. "He's always pushing us to think. He won't let you get careless. So when we go into a game, we think we're ready for whatever someone throws at us."

Like other skills, football skills require the mastering of details, day in and day out. Joe has insisted his players do the small things right: assume the correct stance, take the right angle, eliminate false steps. If each player does his small part, the big play—a "good thing"—will happen.

In *Coaching Winning Football* Joe detailed the approach he used to teach the elementary quarterback-center exchange:

a. *Center Stance*—Same stance as any other lineman. A balanced stance, feet at the same width as the shoulders or slightly wider, depending on the build of the athlete.

b. *Position of the Ball*—The ball is placed in the middle of the stance at full arm's length from the body with the laces facing to the right at about three o'clock for the right-handed quarterback, and to the left at about nine o'clock for the left-handed quarterback.

c. *Two-hand Grip*—The center grips the football with the hands toward the rear of the ball. The hands are placed at opposite sides of the ball with the fingers pointing away from the body parallel with the ground. The thumbs are almost joined at the center seam. The ball is then tilted forward (not more than forty-five degrees) to enhance an efficient snap.

d. *Snap*—The center brings the ball to his crotch, where the quarterback's hands are waiting to receive the ball. The center brings the ball straight up, turning the ball over so that the quarterback gets the opposite end of the ball. The low point of the ball comes up first as the ball turns over.

e. *Feet*—The center must step forward the instant he snaps the ball so that he can get the impetus he needs as a blocker.

    f. The quarterback's hands are joined at the thumbs and spread laterally in such a manner that the hands and fingers pressure the upper portion of the center's thighs. The hands are placed so that they are approximately wrist deep under the center, although this will vary with the size of the quarterback's hands. The fingers are spread and straight to avoid injury and bad exchanges. The hands pressure upward and forward so that the center feels his target and to enable the quarterback to ride the center when he moves on the snap.

    g. *Ride*—The quarterback's hands must move with the center after the snap. We call this the "Ride." The pressure exerted with the hands enables the quarterback to ride the center. The pressure with the hands and the concentration of the quarterback should avoid fumbles caused by the quarterback pulling his hands out too soon.[19]

    "[Joe] comes to practice every day like it is his first practice," said Tom Bradley. "He's excited. He loves being out there." Exceptionally intense and focused, Joe has visualized every play at practice and has known exactly where everybody should be and what each should do. Unlike some coaches, Joe hasn't stood atop a coach's tower, directing the action like a Hollywood director, shouting instructions through a bullhorn. He has been more of a hands-on coach than some of the position coaches. (Sometimes he has taken off his glasses to instruct an offensive lineman in a blocking technique and then wandered around looking for his glasses.) He has moved from drill to drill observing the action. "Zip," he has yelled. "Let's have more zip."

    "Practice good to play good" has been one of Joe's slogans. On the practice field there has been no room for mental errors. The player gets "up" for a game by staying "up" in practice all week. Practice has not meant running the same play over and over again until it is perfect. Especially late in the season, the coaches have looked for perfection on every play.

    He has been a stickler for not practicing bad habits. When Dave Joyner put his hand on the blocking sled, Joe exploded because he thought Joyner was practicing holding. From two hundred yards away, Joe hollered, "Joyner, you stink! Get your hands off the blocking sled!" Joyner got the message. "You didn't want to do it again," he said.

From two fields away Joe noticed that Matt Knizer didn't carry out a fake on a running play. Joe ran over to him to instruct. "You've got to carry out the fake! You've got to sell it. You've got to sell the fake." Joe then got under center and demonstrated the maneuver.

If he has noticed anything, which he invariably has, he has often catalogued it in his mind for discussion later so as not to disrupt the exceptionally organized activity then in session. Or he has written it down. He has carried a pad of paper and a little pencil. "He'd look at you and then write in his notebook, look at you and write some more," recalled a player.[20]

When Joe has screamed and hollered, said one player, "it seems like he's actually *inside* your helmet." "He has the eyes of an eagle," Dave Joyner recalled. "He could see through trees, around corners, through people. If you were doing something wrong, you couldn't hide. I never figured out how he did it." On a few occasions Joe has kept the players at practice for more than three hours because he felt they weren't practicing well enough to win. Sometimes he has canceled practice after ten minutes for the same reason. "Get outta here!" he has yelled disgustedly.

As much as Joe has hollered, he has rarely cursed and has banned profanity by the coaches or the players. When a player has been hurt on the practice field and sworn, Joe has come up to him and said, "You don't need to swear. It's not going to make you feel any better." Normally, the worst Joe has said was "Nuts!" "Occasionally, you would hear something," said assistant Robert Phillips, "but the person swearing was reprimanded by Joe or by the assistants."

He has been a little paranoid about people watching practice, worried that spies might be stealing his schemes. "It was almost like a phobia at times," Mike Irwin said, "to get rid of people on the side who were watching." George Paterno and Bill Zimpfer, the TV announcer for Penn State's games, stopped by once to watch practice. As they were walking onto the field, they could hear Joe yell.

"Who's that?"

Someone told him it was his brother.

"Who's that other guy?"

He seemed satisfied when both were identified.[21]

In *Six Days to Saturday* (1974), sportswriter Jack Newcombe, a Brown classmate of Joe's, detailed six days of preparation for Penn State's tenth game of the 1973 season. With Joe's cooperation Newcombe observed as Joe and his staff studied films, analyzed Penn State's mistakes in the previous game, discussed the weaknesses and strengths of the upcoming opponent, planned strategy, and conducted practices. The book began the day after Penn State defeated North Carolina State, 35-29, giving the Nittany Lions a 9-0 record.

Sunday morning, as Joe met with his coaches to watch films of the North Carolina State game, he was unhappy, particularly with his defense. "Here, late in the season, the team's performance has flattened out," observed Newcombe. "Neither coaches nor players were ready for the option play skillfully handled. Familiar assignments are being done routinely. Players and coaches need a jolt."

At the staff meeting on Monday Joe kept throwing questions out about the upcoming opponent. How much wingback do they use? Do they hook the end? How good a blocker is their tight end? Is he good on sweeps, on straight hits? Joe also asked for statistics from the opponent's last game detailing yards gained against various defenses.

Joe expressed impatience with the poor performance of the defense against North Carolina State. "Are they playing tight?" he asked four defensive assistants. "Is it a question of confidence? We made mental mistakes. We weren't even lined up properly!"

Referring to a player on defense, Joe said, "He never really hit anyone. Is it because he's that tense? He's had a couple of bad games, Jerry [Sandusky]. Maybe you'd better give someone else a shot."

"Nobody's mean on the practice field," Joe continued. "They've had it too easy. All that stuff about being number one!"

On Tuesday Joe called a special meeting with his defensive team. In a loud, controlled voice, he scolded them. "In practice, we're not hitting. We're going through the motions. And it shows on Saturday. The second, the third man through isn't popping. That's why we're not getting turnovers. You're not hitting hard enough. I haven't seen any gang tackling. No one's punishing anybody."

During the week the staff made tiny adjustments to make Penn State's basic plays work against the opponent's defense. Tuesday and Wednesday were grueling practice days. Thursday's practice, run at full speed but without shoulder pads, was more of a dress rehearsal for Saturday and lasted only one hour and five minutes. "We're not going to work very much today," Joe told his coaches on Thursday. "We've had two good sessions. They're getting a little tired. We don't want to leave the game out there." On Friday the coaches worked, but the players rested.[22]

Newcombe observed that to the outsider Joe's schedule for practice late in the 1973 season "reads like some highly technical work sheet to be understood only by advanced engineers." For an eight-minute period, from 4:36 to 4:44 P.M., the printed schedule explained what each assistant coach and each group of players was expected to accomplish in individual drills:

J O H N Gs-Cs (offensive guards, centers) Bull sled Bag drill Downfield Blocking Blocks vs. Shields (names of four reserve linebackers who will serve on defense with blocking shields)

D I C K Ts-Ys (offensive tackles, tight ends) Bull sled Boards (names of reserves on defense)

B O O K E R Xs-Zs (flankers, split ends) SC drill Blocks vs. Shields (names of four reserves on defense)

B O B A-B-Qs (tailbacks, fullbacks, quarterbacks) Ropes Boards Blocks vs. Shields (names of three freshmen on defense)

F R A N A-B Quarterback option drill (vs. three freshmen with shields)

J I M O Ts (defensive tackles) Takeoff Seat rolls Downfield Blocking Follow leader 1/4 Eagle

J T Es-Rxs (defensive ends, right tackles) Quick Bags Leverage Key Fall on Ball

J E R R Y (with a graduate assistant) B-F-M-H (linebackers) Mirror start Score drill Peel drill Bounce P A T (with a graduate assistant)

L-S-R (defensive halfbacks and safety) 1 on 2 Qb-End drill Peel drill

The various defenses the coaches discussed had technical names: 8 Rotate, 6T Rotate, 6 Blow, State Super, 50 Web, State Bullet. Each demanded much from the players—precise lining up, quick mental and physical reactions, and complete follow-through. In its pass coverage against the opponent's "fly" (pass receiver lines up unusually wide), the instructions Penn State's defense had to keep in mind included these technical factors: If Penn State is in a 6 Tough, 6 Gap, 6 Blow defense, it shifts to one-half coverage on the side of the fly. If the defense called is 50 Web or 50 Fritz or 50 Rotate and the fly lines up to the Hero's side, the coverage originally called stays. If the fly lines up away from the Hero, the defense goes to "web" coverage. If the defense is a 3-deep prevent coverage against the pass, it stays the same.

The six days of preparation led to a 49-10 drubbing of Ohio University. (Penn State ended the season with a 12-0 record, ranked fifth in both polls, and John Cappelletti won the Heisman Trophy.) Win or lose on Saturday, Joe was ready to go at 7:30 A.M. on Sunday morning as he convened his meeting with his assistants and prepared for the next game.[23]

A pro scout for a National Football League team observed Penn State's practice in 1973. It was the eighth team he had watched in three weeks, and nowhere had he seen a team practice with such intensity and efficiency. "I see now why you win," he told a trainer. After leaving Penn State, players have often acquired perspective and increased respect for the exceptionally organized and rigorous practices that Joe has conducted. While watching a practice at the University of Pittsburgh, former Lions' center Bill Lenkaitis was shocked by the sloppy, lackadaisical approach. "[The players] just went through the motions," he said. "Joe wouldn't accept that. If you didn't do it right, you stayed out until you did it right." Dennis Onkotz agreed, observing that the practices he experienced in professional football were "unorganized" compared to Penn State's "super organization."[24]

To replenish the team with high-quality student-athletes, Joe became an excellent recruiter. In some ways Penn State's system of recruiting has resembled the approach of other major college football programs. "Before a coach sets foot inside a high school hero's home, he bombards it with mail," observed Ken Denlinger. "Letters. Postcards. Brochures. Pictures." Assistant coaches phone the prospects trying to become like brothers. "They come weekly in the early going," said Denlinger. "Then, near decision-making time, usually nightly and frequently hourly."

At times the process is an unseemly affair for coaches, but it is a dazzling once-in-a-lifetime experience for the recruits. "Suddenly, during the final two-month frenzy, an enormously gifted teenager will find famous coaches seemingly walking right off the television screen to sit down beside him on the living room sofa. They will simultaneously beg and challenge him with a pitch that goes something like: 'Son, you can help us win a national championship.' "

Summer football camps at Penn State have been a fertile source for recruiting high school talent. Besides getting to know many promising young players, Penn State's coaching staff ingratiated themselves over the years with hundreds of high school coaches who were brought in as counselors.

During the fall football season, Joe has sent out stacks of letters offering congratulations to high school coaches in Pennsylvania whose teams were playing well. "We are sure we are interested in some of the boys on your fine team and look forward to contacting them," he has written.[25]

Despite using recruiting techniques similar to other schools, Penn State has had its own unique style, and it has sought a unique type of athlete. In the mid-1970s, Jimmy Cefalo from Pittston, Pennsylvania, a high school running back, was one of the most sought-after players in the nation. In an article for the *New York Times*, Cefalo wrote that he was fourteen when the siege began. Altogether he received 2,856 pieces of mail, was contacted by six U.S. congressmen, a governor, baseball legend Hank Aaron, hundreds of businessmen, and 150 college coaches. He was most impressed with Joe Paterno. "He seemed honest and talked of other things besides football during our meetings," Cefalo wrote. "There were no athletic dorms at Penn State. I stayed on a cot in my host's dorm. Players on the team called Paterno by his first name, and the relationship between players and coach seemed close and genuine."

That Penn State's football tradition has been so successful has made Joe's recruiting easier. The program has turned out dozens of outstanding linebackers, including many who became accomplished professional players. "From the time I was ten years old, I wanted to be a linebacker," Chet Parlavecchio said. "And where else would a kid who wanted to be a linebacker go? You go to Penn State . . . that's Linebacker U."[26]

Joe's system of recruiting has been the opposite of exotic, but its very simplicity has attracted and his methods have worked year after year. Generally Penn State has recruited within a three-hundred-mile radius of the university—Pennsylvania, New Jersey, Ohio, New York, and Virginia. (Usually, Joe hasn't tried to recruit players from California or other distant locations because he didn't think it was natural for someone to go to college thousands of miles away from home. It was hard to keep the boy's morale up. Joe has wanted parents to attend the games because the athlete would feel more support and play better.) Prospects have liked the campus, the chance to play for the national championship, and the chance to go to a postseason bowl game. In Joe's thirty-two seasons as head coach leading up to 1998, Penn State had gone to a bowl game all but four times.

The success of Penn State's players in the classroom and on the field began with the coach's approach to recruiting. In addition to outstanding football ability, Joe has looked for poise, character, pride, work ethic, and academic potential. "If he doesn't like [the recruit] as a person," said Tom Bradley, "we're not going to recruit him. I don't care how good a player he is."

"They recruit good-character kids with academic backgrounds," said Boston College coach Jack Bicknell, who often competed with Penn State for players. "The kid may not have 1,300 on his college boards or be in the top 5 percent of his class, but [to attend Penn State] he has to have a desire to work academically." If a recruit has had an interest in a specific academic subject, Joe has involved a faculty member with expertise in the area. Coaches have talked to high school guidance counselors and gathered academic information. To learn about the recruit's reliability, they have studied his high school attendance record.[27]

"Joe's philosophy, which became the philosophy of all of us, was to recruit character—not just the athlete," said Robert Phillips. While analyzing a potential recruit at a meeting, the staff has often focused on character. "We're always talking about character," said Fran Ganter. "We have turned down so many good football players just because we're not quite sure about his character or how he would fit in."

At a meeting with his assistants, Joe quizzed his staff about their approach to recruiting. "Are we checking the intangible characteristics like Earl Bruce and those fellows used to do?" Then Joe described some of those intangibles. "If the kid belongs to the Boys Club, do you go to the Boys Club and ask the director how he behaves? Do you notice how he treats his parents when he is in their presence? Does he say thank-you? Is he polite?"

Parents who have started off their relationship with Penn State by asking special favors for their son usually haven't heard from Penn State again. "They're giving us a clear message that their kid is likely to be full of 'I' and 'me,' not 'we' and 'us.' Football games are won by what players put into them, not by what they get out of them."

Joe has believed the really ambitious player was flattered when Penn State recruited him. "He knows we're interested in his life and what we can help him make of it, not just what we can get out of him as a football animal."[28]

Inviting both the athlete and his parents to visit the campus has proved an effective recruiting strategy. (Most universities don't invite the parents.) The parents and the athlete have usually arrived on Saturday morning. The parents have been put up at the Nittany Lion Inn on the campus; the athlete has stayed in the dorm room of a veteran player to get a firsthand look at student life. Everything has been done carefully within the NCAA rules; the recruits have not been offered motels, cars, dates, or money.

Coaches at some schools haven't thought living in a dorm would flatter the prospect enough. "They prefer to dazzle the kid with his own importance in a swanky hotel room," Joe said. "That works very well for them—and for us. The two ways help separate our kind of kid from theirs."

They have toured the campus, met with an academic counselor, and dined with the coaches. After attending a basketball game in the evening, the parents have gone to Joe's home. During the recruiting weekends, Sue Paterno has almost been in the restaurant business. She has personally prepared all the food for the get-together with the parents at the Paternos' home on Saturday evening.

While at the Paternos', some of the parents have seemed nervous and sheepish. Writer Bernard Asbell, who observed the Saturday evening scene, speculated that some parents were wondering who was lobbying whom. Was Joe trying to convince them that their son should play for Penn State? Or were they trying to convince Joe that their son should be given a scholarship? Joe and Sue have focused on making everyone comfortable and relaxed. Football "business" has not been discussed. Joe has sat on the floor entertaining mothers at one end of the room; then he has moved and sat down with the fathers. "It was very effective," said assistant coach Ron Dickerson.

Charlie Pittman's parents had been apprehensive when they arrived at Penn State. Shy, products of the black ghetto, inexperienced with sophisticated recruiting, not used to going out to eat and using fancy silverware, they were uncomfortable. Almost immediately, Joe helped them relax. "Joe . . . sensed that my family was not comfortable," Pittman recalled. "He spent a lot of time with them." Joe reassured them that his major concern was that their son receive his college diploma. "They left very comfortable," Pittman said, "feeling that they turned their son over to someone who was going to take special care of their child."

Throughout the evening the recruits and parents have learned about Penn State, and, equally important, Joe and his assistants have gotten to know something about them. "If the kid will not fit in, it usually shows before the evening is over," Joe said. "If we don't like the parents, we get leery about the kid because he is not likely to turn out much different." One father kept trailing Joe around the vegetable trays all evening telling Joe how super his son was. "The kid went to Maryland, pleasing both us and them, I guess," said Joe.

Penn State has meticulously kept track of which weekend visits resulted in the most signees. "Over a nine-year period," observed Denlinger, "the second weekend in December (54 percent) edged the first weekend in February (53 percent). The overall percentage was 45, high considering prospects are permitted just five college-sponsored visits."[29]

"When Joe stops in, that's usually it," said a rival coach in 1987. "It's tough to compete against him in the recruiting game." Another coach recalled sitting in a high school player's living room in 1985. While the coach was talking, he realized the mother was rushing around, cleaning up the house. "I realized Joe was coming in behind me. People clean up houses for Joe Paterno. Not for many other coaches. He is a very, very effective recruiter."

After the staff has made a strenuous effort to recruit a player, with the prospect's decision wavering between Penn State and another school, Joe has decided to visit the young man. "I better get out there," he would say. "You just breathe a sigh of relief," said Fran Ganter when Joe has decided to visit a key recruit. "He says all the right things and he's sincere."

On a visit to a recruit's home, Joe has drunk coffee with the parents, joked, and teased. Then he has explained how it would be if their son went to Penn State. If he was good enough, he would play. If not, he would still get his degree.

"He wasn't like any other recruiter," linebacker Bruce Clark said in 1976. "He sounded more like a friend. Nothing hard or pressing. He said most guys he gets graduate. I had friends check that out, and it's true. Paterno never cut up other schools like some coaches who came."[30]

"Joe is a great closer," said Allen Wallace of *SuperPrep Magazine,* a California-based recruiting publication. "He's just super when he goes into a recruit's home. He has a good sense of humor and he just makes people feel at ease."

"He's just a supersalesman," agreed quarterback Chuck Fusina in 1978. "I'm in marketing, and . . . I'd like to someday be able to sell a product as well as he sells this university."

Joe has had phenomenal ability to remember the names of recruits and their parents, plus details of the family's circumstance (whether, for example, the father was deceased). He has made it a point to prepare himself before each visitation. At times it has seemed he was recruiting parents more than the player. He has known that most athletes listen to the advice of their parents; parents have made it difficult for the son to reject the parents' choice.

"My parents were more impressed with him than any other coach," said former star quarterback Todd Blackledge. Joe sat on Blackledge's La-Z-Boy chair. "He asked if he could take his shoes off," Blackledge recalled. "He made himself at home. That really made an impression on my family."

"Joe was more at ease than any coach that came by," said the father of Bobby Samuels, who Joe was recruiting in the late 1980s. "A . . . lot of coaches when they go in black families' homes feel sort of intimidated, I think. And they sort of shy back a little bit. Joe wasn't that way. He was really down to earth."

Joe has ingratiated himself with family members and has struck the family as sincere. (Joe would *never* say, "I look at your mother, and I know why you are an outstanding young man.") On the phone Joe told a prospect: "I'll be up Monday night. Dinner? I don't want to impose. Sure, tell your mother to make some of that good Italian food and I'll bring an opera record. Just show me the wooden spoon, I'll help her with the sauce."

Joe and his assistants have been honest with the parents but have tailored their presentation to the parents' concerns. "As you get to know

Paterno has long been considered one of the best salesmen in college football when it comes to recruiting players. His particular strength is ingratiating himself with the recruit's family members. (Allsport USA Photo by Rick Stewart)

each family, you . . . know what they want to hear so you dwell on those things," said Robert Phillips. "Joe always appealed to the academic side as much as to the football [side] because for most parents, down deep, that is what they wanted to know."[31]

In a 1987 feature story about Joe's recruiting, writer Jay Searcy described Joe's confidence and flair. The names and the location changed but the story line seldom varied. "Paterno moves quietly into enemy recruiting territory, subtly casts a spell on his subject, warms Mama's heart, charms Daddy, excites the neighborhood, then waits patiently for the magic result. Voila! Another of America's prize athletic talents rides off to Happy Valley, U.S.A., home of Joe Paterno's no-frills, no-nonsense finishing school for football players."

While recruiting Leroy Thompson at his home in Knoxville, Tennessee, Joe teased with Thompson's mother about rival coach Johnny Majors of the University of Tennessee. He told Mrs. Thompson he had something very serious to tell her, but it was off the record. (At first she fell for the yarn.) Claiming he had received a phone call from the Tennessee coach, Joe said, "Coach Majors called me and said, 'Joe, I've got this kid down here named Leroy Thompson who is a great athlete, and I need somebody to come down here and take him off my hands. Would you mind coming down to Knoxville and sign him.'" The Thompson family howled. "That broke the ice, you know," said Mrs. Thompson. There was more teasing, leading Mrs. Thompson to declare later, "You know, he was just so *eeeeasy.*"

Then Joe talked at length to the family and to Leroy about academics at Penn State. "Other coaches talked about academics, too, you know," Mrs. Thompson said. "Like they said Leroy would have a four-year scholarship; and if he got hurt he would still go to school. But nobody put academics first like Paterno."

Throughout the visit Leroy hardly said a word but listened intently. "If you come to Penn State," Joe told Leroy, "I'm going to work you. This person you see sitting here isn't going to be the same person you'll see out there on that practice field."

"You know, Leroy," Joe said, "it would be wrong for me to make a lot of promises to you and say you're going to start, or do this or that. I've got to be loyal to the other players I have. I could tell you that, and then when I go back to them, what do I say?"

He told Leroy that he would get an education, that he would be tested for drugs ("not because I think you have a problem, but because I don't want you to get one"), and that he would get an opportunity to play like everyone else.

Joe's visits to the Thompsons' home became media events. When Joe and Leroy rode somewhere to talk privately, a local radio station interrupted a show to report: "Leroy Thompson and Penn State coach Joe Paterno have just left the Thompson apartment in Leroy's 1979 Mustang. They turned north on Dandridge Avenue and . . ."

Joe left the Thompsons at midnight, but the family was too excited to sleep, talking about Joe's visit far into the night. "So that's the Legend," Mrs. Thompson said. "I don't know Joe Paterno the coach. The person I saw was Joe Paterno the man, and I like him." Thompson eventually signed with Penn State.[32]

Joe has pushed for streamlined recruiting rules and more severe penalties for violators. He has felt that many NCAA rules were needlessly handcuffing, stupid, and begging coaches to cheat. Nonetheless, he observed in his autobiography, "I think most new rules are better—at least no worse—than the freewheeling ways of recruiting in the old days."

Like many coaches, Joe has found it difficult to follow every complex NCAA rule. What was "excessive hospitality"? Were two steaks excessive? While recruiting Leroy Thompson, Joe wanted to take the athlete for a private ride in his rental car, unaware that such a ride was against recruiting rules. When he asked his assistant for the keys, the assistant stopped him.

At times Sever Toretti suspected that, unbeknownst to Penn State's coaches, a zealous alumnus may have violated recruiting rules. "On a couple occasions I was a little concerned about how this kid made his choice with us. But I was never able to find [what] was done. I suspected maybe some alumnus was doing something for this kid." Jerry Sandusky speculated that Penn State's coaches had accidentally violated rules that they didn't know existed. "I'm sure we have [inadvertently] violated rules at different times."[33]

Ironically, an NCAA rule that Joe helped enact was one he wound up breaking. At the NCAA convention in 1982, Joe was a leading advocate of a provision that prohibited head football coaches from being present for the signing of a recruit. "I think getting the head coach out of the signing is good," Joe had said. "It used to be the head coach hopped [into] a plane, signed one kid at eight o'clock, hopped [back into] the plane, signed another at nine, and another at ten. Now the head coach isn't allowed to be involved in the signing. Only the assistants can sign players."

Nonetheless, in February 1985, Joe was present at the Montclair, New Jersey, home of Quintus McDonald, a premier linebacking prospect, to witness McDonald sign his letter of intent to attend Penn State. All during the recruiting process Quintus and his mother had indicated that if Quintus signed with Penn State, they wanted Joe to be there when he signed. Therefore, McDonald and his mother requested that assistant coach Fran Ganter and Joe attend the signing in Montclair. But when a New Jersey newspaper reported Joe's presence at McDonald's signing, it set in motion Joe's first brush with the NCAA.

Joe was dumbfounded and apologetic. He thought the rule applied only to national letter-of-intent day or twenty-four hours thereafter. "Because this was nine days after the signing date, I simply did not think of a violation. I would not knowingly or intentionally want to break the rules. But I'm aware, of course, that ignorance is no excuse."

Joe's presence at McDonald's signing was out of character and embarrassing, but no criticism or sanctions resulted. An NCAA official correctly described the incident as "isolated, minor, [and] inadvertent," and the matter was dropped.

There have been, however, elements of insincerity and deviousness in Penn State's recruiting. While recruiting a player, Joe has taken the time to write the prospect, sit in his living room, and joke with his family. "That suggested an intimacy that almost never happened once they got to campus," Denlinger noted. "There wasn't much time in Paterno's life for chitchat, let alone the sort of relatively close relationship nearly every player had enjoyed with his high school coach."

The new recruits have often been shocked when they arrived at training camp and faced a military-like regimen and saw the dark, hard side of Paterno. "The Paterno they had been drawn to on television, the Paterno who had charmed them and their parents, the Paterno who had enthralled much of the country with his wit and enlightened thinking about big-time sport was not the Paterno they were now seeing up close and very personally," Denlinger observed. "This Paterno was a screamer. The calm voice that had inflated their egos several months before was very quickly cutting to the core of their self-esteem. His voice was high-pitched and distinctive; his manner was anvil-hard and blunt."

Assistant coach Tom Bradley's zest in recruiting was such that an oil spill near Pittsburgh was sufficient reason to pitch Penn State at the expense of its arch rival Pitt. "He called one night," a recruiting prospect recalled, "and mentioned that Pittsburgh didn't have water. So he turned on some water at his place and put the phone by it. Then he took a big gulp of water and said: 'See, we always have water at Penn State.'" During a parade, Bradley hopped from place to place, waving wildly each time the truck carrying two recruiting prospects passed, making sure they noticed him and how much he cared about them.[34]

Overall, though, Joe has earned accolades for his honest recruiting. Ron Bracken learned from talking to Penn State's players that the overwhelming majority said they had come to Penn State because of the low-keyed, honest manner in which they were recruited. Penn State's recruiters usually didn't hound them, didn't criticize other schools, and didn't make grand promises. "[A] thing I respect about Joe Paterno is that he plays and recruits within the rules," said Ohio State's coach Woody Hayes. "Not everybody does." One hundred schools recruited halfback Joel Coles. Some offered illegal inducements—money, a car, clothes, a scholarship for his sister and one for his girlfriend. And what did Joe Paterno offer? "A scholarship," said Coles. "Period."[35]

Despite the hard work, Joe has found his job stimulating and fulfilling. He has enjoyed the planning, the organizing, the camaraderie, and the challenge of motivating young people and his staff; it has been exciting to work toward a common goal and to watch young men develop their skills and mature. The give-and-take during the game, the quick decisions that need to be made—all of that has been fun for him.

Nothing has thrilled him more than being in a locker room before a big game. "To see these men who are so strong, so aggressive, so ambitious, so determined to be recognized—to see them lose themselves in something bigger than they are at that moment," Joe said, "it's really almost an act of love."

Before the team has run onto the field to start the game, Joe has had them kneel down and pray the Lord's Prayer. "To gather a team around you just before a big game, to look at grown men huddling close to each other with tears in their eyes, each one taking the hand of another on each side until everybody and every soul in that room is connected, each pledging to give and to expect the best, each becoming part of all the others—to look into those strong faces that say 'If we can only do it today'—to be there is to see and touch and be touched by people who have joined a cause that they have made bigger than themselves. If they can do it here, they will be able to do it anywhere."

"There are few things that people will do in their lives that sixty thousand people will cheer them for," Joe observed. When an assistant coach expressed the wish for "six more days" to study film of an upcoming opponent, Joe dissented. "If you had six more days, you'd want six more. I wish we were playing right now." Syracuse coach Dick McPherson once told him: "I love coaching. The only time I don't love it is on Saturdays." Joe was incredulous. Saturday's game was the best part of coaching for him. "Maybe I'm different," he said. "Maybe I'm crazy. But I *live* for fall Saturdays."[36]

Paterno can yell with the best of them, as he does here in barking out instructions during the 1997 Fiesta Bowl, which Penn State won, 38-15, over Tennessee. (AP/Wide World Photo)

Naturally, Penn State's fans have intensely identified with the team's fortunes. Joe has felt pressure not to let down all the people across the state who have so vicariously identified with the Penn State program. "It sounds crazy, but a football game can ennoble these guys, enrich their lives." People have lost themselves in the "aliveness" of the game. "If we want to define art as something that adds a special quality to our lives, if I can look forward to the Pittsburgh Symphony playing Beethoven for two hours and come home feeling better for it—if that constitutes a working definition, then football is an art form."[37]

~6~

PROFILE: PLAYER RELATIONS AND THE GRAND EXPERIMENT

"UNIFORMS AREN'T IMPORTANT," SAID DAN RADAKOVICH. They haven't seemed to be at Penn State. Sportswriters have often joked about the Lions' spartan uniforms: white jerseys, with no names on the back, no stars on the helmets, no frills, plus plain hightop black shoes. Dressed like "nerds," Penn State has been "the Team in the Plain Wrapper."

The uniforms, though, represent tradition. Sterile and merely functional, they were supposed to encourage selflessness and discourage individual flamboyance. Before the Orange Bowl contest on January 1, 1986, the team eschewed the traditional orange ornament on their uniform. "Joe held up these little miniature oranges next to a jersey so we'd have an idea what they'd look like," recalled safety Ray Isom. "Then, one by one, you'd hear guys saying, 'Nah. Forget it—too gaudy. Wouldn't look right on us.'" To his surprise Isom agreed. "Like most of us, I hated our uniforms at first," he admitted, smiling. "Hey, you figure you're playing for Penn State, playing to be number one, you should dress the part, right? Something shiny, something sharp. But it doesn't take long before you realize it's what's inside that counts. The rest is nothing but window dressing. It doesn't mean a thing." When asked about the painfully plain uniforms, Joe laughed. "I've always been for simple things," he said. "I guess [the uniforms say] something to kids about team-oriented play and an austere approach to life."[1]

Joe has tried to indoctrinate his players in "the Penn State way." He has encouraged pride, making his players feel they were part of a

Penn State's uniform style always has been noticeably traditional, even drab, although the coach has occasionally stretched the limits of fashion taste. (Photo courtesy of Penn State Sports Information Department)

special team, a special university, one that was worth making sacrifices for. "If you're the kind of guy that we call the 'we and us' people that can work with the group, by being unselfish, benefits will accrue to you," he has preached.

Prominently displayed for the players near the team meeting room has been the message:

> The bruises
> The pain
> The mud
> The pulled muscles
> The chalk talks
> The long hours
> Are all worth it
> Because when you are part of a team,
> you are better than you ever could be alone.

Joe has lectured incoming freshmen players about rules and expectations. Each has represented not only himself individually but also the team and everyone who had played before them at the university. "Penn State has a tradition. You are now a part of this tradition and with that comes a lot of responsibility and rewards. Part of your responsibility is to uphold the image of Penn State football."

To enhance the image of the Penn State players Joe has required them to wear ties and blazers on trips. "Personal cleanliness and good grooming are signs that a person has respect for himself," he said. "[If] you have no self-respect, you can't expect other people to respect you either." A neat appearance helped overcome the "dumb animal" image many people had of football players. On a trip to the Cotton Bowl, Joe was probably delighted that his well-dressed Nittany Lions were praised for their "look of pride and class."

Assistant coaches have worn a dress shirt and tie to the office every day, a dress code Fran Ganter doubted ten coaching staffs in the country have adopted. "When I was younger," reflected Ganter, "I thought it was crazy. . . . Now I take great pride in it. It is something we stand for."[2]

In 1971 Joe publicly seemed open-minded and liberal in his attitude toward the personal lifestyles of players. "What difference does it make how long a kid's hair is? That doesn't have one single thing to do with discipline. When it comes to hair, dress, or living habits, I think college football players are old enough and men enough to handle these things themselves." Subsequently, he changed his mind and took a more rigid, doctrinaire position on the grooming habits and manners of his players.

Certain things were "right," Joe came to believe after 1971. The players should not have shaggy hair or wear earrings. They should wear socks when they wore long pants, especially when they attended church. After seeing a player at church dressed sloppily, Joe called the young man into his office for a chat. "Why don't you put on a nice shirt and put a pair of socks on?" he advised.

"He didn't like to see hair sticking out of the back of the helmet," observed Todd Blackledge. When Blackledge's hair grew too long, Joe teased him, calling him Shirley. At a banquet in 1976 he became visibly upset to see an ex-player with muttonchops. He didn't allow one bearded graduate to appear in the team's 1975 highlight film. "I don't want a player to be ahead of his style," he said in 1976. "That's just a gut feeling I have. Yet I want them to be free spirits off the field, intellectual, inquiring. You have to be flexibly inflexible."

Joe's office overlooks the entrance to the locker room. Once, as Matt Knizner and a group of players were about to enter, one player stepped off the sidewalk onto the grass. The window opened and Joe yelled, "Get off the grass! Stay on the sidewalk!"

It has not just been players who are to follow Joe's rules; everyone associated with the Penn State football team has had to follow them as well. Penn State's team physician Dr. James Whiteside and other medical personnel were walking back from a meal with Joe when they walked on the grass instead of the longer way around on the sidewalk. "Joe pointed out to us," said Whiteside, "that the walk was made for walking and the grass was made to be appreciated. He treated us all the same way."

Joe has expected visitors who traveled with the team to abide by the rules as well. Players have not been allowed to order an alcoholic drink aboard the plane, so neither can the visitors. Because ties have been mandatory for the players on trips, and Milton Bergstein, a business professor at the university and major football booster, didn't have one on, Joe approached him. "You know the rules for our travel," he told

Bergstein. "The players on our team know you. Some of them look up to you as a role model, as a professor. And you're not wearing a tie. . . . If you want to travel with us you'll have to wear a tie from now on."

To some players the rules have seemed petty and Joe's anger irrational. For them the rules have intruded on privacy and stifled individuality. "As far as your drinking habits, your social habits, how you wear your hair, whether you shave or not is your business," one player argued. "That's your lifestyle, your choice. Imagine if your calculus teacher said: 'Hey, you can't wear an earring in here. And go cut your hair.'"

Penn State was one of the first major football programs to test for drugs. In the fall of 1986 the players were tested four times, and no one tested positive. "On a football field," Joe observed, "you have a bunch of people who come together and say they are a team. They are going to work together to have the best team they can. You have to depend on each other. If you have a couple of guys who are half-shot with drugs, that is a problem."

Drug testing has also helped the young players overcome peer pressure. They could say, "I can't do that. I might be tested tomorrow. It might ruin my career." Joe explained: "You create artificial props for them, until they get to the position where they can handle it themselves."[3]

Using a variety of approaches, Joe has pushed his players to improve. "Basically, he's a driver," said his friend Steve Garban. "He drives you to work hard. He drives you to discipline yourself. He drives you [toward] perfection."

He has known how to upset a player's sense of well-being in order to get the player to exert himself more. If a player has done poorly in his academic work, skipped classes, violated rules, or caused a disturbance on campus, he has found himself in Joe's doghouse. Joe has sat him on the bench, yelled at him more, or regulated his academic life. Some excellent football players have aroused Joe's ire because they haven't dedicated themselves. He has assigned each assistant coach the responsibility for advising several players, to keep an eye on them, to make sure they have studied and attended classes.

Joe hasn't wanted any one player to become a "star." "He was dealing with 120 guys who had big egos," halfback Curt Warner observed. "Guys that were high school stars. Guys that were pampered and babied. He didn't allow any of that at Penn State."

"Don't baby the star," Joe advised coaches in *Coaching Winning Football*. "I'm tougher on my best players on the practice field than I am on anybody else—so that the squad knows that these stars aren't special. If a kid has too much of an inflated ego to be able to play in a team fashion, I'll take him out for a while, until he realizes you can play the game without him."

Joe has sent home players from bowl trips on several occasions because they violated team rules, and he has benched star players. In 1971 Franco Harris, a future professional star, was an outstanding fullback whose rebelliousness irritated Joe and finally led to major disciplinary action. While preparing for the Cotton Bowl, Harris arrived late for practice. "Don't be late tomorrow or I'm going to demote you," Joe told him. The following day Harris again arrived late and Joe demoted him, making him wear a freshman jersey at practice. At the Cotton Bowl Joe did not allow Harris to start the game and played him only sporadically. "At Penn State, I really didn't work hard enough sometimes," Harris later conceded.

Nor has Joe wanted "hot dogs" on his team, players who danced or boogied in the end zone after a touchdown. "Those stupid dances ridicule your opponent," he declared. He has taught players to cross the goal line and simply hand the ball to the official.

Joe has tried to teach "hotheads" to keep their composure. "They're usually the best competitors and the other teammates will respond to them. So you want to keep them around. But you want them to be poised, rational competitors."

When a player has shown up late, dropped a pass, busted a play, or put out less than 100 percent, Joe has been caustic and shrill, like a terrier snapping at the heels of breeds far bigger than he. More than one player has expressed an urge to bury an arm down Joe's throat, but no one has ever dared do so. "There were times when you wanted to walk up and punch him in the nose," recalled tight end Mike McCloskey. "Then you would realize that he was yelling and screaming for your own good. He was trying to make you a better football player and a better person."[4]

Sometimes, after Joe has yelled at a player, he has visited with the young man in the locker room or in his office. "Do you understand why I'm up and down your back? Do you realize that I think you can be awfully good, but you're not paying attention to details? You're sloppy. You don't seem involved. You're not approaching the practice field with the right attitude. I'm going to chew you up and down until I get you where you're good."

Sometimes Joe has verbally lambasted an innocent player. Radakovich remembered one incident in about 1967. "[Joe] was wrong in doing it," said Radakovich, who expressed his displeasure to Joe. Then Joe apologized to the player. "I thought that showed a lot of class," Radakovich reflected. Joe made mistakes, Radakovich believed, but one of his finest attributes was his willingness to "correct them."

Joe has been consistent, a trait appreciated by many players. "Joe seemed always to be the same," Blackledge said. "You always knew what to expect from him." He has also been stern but fair. "You'll get a second chance," said Dennis Onkotz, "but don't expect a third."

"I don't think Joe asks too much of his players," Onkotz contended. "To play this game, you have to be mentally tough, and the only way to become mentally tough is to be pushed. A lot of people don't know what it's like to be really pushed. When it happens, they think they're being abused. There's a difference between being pushed and being abused. There's a line and, personally, I don't think Joe oversteps it."[5]

Joe has not lavished praise on his players for the same reason he hasn't painted stars on their helmets. He has wanted them to expect good plays and winning as a natural expression of the Penn State tradition. "You're supposed to make good plays," he has said; "that's why you're here in the Penn State program. If you work hard and you're a good athlete, you're gonna make good plays. Simple as that."

In some ways he has been liberal in his personal relationship with players, encouraging them, for example, to call him by his first name. "How's it going, Coach Paterno?" said linebacker Greg Buttle. "Just fine, Player Buttle." Buttle laughed and explained. "He wants us to call him Joe. I can't do it. I call him Coach Paterno. So he calls me Player Buttle. It was tough for me at first. In my freshman year I never talked to him. . . . Then when you start playing—well, now I talk to him like he was my dad."

As co-captain, Steve Smear met with Joe to discuss team rules and problems on the squad. "He might not always agree with you," said Smear, "but he would listen to you and he would give you a reason." Sometimes Joe replied to a request with a qualified assent. "I'll go along with this, but I'm going to be watching it very closely."

In games Joe has wanted his players to gamble, to take a well-considered chance. "Don't stand around and wait for something to happen," he has constantly advised. "Don't be afraid to take chances. Gamble. Be reckless. Make things happen!" Recover a fumble, force an interception, block a kick, create confusion in the opposition. "We want to make our opponent afraid to make a mistake. That's when they make 'em and we'll take advantage of it."

He has encouraged his players to defy him. "[If] you're a defensive halfback and you're playing in a zone defense and I tell you to play deep, but you just know that the next pass is going to be a short flat one—and there will be times when you just *know* it—and you don't go against everything I've told you, if you don't gamble for the interception, then you're no damn good."[6]

Joe has motivated his players primarily by his intense competitive drive to win and by the exceptional quality of his training and coaching. "We didn't have a lot of psychological stuff," said Radakovich. Developing an excellent attitude, however, is crucial for a football player. Every player must sustain his discipline, focus clearly on the goal, psyche himself up, systematically build confidence, and take personal responsibility for his play.

Joe has occasionally delivered a motivational speech, but the Knute Rockne approach has not been a constant source of motivation. He has thought that players were too sophisticated and knowledgeable to fall for the Win-One-for-the-Gipper routine. "You can't, all of a sudden, change things around with a thirty-minute talk." Joe's message before a game has usually been simple. "We have a chance this weekend to see how good we are against a darn good Notre Dame football team. Let's go out and have some fun. This is what we get ready for. We want them to play their best so that if we're successful, we can walk off and say, 'Gosh darn it. They played their best and we played well enough to beat them.'"

During halftime he seldom has screamed and hollered. "I don't remember that in four years," said Buttle. If an assistant coach flew into a rage, Joe would say, "Come on. Calm down."

"When we get in at halftime, I don't want to start talking right away," Joe said. "I'll get my assistant coaches around me and ask their opinions as to what's going on. Then I'll talk to my key players. I consult with a lot of people. Then I take a couple of minutes and think about what we should do. Then I tell my squad, specifically, if and how we should adjust our plans."

At halftime he has let the enthusiasm rebuild. When it was time to return to an intense battle with Ohio State in 1978, Joe said, "It's all yours now. All you have to do is finish the job. We're not going to sit on any three-point lead. We're going to play this baby like we were behind, like we are *desperate*. Before the game I told you I thought we were better. Now we know it. Right?" "*Right!*" After defeating Ohio State, Joe climbed to a bench, spread his arms, and, smiling broadly, told his players they had done a great job but not to become overconfident. "We're going to get better. So keep your feet on the ground."[7]

Preparing for difficult games against Alabama, Nebraska, Notre Dame, or an arch rival like Pittsburgh, Joe has toned down his abrasive remarks because he has known the players would be ready. "He was most obnoxious when we were playing teams like Rutgers or Temple," Blackledge said, referring to teams Penn State was heavily favored to defeat. "The hardest we practiced was for the team he knew we could beat, 70-0, and we knew we could beat, 70-0," agreed Buttle. "The team he knew we would have a rough time with he would say, 'Okay, guys, let's relax.'" He has wanted the team intense but relaxed. Buttle added, "He was a little more intense on little things for the big games and less intense in his demeanor. He was more intense in his demeanor for the easy game and less concerned about little things."[8]

Losing games, practice drudgery, injuries, and little playing time all have hurt morale. He has strived to keep the team together and to maintain morale. Following a tough defeat, he has urged them to focus on the next Saturday afternoon's game. In 1974, after losing to Navy, 7-6, players expected Joe to explode. But he immediately began looking ahead. He never said anything critical to any player on the team. "We lost the game," Joe said. "Let's go to the next game."[9]

An excellent halfback, who had many scholarship offers, came to Penn State as a freshman, but on the practice field he was disappointing, showing less and less of the talent that had made him such an outstanding prospect. Complaining of minor ailments, he quit the team and returned home. Joe contacted the young man and also conversed with the player's high school coach, principal, and father. Joe concluded that the freshman's real problem was lack of confidence. When another player moved ahead of him in the depth chart, he became discouraged and quit, using injuries as an excuse for returning home.

Joe told the freshman his situation was not unique. "It happens to many good players who come here. They see others who are just as good on the field. They get discouraged because they're not playing all the time, as they did in high school. If everyone who became discouraged, who got down on himself, dropped off the squad, we wouldn't have many players left. At one point or another it happens to almost every member of the team." Subsequently, Joe arranged for the freshman to reenter the university and rejoin the team.

The young player's crisis was a familiar morale problem for Joe. The coaches constantly sought to bolster the morale of all the players. "You don't have to concern yourself much with how a first-stringer feels," Joe said. "The real test is whether the last substitute has good morale. If he has, it means everybody has."[10]

Joe has encouraged his players to be totally self-confident—to think of themselves as "demigods, able to do wondrous things." When the coaching staff or players have been discouraged or doubtful, Joe has interjected to enhance self-esteem and a positive attitude. "The minute I have the feeling they have doubts concerning . . . [their] ability to do it . . . then I immediately want to jump in there and . . . talk about how good the kids are and what a great job they've done."

He has tried to keep his team calm and poised. Before playing Ohio State in 1978, he cautioned his staff to make the final practice day a "positive" experience. "We'll make mistakes, but we don't want to get them nervous about themselves now." Players shouldn't become too emotional about an upcoming game. To him poise was common sense. "Football is a game of concentration," he said. "I just don't see how you can concentrate on what you're supposed to do with all that jumping around and yelling."[11]

"He wants to create people who will come out of this institution and will contribute greatly to society and will have learned a great deal about life," quarterback John Shaffer said in 1986. "You learn to grow up and face the everyday things in life," Curt Warner recalled of his Penn State experience under Joe. "I appreciate all the things I learned up there. He was tough. He was a disciplinarian. But we needed that. We were a bunch of wild kids going to school, and it kind of molds and shapes you, builds a little character in you. At first you might not like it, but down the line you really appreciate it."

In 1981, while Penn State was losing, 14-0, to arch rival Pittsburgh, Joe guided and reassured his team. "Don't panic," he told them. "Stick to your game plan." Subsequently, Penn State's offense caught fire and the Lions won the game, 48-14. Afterward in the locker room Joe quieted his celebrating players. "Look," he said. "I don't want you to remember how you feel right now. You're feeling pretty good. But I want you to remember how you felt when you were down, 14-0, in a national television game and you were about to get your face put in the mud and have somebody rub your noses in it. Remember how you kept your poise and held hands and pulled it out. Those are the things to remember, because you're going to be down, 14-0, a lot of times in your life."

A perceptive judge of the character of his players, Joe has seen the intangibles in those who were not exceptionally fast or strong. "Joe always seemed to pick out the guy who had character [or an] intangible that made him a little quicker reacting to things which made up for the lack of speed," said Robert Phillips. "He has played some kids . . . that the rest of the staff [didn't think were as capable]. But the boy he picked [almost] invariably became an outstanding player."[12]

Because Joe has been tough and demanding, he has offended some players. "Complaining actually is the best part of this place," a player observed. "Just bitching about Joe. That's what we enjoy most. And we do it constantly." The same player described life with Paterno as "like playing for your dad in a bad mood." For years disgruntled players called Joe "the Rat" behind his back, partly because of his high-pitched squeaky practice-field voice and his vaguely rodentlike facial features.

To some players Joe has seemed like a brusque businessman, cold and aloof, who coached through intimidation. They have resented his verbal assaults. In the late 1960s a few players reacted angrily to Joe's seemingly arrogant ranting during halftime of a game against Syracuse. "If we lose this game," some remembered him as saying, "whatever you do, don't embarrass *me*!"

"The image of Joe as a kindly fatherly figure that is beloved by his players is not really accurate," contended sportswriter Ray Didinger of the *Philadelphia Daily News*, who wrote a critical series of articles on Joe in 1982. "There is no relationship between the players and Joe Paterno," charged former player Rocky Washington in 1985. "He is not a players' coach. You deal with the other coaches if you have problems. It is diffi- cult for most players to go to see him because they fear him."[13]

"Joe used the fear-of-God approach," argued Tracy Hall, a wide receiver from New Jersey, who played two years at Penn State before trans- ferring to Temple. "He let you know your fate was in his hands every day you went out there. His practices are always closed. It's just you and him behind those gates. That's a weird feeling. [The players] used to call him 'Big Daddy' because he held the power. I wish I could have worn a tape recorder on that field just one day. You wouldn't have believed the way Joe got on guys. He'd tear 'em apart in front of the whole squad, so they lost all respect. . . . Joe says winning isn't everything. Well, he could have fooled me. He seemed obsessed with winning." (When asked to comment on Hall's criticism, Joe suggested Hall may have had an axe to grind because he didn't play much.)

Neal Smith, an All-American safety in 1969, also outspokenly criticized Joe, contending that Joe's image was phony, that he cared more about winning football games than advancing the college education of his athletes. "Paterno wants the public to think he's concerned about his players' getting an education," Smith charged. "Don't believe it. Like any other big-time coach, he's all football. I don't really know the coach's priorities, but winning football games was right up there. You have to respect Paterno for his football knowledge, but not as a person."[14]

Others have felt that the detracting players were wrong in their criticism. "They never should have played anyway," observed Dave Joyner. Greg Buttle agreed: "The truth of the matter is that everyone who was in Paterno's doghouse while I was there deserved to be in his doghouse."

Asked to comment on the complaints from a few former players, Joe replied that he never tried to win a popularity contest. "I'd expect there are a number of kids who resent me," he said. "That's only natural. You can't deal with as many people as I've dealt with and be as demand- ing as I've been without having people resent some things." Joe has pre- ferred to challenge his players. He hasn't wanted them sitting around ten years later saying, "Paterno was a nice guy, but he just didn't know how good we wanted to become."

George Paterno has understood how his brother could rub some people the wrong way. "Joe has no time for goof-offs," George said in

It's time for pre-game calisthenics before the 1995 Rose Bowl kickoff against Oregon, and Joe is giving his players a pointed pep talk as they loosen up. (AP/Wide World Photo)

1982. "If you let down, you're gonna hear about it. If you don't like it, that's too bad."

For Harrisburg sportswriter Ronnie Christ, who covered Joe for many years, it wasn't unusual that some of Joe's players didn't like him. "Show me any man who has coached that long and I'll show you a man who is disliked by a certain percentage of his players. Especially the disgruntled ones who have an axe to grind. Or those whose personality and ego clashed with Paterno's."

"I've seen him yell and scream," Christ continued, "but he's a piker compared to many of his colleagues. Every coach is a tyrant of sorts. Any football fan who thinks their favorite coach doesn't berate his players at times doesn't know a thing about the game."[15]

Those who initially criticized Joe, but later appreciated him and praised him, comprised a large club. In 1973 Jack Ham, Penn State All-American linebacker in 1970 and later star of the Pittsburgh Steelers, was prominently quoted as saying: "All of us disliked Paterno. It made us closer. He was very cold to his players, very impersonal."

Fifteen years later Ham was talking differently. "I didn't realize it at the time, but to have a guy like Joe Paterno as your head football coach—a guy who is concerned about football but also how you turn out as a man—was important to me," Ham reflected. "I was lucky to have four years with Coach Paterno." One of the reasons Ham chose Joe to introduce him at Ham's induction into the Pro Football Hall of Fame in 1988 was because Joe "probably had more of an impact on my life than anyone else."[16]

Matt Bahr, star place-kicker in 1978, found it difficult to play for Joe. When Bahr wasn't kicking well in practice, he heard a high-pitched Brooklyn accent yell at him, "Hey, Bahr, will you kick the ball? Ah, get outta here." Bahr didn't like Joe while he played at Penn State. As the years passed after his graduation, Bahr appreciated Joe more. Ironically, he liked Joe for the same reason he didn't like him when he played at Penn State—that insistent devotion to excellence. "He wants you to achieve more than you believe yourself capable of, which then prompts you on to greater heights," Bahr said in 1986. "You feel like what you do is never quite good enough, [but] that's what a coach is for—to make sure you excel. Today, looking from the outside in, I realize why he did what he did."[17]

Paul Gabel, a 1974 Penn State graduate, had an unpleasant experience playing for Joe. "What bugged me most was being belittled in front of [my] peers, being told in front of the team that you stink, that you are a baby, that you are a nothing." Gabel suffered from asthma and normally took shots to control the disease, but the summer before his junior year he discontinued his shots and reported to training camp with congestion. On the second day of the August drills, he was running sprints after practice when he felt an attack coming on. "So I slowed down," said Gabel. "But [Paterno] starts screaming, 'Get it out, get the lead out, start moving,' so I pushed myself. I went beyond what I should have done and I collapsed right there on the field. When I came to, everybody was around me and I could hear Paterno yelling and screaming, 'Get up, get up, you are a baby.' My pulse went up to about 210. The doctor had to shoot me with depressants to get me down."

Gabel's public comments damaged Joe's reputation, but later there were apologies all around. Subsequently, Gabel softened his attitude. Joe was tough and yelled at players, Gabel said in 1987. "But more chances than not, he was right. My attitude toward Joe changed in the past seven or eight years—after I had my own kids and I began to understand what he was trying to do for us." As for his collapse on the field, Gabel now says, "Joe probably wasn't aware of what happened to me."

In his autobiography Joe apologized for mistreating Gabel. "I think Paul understood that perhaps he hadn't made the complete commitment I was asking him to make and that I pushed him to make him better than he was. But I didn't allow for his legitimate health problem. I expected him to be like me when I was a kid. If I got hurt, I played hurt. But asthma is not the same as a hurt arm or stabbing your lip with your own teeth."[18]

For the most part, Joe has won praise and respect from his players. Many have been effusive. He left an indelible impression on Greg Buttle. "Three things would sum up the program in a nutshell—character, discipline, and responsibility," Buttle said. "We were taught all three of those traits on and off the field by all the coaches."

Joe's relationship with his players has often resembled a teenager and his father—strained at times but usually improved as the years went by. "Joe Paterno is sort of like your parents," Charlie Pittman said. "You don't appreciate them until you get older and become one."

"You know when you're seventeen and you don't think your father knows anything?" quarterback John Shaffer observed. "Then, when you're twenty-two, you wonder how your father learned so many things in the past five years. That's how you feel about Joe."

"The older I get, the smarter Joe Paterno is," observed tight end Ted Kwalick. "I probably hold the Penn State record for being called on the carpet when I was there." Kwalick hadn't talked with Joe for many years, but when Kwalick's father died, "I got a note from Joe, which shows you what kind of guy he is."[19]

Gregg Garrity and Kenny Jackson were the starting wide receivers on Penn State's 1982 championship team and later teammates with the Philadelphia Eagles. "I don't know too many players who really liked him while they were playing for him," Garrity recalled. "He was so tough on you, so demanding. He's such a perfectionist that a lot of times you think he's just nitpicking. But once you get on with your life, whether it be football or in business, those small things seem to add up, and they help you out a lot. He's more interested in his players than he is in himself. That's very rare. A lot of coaches will do anything to win to keep their job."

Jackson, who later became an assistant coach at Penn State, thought that Joe made his life better. "He taught you that football is a game and if you don't keep it in perspective, you can forget what life's about," Jackson observed. "I think he's a better teacher than a coach. He's not a great tactician. . . . But he's a tremendous motivator. He has a tremendous amount of pride, and when he looks at you and says you can be the best, you really believe it. He's a special man. You don't realize it until you go on in life and see other people. He's done what he's done in a fair, honest way."[20]

Joe helped Charlie Pittman build his confidence. An outstanding halfback for Penn State's undefeated 1968 and 1969 teams, Pittman initially had doubts about his ability. A bashful, inner-city black youth, he was uncomfortable at Penn State as a freshman. He questioned whether he belonged, whether he was good enough. During the spring practice of Pittman's freshman year, he overheard Joe speaking to another person in the locker room. "Here's the guy who's going to make me a great football coach!" Joe exclaimed, referring to Pittman. Joe had sensed Pittman's uncertainty. "Just that statement did so much to boost my confidence," Pittman remembered.

Because Pittman was unresponsive when a coach hollered, Joe motivated by putting his arm around his halfback before a game and saying, "Charlie, we need you. We need a good game out of you today." Pittman led Penn State in rushing for three consecutive years and scored thirty-two career touchdowns.

Joe made Pittman promise that he would eventually earn his MBA. After playing three years of professional football, Pittman returned to school and earned his MBA in 1976. Subsequently, Pittman worked as an executive for the *Erie Times* newspaper, where he tried to apply Joe's philosophy. "Today I think about winning and being the best I can be," said Pittman. "I always apply the principles from football to what I do on a day-to-day basis. The way Joe Paterno motivated his people, that's the way I try to motivate my people in the newspaper business."[21]

Having developed special affection for his players, Joe has had bittersweet thoughts when they graduated. "To some coaches," he said, "graduation is disaster, the enemy. All the things I believe in force me to celebrate graduation as achievement, as victory. But a secret part of me weeps inside at commencement. Like any professor, I hate to see those kids leave their dependence on me. Like any father, I hate to see them leave home. Like any coach I hate to lose those players."[22]

Penn State has never been known for the number of blacks on its football teams. Indeed, in the 1940s and 1950s there were only a few—Jesse Arnelle, Rosey Grier, Lenny Moore. There were five blacks on Joe's unbeaten team in 1968; and eight on the second undefeated club in 1969. However, at the beginning of the 1970 season three of the four backfield starters were black.

Having been called a wop and a guinea as a youth and being the target of snobs at Brown University, Joe felt sensitized to a "lifelong empathy" with blacks. He was correct in his self-assessment, but the environment at Penn State was not always conducive to wholesome race relations.

For many years Joe made a point of rooming a black with a white player, figuring that if they were going to play together they should live together. Jesse Arnelle thought Joe treated black players fairly in the early 1950s and, more than anyone else on the coaching staff, sensitively expressed interest in civil rights. As Arnelle walked onto the practice field in 1954, Joe called him aside and asked, "Jesse, did you hear?" Arnelle thought something tragic had happened. Joe continued, "The Supreme Court [in *Brown v. Board of Education*] just struck down the separate but equal doctrine." Arnelle was elated. "I knew exactly what he was saying. It was an important moment in my life. It was an important turning point in race relations in the United States. And Joe understood it perfectly."[23]

Dave Robinson, a receiver and linebacker, was the only black on the traveling squad in 1962, the year he was a consensus All-American. (Later he starred with the Green Bay Packers.) That year Penn State played Florida in the Gator Bowl in Jacksonville, Florida, but on the team's flight to Florida, bad weather forced the plane to land in Orlando. When the hungry players and coaches entered the airport restaurant and began ordering, the restaurant manager enforced the segregation ordinance and prevented Robinson from eating with his white teammates.

Angry, Rip Engle ordered his team out of the restaurant, gave each player expense money, and told them to eat somewhere else. The gesture relieved the immediate problem, but Robinson still needed somewhere to eat. "What good is this expense money if no one's going to let me in to eat?" he thought.

Enter Joe. He said to Robinson, "Come on, come with me." Joe took him to a coffee shop where they had lunch together. "I had the feeling," Robinson recalled, "that if they threw me out, they were going to have to throw out Joe, too." Penn State lost to Florida, 17-7, but Robinson barely remembered the game, only the incident. "I was not accepted in the South, and I would rather not have gone through [an] experience like that," Robinson said. "But I did, and Joe helped me, and I think it made a better person out of me."

"I'll never forget the look on Robby's face," Joe recalled indignantly. "Here it was 1962 in the land of the free and a restaurant in Florida refuses to serve an intelligent human being like Dave Robinson because his skin is a different color." Joe vowed that he would never permit any of his players to be embarrassed again. Five years later, when the team played in the Gator Bowl, Penn State officials scoured Florida looking for a pregame training site where blacks would be accepted. Joe wanted assurance that his black players would not be embarrassed.[24]

In his early years as head coach Joe was optimistic in his outlook about the progress of blacks. "I think it must be exciting to be a young black kid today," he said of the black protests in the 1960s. "All of a sudden, they're part of a race that has finally become aware of its great potential. They're on the move, making progress, and every day is kind of a challenge."

Some universities have exploited black players, recruiting them to play football, but ignoring their academic progress. Given snap courses to remain eligible, they have never received a decent education and many haven't graduated. Joe has deplored the policies of some of his coaching peers. "It's part of the winning-at-any-cost philosophy that some coaches have," he charged.[25]

Joe advised Charlie Pittman, "Charlie, don't just stay with all your black friends on campus. Mix with the other [students]. Learn how they live. Get exposed to their way of doing things. . . . If you don't learn to share and mingle with other people, you're going to miss out on some good things in life."

In retrospect Joe has occasionally appeared patronizing and condescending. In 1971 he said he wouldn't mind if his daughter dated a black. Referring to the two black Penn State stars of the late 1960s, he said, "I once told Charlie Pittman and Jim Kates, two of the finest human beings I have ever known, that if my daughter came home with either of them, my wife and I would be very happy. And I meant it."[26]

In 1970 Joe started a black, Mike Cooper, at the key position of quarterback, and the resulting controversy, plus the subsequent demotion of Cooper, caused anguish. Cooper won the starting assignment over a white quarterback, Bob Parsons. No matter whom he selected, Joe was bound to lose. In his autobiography he reflected: "If I picked Cooper, it was because he was black. If I picked Parsons, it was because Cooper was black."

When Cooper proved ineffective and Penn State lost three games early in the season, an avalanche of hateful phone calls and letters descended on the Paterno home. "Is the nigger lover home?" one caller demanded. Sue Paterno usually answered the phone. Another caller seethed at her, "You tell that son of a bitch we're going to get that nigger." About two hundred letters poured in as well. "Many of them, anonymous of course, were just as ugly as the calls," Joe said. Because both Cooper and Parsons were ineffective, Joe transferred John Hufnagel, who was white, from defense to quarterback, and the team improved dramatically, finishing the season with a 7-3 record.

After Joe benched Cooper, hate mail poured in from the other side. Now Joe was accused of "caving in" to racists. "Letter writers on both sides were too deeply trapped in their prejudice or their 'raised consciousness' to accept that I had made a football decision, not a political decision. In my view, callers of both stripes were racists of two different kinds."[27]

There were 1,200 blacks at the State College campus in 1972, but the figure dropped to only 939 in 1976. In the fall semester of 1982, the university enrolled 32,937 students, but fewer than 1,000 were black— about 3 percent of the student population. Only 1.5 percent of the faculty was black, and the dearth of black administrators at Penn State was chronic. Penn State's athletic department was virtually devoid of blacks as well; in 1983 only one part-time administrator, Don Ferrell, worked on the staff.

Excellent black high school students have attended universities like the Ivy League schools or universities that granted more financial aid than Penn State. Although a lovely community, State College is decidedly white and middle class. In 1983 the city was only .5 percent black and most of the blacks were associated with the university.

Social life has been a major problem. "Socially, the entire area, on and off campus, is a virtual wasteland for blacks," observed Ron Bracken in the *Centre Daily Times*. No black bars, no black radio stations, no black theaters, no black churches. For a long time no barbers in State College would cut the hair of a black person because they had no experience doing it. For many years there were no black clubs on campus, and fraternities wouldn't admit blacks. The nearest urban center was a four-hour drive.[28]

In 1969 Jesse Arnelle was invited to give a speech at Penn State (and to accept an award as well). After agonizing over his speech, Arnelle decided to focus on the lack of racial diversity at Penn State. "I felt so strongly about it," Arnelle recalled. "I knew [Penn State] could do better" in attracting racial minorities. Arnelle sensed that Penn State officials had mixed reactions to his speech, that some didn't want to hear his message.

But Arnelle was delighted with Joe Paterno's reaction. "Joe came over to me after the speech," Arnelle said, "and looked me in the eye, shook my hand, and said, 'Jesse, I am awfully proud of you. I am awfully glad you made that speech. A lot of people here may not understand, but I know what you are talking about and you're right and we're going to do better.'"[29]

Penn State subsequently tried almost everything to solve the problems—forming committees, starting commissions, initiating minority programs, hiring affirmative action coordinators, a minority affairs director and black recruiters, and instituting a Black Scholars Program. Still, the university's efforts mostly failed to recruit more blacks. "I wish I could report a better result in terms of figures," President John Oswald sadly observed in 1983.

Arnelle expressed disappointment in Penn State's inability to recruit blacks but put the problem in perspective. "I don't think any major white university in the country can point with a great deal of pride to the job they've done overall," Arnelle recently said. "Every major white university in the country has tried very hard to recruit black students, some with mixed returns. At Penn State, it is not from a lack of desire."

Nonetheless, the small number of blacks on Penn State's football teams was disconcerting. A week after the loss to Alabama in the 1979 Sugar Bowl, Joe received a phone call from Charlie Pittman. "I told Joe I was embarrassed," Pittman said. Not by the loss. Pittman was embarrassed by something else he observed on TV. He said, "Joe, Alabama had more black players on the field than Penn State. *Alabama*." Penn State had all white backs, all white receivers. "Hey, Joe, there's something wrong here," Pittman told his former coach. "Charlie, I'm embarrassed by it, too," Joe responded. "We've got to have more black players playing here, and I am going to do all I can to get them."[30]

In the mid-1970s Joe fielded nearly all-white teams, coinciding with the drop in black enrollment at Penn State to an all-time low in 1975. He said he could not find black players who were good enough athletes and good enough students to compete academically at Penn State. "The ones I found, I was competing against the Ivy League for." Joe was always reluctant to recruit players who did not have a good chance of graduating. But in order to bring in more minority students, in the early 1970s he approached President Oswald and asked for special admittance for a few students who could not normally meet entrance requirements. The special admittance policy, known as a "Presidential Special," allowed an athlete to be admitted by the university president even though he did not predict a 2.0 on a 4.0 grade-point scale. From 1971 through 1980 twenty-four minority students were admitted to Penn State under the program; twenty were retained and eleven graduated, thus yielding a 55 percent graduation rate. (Minority student-athletes admitted under normal procedures for the period 1966–1980 graduated at the higher rate of 71.2 percent.)

"I don't even like to think about the number of black players we have," Joe said in 1983. "I have no quota. The years we didn't have a lot of blacks on the squad was because the ones we wanted, the ones who were good enough students and good enough players, were going to the Ivy League. I would be shocked if we did have a [racial] problem. That doesn't mean that the kids on the squad all love each other. You will always have personality conflicts between whites, between blacks, and between blacks and whites. But I don't know of any racial problems."[31]

By the early 1980s Joe had come to believe that the national attitude of "helping" minorities had gotten to the point where it was doing more harm than good. Reminding young people every day that they needed help convinced them that they were not as good as others. He believed in demanding reasonable standards and then pressuring the student-athlete to get the best out of him.

Penn State was an awkward environment for black athletes, but he thought they were better for it. "[Penn State] is an open society in a lot of ways. I preach that to the [black] players all the time. I tell them if they can handle this environment, they can sure handle any other environment." Although they might not like having white middle-class attitudes shoved down their throat at times, they were still going to have to handle a white middle-class society after they graduated and were going to have to understand it to handle it.

Many praised Joe's approach to race relations. Sportswriter Bill Lyon thought Joe "felt very strongly on racial minorities issues." Black assistant coach Booker Brooks observed that Joe wanted black players to come away from Penn State with a fine education and a comfortable feeling about living within the white world. "I agree with him," Brooks said.

Carl Cayette, a black Penn State running back (1969–1972), lauded his experience with Joe and Penn State. "We have to learn how to live in a *total* society, not just a black society. Penn State teaches you that, in addition to everything else. There are other colleges where you might get the same degree, but not the same education. . . . And Joe does care, he does listen," Cayette said. "I remember leaving his office and him telling me, 'Carl, if I were black, I'd feel the same way.'" Black assistant coaches also expressed affection for their boss. Assistant Ron Dickerson thought it had been a "great opportunity" to work for Joe, "to have been around him."[32]

The Grand Experiment has consistently remained the focus of Joe's concern. He has readily admitted that the high-minded concept was partly "a recruiting cliché." Still, he has deeply believed in his vision of the ideal student-athlete and has consistently conveyed his convictions to his players. He has wanted his players to develop discipline, a work ethic, and attention to detail, not just on the football field, but in the classroom and in their whole life. The traits should become an instinctive habit, ingrained in the player's character. "We are old-fashioned," he proudly told his players. "We are going to go to school every day."

After Penn State lost to Navy in September 1974, freshman Jimmy Cefalo and other players anticipated a severe tongue-lashing from Joe at the next team meeting. Indeed, when Joe arrived, his jaw was set, he looked grim, but his message surprised. "So far," Joe snarled, "we've had a lot of fun playing football, and we've only taken time out to register for classes. Those classes start on Monday morning. None of you has any excuse for flunking, and I don't want you to let yourselves or your families down. Let's really hit those books."

"Right away," Cefalo said, "I knew there was more to life than football."

John Coyle became Penn State's faculty representative to the NCAA in the fall of 1970, just after Joe had established a national reputation by going undefeated for two consecutive seasons. During Coyle's first year in the new position, his friends teased him about having to confront the renowned Joe Paterno. "Hey, John, what are you ever going to do if you have to declare one of Paterno's starters ineligible?" said one friend.

"Well, I'll cross that bridge when I come to it," Coyle responded, "but I guess it could be traumatic."

Three years later Coyle received records from the registrar's office indicating that two football players—one of them a starter the year before—were scholastically ineligible. Inadvertently, Joe had received copies of the records shortly before Coyle. Joe immediately phoned Coyle and explained the problem with the ineligible players. "John, I just want to let you know . . . that two of the people on my team are not going to be eligible this fall because they didn't do what they were supposed to in summer school, and their grades aren't up to par. So don't be surprised when you see the records."

"I didn't even have to tell him," Coyle reflected. "He told me ahead of time. There were no questions, no problems."

"That is the kind of relationship I've had with him over the years," said Coyle, who continued as faculty representative to the NCAA. "He has never ever questioned anything that I have done with respect to his team. If I declare [players] ineligible, there are no problems, and no questions. We just work to get them back on track."

Joe has encouraged his players to take part in the same academic and social experiences as other students. Joe had enjoyed mingling with different types of students at Brown, including nonathletes. At Brown football players weren't locked away in a plush, carpeted athletic dorm like the one Coach Bear Bryant built at Alabama. "Maybe Bryant believed in protecting his Red Tide from the mental distractions of a university," Joe said. "He sheltered his squad of stars from the student who didn't play serious football. Thank God I wasn't 'protected' that way at Brown." Utterly opposed to a "football dormitory," he has preferred, instead, that his players live in campus residence halls and fraternities where they could participate in campus life. No easy courses have been created for those who were floundering academically. And there have been few other prerequisites common at big-time football powers.

Football makes academic excellence very tough to achieve. "Mostly, a player is weary before he even walks into a classroom in the fall," observed Ken Denlinger. "That's because of those energy-sapping two-a-days, plus scrimmages, that begin in early August. A player is physically drained and mentally uneasy because of the keen competition for positions, and then he has to go to class."

"College even without football takes a good deal of discipline," Denlinger added. "College with football almost requires the sort of forced time management that Paterno uses at Penn State: study hall each night for freshmen and upperclassmen with grade-point problems."

Despite the rigor, Joe has urged his players to enjoy the experience of college. "It should be the four greatest years of their lives," he said. "It's the only time in their lives when they're free, when they have the opportunity to choose what they want to do and when they want to do it. . . . I tell the kids, *enjoy* yourselves. There is so much besides football. Art, history, literature, music, politics, the changing society."[33]

He has wanted players who wouldn't taunt opponents, who would be gentlemen and in some cases scholars. He has occasionally used football as a carrot to motivate his players to study. "Okay, you like football?" he has told them. "Well, you can't play unless you go to class, get good grades, and stay out of trouble. You can't be part of our program unless you do things *our* way."

"Get involved," Joe has hounded his players. "Don't let the world pass you by. Go after life. Attack it. Ten years from now I want you to look back on college as a wonderful time of expanding yourself—not just four years of playing football."[34]

After defensive end Bruce Bannon was excused from spring practice to do research on a geology project, Bannon framed his project and presented it to Joe. Bannon graduated with honors in geologic science. "Joe Paterno's first job is to win games, but I think he does his best to help players," Bannon said. "He really does emphasize academics. There're not many coaches who do."

Mike Reid, an All-American defensive lineman in the late 1960s, was an accomplished musician. "There was no way I could get my music courses changed to a certain time," Reid said. "I had to take them when they were available, and they often collided with spring practice times. But there never was any question about whether you would go to practice or to class."

When linebacker Shane Conlan arrived at Penn State in 1982, he was ready to play football but couldn't have cared less about his schoolwork. "I thought I was going to play football the rest of my life," he reflected. "I didn't think [school] was important." Slowly, he changed his mind. His coaches, academic advisors, and older players drilled it into his head: Go to class. At first he resisted. "I had a rough couple of years," he said. "There were times when I said, 'This isn't important.' But Joe drilled it in me. Now I'm glad it happened."[35]

About an academically unmotivated player, Joe said: "I'm still feeling my way about how to get it out of him. He's not afraid of me yet. Somewhere down the line, I gotta scare the hell out of him. I'm trying to pick my spot." Another player recounted Joe's efforts to straighten him out. "Joe lectured me. Lectured me. Lectured me. Lectured me. And lectured. He'd call me in there every two weeks. Toward the end of the year, it was two times a week. He gave me a lot of chances. He liked me a helluva lot when it came to football. He wanted me to get my act together. I'm spoiled as hell. My dad would give me anything. My grandmom, too. Spoiled from day one. Still am. Joe wanted to make me a man. I really respect Joe. I have no resents [sic]. Just regrets."[36]

Defensive tackle Bob White became a legendary success story for the Grand Experiment. A three-sport star in high school, White was recruited heavily by a dozen major schools. He wanted to attend Penn State, but Joe was reluctant to take him because of his academic deficiencies. White was perplexed because nobody else was complaining about his grades. "He had a 2.0, which will get you a scholarship and maybe a Firebird most anywhere else," observed a story in *Sports Illustrated*. "Why should he hit the books in the *summer*, for crying out loud, when everyone else was hitting keggers? Why should somebody be so worried about him?"

"I didn't see how we could take him," Joe recalled. "Impossible as this may sound for a Pennsylvania high school, here was a kid who had never read a whole book!" How could White remotely hope to do college-level work?

After Joe's assistants urged him to give White a chance, Joe offered the young man a deal. Joe would accept him if White agreed to extra tutoring in English in the summer from Sue Paterno. White concurred. Starting with *Huckleberry Finn*, Sue required him to read a dozen books and to write a paper on each. Initially, White struggled with college, but he improved as a student and graduated, and he was a charming, enthusiastic, and spirited team leader on the 1986 national championship team. "I'm so happy about the way things turned out for me," said White. "There was a time I never really thought I'd get through college."[37]

In one notable case the Grand Experiment touched Joe's own staff. Ron Dickerson coached the defensive secondary at Penn State from 1985 to 1991. At a team meeting Joe asked his players, "How many of you guys have read a [serious] book in your life?" Most of the players raised their hands. "[It] surprised me," reflected Dickerson, whose coaching career had included stops at five other universities, "because at some of the other schools I've been at, if that question was asked, I know that very few of [the players] would raise their hands."

Joe's challenge prompted Dickerson to reflect on his own reading habits. "I've only read about five or six books [in my life]," Dickerson thought. From then on Dickerson made a dedicated effort to improve his mind, rising early in the morning to read. "I *made* time to sit down and read," he recalled. "[Paterno] brought it to my attention." Dickerson completed more books during his stay at Penn State than he had read in his entire life.[38]

"I played with guys in the pros who never graduated from college and never thought about graduating or going back for their degrees," observed Greg Buttle. "All they did was play football because they thought football was everything."

"I think [Joe] takes a lot of pride in the fact that a number of his student-athletes have gone on to make marks in the world," said Chuck Burkhart.

Joe has brought books and articles to team meetings, citing passages for the players, usually on an inspirational theme. He has made his points by quoting from the *New York Times* and the *Wall Street Journal*, and from philosophy and literature. On one occasion he read from an article about the dedication of professional musicians. The lesson he taught was that, like great musicians, great football players must think about their work every day. "You can't ever take a day off," he said. "You've got to do something to improve every single day."

When Joe met with Don Ferrell, the academic-athletic advisor since 1982, he peppered Ferrell with questions about players. Is the player in the right major? Do we need a summer school? Do we need to get in touch with the parents? What do you think I should do? "He is interested in every one of the kids he brings here," Ferrell observed. "He fathers every one of them."[39]

There have been many instances where Joe has sat out excellent players because they were not performing in the classroom. On several occasions he hasn't allowed a player to take part in spring practice because the player wasn't studying. Banishment from spring practice is a severe penalty because many positions are set after the spring. "If you don't take part in spring practice, it is not very conducive to winning a starting spot on the team," said Booker Brooks.

One outstanding player, a potential All-American, was about to enter his senior year when Joe learned the young man wasn't studying. Joe warned him that he might not play in his senior year. Technically, the player remained eligible, but Joe expected more academic effort. When the player still made only a minimal effort in his studies, Joe did not allow him to play in his senior year. "[The player] would have helped the team immeasurably," observed Brooks.

Joe has phoned former players, some in professional football, and urged them to return to school. "Remember, I promised your family that you're going to graduate," Joe told one player. "I want you back here."[40]

When Joe initially talked about the Grand Experiment, some had viewed it as noble enough, but impractical, unrealistic, and probably impossible. "Hardly anybody thought it would really work," said sportswriter Bill Lyon. By setting lofty standards, Joe made himself a target and could not afford to stumble or fail. As best he could he has tried to keep boosters and alumni from interfering with recruiting. He has worried that a booster or an alumnus would break an NCAA rule. "A guy walks into your locker room and sees a kid doesn't have a topcoat or something. And, just out of sympathy for the kid, he puts twenty dollars in his hand. Or a kid's going out with his girl and [the alumnus] sees them downtown and picks up the dinner check. They're all breaking rules. But how do you control it?"

Joe could imagine the headlines if one of his players posed for a poster or took fifty dollars for appearing on a radio show. "Sometimes, I hope the NCAA would audit us so we could see if we are really as clean as we think we are," he said.

Nobody on the football staff is supposed to approach a professor asking to "go easy" on a player's grade. The faculty member teaching a course should have complete autonomy in grading student-athletes. "I have never been approached relative to a grade, and I could have been," said a Penn State professor. "We *never* tap a professor for a little 'special understanding,'" Joe said.[41]

Before a Wednesday meeting of the Nittany Lion Club, Milton Bergstein approached Joe about an academic problem with a player.

"Joe. One of your players has cut my class a couple times."

"Did you speak to him about it?" said Joe.

"Yeah I did, but I'm not going to speak to him again."

"Good," said Joe. "If he cuts any more, flunk him."

"What if he's your quarterback?"

"I don't care. If he gets by with cutting your class, he'll ruin my locker room. He'll tell everybody. . . . The first thing you know, everybody will be thinking that is okay. I don't want to know who he is. Just flunk him."[42]

There was one controversial exception. Although neither the university nor Joe Paterno condoned placing pressure on a faculty member to give higher grades to athletes, an overzealous athletic advisor did infuriate some faculty until he was quietly asked to resign.

When Frank Patrick retired in 1977, after twenty-five years of coaching and academic advising, the university hired Dr. Frank Downing to replace him as director of the academic-advising program. Downing stated publicly that the purpose of the academic advising was to assist the athlete in becoming independent. However, some charged that Downing interfered with faculty on behalf of student-athletes, creating intense resentment. Downing irritated faculty by constantly checking on the academic progress of players. "He would call faculty members and see how [players] were doing in class, see what their grades were," said John Coyle. "Some faculty thought that was bothersome. They didn't think they should have to respond to those types of inquiries." Irate faculty complained about Downing's alleged interference and intimidation, including John Romano, associate dean for undergraduate studies in the College of Liberal Arts, who claimed he received three phone calls in one day—the last at 11:30 P.M.—from Downing concerning a student. "I think [Downing] was acting on his own," said a Penn State professor.

Standout defensive lineman Matt Millen told *Sports Illustrated* that Penn State stressed "the image" too much and singled out Downing. "I remember the academic advisor, Frank Downing, telling me to carry a briefcase when I went to class and sit in the front row and raise my hand and ask a lot of questions. 'Good for the image,' he said."

Because of the complaints, Joe felt compelled to make a change and huddled with President Oswald. "I was informed that there had been enough negative comments about [Downing] that a change needed to be made, and I supported this," Oswald said.

After Downing was quietly dismissed in 1982, Joe commented that he and Downing had agreed on philosophy, but admitted that problems had existed. "[Downing] did not know when to back off," Joe recalled. "Everything was urgent, and he alienated people. His style was [abrasive]."[43]

Overall, though, Penn State has been remarkably consistent and successful in abiding by NCAA rules and by the ideals of the Grand Experiment. Joe's success in producing the student-athlete is partly illustrated by his nineteen first-team Academic All-Americans, ten Hall of Fame Scholar-Athletes, and fifteen NCAA Postgraduate Scholarship winners. Under Joe's leadership the Penn State football program has never been accused of seriously violating the rules of the NCAA. "As far as I know," Jim Tarman said in 1983, "we've never been investigated. I can't say that we've never been turned in, because you never know when somebody may make a phone call."

"When I say we're honest," Joe said in 1983, "I mean that we're as honest as it is possible to be. It's a relative term because, after all, we are human. We may not be simon-pure. The rule book is vague in some areas. You could probably nitpick and find something we did that was unintentional."[44]

In the 1980s hardly a press conference went by without someone asking Joe his views on cheating, NCAA rules, improved admission standards, college play-offs, freshmen eligibility, agents and the NFL draft, redshirting, and other problems. Such was life for the dean of college football coaches. Although some thought he was patronizing and condescending, most people admired his reformist ideas and especially his courage and fortitude in speaking out. For years Joe seemed to be a voice in the wilderness, crying out for sanity in the operation of big-time college football.

He directed many of his suggestions at decreasing the high cost of sports programs: limit grants-in-aide, cut traveling squads, reinstitute one-platoon football. He also spoke out against excessive redshirting and the lack of appreciation for eastern football. "What's the use of being against something if you don't talk about it?" he said.[45]

The classic Paterno pose suggests satisfaction with his Grand Experiment, both on the field and off. (Photo courtesy of Penn State Sports Information Department)

In his biography by Hyman and White, Joe criticized Little League and opposed any organized athletics for youngsters under fourteen. The youngsters were not emotionally prepared for intense, highly organized, pressurized sports, he reasoned.

"Whatever happened to the good old days when, if you felt like playing baseball, you rounded up some of your buddies, got a bat and a ball, and went out and played? What do we do now?" Joe said, answering critically: "We dress up our kids in uniforms, give them professional equipment, tell them when to practice and when to play, organize their games for them, give them officials, and put them in the hands of some guy who doesn't know the first thing about the sport or what's good for an eight-year-old."[46]

Sometimes his judgments have been dubious or overly harsh and understandably caused resentment. In the early 1970s, for example, he castigated the Ivy League for being content to play one another instead of enhancing the prestige of eastern football by scheduling intersectional powers. "It would help the eastern image if the Ivy League got away from its incestuous relationship," he said of the Ivies whose administrations were trying to de-emphasize football and concentrate on academic excellence. "They won't venture out of their own league, yet they want to be considered the equals of the independents who play tougher schedules." Joe continued abrasively: "They talk about competition and how their good teams can play with anybody in the country, but they sit in their ivory towers and never give their teams a chance to prove it. They should put up or shut up!" Such comments did not endear him to some colleagues in the Ivy League.[47]

Joe has detested unscrupulous coaches, college administrators, and university presidents who accepted athletes who could barely read or write only because they could perform on the gridiron. They have intentionally broken the rules, cheated young players out of an education, used them, and then cast them aside. "That stinks," he said. "[If] we can't look to our colleges for integrity, where can we look?" In the mid-1980s it was made public at Southern Methodist University that boosters, with the approval of top officials, had made secret payments to players. "It's unbelievable to think that kind of corruption came right from the top of the power structure," Joe said, and he supported the NCAA's draconian penalty against SMU.

Compared to his peers, Joe has considered himself lucky to be insulated from the temptation to violate rules. "I'm a full professor here," he observed. "I'm not at the mercy of alumni; they can't interfere with me. I've never had the dilemma of whether I should have to cheat to save my career." The people to blame for recruiting violations have been college faculties, administrations, and—yes—the NCAA. The NCAA needed more investigators on the road digging up rules violations.

"I don't think the NCAA does enough to seek out the recruiting cheaters," Joe charged in 1971. "They've passed too many rules that they can't enforce, and half the time the rules are so ambiguous that you don't know what's legal and what's illegal. What the NCAA should be doing is policing college football instead of waiting for a school to squeal on someone before they start an investigation. They should have a dozen investigators checking up on people and looking into suspicious actions. If the coaches knew that the NCAA was snooping around, they would be more reluctant to cheat."

The NCAA could do a lot more to help schools cut expenses, Joe also insisted in 1971. "The first thing would be to place limits on recruiting. High school youngsters should be limited to visits to only three or four schools, there should be a ceiling on recruiting budgets, and the length of the recruiting season should be shortened." (Some of Joe's suggestions were later implemented by the NCAA.) Nonetheless, he has deplored the proliferation of NCAA rules, rules that explained rules, unenforceable rules, impractical rules. "If someone calls NCAA headquarters in Mission, Kansas, and asks three officials for interpretation of a single rule with a single set of facts, at times he'll get three different answers."

Asked in 1986 what he would do if he were the executive director of the NCAA, Joe responded: "I would get a group of five or six people from different areas of intercollegiate football. We'd sit down and take a look at the rule book, divide it into maybe five sections: eligibility, definition of amateurism, ineligibility, recruiting, academic standards. . . . Then, with the help of these people, I would appoint committees in each of these areas and I would give them a year to write rules that are pertinent to this day and age. Then, instead of having an NCAA convention for two days, you have a ten-day constitutional convention where you vote on the recommendations of these committees."[48]

He has been particularly opposed to allowing freshmen to be eligible for varsity sports, but practical considerations have led him to play freshmen like everyone else. It was wrong to allow an eighteen-year-old to check into college and immediately get swallowed up with high-pressure, big-time football. In some cases the youngster was on the football field before he attended his first college class.

Allowing a freshman to be eligible for the varsity robbed the student-athlete from spending a year on the campus somewhat anonymously without a football reputation. "If a kid is thrust immediately into the spotlight of being a football player, there aren't many people on the campus who are going to stop him and ask him much about history or art or music," Joe argued. "They're going to ask him about the football team."

Supporters of freshmen eligibility have argued that without it schools would need to increase the number of scholarships, raising costs. Yes, universities were trying to get their "money's worth," Joe conceded, adding caustically "by squeezing four years of playing time out of a kid, further exploiting him for the sake of the school, not for the good of the young athlete himself."

Joe's solution? "If everybody has a limit of ninety-five scholarships, and everybody has twenty-five for freshmen who are not permitted to play, then everybody plays with seventy scholarship players. Is seventy not enough?"[49]

Beginning in 1974 Joe worked some freshmen into the lineup for the pragmatic reason that their widespread use by opponents made it necessary, particularly as a recruiting ploy. "I have to play our freshmen or we would not be able to recruit the players we do," Joe said sadly in 1980. "Kids get told they will play their first year. It's a vicious cycle." Like everyone else, Penn State took advantage of the rule, but Joe still thought it was an awful rule.

In his autobiography Joe expressed disappointment with himself for not following completely his convictions on freshmen eligibility. Opponents had put him in a bind. "I lacked the toughness and resolve to rule flatly that freshmen would not play for Penn State." He referred to himself as a "phony and [a] hypocrite," because "I knew it would hurt our recruiting—when other coaches were actually promising some hot prospects that they'd play as freshmen—and would shave our chances of winning championships."[50]

Both the Associated Press and United Press International conducted a weekly press poll to rank the top teams in the nation. Because there was no system for determining the relative strength of teams or a national champion, the polls became a powerful symbolic substitute. Many fans agreed with writer Dan Jenkins: "I . . . will assure anyone who is uncertain about it that there is no drama, suspense, excitement, thrill or feeling of necessity in sport that can equal the countdown to an opening kickoff between two great teams or contenders for that elusive, cantankerous, agonizing, dreadful, and wonderful thing called number one."

Since 1969 when President Nixon proclaimed Texas number one and the wire services followed suit, Joe has publicly endorsed a college football play-off system. "Paterno has at least three reasons for wanting a play-off," Bill Lyon wryly observed. "His 1968 team, his 1969 team, and his 1973 team. Each went through the regular season without a loss, each won the Orange Bowl, and each could only look on forlornly while other schools were crowned mythical national champions." In 1978 a writer joked that Penn State would never secure a number-one ranking from biased southern and western coaches and writers until it defeated, on successive Saturdays, "Ohio State, Notre Dame, Oklahoma, Alabama, and the 82nd Airborne Division."

Throughout the sports world—all sports—champions have been determined on the field of play. Except one—college football. (Even the champions of lower divisions of college football have been decided on the football field). Joe's guiding principle has been his love of competition. He hasn't wanted someone *deciding* how good Penn State was. "If your team beats us, you're better than we are. But don't tell me—or have the president or anybody else tell me—you're better than we are and then not want to play us to prove it."

In any discussion of play-offs, coaches and athletic officials feared antagonizing the bowls, specifically the New Year's Day bowls. No one wanted to offend them because they paid exorbitant sums of money, had helped establish college football, and brought national exposure. Joe's solution was to incorporate the bowls into the play-off process by having the four semifinalists emerge from the winners of the four major bowls.

Players wouldn't lose time from classes because the play-offs would take place over Christmas vacation, he argued. In any case, few complained about the long college basketball and baseball seasons and both sports have play-offs. The earnings from the football play-offs could go into a special account earmarked for college athletic programs suffering from financial adversity. "We could make an out-and-out grant, say, to Evansville," Joe proposed, "where the whole basketball program was wiped out in that plane crash [which killed the entire team]. Or we could lend Bucknell $200,000 at 2 percent to rebuild their facilities."

By the late 1980s Joe was proposing that the small number of top-ranked teams that emerged as winners of bowl games, supplemented by a panel of coaches and sports journalists and computer calculations, could name four top contenders.[51]

Joe and a few other coaches have supported paying college players a monthly rate to perform. Before the NCAA tightened its rules, players used to receive about fifteen dollars a week. Joe has wanted to return to the practice and pay the modern athlete a modest stipend. He has encouraged his players to enter the mainstream of college life, but many haven't been able because they had no money for a movie or a hamburger. Consequently, they have often been embarrassed and humiliated. "I'm not worried about the kid who comes from the middle-class family. I'm talking about the poor kid who literally doesn't have a buck in his pocket. I am for giving the kids the equivalent of what we used to give them."

The NCAA rules systematically ensure that broke players stay broke. Said Joe, "We encourage whole universities to worship them as stars. Then we embarrass them so mercilessly, the weaker characters among them go out and break laws. I'm no softheaded excuse maker for kids who do wrong, but time and again I've seen good kids break under the money stress we put on them."

Athletic directors complained that paying athletes would add too much strain on the budget. But Joe dissented. "We do too many things where we don't take the kid—the football player—into consideration. . . . It's worse to be poor when everybody around you isn't poor."[52]

Joe played an active role in the College Football Association (CFA), formed by about sixty major football schools in 1976 to lobby on behalf of large football programs that felt outnumbered by smaller schools within the NCAA. The CFA threatened to secede from the NCAA, discussed the possibility of a football superconference, and considered establishing a separate television package. Joe was the first chairman of the CFA's coaches' committee from 1977 to 1984, and supported academic reform and higher standards. Charles Neinas, executive director of the CFA, cited Joe's "prestige, ability, and peer respect" as extremely vital to the success of the organization. Gene Corrigan, athletic director at Notre Dame, added that when Joe directed the coaches' meetings, "what came out of those meetings was very productive."

Joe's leadership in the CFA was instrumental in uniting Division I football coaches, improving academic standards for players, requiring players to meet the same academic standards for graduation as other students, reducing the recruiting calendar, and formulating stricter penalties against coaches who cheated.[53]

Joe has felt strongly about his players graduating. "To use a boy for four years and to let him not earn a degree is wrong," he often said. For years Joe exaggerated Penn State's graduation rate for football players, possibly to gain a recruiting advantage. Media accounts often used graduation rates as proof of the success of Joe's Grand Experiment. "More than 90 percent of his athletes eventually graduate," praised an article in the *Saturday Evening Post* in 1983. The 90 percent rate (which others also cited) was inflated, but Penn State did graduate its football players at an excellent rate.

Schools have determined graduation rates in different ways, making it difficult to make comparisons among institutions. In his doctoral dissertation, Dennis Booher computed the graduation rate for football players at Penn State at 86.6 percent for the years 1966–1979. "Despite differences in computing graduation rates," observed Booher, "the method used by Penn State seems reasonable . . . [and] the 'Grand Experiment' has been successful when compared to most major college football programs."

Of the forty-one Penn State players who were playing in the National Football League in 1982, the *New York Times* reported that thirty-eight had earned degrees. "Only Notre Dame has done better," said the report. In a respected survey conducted from 1981 through 1992 by the College Football Association of its members, Penn State tied for fourth (behind Notre Dame, Duke, and Virginia) for the number of years it graduated its football players at a rate of 70 percent or better.

Despite problems and limitations, there has been an overwhelming feeling that Joe Paterno was trying to do something eminently right at Penn State, and he has won widespread praise for his coaching, for the Grand Experiment, and for his reformist philosophy. "I think Joe represents what most people would like for college athletics," said Oklahoma coach Barry Switzer. "At a level of sport often muddied by unprincipled men," commented a sportswriter in the *Pittsburgh Press*, "Paterno has achieved glittering success while playing by the rules."[54]

~7~

PROFILE: PERSONALITY, VALUES, CRITICS

IN SOME WAYS JOE HAS LED A SIMPLE, QUIET, MODEST LIFE. HE HAS PREFERRED TO BE ALONE OR WITH HIS FAMILY, AWAY FROM THE PUBLIC EYE. Because of his lifestyle and because he has not been a drinker, carouser, or womanizer, he has not been portrayed in the tabloids. "From that standpoint," said professor Ron Smith of Penn State, "he is kind of dull and boring."

"As coaches go," wrote Jim Carlson in the *Centre Daily Times*, "[Joe] . . . isn't one of the more colorful."

For the most part Joe has been a creature of habit who established routines consistent with his life in football. Year after year he has conducted the same kinds of meetings and practices, walked the same sidelines, gone through the same rituals, held the same job at the same university, with the same wife, home, and values.

Besides fulfillment in his work, his needs have been elementary. "I believe in very simple things," he said. "I do not drive a big car, and I am not interested in having a big car. We have a nice house, but it is not really fancy." He loves his family, good music, reading, long walks, and stimulating conversations. "I am not very complex."[1]

In other ways, though, Joe has been mysterious and hard to categorize. He has displayed different moods and a multifaceted personality. Some people have had difficulty understanding him. "Every time I get a lead or think I have one, I find out it is wrong," said former linebacker Ron Hostetler, class of 1977. Jim Tarman said in 1983: "I have known him for twenty-five years, and yet I am not sure that I really know him yet." Joe has kept his own counsel, has been self-reliant, and hasn't sought a lot of advice. "Maybe because I make decisions and I do not explain them to people makes me [appear] complex," he said.[2]

Joe hasn't had many close friends. ("A lot of acquaintances," he said, "but very few friends.") He has not been an easy person to get to know well and hasn't taken enough time to cultivate friends. "No one . . . gets that close to him except his family," said Don Ferrell. "That's the way he wants it." "I have always been very secretive in my real feelings," Joe told Bill Lyon in 1983. One of Joe's confidants has been his brother George, who has managed nicely living within the shadow of his famous brother. George became head football coach and subsequently an athletic administrator at Kings Point, New York, and the television analyst for Penn State's football games. "I don't shine his shoes; in fact, we fight a lot," George said. "But I do look up to him, and not many brothers can say that."

Angelo and Florence Paterno profoundly influenced Joe. Angelo provided a model of hard work, determination, ethical behavior, and intelligence; from his mother, Joe inherited charm, ambition, aggressiveness, and a strong physical constitution. "Our mother's side was street-wise, charismatic," observed George Paterno. "On our father's side are a lot of lawyers and educators. Joe is a mixture of both."[3]

Early in his head-coaching career Joe sometimes directed biting remarks toward his assistant coaches. "He had a tremendously sarcastic sense of humor," said George Paterno, "which would make you want to crawl [into] a hole." If a receiver dropped a pass in the end zone, Joe would say sarcastically to the coach of receivers, "You did a good job there!" Later he mellowed and accepted less than perfection. "He [now] realizes that nobody is perfect," George said. "He puts up with more human error than he would tolerate when he was young—including his relationship with me."

Joe has never allowed angry confrontations to result in lasting bitterness. "We've had shouting matches you wouldn't believe," said Jim Tarman, "and I've come home in a blue funk and found out I had to be someplace that night with him, and I almost wouldn't go. And then I'd see him, and it was like nothing had ever happened."

Usually, Joe has kept his emotions under tight rein, remaining on an even keel, not allowing himself private celebration after a major victory. "I can't afford that to happen," he said. He has been fond of quoting Winston Churchill's remark: "Success is never final, failure is never fatal." He has tried not to be too elated over a victory or too depressed about a loss. "I look for the lesson in it," he said.[4]

Joe has liked being in control. "If he walks into a room, he wants to be able to control what's going to happen in that room," Ron Bracken observed. Joe was most responsible for hiring Jim Tarman as Penn State's athletic director, creating an awkward situation. Technically, Tarman was Joe's boss, but few believed that in a confrontation Tarman would prevail. Actually, they cooperated and discussed problems, reaching agreement on most issues by consensus. (Tarman denied the widespread belief that Joe actually ran the athletic program. "No," Tarman insisted. "[Joe] doesn't run the athletic department behind the scenes.")

Rigorously self-critical when things have gone wrong, Joe has repeatedly put the scourge on his own back. "Joe Paterno can flatten you with his honesty about himself," said a reporter for the *Washington Post*. Joe has talked about his weaknesses and mistakes. "One of the biggest sins is to imagine you have no faults," Joe said. "Worse is to do nothing about them."

Perhaps his attitude has been partly a method of deflecting criticism, but he seems sincere. After a disappointing 7-5 record in 1976, his worst record since his first season, Joe told a Philadelphia audience: "I think we had a mediocre football team because of the coaching. . . . To be quite frank with you, I got involved with making a lot of speeches where I could make some money. I have five kids, and I felt maybe I'd better make it. You don't realize it, but all of a sudden you're away from your squad. I didn't know my football team this past season, and I'm going back to learning a little bit more about the people we're coaching and maybe I can do a better job with them."[5]

He has been witty, articulate, and straightforward, saying what he thinks and believes. Being a highly successful coach has led reporters to his doorstep, giving him a forum for his views. Winning football games has given him power, and "I work it for all it's worth." Once he became successful, he hoped people would listen to him. "I've always been the kind of guy who wants things to go my way," he said.

"Joe is a zealot," George Paterno said. "He understands that to get people to listen to you, you have to have a position of power or you have to have notoriety. . . . He's preached about the hypocrisy of college athletics; he almost pontificates."

Joe has kidded people with friendly put-downs, endearing himself to others. "He is a tease," said David Gearhart, an administrative officer at Penn State. If Joe phoned Gearhart at 8:00 A.M. but Gearhart didn't show up for work until 8:10 A.M., Joe later said, "What are you doing? Sleeping in this morning?" Staff members kidded Gearhart that he had "arrived" because Joe Paterno teased him. "People he likes, he generally does tease," said Gearhart.

"He knows all about the ironies of life," writer Bernard Asbell said. "He's just a funny man." In public and in interviews Joe has usually been easygoing and charming, splashing his conversation with humorous asides and self-deprecating jokes.

He has had a flair for clever one-liners, delivered in his thick Brooklyn accent. Someone asked him how a defensive end named Lincoln Lippincott III had ended up at Penn State. "He was looking for Princeton and got lost," Joe responded. After the 1967 Gator Bowl, when Joe's dubious gamble failed on fourth and one, allowing Florida State to gain a tie after trailing by seventeen points, Joe was asked about the possibility of putting a dome over Penn State's Beaver Stadium. "Frankly, I'm against it," Joe answered. "I don't want to work in a place where they can hang things." At the 1969 Orange Bowl banquet, as Kansas coach Pepper Rodgers intoned a long opening monologue, Joe finally leaned over his microphone and interjected, "I would just like to say one thing to Pepper. Hello."[6]

In 1979 a reporter for the *Washington Post* followed Joe into a restaurant on campus and was struck by his nonchalance. He sounded like a Brooklyn Rocky:

> 'Hey, hiya, cap'n,' he says to a mailman at the door to the inn, cuffing him affectionately. 'How are ya? Been out to the Elks lately?'
>
> 'When are you going to sign that book, Joe?' scolds a matronly woman in the dining room.
>
> 'Well, when are ya going to bring it in, buddy?' he fires back, giving the lady a small hug, aware he has an audience. 'I mean, if you weren't out running around every night. . . .'
>
> 'Whatcha got here, chicken *cac-ci-a-tor-e*?' he says to the white-jacketed waiter at the buffet line, peering into a pot. 'Got anything for a diet?'

Joe has often been kind to players, ex-players, staff, and assistants. On the Friday before a home game, with Gregg Ducatte's wife pregnant and the team quartered in a motel out of town, Joe kept calling Ducatte's wife, inquiring about her condition, and then relayed the information to Ducatte. "He was concerned about her," Ducatte recalled. "He knew it was a difficult time."

"He is always there for you when you need him," said assistant coach Tom Bradley. "He is there for your family. He has done numerous things for my family without [my] asking him."

As the years have gone by, he has become increasingly more compassionate and sensitive about other people's problems. He has written many personal notes to friends and acquaintances who suffered some misfortune. Ernie Savignano had been an assistant football coach at Brown while Joe played, and when Savignano died, Joe wrote a personal note to his wife, Barbara: "I just heard about Ernie. What can I say? He was a wonderful person and I'm very sorry. I wish I could do something to help except to let you know how many share your grief."

It has not been unusual for him to leave a meeting to make calls for players. He has continued to open doors for players long after their careers at Penn State were over. In the early 1980s defensive tackle Greg Gattuso left Penn State, without having graduated, to play professional football. But when the Washington Redskins cut him, he was in deep trouble—with no job and no degree. His father urged him to ask Joe Paterno for help, but Gattuso was reluctant. Finally, he did call Joe, who helped him reenroll and provided him a job as a graduate assistant coach. "That was something really important for me," Gattuso said. "It made me understand that he really does care about his football players."

When former quarterback Chuck Burkhart returned to visit Penn State after a long absence, Joe greeted him warmly. While chatting with Burkhart, he grabbed a football and said to Burkhart's nine-year-old son, "This is one your father threw when he was here."

"When I see him, he's always interested in what *I'm* doing," marveled Marty Gresh, Joe's former teammate at Brown.

After Don Sheffield, an athletic department staff member, completed his Ph.D. and sought an important job in higher education, Joe provided assistance. "Tell me how I can help you to get where you want to go," Joe said to him. When Sheffield injured his foot, Joe phoned him at the hospital. "He . . . took the time to call me to see how I was doing," Sheffield reflected. "There was a genuine concern for me."[7]

Joe's approach to ordinary tasks has been practical and immediate. "I get up in the morning, and there's something to be done. It might be mowing the lawn, it might be working out a defensive play. I just go about getting it done." He has described himself as "a 'let's go out and get better' kind of guy." If faced with a challenge, "let's lick it."

For the most part, though, he hasn't been interested in the mundane or the commonplace. He has absolutely no interest in how mechanical things work or in fixing his car. He relates to courage, gallantry, sweeping battles, men looking into their very souls in moments of extreme duress. Kipling, Homer, Virgil, Napoleon, Churchill, General George Patton.

"I've always dreamed about doing difficult things," he said. He has been fond of quoting Robert Browning: "A man's reach should exceed his grasp, or what's a heaven for?" The coach must set lofty goals and make sure that his players aspire to the highest goals they can achieve.[8]

Because he has been a romantic and an idealist, who has seemed to joust at windmills, some have compared him to Don Quixote, the literary hero created by the great Spanish writer Cervantes, who was a selfless, idealistic reformer with sterling morality. (A statue of Don Quixote, a gift from Joe's classmates at Brooklyn Prep, stood on Joe's stereo at home.)

Like watching Errol Flynn and Douglas Fairbanks Jr. dueling and jousting in medieval courts in the dramatic movies he saw as a youngster, experiencing college football's game day, with its vast stadium, colors, precision bands, cheerleaders, and football warriors, has excited Joe. "In September we melt, but we joust," Joe wrote in his autobiography. "In December we can hardly grip the icy ball, but we joust. In rain, in snow, we suffer, they suffer, we're determined to win, they're determined to win, and the contest pursues its fate."

"He would have made a good general," commented Bill Lyon. Indeed, Joe loved the movie *Patton* (1969), and for several years after seeing the film, he often referred to it in conversation, comparing the qualities of General George Patton to the qualities needed in an excellent football coach. (Joe carefully disassociated himself, though, from some of the controversial ideas and actions of the World War II general.)

"Every football coach ought to see the movie *Patton*," Joe said. "He had the ability to rally people around a cause, to get them to make greater sacrifices than they thought were possible. He had the ability to get people to do things by the sheer power of his personality, by his drive and his inspirational qualities. In that respect, he was fantastic." An analogy could be made between General Patton and football coaches, Joe thought. "[Patton] said he always dreamed of leading a great army in a dangerous battle. I think all football coaches, on the day of a game, basically . . . think of themselves as leading their teams into great battle." The coach who didn't get excited ought to get out of the business and be something else, "maybe a stockbroker or an insurance salesman. He isn't much of a coach."

"Of course, with our society, with the way things are now, you never even think about war," Joe reflected in 1983. There was nothing romantic or heroic about the slaughter of modern warfare. It was repugnant. "War is a horror. But I think sometimes that sports is war's replacement. I know, for me, that was the magnet of athletics. The romance, the glamour, that was what attracted me. It still does."[9]

"What I like to do is fool people," Joe teased. Sometimes, as he has pranced up and down the sidelines and yelled, he has thought of himself as an actor. "Sure, sometimes it's an act, just to stir things up, to get my players emotionally charged up." Every football coach must be a bit of an actor. "Some of us do it a little better than others," he said.

Although idealistic, Joe is also realistic and pragmatic. "He's calculating, and he always has a plan," said Jim Tarman. George Paterno described his brother as a "Byzantine humanist," meaning that Joe used intrigue to accomplish humanistic goals. "In our world, to get the greater good [which we learned from the Jesuits], you have to make the right moves within the maze," George said. "[Joe] has a genius for that."

Joe has been intellectually curious and open-minded about books and educational experiences, but he has rigidly adhered to traditional values—hard work, discipline, fairness, sacrifice, commitment, loyalty, pride, and the pursuit of excellence. "He has certain things set in his mind," said his youngest child, Scott. He has strived to be the best and has been intensely competitive. "I just do not like being involved in anything unless it has a chance to be the best. I do not like to be around people who do not want to be the best. That includes the football team and the

Joe loved the movie Patton *and often said that some of General George Patton's qualities were the qualities needed in an excellent football coach, such as not being shy when it comes to getting a point across. This scene is from the 1998 Citrus Bowl, which the Nittany Lions lost to Florida, 21-6. (AP/Wide World Photo)*

university. We have limited our goals and how good we can be for a long time. I would like to be the number-one football team, the number-one university. I like to be good at everything we do."[10]

People have valued his loyalty. Despite plenty of financial incentives to leave Penn State, Joe has stayed for almost half a century. "I kind of like the idea of somebody who has spent his entire life at the same institution," said Bill Lyon.

Fundamentally, Joe is a "happy, positive person," Sue Paterno believes, but he has been exceptionally intense about his work. "If practice has been bad, it's usually not a very good dinner," Sue said. "But he'll yell and get out whatever's bothering him, and then he's fine." Some people have ulcers; others are carriers. "Joe is a carrier," said Sue. Jerry Sandusky quickly corrected those who thought Joe was usually calm and nonchalant. "He's an intense man, don't be naive. There are extreme demands." Half-jokingly, Sandusky said that Joe would not play golf because he didn't do it well. "That's the way he is," Sandusky said. "He has so much pride in everything he does." George Paterno's assessment of his brother has remained the same: "Joe's the most intensely competitive man I've ever known."[11]

Joe has worried about social problems as well as his football team. (He was a "born brooder," said a writer for *Sports Illustrated*.) "I worry about kids today," he said in 1986. "[When] I was a kid, you *never* heard about a kid committing suicide. The choices just weren't that hard. You had it all laid out in front of you. Your church told you what to do, and your parents told you what to do, and you knew what was right and wrong. But now kids have so many choices to make, so many people to listen to, no direction. Now you hear of kids committing suicide every day. It's very frustrating for me."[12]

Despite his brooding, Joe has taken disappointments in his work as a challenge. After a loss to arch rival Syracuse, he spent hundreds of hours studying Syracuse, planning for his rematch the following year. "I've always been a believer that if somebody beats you, that's fine, but there's always another day and you plan how it's not going to happen again. I've never been the kind of guy who felt sorry for himself when I got licked, no matter what it might be. A lot of times you deserve to get licked; it's your own fault."

Joe has thrived on adversity and has been strongest and most resolute when the situation was toughest, motivating those around him to overcome the difficulty. Aeneas, posting himself at the head of his bloody and broken army, raised his sword and rallied his troops. "The great leader and his men take on the enemy one-on-one, turn the day around, and win it," said Joe. "That kind of image excites me." When the opposing team has been leading, has had fewer injuries, or has had some other advantage, Joe has been concerned, but his worrying has spurred and stimulated him. "I feel most alive surrounded by other people's doubts," he observed, "when all around me it seems my forces are on the verge of collapse."

For him the best games have been hard-fought, well-played, hairline-close contests. Such games resemble tragedy in the theater.

"A tragedy usually ends with the stage strewn with bodies from both sides of a struggle, and you can't tell who won and who lost," he said. "Victory is contained within defeat, and defeat is contained within victory. That's the way it is in the best of games." What mattered most in sports was not victory but the magnificence of the struggle.[13]

Competition should be related to compassion. "The more you pit yourself against the other guy and he pits himself against you, the better you understand each other because you're both struggling for the same thing in the same way." However, it has been difficult for him to convince his players to be gracious losers. "I say to my kids, 'Play the game and respect the other guy.' If the other kid is no good, it's not enjoyable to play. I never want to play handball with somebody I can beat. It's hard to get kids to understand that."

Obsession with winning has grown out of confusion between the values of success and excellence. Success and excellence are not the same, and Joe has emphatically preferred excellence. "Excellence grows from within a person, is largely within that person's control and its meaning lasts," Joe wrote in an eloquent article for the New York Times in 1989. "Success is measured externally, by comparison against others, is often outside our control, and it is perishable."

He has repeatedly told his squad: "I hope the other side plays well. I hope they play to their limit, because if they don't, there's no fun beating them. We want opponents who make us play better than we think we can play."

He has not always understood the distinction between success and excellence. Reflecting on his early coaching career, he thought he had been too consumed with wanting to be successful. Headstrong and insecure, he had mistakenly charged down the wrong road. "The road was called Success," he said. "It was called Winning. It was called Don't Lose, No Matter What. I didn't yet know that there was a different route with different scenery called Excellence. And if I did know of that other road, I wasn't yet ready to appreciate its difference."

Of all places, the university should understand the difference between success and excellence and find meaning in losing. The university, Joe observed, "keeps alive the classical epics of Homer and Virgil, the trials of Odysseus and Achilles, heroes of battle who sometimes won and sometimes expanded the meaning of losing."

Joe has influenced those who work for him to strive for excellence as well. "During football season I just knew I was going to work seven days a week," reflected John Morris, former director of sports information. "I was going to be in there every Sunday as early as the coaches were . . . helping whatever way I could to keep that thing going."[14]

Joe has deplored the permissiveness of modern parents, the tolerance of sex before marriage, the unwillingness to enforce strict rules. Young people need rules. "If I have trouble getting the value of rules out of my system, maybe it's because I'm a man of a game. Without strict rules—strict rules—games can't be played."

Joe has endorsed traditional moral and family values. "He really thinks a woman should be home with the children because we both agree that a mother is probably the best teacher they will ever have," Sue Paterno said, adding, "I don't object to that value because I feel the same way." At a private meeting Joe expressed disgust for a coach on another team who had left his wife and was living with another woman. "He sure didn't like that sort of thing," said Dr. Harry Weller.[15]

Early in his career Joe stereotyped women and their attitude toward athletics. In 1971, while criticizing organized sports for youngsters under fourteen, he said that one problem with Little League was "too much of the woman involved in a boy's life." Women had a tendency not to appreciate the great joy in sports participation, even in the disappointment. "Women try to shield their kids from disappointment, to feel sorry for them when they lose. As a result, kids lose some of the joy that comes out of just playing a game."

He had difficulty adjusting to women in sports competition and underestimated the importance of discrimination in women's athletic programs and women's desire to compete. A major legislative controversy dominating education in the 1970s concerned Title IX of the Educational Amendments Act of 1972, banning discrimination on the basis of sex in education. The act required universities that received federal assistance to provide equality in their athletic and physical education programs. Shortly after the passage of Title IX, confusion reigned about the implications of the law and the future of women's athletic programs. It was clear, though, that universities needed to take some immediate action to meet the implementation deadline of July 21, 1978, or they might lose millions of dollars in federal financial assistance.

Discrimination against women in sports was pervasive. "There may be worse forms of prejudice in the United States, but there is no sharper example of discrimination today than that which operates against girls and women who take part in competitive sports, wish to take part, or might wish to if society did not scorn such endeavors," said an article in *Sports Illustrated* in 1973.[16]

At first Joe did not fully appreciate the problem. He favored various improvements in women's sports at Penn State but adamantly refused to endorse the most crucial improvement of all. He said he supported equal rights, equal facilities, quality coaching, and first-class travel, but he refused to support equal athletic scholarships. He and other male coaches in the American Football Coaches Association tried to testify before Congress against Title IX. (Some of the coaches testified, but Congress ran out of time to hear Joe's presentation.)

Understandably, Joe feared that proportional equality in aid to women athletes might cause financial ruin to universities like Penn State. "Any sport which makes money shouldn't be included," he insisted. "Football is the only sport at Penn State that brings in the money. We don't get any money from the state and we don't get any federal aid. If you chip away at the football program you cut into your revenue-making. And that means fewer facilities."

In 1975 about two hundred of Penn State's five hundred male athletes (40 percent) had scholarships, but only eighteen of two hundred female athletes (9 percent) had grants-in-aid. If the U.S. Department of Health, Education, and Welfare enforced literally the Title IX guidelines, Joe argued that the money for the new scholarships for women would have to be taken from men's teams in soccer, lacrosse, golf, and tennis. "You protect football," he said, "because football is the moneymaker." He worried that eventually there would be only two types of scholarships—for football and for women.[17]

In some ways Joe supported women's athletics at Penn State. When the university's women's basketball team was placed on probation in 1979, he was understanding and supportive. Sometimes, though, he patronized women. "I'm for everything Title IX wants to do for women in sports, *except* giving them an equal number or percentage of scholarships," he told the Football Writers Association of America in August 1975. "We [men] are so screwed up in scholarships that the women ought to be smart enough to avoid the same rat race."

"Joe Paterno really doesn't like to have women at all associated in any way with the football team," contended a Penn State faculty member, adding that Joe "almost has a tremendous fear of women." Joe reacted angrily to having a female athletic trainer for football. In the fall of 1981, Debra Alston, a varsity gymnast and athletic training major who had worked with a variety of sports, requested assignment to the football team. According to Alston, Joe resisted, but under pressure yielded, allowing her in the locker room, but not permitting her to travel with the team. When she did accompany the team to a game at the University of Pittsburgh in November 1981, she claimed that he became "very upset and yelled at the assistant coaches."

Caught in a dilemma between the need to allow equal access by the media and his distaste for having female reporters in the locker room, Joe barred *all* reporters from the locker room. All interviews with players would be conducted outside the locker room. Modesty was the issue. "It is a clear-cut moral issue as far as he's concerned," observed the *Centre Daily Times*'s Ron Bracken. "You don't want women in the locker room with naked guys."[18]

Slowly Joe changed his attitude about women in sports. He was shocked to see the competitive fire of Penn State's women's lacrosse team as they banged into opponents with sticks, and he admired the talented Penn State women's basketball team. "Women's sports have arrived," he said in his autobiography. "They give women another way of feeling good about themselves. They've made it no longer necessary for women to feel that they have to be the support of men's glory." He also apologized for his partiality against women. "I was condescending about women's new interest in competitive sports," he said. "I didn't believe women really understood what competition meant."[19]

Joe has absorbed some of his values from his Catholic upbringing. "Being raised Catholic," he said, citing one example, "we were told about making sacrifices." Sometimes he has spoken as if he possessed strong religious faith. "All of the decisions I've made in my life, personal and otherwise, have been based on my feelings that I had a responsibility not only to myself and my family but to my church and my faith," he said in 1987.

Before the children went to bed, Joe knelt down with them and prayed the Our Father and Hail Mary. "We all prayed together before we went to bed," said his son Jay. "He is not religious in the sense that he goes to church every week," said his son Scott, "but he has a very strong religious presence. [God] is important to him; God is a part of his life."

Periodically, Joe has had his players pray, but never for a victory. "I figure He's got better things to do," said Joe. "The idea of God taking my side in a football game embarrasses me." He praised Vatican II and Pope John XXIII for instituting ecumenism, urging Catholics to accept and respect other religions. ("A voice inside me yelled, 'For crying out loud, what have we been waiting for?' ")[20]

For the most part, though, Joe's practice of his religion declined after he graduated from high school, probably confirming his parents' fear that his Catholic faith would erode if he attended Brown University. Having grown up a very traditional Catholic, he found it difficult to relate to the church after the changes brought about by Vatican II. "It has been hard for me to accept some of the things said by more liberal people in the Catholic Church," he said in 1987.

He resented the changes in the Mass brought about by Vatican II, particularly the dropping of Latin. The meaning of the Mass had been taken away and an ancient, venerated ceremony abandoned. Furthermore, how could something be right one day but suddenly not right or not necessary the next—especially on matters related to eternity? "It's a rare day that I don't think about my obligation to God, but I wish the church hadn't changed the rules on me," he said.

Sue has been a devoted churchgoer and the children were raised Catholic, but Joe has attended Sunday Mass intermittently. "I go to Mass," he said, "but I am not there every Sunday." A major reason for missing Sunday Mass during the football season was the heavy workload of the coaching staff on Sunday morning.

In 1986 William Schreyer sponsored Joe for knighthood in the Order of Malta, a prestigious and elite Catholic layman's organization. (Schreyer himself was a member.) Nominees had to go through a screening process and be approved by the Vatican. Schreyer had done extensive preparation for Paterno's acceptance and only needed Joe's approval.

Joe was flattered by the offer but told Schreyer he needed time to think about it. On August 3, 1986, in an anguished handwritten letter, Joe rejected Schreyer's offer:

> This is a tough letter for me to write because of my deep appreciation of the time and effort you must have put into making it possible for me to be a candidate for Knighthood in the Order of Malta. But really, Bill, it would be wrong and probably hypocritical for me to attempt to be a member of the order. I could give you a lot of reasons for this, but suffice it for me to say I'm really not a good enough Catholic to seek such an honor. I believe in the Church, but I am an inconsistent participant. I try to contribute financially as generously as I can, but I do very little in the ways of corporal mercy. There are so many men in State College who are really soldiers of the Church that I'd have trouble looking them in the eye if I accepted this high honor. Without appearing to be eating "humble pie," I know where I am good and where lacking and I have never wanted to be a phony. To aspire to this honor is something I haven't earned, and I can't do it.

Schreyer was deeply impressed with Joe's thoughtful and humble response. "That's why Joe is such a good friend and why I hold him in such high regard."[21]

Overall, Joe has been known more as a moral man than a religious person.

Because Joe graduated with a degree in literature from an Ivy League university, loved literary quotations, listened to opera, rubbed elbows with a few professors at Penn State, earned tenure and full professorship, and was intellectually curious, sportswriters and others inflated his intelligence. Sharpening their skill at hyperbole, the media have often described him as a "serious intellectual," a "modern Renaissance man," who "inhaled" Kipling and Homer, "devoured" *The Iliad* and *The Odyssey*, and could speak intelligently on "any" subject. "Joe often can be found roaming the Penn State campus to seek out a professor for a bull session on the humanities," said an account in the book by Hyman and White. "Start preaching the winning-is-everything philosophy to Joe Paterno and he'll likely excuse himself and go sit in on some Penn State profes-sor's lecture on Greek mythology," wrote a reporter for the *Dallas Morn-ing News*. In *Sports Illustrated*, writer John Underwood suggested Joe possessed formidable intellect when he observed that Joe worked in his office at home "surrounded not by trophies or portraits of himself but by volumes of Homer, Descartes, and Thomas Aquinas."[22]

Actually, Joe isn't a genius or a modern Renaissance man, but he is intelligent, more intelligent than most—perhaps all—of his coaching peers. Most coaches are relentlessly single-minded and know little beyond the world of football. Joe has been an exception. "How many [coaches] write opinion pieces for the *New York Times* and throw in words like 'sophistry,' 'proselytizing' and 'mendacious'?" Rick Reilly pointed out in *Sports Illustrated*. "How many even read the *New York Times*?"

In his commencement address at Gettysburg College on June 3, 1979, Joe talked about Plutarch's *Lives*. "[Every] once in a while I go to the *Lives* again just to read about certain people who are heroes of mine." The *Lives* gave Joe insights into human nature, "on how to adjust to situa-tions, to understand what drives people, how people build organizations, how people allow organizations to collapse, how leaders lead people, how they motivate people. You read the *Lives* and you can understand what people mean by writing clearly and precisely, without redundancy, with-out wordiness."[23]

Some of his literary interests carried over from his high school and college education (Virgil, Robert Browning). On occasion he has attended meetings of the English department's literary club, listening, for example, to the analysis of twentieth-century authors by Hemingway expert Philip Young. Joe usually listens quietly and respectfully to experts like Young, absorbing information in the other person's area of expertise. ("Never argue with a man on his own ground," he said with a grin.) Once Joe addressed a faculty forum on the relationship between football coach-ing and the *Aeneid*. ("Just a little something that came up at the last coaches' convention," deadpanned Rick Reilly in *Sports Illustrated*.)

While working in his office at home, Joe has listened to Beethoven, Verdi, or Puccini. He and Sue have enjoyed attending the opera on campus and in Pittsburgh or Philadelphia. During a flight to San Francisco with Dean Robert Scannell, Joe talked about athletic department business one-quarter of the time; for the rest of the trip he conversed intelligently about politics, world affairs, wines, and New York City restaurants.[24]

Joe's reading list in the summer of 1987 included Gore Vidal's *Empire*, Virgil's *Aeneid*, Richard Nixon's *Leaders*—his copy a gift from Nixon himself—and Allan Bloom's *The Closing of the American Mind*. "Whenever I get together with him," said Fr. Thomas Bermingham, "he still is avid to talk about what I'm reading and what he should read. . . . He is a man of intellectual hunger."

At social outings Joe has preferred to discuss literature, politics, or international relations. "He didn't like to talk shop at all," observed an assistant coach. "He likes to debate," said John Coyle, "but he listens to what the other person has to say. . . . He doesn't get on a soapbox."

Sportswriter Ron Christ was amazed at the breadth of Joe's interests during the Friday night gatherings with reporters in the 1970s. "Here was a guy, on the eve of a big football game, and we'd be sitting there arguing about . . . Nixon, John F. Kennedy, an art exhibit on campus. . . . Almost none of it applied to football." Bill Lyon, who also attended the Friday sessions, had majored in literature in college and enjoyed discussions with Joe about Twain, Hemingway, Browning, and Shakespeare.

Joe does not have a good memory for details about his past unless it has something to do with football or his coaching. He has focused on the present and the future. "The past does not stick in his brain very well," said Bernard Asbell, who assisted Joe in writing his autobiography. However, "He'll remember remarkably the sequence of plays in a game twelve years ago." For the most part, Joe has applied his fine mind to his coaching. "Joe is mostly an idea man," Sue Paterno observed. "He has good instincts. He has an ability to see what lies ahead, what should be done."[25]

In the mid-1980s Joe received about seventy letters a day and several hundred speaking requests each year. Much in demand as a speaker at high school banquets, he has usually mesmerized his audience. "He is a tremendous speaker," said Dr. David Yukelson, sports psychologist at Penn State. "The [high school] kids are in awe because of the enthusiasm, inspiration, and magnetism that Coach Paterno gives off."

"Listening to Coach Paterno's talks gives me chills," added Yukelson. "He is so inspirational."

Drawn to Joe's uniqueness and reformist philosophy, the media have helped form Joe's public image. He has been the "saint in black cleats," said one reporter; "the conscience of college athletics and their most viable crusader," another intoned. "Admirers think of Paterno as a symbol for everything that college athletics should be and would be if their mentor had his way," Mark Johnson reported in the *Dallas Morning News*.

Rejecting $1.4 million to coach the New England Patriots in 1973 won him praise for standing by his principles. Six years later the normally sharp-edged CBS television show *60 Minutes* glorified Joe before the 1979 Sugar Bowl contest. The segment was so gushing it could have been used as a Penn State recruiting film. ("We only do shows like that on guys who die," said a CBS staff member.) Columnist Pete Axthelm of *Newsweek* observed sardonically, "It isn't easy to play a championship game when everyone insists on interrupting to tell you that you're perfect." In one segment viewers looked over the shoulders of Penn State's players as they studied—at their football lockers. "Watching the program," Axthelm teased, "a fan might have assumed that Paterno is coaching 125 walk-ons from the physics department, most of whom elected to play at Penn State in a narrow choice over Harvard and the Sorbonne."[26]

Conscious of his public image and aware that many people look up to him, Joe has tried to appear poised and self-confident, but this role has caused inner tension. "I don't always have [confidence]," he confessed to Bill Lyon in 1983. "I'm human. I have weaknesses, shortcomings; there are times when I am overcome with self-doubts, just like anyone else. Sometimes you just have to be an actor."

At times he has sought to flee his own legend. "Everybody thinks I'm obnoxious," he exclaimed in 1987. "I think I'm obnoxious. My wife thinks I'm obnoxious. Because we were successful, and because I shot my mouth off, we got this reputation."

Former players and others who have known Joe have repeatedly been asked if Joe's image reflected the real person. Is Joe Paterno real? Does he really believe in that Grand Experiment? Does he actually put life experiences before winning and losing football games? "[He] seems like he is too good to be true," observed Charlie Pittman. But Pittman reflected the attitude of most people who knew Joe when he answered resoundingly: "Yes, Joe Paterno really is real."[27]

In 1973, shortly after he rejected the offer from the New England Patriots, Joe attended a basketball game in the recreation building on the Penn State campus. During a lull he left his seat and started making his way to the men's room. A few fans noticed him and began clapping. Soon the whole section was standing and applauding. By the time he reached the exit, embarrassingly waving, seven thousand Nittany Lions fans had risen in tumultuous tribute to their football coach.

On other occasions Penn State fans have chanted, "I say JoPa, you say Terno; I say JoPa, you say Terno; JoPa! Terno! JoPa! Terno!"[28]

Because he has been exceptionally successful, held the limelight in the media, and been the "conscience" of college athletics, Joe has become a celebrity. A "funny thing happens when Joe starts to speak," wrote Rick Reilly in *Sports Illustrated*. "Two-hundred-eighty-pound linemen, college presidents, NCAA honchos, network biggies, and even your basic U.S. vice presidents cross-body block one another to get near him."

Fans have boldly rung the doorbell at Paterno's front door, seeking Joe's autograph on footballs, books, pictures, metal trays, golf balls. One man manufactured his own beer and wanted Joe to sign the label on the bottle. Usually, Joe hasn't been home, making it necessary for Sue to fend off the enthusiasts. Townspeople have stared when Joe walked by. He has been their place on the map, their intimate piece of fame and recognition.

While walking through an airport, Joe has barely been able to take a step as fans and autograph seekers swarm around him.

"Joe, can I have your autograph?"

"Hey Joe, we really believe in what you stand for."

"My kids, I tell them about you all the time."

"Hey Joe, you're wonderful." After one autograph seeker breaks the ice, others follow. "I hate to interrupt, but . . ." Some haven't had paper. "Do you have paper?" they have asked Joe.

Joe's renown has been a public relations bonanza for Penn State. William Schreyer observed: "Joe is the icon of Penn State. Wherever I've traveled in this country or even around the world, [I'll] mention Penn State and invariably someone will say, 'Yes. And that coach Paterno you got. What a great guy and what high standards he sets, the high academic success of the student-athlete.'"

"He is one of our icons," echoed David Gearhart, "someone who is bigger than life who has become larger than football itself."

Upon learning that Joe Paterno had arrived in Sun Valley, Idaho, to speak to a convention, reporters at a small Idaho newspaper were thrown into a tizzy:

Our government reporter, always more interested in a rapid kayaking stream than cracking a cold one in front of a football game, said, "Someone named Joe Paterno is talking to this convention up in Sun Valley tomorrow. Want anything on it?"

"Joe Paterno? Here?"

"The football coach?"

"From Penn State?"

Snapping away fast and furious, like wags in a postgame locker room, the comments were immediate. Everybody dropped projects. Cynical reporters left their chairs. Features waited. News stories were delayed. Suddenly, in the middle of summer, the newsroom was talking football.[29]

Two things have irritated Joe about his celebrity status. He has been nervous and afraid that people have judged him as too exemplary. "I don't want to be a phony. There are good things about me and there are bad things about me. I try to overcome the bad things." Fame also has interfered with his personal relations with his family. "[Fame] really deprived me of a lot of quality time with my kids," he reflected. "I really resented it when the kids were young." With his children now older, that problem with fame has diminished.[30]

Joe's statements and actions have sometimes contradicted, as if there were a conflict between his head and his heart. He has been most ambivalent about the nature of coaching and college football. Like his father, Joe wants the game to be fun. The authoritarian coach was obsolete, he preached. He quoted the Dutch historian Johan Huizinga's *Homo Ludens* (1938) that the imaginative faculty was encouraged by free play. Joe has encouraged his players to be free spirits—intellectual, inquiring, questioning, experimenting. However, in reality big-time college football has become hard work, serious, structured, disciplined, scientific, and efficient. This could murder the spirit. "He finds himself ambivalent," said Bill Lyon, "the philosopher at war with the coach. He wants to nurture the creative spirit, and yet at the same time he must do things that may crush it."

Was there a conflict? Joe was asked. "It is a conflict. It is very difficult to look at [college] football and say, 'Let's have some fun.'" In Joe's case, though, his work has been fun. "I enjoy my work." As for the players, Joe has contended, although practice has been difficult, it has been essential to prepare them expertly. Then, after the fun of Saturday's game and after they've risen to the challenge, "they feel good about themselves."[31]

"I hate to lose. God, I hate to lose," Joe said. "Ever since those kid days of stickball in Flatbush, of boxing my cousins in Coney Island, of my mother insisting, expecting, that I be the best, I have never learned how not to hate losing."

He continued: "Yes, I know, I preach a lot about being willing to lose, that there can be valor in losing to a better opponent. Yes, I know it seems contradictory, inconsistent, maybe even hypocritical. I'm sorry about that. The world is a more complicated and ambiguous place than I wish it were.

"I'll say it again: To win right, you cannot be afraid to lose. But God, I hate to lose."

The paradoxes have nagged at Joe. When asked about them, he has conceded their existence. "Sometimes, frankly, I find it hard to dissect my thoughts." After noting an inconsistency in his beliefs and feelings, Joe observed in his autobiography: "I didn't promise, when I started this story, to be consistent or to resolve contradictions."[32]

On April 19, 1983, Joe delivered a pep talk, but instead of X's and O's, the subject was politics and human needs. Instead of an audience of football coaches, his audience consisted of Governor Richard Thornburgh, state senators and representatives, and economists and business leaders attending a conference on Pennsylvania's economic future in Harrisburg. He spoke on improving education, economic change, and political malaise. "You owe it to the people of this state to get over political pettiness," he told them. "We've got to be a 'we' and 'us' people. Unless you take a team approach, nobody, nobody, will be able to say we're number one."

The legislators had to be prepared to make tough decisions. "The minute we elect a governor or a president, our two-party system sets out to embarrass him," he said. "In times like this, it's almost criminal to undermine our leaders."

Joe's speech reflected his consuming interest in politics and his fascination with the entire political process. Angelo Paterno had intensely admired Democrat Franklin D. Roosevelt, but Angelo's oldest son turned out to be a Republican. "If my dad knew that," said Joe, "he'd turn over in his grave."[33]

"We talk about [politics] a lot," said Sue Paterno, "our hopes and frustrations." Joe supported Republicans because of the GOP's emphasis on fiscal responsibility, traditional values, and opposition to federal welfare programs. On the other hand, he had a strong social conscience and worried about the inner city—the poor, the homeless, and the urban underclass. "Joe is a liberal person who has conservative values," observed George Paterno.

Another reason Joe became a registered Republican was because Republicans dominated in his congressional district and joining the GOP was the only way to have a meaningful vote in the primary election. "It was a politically expedient thing to do," he said. U.S. Congressman William F. Clinger Jr., who represented Joe's Republican district in central Pennsylvania, brought Joe into politics in the mid-1970s by taking him to a fund-raiser for Gerald Ford. (Joe was not married to the Republicans. He admired some Democrats, including New Jersey's senator Bill Bradley, New York's former governor Mario Cuomo, and John Kennedy.)

Joe disliked the approach Democrats took to solving poverty. "I became dubious of the way the Democrats were doing things, particularly in the inner cities, with welfare and the buying off of people." Joe has preferred programs that helped the poor help themselves. "For that reason," he said, "I started to get to where I was a little bit more conservative." Only a bit more conservative, though, because he categorized himself as a "liberal" Republican.[34]

Because of Joe's stature, prestige, name recognition, and interest in current events, some have speculated that he might run for U.S. senator, governor, or lieutenant governor in Pennsylvania. Many people have admired his coaching success, outspokenness, and values, and perceived him as honest, sincere, and charming. "One suspects [Joe] would be candidate Paterno with the proper amount of coaxing," said a sportswriter in 1969. "I can see Joe sitting in the governor's chair in Harrisburg," said a long-time admirer.

In 1974 Republican gubernatorial candidate Drew Lewis urged Joe to run with him for the position of lieutenant governor. Joe refused because he didn't want to give up coaching and didn't think he would be an effective officeholder. "I would have been a lousy lieutenant governor," he reflected. "All I would do is help [Lewis] get elected. If something happened to him, I wasn't prepared to be governor. . . . I don't have the [political] connections." (Lewis ended up losing to the Democratic incumbent, Milton Shapp.)

Actually, Joe would rather be a kingmaker than a king. Uninterested in being a candidate himself, he has preferred to assist someone he admired by making speeches, conducting research, organizing rallies, and directing strategy. "If a John Kennedy came along tomorrow and I could get involved with him, . . . I think I'd like to do that," Joe said in 1982.[35]

Meanwhile, except for a circulation problem in the veins behind Joe's left eye for which he underwent treatment, Joe's health has remained consistently excellent. He has exercised mainly by walking. With his black, slicked-back hair, he looks years younger than his actual age. "He is an intriguing mixture," observed Bill Lyon, "at times resembling a paternal uncle, at times something more vaguely sinister; he has never been accused of possessing a matinee idol's profile, but there is a sense of power there, a face that suggests a deep reservoir of strength."

Still, Joe has been the caricaturist's dream with his thick bifocals that tint in the sunlight and his large prominent nose. "It's an honest face," said an observer, adding frankly, "There's not much else it could be. It has a powerful, decent homeliness." Commentators have compared his facial profile to the hood ornament on a 1956 Plymouth and likened him to a CPA for an olive oil firm, a getaway driver for the mob, a New York detective, a Shakespearean researcher, and the saxophone player at an Italian wedding.[36]

"Paterno has the build of an old G.I. Joe doll, all detachable rickety parts," wrote a sportswriter in 1976. "His feet stand out, separate and overlarge, the way your feet would look with three pairs of rubbers on. Each lank shin indecently shows sock to the five-inch line. Paterno strides bowlegged: right knee and left knee have never been on speaking terms."

On the sideline Joe's wardrobe has looked nerdy—rolled-up slacks, white socks, and black gym shoes. *Sports Illustrated*'s Rick Reilly thought that Joe wore his pant legs like a person living "in continual fear of a flash flood."[37]

Joe's position as tenured professor has given him financial security, academic respectability, and has reinforced his belief in the beneficial coexistence of academics and athletics. He seldom has talked about his

Guess who. (Photo courtesy of Penn State Sports Information Department)

salary except to say that he made more money than he ever expected to. Although he earned more than a hundred thousand dollars from all sources in the mid-1980s, his income was barely in the top twenty among the nation's most highly paid coaches. He could have doubled or tripled his income easily if he had wanted to sell his name, as many coaches did. Joe received the same 75 percent tuition reduction for his children at Penn State as any secretary, maintenance worker, or faculty member at the university.

"How much money does a man need?" Joe said. "I have a nice home, money in the bank, everything I want. . . . I've never wanted to count money."

"He wouldn't know what to do with a great quantity of money," observed George Paterno. "He doesn't think you should have a great quantity of money. If you get above a certain amount, you should share it." Joe has contributed to various charities and has often made public appearances and speeches for free.[38]

Although Joe has been altruistic and uninterested in a better car, a bigger home, or luxurious vacations, he has worried about the financial security of his family. A few months after the victory over Miami in the

Fiesta Bowl, the credit card people came calling. They wanted Joe to join Ray Charles, Candice Bergen, Tip O'Neill, Wilt Chamberlain, and Willie Shoemaker in a series of print advertisements. "All they asked was that they take my picture and pay me for it," Joe said. "I thought it was pretty good. As ugly as I am, people pay me to take my picture."

The vice president of a booking agency thought Joe could command about seventy-five thousand dollars for a regional commercial in 1987. "[Paterno is] seen more as an educator and a real statesman of college football," said the official. "There's probably not another coach that leaps readily to mind."

"He is very, very cautious and reticent about what he does in the commercial field," said Ed Keating, who handled Joe's endorsements at Keating Management Agency in Cleveland. "He doesn't do anything during the season, first of all. I think more importantly, he only does a few, very high-quality endorsement arrangements." Joe has been cautious with his investments as well. A close friend thought that Joe made careful and thoughtful investment decisions. "He does intelligent things with his finances rather than get involved in harebrained schemes. He uses good common sense."

In 1987 Joe became testy when a reporter asked him why he appeared in a television commercial advertising the Yellow Pages. (Critics charged that Joe had gone commercial.) One reason, he replied, was because the Pennsylvania telephone company had donated a large sum of money to Penn State. But he also suggested that he needed the money. He would do more ads in the future, he said, because "some people out there resented the fact that I did the commercial and I don't think that they had any right to resent it. All right? I'm going to do them, and I'm going to do them for some money, okay? And, I don't care what [critics] think. To be very honest with you, I think there comes a time and place where I ought to be able to do something that I want to do if it means a couple of bucks for my family."[39]

Although Joe has earned mostly accolades for his coaching and his values, a few critics have accused him of being self-righteous, dictatorial, secretive, quick-tempered, and hypocritical. The Grand Experiment was merely a public relations ploy, some thought. Detractors have referred to him derisively as Saint Joe, the Evangelist, Goody Two-Shoes; they have charged that his squeaky-clean image has been more perception than reality; and they have contended that he has been fortunate that the remote location of State College has isolated his program from inquisitive reporters from large metropolitan newspapers.

The major irritant has been his air of righteousness. "If Sominex can't put you to sleep, Paterno will with one of his holier-than-thou speeches," commented ESPN college football analyst Beano Cook. Former sports publicist at the University of Pittsburgh, Cook thought Joe had changed from a fun-loving leader to a "classless bully," consumed with ambition. "If he doesn't get his way, he pouts and tries to bully things," Cook said. "Sometimes he's successful because Penn State has been successful." On one occasion, Cook charged, Joe complained publicly about the seats his wife, Sue, received for a game at Pittsburgh. "That was classless," said Cook. Cook thinks Joe practiced convenient morality. "When it is convenient to have principles, he has them. When it isn't convenient, then he doesn't have them."[40]

One of Joe's coaching rivals, who chose to remain anonymous, thought Joe pontificated. "If Paterno would only stop telling other colleges how to run their programs, professors how to teach, politicians how to solve the world's problems, reporters how to write, and artists how to paint, he could have more time to do the thing he does best—coach Penn State's football team."[41]

Critics have disliked the secrecy that surrounded the Penn State program—closed practices, not identifying the names of new recruits or injured players, not listing freshmen in the press guide. It has been difficult to get inside the program. Neil Rudel of the *Altoona Mirror* called Joe a "control freak."

When Jay Searcy returned from Knoxville, Tennessee, after interviewing Penn State's new recruit, Leroy Thompson, he received a phone call from Penn State's sports information director, apparently acting on orders from Joe. "You know how Coach Paterno feels about publicizing his recruits. He's upset. I'm calling to protest." The objecting phone call spurred Searcy to summarize publicly Joe's alleged dictatorial traits in the 1987 feature story the writer composed for the *Philadelphia Inquirer Magazine*. "Any other college coach would be bragging about signing an athlete of Leroy's abilities," Searcy wrote. "Not Paterno. It's an example of his attempt at total control. He has never allowed any of his five children to be interviewed, and two of them are grown and living independently.

To a degree, he controls what his players wear, how they speak and to whom, what they say, where they go, when they go to bed, whom they hang out with. He even assigns roommates. He forces the media to meet him on his terms. Practice sessions are closed. Player interviews are by permission only."[42]

Some of Joe's coaching peers have suggested that Joe's lofty image and the Grand Experiment were exaggerated. Said the prominent and respected Michigan coach Bo Schembechler, "Nobody is that good, and no program is that perfect." Critics also have thought that Joe seemed to play too many different roles to be authentic. Alternately he has been an actor, a preacher, a father figure, a shouting agitator, a Renaissance man. "Nobody can be all those things," said an observer. "So [cynics] call him a fraud. Pompous, they say. A hypocrite." Joe also has had to read critical comments in the newspaper from a few disgruntled former players who didn't like his drill-sergeant approach at practice or were not good enough players to crack the talent-rich Penn State lineup.

That the pervading image of Penn State has remained squeaky-clean may have stimulated envy. It seems people always have been looking for chinks in the Penn State armor. "Penn State was always coming off as the vestal virgin," Lyon observed, "while every other member of the NCAA was a harlot." Some have wearied of Joe's message. To them he has been talking less and preaching more. Lyon observed of the attitude of skeptics: "This man was saying that Penn State was doing it 'the right way.' By implication, that meant everyone else was doing it the wrong way."[43]

Some critics have thought that Joe was doing a good and ethical job as coach but that he was mired in the hypocrisy of all big-time college athletics. "The hypocrisy of amateurism is tolerated because of the importance of football to society," said Ron Smith, professor of sports history at Penn State. "Society wants it, maybe needs it."

A persistent gadfly critic, close to home, has been John Swinton, an instructor of hotel and restaurant management at Penn State. A fine writing stylist, a long-time advocate of players' rights, and a critic of intercollegiate revenue-producing sports, Swinton has tried to keep Joe's admirers from becoming too satisfied. For over two decades he has lambasted Joe, the football program at Penn State, and college football generally before audiences on the Penn State campus; at the Rotary Club in State College; during radio and television interviews;

and in scores of articles in Pennsylvania newspapers, plus the *Wall Street Journal* and the *New York Times*.

"I'm not criticizing Joe Paterno," insisted Swinton; "I'm criticizing his profession. He's the water lily in the cesspool." According to Swinton, the real Joe Paterno is not what Joe Paterno says he is or what the sports media say he is. Joe uses "underpaid, overworked, special-purpose students" to raise revenue for Penn State. Big-time college football has exploited athletes and taken the joy out of playing a game. "Paterno says football should be fun," Swinton argued; "yet he won't open practice to see if they're run in a humanitarian way. He says he graduates a lot of players, but I've challenged him and I haven't seen the statistics."

Despite substantial evidence to the contrary, Swinton contended that Penn State players were given preferential treatment in the classroom. Football players received "all kinds of breaks," he said; faculty members had been arm-twisted to provide better grades for football players.

The shallow sports media, said Swinton, have exaggerated Penn State's Grand Experiment which, in reality, was merely a public relations ploy to recruit athletes. The media also have exaggerated Joe's virtues. If Joe quoted Robert Browning, that made him a scholar. "If he sits down and listens to a Verdi opera on a record player, he is an intellectual. If he wins, he is good. If he talks about integrity, he has it. This is what the sporting press does." Joe isn't naive, said Swinton. "If he can gain integrity by discussing integrity, he'll discuss it."[44]

However, Swinton has often distorted Joe's statements, taken others out of context, and exaggerated Joe's weaknesses and mistakes. Penn State's players have not been victims of exploitation for doing something they willingly and eagerly wanted to do. The players have regarded it as an honor to have been offered a football scholarship by Penn State. "And any further enhancement of the university's reputation also enhances their reputation," argued a critic of Swinton. "Any money gained helps pay for their tuition, room, books, and board, as well as providing golf courses, tennis courts, swimming pools, and other recreational facilities, which are used by faculty, staff, students, and the general public."[45]

Never professing to be a saint, Joe has readily accepted much of the criticism. Despite the complaints by a few discontented players, the vast majority of former players have thought Joe treated them fairly, were not offended by his yelling, and deeply respected his coaching and his attempt to improve their lives.

To critics who have charged that he has driven his players too hard and caused them mental anguish on the practice field, and that this behavior and approach hasn't squared with his contention that he wanted his players to enjoy their entire college experience, Joe responded: "This is a tough game, and it requires discipline. If I feel someone is not performing up to his potential, I'll get after him. Isn't that what any good teacher would do? I regard [football] as an extension of the educational process. Just because it's outdoors doesn't mean it's recess. There are demands. The [players] know that when they come here."[46]

Joe has had justifiable reason to be upset with some of his critics. In November 1982, sportswriter Ray Didinger wrote a long, critical, and widely publicized five-part series about Joe in the *Philadelphia Daily News*. The series portrayed Joe as an "autocrat" who craved "power and control"; his defeat at the hands of Alabama in the 1979 Sugar Bowl exposed his weaknesses as an offensive strategist and tactician; black players complained of the alien atmosphere at Penn State. The series was dotted with unflattering references to Joe—"shrill tyrant," "egotist coach," "cold and aloof," "caustic and abusive." Didinger quoted Joe's rebuttals and praise from some admirers, but within the context of the hostile series their remarks seemed insipid.

Didinger's editors made the articles appear exceptionally hostile by sensationalizing the series, lifting the most inflammatory quotes, setting them up in bold-face type, and changing the title from Didinger's preference, "Paterno," to the more sinister "The Real Joe Paterno." Editors entitled one article "Joe Paterno, An Ogre on the Practice Field." (The editors at the *Daily News*, a street-corner newspaper, not home-delivered, wanted the series to catch the eye of commuters and promoted it heavily in radio advertisements.)

"It seemed to prejudice a lot of readers before they ever got into the story," Didinger later conceded of the sensational captions. "It was the one time since I've been with the *Daily News* that I thought something I had written was kind of misrepresented to the public and it caused quite a stir."

Didinger still insists his critical series was basically accurate: "The image of Joe as a kindly, fatherly figure that is beloved by his players is not really accurate. Most of the players I spoke to, even those who really liked him, admitted that he was a hard guy to talk to; that he was kind of off by himself; that he was aloof; and that he was a very, very stern taskmaster on the [practice] field."

When Joe learned about the series, he was indignant. "I don't think you're being fair with this," he told Didinger. "We believe we stand for a lot of good things." Subsequently, Didinger reflected, "It was pretty obvious that I was persona non grata [at Penn State]."[47]

Some coaches, while not critical of Joe, have believed his image was due partially to effective public relations. Other universities have been doing the same things as Penn State but with less publicity. "What they do is excellent, and they deserve the image," Oklahoma coach Barry Switzer said. "But there are other schools around [doing it]. Penn State simply has done a better public relations job. They go out and sell it. Joe is terrific at selling it."

Part of the problem between Joe and his critics have been different perceptions. What Joe has perceived as standing by the courage of his convictions, others have interpreted as stubbornness and self-righteousness. "You think you're sticking by your guns and other people think you feel you're above it all," Joe said. "Or that you're a pompous jackass."

"I don't like to put myself up as a do-gooder, but I am," said Joe. "We have an obligation to try to make these athletes better people. If a kid goes through here and can't read and write but can knock people down, is that good? We've got more of an obligation than that."[48]

Some of the criticism probably has stemmed from cynicism. George Paterno observed of his brother: "We need heroes, and then when we get someone who is, who has a good image, then right away we start taking shots at them. Maybe some people are jealous of Joe, maybe they resent his fame, maybe they'd like some for themselves. It seems that whenever you challenge the system, they want to undercut you." Joe has won without cheating and criticized those who did cheat. "That makes people uncomfortable," George said. "It makes them feel uneasy. Maybe even guilty."

Sue Paterno became upset when detractors charged Joe and Penn State with hypocrisy. "Why can't people accept things the way they are? We never said Penn State was perfect, but we work hard at doing what we think is right."

"I disagree with [the critics]," said Booker Brooks. "I think that the Grand Experiment worked and worked very well. If I were a head coach, I'd do it exactly the same way."[49]

Sportswriter Bill Lyon tried to put some of Joe's weaknesses in perspective. "I think there is some pettiness in him. I think there is a trace of hypocrisy in him. But that is true of all of us." Lyon discounted criticism of Joe from some of his media colleagues. "I think they have a blind spot where he is concerned."

"There's one thing you have to say about Joe Paterno," contended Ron Christ. "If there were more coaches like him, there would be a lot [fewer] schools on NCAA probation and a lot more players leaving college with degrees."

"He is an honorable man," insisted sportswriter Ralph Bernstein, "in that he practices what he preaches. . . . I always put aside those detractors because if they had anything they could find wrong with Penn State's program, you can bet . . . that Penn State would have been on probation by the NCAA a long time ago. Coaches won't hesitate to cut the next guy's throat if they think they can get an edge. And if they could find anything wrong in Paterno's program . . . at Penn State then [Penn State] would be with the Oklahomas, and the Southern Methodists, and the Houstons and the other schools who are all on probation. But you don't find that at Penn State."

"One of the things that has appealed to me about him is that he is the least exploitative person in that profession that I have ever encountered," said Bill Lyon. "I have a very harsh yardstick by which I measure a coach. And that yardstick is: Would I turn my sons over to this man for four years? And in the case of Joe Paterno, I could say yes without qualification."[50]

~8~

PROFILE: PUBLIC SERVICE, FAMILY, LEISURE

THROUGHOUT HIS HEAD-COACHING CAREER AT PENN STATE, JOE HAS DEDICATED HIMSELF TO NUMEROUS CIVIC EVENTS AND CHARITIES. Over a three-year period in the early 1970s, he helped raise money for the Boy Scouts by speaking at Scout-sponsored events, served a one-year term as state chairman of the American Cancer Society, worked on the national sports committee of the Multiple Sclerosis Foundation, and was appointed to Pennsylvania's Citizens' Committee on Basic Education.

Over the years he has assisted local community projects as well. After a press conference, he hustled to a meeting of transportation experts studying expanding roads leading into State College. "Imagine Woody Hayes interrupting his football preparation to talk about streets," commented a reporter.[1]

Most of his efforts, though, have gone toward improving the quality of Penn State. "It sounds corny, I guess, but I have a dream," he said in 1971. "I'd like to see Penn State number one in everything." Later he conceded that at the time the university was "more-or-less [an] ordinary state university." Using his energy, determination, and prestige, Joe became one of Penn State's greatest fund-raisers, trying to transform the ordinary university into an excellent one.

During the 1970s Penn State had struggled to maintain an income adequate to its needs. Inflation and a gradually declining Pennsylvania economy lessened the ability and the will of state government to support higher education and placed Penn State in precarious financial position. A survey by the *Chronicle of Higher Education* in 1978 reported that Pennsylvania ranked forty-fourth among all states in per capita spending on higher education. The *Chronicle* also reported that Penn State's endowment ($11.3 million) ranked only 103rd among America's colleges and universities. The Harrisburg *Patriot-News* stated on March 20, 1977, "Penn State is in deep economic trouble—not the type that will force it to close its doors tomorrow but a problem that, should it continue, would doom the university to mediocrity."[2]

Joe's speech to the university's board of trustees in January 1983 helped stimulate fund-raising at Penn State. His call for fresh ideas and money for endowed chairs and libraries galvanized the university into a fund-raising mode. "I had met a lot of people over the years who said they would be willing to help us become a great university, whether by making a gift or in some other way, if only they were asked," he recalled. "But they had never been asked. We as a university were relying too much on state appropriations and tuition. We had asked alumni to give but not in a big way."

In 1984 during a speech to hundreds of university officials, faculty, students, and Pennsylvania governor Dick Thornburgh, Joe focused on the need to raise scholarship funds to attract the very best students. Scholarships gave students the chance to be "good people, sound citizens, and good leaders." The world needed people with enough courage to be different. "Martin Luther King Jr. was different; Bobby Kennedy was different; Anwar Sadat was different. Our only hope is in our young people and we have to prepare our young people."[3]

Joe and Sue have focused much of their efforts on improving Penn State's libraries. In 1977 the Pennsylvania Library Association had recruited Joe for public service announcements. On the radio Joe proclaimed: "I'm a K-N-O-W-body. That's why I join the K-N-O-W people at the library."

Before Joe made calls on others for a donation to a library fund, he and Sue followed the traditional rule for all fund-raisers: They made a major gift of $170,000 to expand the university's library collection. The gift started the Paterno Libraries Endowment, whose principal reached $3.5 million by 1995. "I knew when I got involved in the campaign that Sue and I would be asked to make a serious financial commitment," Joe explained. "You can't ask others to give when you aren't willing to give." Joe also pledged his 6 percent royalties from sales of stand-up Joes, the life-size cutouts of himself.

Why focus on the library? Joe's efforts grew out of his long-time love of books and his belief that the library was the heart of a university. "Professors can come and go but if you have great books for the people who want to do research . . . the library is essentially a university all by itself."

The Paternos' contributions to the library served as a magnet, capturing the attention of potential donors. Nancy Cline, dean of university libraries, thought people wanted to honor Joe. "Many people want to give a gift to Penn State that signifies their loyalty to the coach, their [admiration] for him and what he has stood for."[4]

Even more important has been Joe's assistance to the first significant fund-raising drive in Penn State's history. Both Joe and Sue served on the National Development Council, the university's major volunteer fund-raising advisory board. In 1984 the National Development Council started the Campaign for Penn State, a six-year plan to raise $200 million mainly for endowed chairs and scholarships. The drive was designed to put Penn State on the fast track to becoming a premier public university. Dr. Bryce Jordan, the new university president, selected William Schreyer to be chairman of the campaign. Schreyer, a Penn State graduate and head of Merrill Lynch, made it his first priority to name Joe as vice chairman of the fund-raising effort.

Joe jumped at the opportunity. "I didn't feel I was obligated to do it," he said. "It was something I wanted to do." Jordan credited the bold challenge Joe laid before the trustees in his 1983 speech for helping to stimulate the campaign. "The fund-raising campaign was just a gleam in the eyes of some people when Joe addressed the trustees," said Jordan. "I think his conviction helped make it a reality. . . . There isn't a football coach in the country who could do for a school in fund-raising what a Joe Paterno can for us. That's largely because he has always supported the academic side of this university strongly."

Joe has written hundreds of letters and made scores of phone calls. In Kansas City, Saint Louis, Denver, Phoenix, Los Angeles, San Francisco, and Florida, as well as stops throughout Pennsylvania, Joe has used his persuasive powers with the alumni. "I was with him during one twelve-day swing, and by the ninth, tenth day I had had it; I was ready to go home," said Dave Gearhart, Penn State's vice president for development and university relations. "But Joe was still going strong."

In the winter of 1987, Joe was delivering nearly a speech a week for Penn State fund-raising events. "All of a sudden we're looking at ourselves as a university and we're finding out we're pretty darn good," he gushed. "And we have a chance to be great! And I've gotten caught up in that." After calling on a wealthy Pennsylvania banker, Joe returned to his office and proudly announced, "That's another million."[5]

While enthusiastically touting the academic improvement of the university, he occasionally has exaggerated both its academic quality and its national ranking among universities. "Penn State has become one of the finest educational institutions in the country," he declared in 1990, and was "definitely among the top ten universities . . . in all respects." (Prominent national surveys consistently showed that Penn State was improving but did not indicate it was near the top ten among universities.)

Joe hasn't been content to be a figurehead; he has wanted to be an integral part of the fund-raising projects. "We knew he wouldn't be comfortable in an honorary role, and our donors appreciated his hands-on approach," said Gearhart. "That's one of the big reasons he performed so ably as a vice chair." "Joe's the sizzle on the steak that's making the difference in this campaign," Schreyer said. With the six-year campaign only three years old, Jordan and Schreyer announced an expanded goal of $300 million and the campaign eventually raised $352 million.

With the conclusion of the Campaign for Penn State, Joe indicated that he would like to continue fund-raising. "We felt that we had to be sensitive to demands on his time and to involve him only in new projects that he was comfortable with," said Gearhart.[6]

Joe's next project was to help raise over $20 million for a new athletic arena that the university could also use for academic and entertainment events. The 16,500-seat facility, named in honor of Bryce Jordan, who retired in 1990, would replace an outmoded structure. Again Joe used his visibility and wide circle of contacts to good advantage during the eighteen-month drive. The campaign ultimately raised $22.5 million, which was matched by a $33.8 million state appropriation. The Bryce Jordan Center opened in January 1996.

Joe researched the potential donor he was about to approach, learning about the donor's background and previous contributions to the university. "He knows who the potential donor is before [he visits]," said

Schreyer. He was not reluctant to ask for large donations. At times he even jumped ahead of others who felt the prospect needed more warming up.

In soliciting a potential benefactor Joe was energetic and straightforward:

> I'm here because I believe in Penn State and I know if we're going to be the best we can be, and if we're going to move up to the top ranks of the great public research universities, we are going to have to do it through private support. We are not going to be able to rely on the legislature . . . [or] tuition dollars. We've got to go out and get it ourselves.
>
> If you look around the country and look at those institutions, both public and private, that are the best institutions in this country, the way they got there was through private philanthropy.
>
> Penn State has got to do the same thing. I'm here today to ask you to help us. We need your help. I'm committed to it. I've already made my commitment to this particular campaign, and I'm here to ask you if you'll make yours.

Then Joe would turn the meeting over to Gearhart, who explained a specific project—a scholarship fund, an endowed chair, or the convocation center. Generally, Joe made the final sales pitch. "We've got you down, Jim, for a million-dollar gift, and I hope you can do that."

Joe's renown allowed easy access to offices in downtown Philadelphia and Pittsburgh. "Because Joe had become an icon, whatever he says people hang on his every word," said Gearhart.[7]

At meetings Joe pushed the National Development Council in the same way he has pushed his football team. Strive to do better than you think you can. "Generally, Joe is for pushing the goal up as high as we can," said Gearhart. He ended up being a cheerleader, rallying the troops. Joe told fellow members, "If we want to compete academically in the Big Ten, if we want to be one of the best national public universities, . . . we've got to have the resources to do it." On another occasion he exclaimed, "Come on! We can raise that goal!"

Joe's optimism has created problems for the development office and for other members of the National Development Council. "Joe can be tough . . . and difficult," Gearhart said. "He can push the goal up so high that it could be unrealistic. Sometimes we have to say, 'Well, Joe, let's start off at this level and then we'll move up higher.'"

"There isn't any [fund-raising] goal he doesn't believe we can achieve or exceed," observed Schreyer. Was Joe being realistic? "Being chairman of the campaign," Schreyer commented wryly, "I thought sometimes he was unrealistic." Although Joe argued with the staff and other members of the National Development Council, he loyally accepted the final decision. "Once the decision is made," said Schreyer, "and he buys into it, then he is right on board, and he will do whatever he is asked to do."[8]

Sue Paterno also has been an integral part of the fund-raising efforts. Besides serving on the National Development Council, she has been a member and, for a while, the chair of the Libraries Development Advisory Board. ("When they get him," Sue said, "they get me for free.") About six times a year, after every home football game, Sue and Joe have hosted a dinner at their home for benefactors and other friends of the university—as many as fifty people. Sue has issued all the invitations, cooked the entire meal, and hosted the cocktail party that preceded the dinner. (The Paternos have paid for the dinner and the drinks themselves.) Following the game Joe has showered, then has arrived about forty-five minutes into the festivities and visited all the tables. "It is a very prized invitation," Gearhart said. "It is absolutely incredible." The dinner has not been officially billed as a fund-raiser and no one has asked for money, but because of the warm feelings of the guests, the event later turned into philanthropy for Penn State. (At the conclusion of the dinner at the Paternos', Joe has risen and said humorously, "There is no free lunch, but I'm not going to make you pay tonight." Everybody has laughed. "But one of these days we are going to come get you.")

Nancy Cline observed that by welcoming people into her home and adding her personal touch, "Sue makes our donors feel very special and very important. The informal set of connections she's made for the libraries and the university have immense value for development efforts."

Sue has listened carefully at meetings of the National Development Council and studied newspaper accounts of benefactors and potential benefactors. "Interestingly," Gearhart observed, "I'll notice how she will kind of monitor what we're doing. If someone announces a big gift, even if

I don't prompt her, the next year [the benefactor] will show up at one of the dinners simply because she's read the announcement in the paper."[9]

The fund-raising effort that most reflected the interest of Joe and Sue was the campaign to raise money to construct a new addition to the library on the University Park Campus. In the fall of 1992, university president Joab Thomas selected Joe to head the effort, initially setting a goal of $5 million. The addition was desperately needed. "The number of library patrons had increased fourfold (to 1.5 million annually) over the previous twenty years," observed Michael Bezilla. "The collections were steadily growing, but the library itself had not grown physically since 1972." University officials knew that state funding for the library expansion was unlikely unless Penn State could show a major private commitment to the project. Fund-raising for the library was difficult because, unlike colleges, libraries do not have alumni to target for donations. No one knew for sure how strongly alumni, faculty, staff, and students would respond.

Again, Joe and Sue led by example, pledging $250,000 to the project. "I have made some investments and had some things that have come to me as a result of being a football coach—shoe contracts and things like that," Joe said after the donation. "I felt it was only fair that I do my share."

Joe Paterno was an "absolutely perfect choice" to head the Campaign for the Library, said Thomas. "We enjoyed the best of both worlds in the campaign," he observed. "People who might not have had an affinity for the library responded generously because they liked and respected Coach Paterno personally. Other benefactors responded because he had the credentials to be a convincing spokesperson for a project that was at the academic core of the university."

Joe met with the library's faculty and staff, urging all of them to donate, and faculty/staff participation in the Campaign for the Library was nearly 100 percent. Although the original goal was $5 million, Joe insisted that it be raised to $10 million. "Those of us who work at fund-raising as a part of our jobs took a deep breath," said Nancy Cline. "A lot of us felt we ought to start off a little slower, and not try to go for such a big goal," said Gearhart. Joe refused to back down. "If you want me to lead this, we're going to go after $10 million!" Gearhart and others disagreed. "We had just finished a major campaign," said Gearhart, "a

$23 million campaign [for the Bryce Jordan Center], and there was a little donor fatigue among some of our donors. We were a little worried that we may not be able to go out and quickly raise this money." But Joe was adamant. "You've asked me to do this, and I'm going to do it, but we are going to do it this way. Here's the goal I want to achieve."

The library fund-raising effort more than accomplished Joe's optimistic goal. The eighteen-month campaign raised $13.75 million from private gifts; the state kicked in $14.8 million. Construction on the five-story addition began in April 1997.[10]

Joe has had difficulty squeezing in the time for fund-raising, but the staff of the development office has done most of the preliminary work. He confessed that "maybe I've overcommitted myself in other areas—I have a tough time saying no to people for worthy causes," but quickly added that development work for Penn State was never a problem. "I didn't hesitate, and still don't hesitate, to say no to requests from Dave Gearhart or others if the football schedule demands my time."

The development office has tried not to bother Joe from July through November, his busiest coaching period. Spring has been the best time to use his services. Once, in 1995, Joe took time off from his coaching on the Friday afternoon before a Saturday home game to sit through three hours of a fund-raising meeting. In December 1995, as Joe prepared his team for the Rose Bowl, a prominent benefactor requested that Joe speak at a chamber of commerce dinner in Wilkes-Barre on December 15. Gearhart didn't think Joe could make the commitment but asked him anyway. "That is an awful time," Joe responded. "But for this gentleman, because he has been so generous to the university, I'll do it."[11]

Ed Hintz, one-time president of the National Development Council, speculated about a subtle intangible benefit the fund-raising efforts had on Joe: "He felt at the end of the campaign as if he truly belonged with the people who were also raising money, who were CEOs of Bell Companies and big, big companies. And I guess in a sense, emotionally, he may have felt that he was just a football coach. And even though these people would have given their right arm to spend a lot of time with him, and enjoy his company, I don't think that he really felt their equal until the campaign was completed."[12]

Assessing his own career as a fund-raiser for Penn State, Joe sees his most lasting contribution as that of popularizer. "If I had an important role in development, it was in helping to change the whole mentality of giving. The whole idea of participation has changed at Penn State over the last ten years or so. More and more people are feeling an obligation to give, even if it's just a hundred dollars or so."

Sue Paterno didn't think Joe's brother George understood the depth of affection and loyalty the couple had for Penn State. "Why are you killing yourself?" George asked late one night after the Paternos had hosted a fund-raising event in their home. "Why do you do all these things?" Sue told him: "George, it is because we are committed to the university. We want to leave it in the best possible shape we can."

The National Development Council's next major campaign venture is to raise between $750 million and $1 billion in seven years. Joe talked eagerly about the upcoming challenge. "This next campaign should be our defining moment as a university. It should enable us to take our place among the elite universities of this nation."

To honor the Paternos' service to the university, in July 1994, Penn State's board of trustees named the new library addition the Paterno Library. "Sue and Joe Paterno are legendary at this institution," explained Joab Thomas. "This new library will stand as an appropriate tribute to all that they have done for Penn State." When Joe learned of the honor, said Sue Paterno, "he was stunned and in a state of shock. It was overwhelming."

In 1998 the Paternos made their largest donation to Penn State: $3.5 million toward new teaching positions, scholarships, a new interfaith spiritual center, and a sports hall of fame. "It just seemed like I ought to give it back," Joe said.[13]

"We get little information on the private life of Joe Paterno," observed sportswriter Ron Christ. "His private life is very private." Besides being intensely private, Joe has budgeted only a small amount of time for his family and his leisure. Sue and the children have had to withstand the hectic September-to-November regular season, usually a postseason bowl game, followed by the recruiting season, spring practice, the Blue-White scrimmage, planning sessions, preseason drills, and

Joe and Sue Paterno weren't the only Penn State folks smiling on this occasion. The Paternos share a laugh and a lot of their assets at a January 1998 press conference, when they announce their $3.5 million gift to the university. (AP/Wide World Photo)

then the September kickoff again. When a reporter asked Sue about the problems of being the wife of a college football coach, she answered candidly: "You are a single parent. I don't know any way around that."[14]

Bright and humorous, Sue Paterno is Joe's partner, best friend, and confidant. A full-time mother, jill-of-all-trades, and a proverbial hostess, she has sewn, cooked, managed the household and children, and entertained the parents of recruits, friends, and potential donors to the university. Preparing a dinner party for forty, Sue spent two days cooking manicotti and lasagna. "Joe and I think if you're going to have someone to your home, it should be *your home*," she said. She has tutored players in English. (Several times Joe accepted a new recruit only with the stipulation that he accept tutoring from Sue.) She has also suffered from severe back problems for which she has had major surgery four times.

"I call her Saint Sue," said George Paterno, referring to Sue's exceptional dedication to her husband, children, and Penn State. "She should get a lot of credit for [Joe's] success." Bernard Asbell observed: "She is the most striking combination of old-fashioned devoted wife who makes the way for the accomplishful husband, . . . and at the same time has an absolutely strong sense of independence that [Joe] respects. There is nothing demure about her. She speaks her mind openly and quite freely." She has spoken openly and freely with her husband. If Joe has complained about a bad day, Sue has set him straight. "She is the balance in his life," said Scott Paterno.[15]

Joe always has spoken affectionately and gratefully about Sue, telling reporters that she was strong, intelligent, a good mother, and his closest friend. "I will always treat women well," observed Scott Paterno, "because my father treated my mother like she walked on water. He has never raised his voice at her in front of me. (I don't think he did in private either.) He was never disrespectful toward my mother."

The Paternos' first child, Diana Lynn, was born in 1963, followed in 1965 by Mary Kathryn, David in 1966, Joseph Junior ("Jay") in 1968, and George ("Scott") in 1972. They have spoken affectionately and gratefully about their mother as well. "My mother has been more of a part of my life than my father has," said David. "My mother . . . is the family. She has worked at our family even harder than my father has worked at his job. She has put her family ahead of herself so many times."

"Not to take anything away from my father," agreed Jay, "but my mother did most of the work raising us as we were growing up. She was there for us all the time, and she was there for my father all the time."

Sue listened to the children's complaints, provided the most motivation, and celebrated achievement. When the children needed discipline, she was the primary disciplinarian. Only when a problem became serious did Joe sit down and talk about it. "Until it became a real serious problem, where my dad needed to intervene, my mom could handle it," said Jay.

For many years Joe walked home after practice. "It was very important for Joe to walk home when the kids were young," Sue said, "so he could clear his head before he came in the door." The pressure of Joe's work sometimes affected the family. "You have to be good tonight," Sue carefully instructed the children. "It's a big game this week. Don't fight at dinner tonight."

Joe felt guilty not giving more attention to his children. He could vividly remember former players and details about football games a decade earlier, but he had trouble remembering his children's birth dates. Sometimes when he was with the children, his mind wandered. "When they were young, I used to take them out to the swing," he recalled, "but even though I was talking to them, I wasn't really there. I was never able to give my all to them."

"He is really concerned that he is not spending enough time with his family," observed Jim Tarman in 1982, "that his kids are growing up and he really doesn't know them."

"I've gotta be a father first," Joe told a reporter in 1982. "If I'm a failure as a husband and father, then nothing else is important."[16]

On Christmas Day, Joe spent a few hours with the family opening presents and eating dinner. But even on this major holiday, he slipped away to his den to work, rejoining the family again later. "Work was always on his mind," said David, who added it didn't bother him that his father worked so much. "No. Not at all. I admire how hard he works."

Diana said she didn't feel cheated either. "It would have been nice if he could have gone to more sporting events, or PTA meetings, or open-house nights at school, but I never felt that I missed out on anything because I knew how much he cared about us."

Joe's preoccupation with work seemed to have the most unsettling effect on Scott Paterno. "It was very difficult," he said. "My father and I did have some problems [and still have problems] because he was not around a lot when I was a child." The time they did spend together was enjoyable and special, but, Scott added, "I would have liked to have spent more time with him when I was growing up." Still, Scott enjoyed the fruits of his father's success—trips to bowl games, visiting the White House, and meeting President Bush. "I have the highest amount of respect for my father," Scott concluded, "because he has never wavered from what he believed."

When Joe wasn't working, his family appreciated that he didn't spend his meager free time bowling, golfing, or drinking beer with friends. He was usually home with his family. "He had very little time for us," said Mary Kay, "but whatever free time he had he did spend with his family." The Paternos took family vacations to Disney World, Williamsburg, Washington, D.C., Philadelphia, Boston, California, and usually spent two weeks at their home on the New Jersey shore.

When the children were young, Joe played board games (Monopoly and checkers) and wrestled with them. While playing Monster, he stomped, snorted, and prowled through the basement looking for his children in hiding. He also enjoyed reading to his children. "His quality time with them was reading to them," observed Sue. Not wanting his children to read "trash," he encouraged them to read excellent books.

Because Sue and the children wanted to eat with Joe in the evening, if he returned home at 8:00 P.M., the family ate at 8:00 P.M. The evening's dinner table was a time for each child to converse. "Everyone got to contribute," said David. As the children grew older, animated discussions of politics, literature, and current events dominated after-dinner conversation. The arguments stimulated both Scott and Jay. "You had to defend what you said," Scott observed. "It taught me how to think critically."

"It always strikes me how much knowledge that my parents have," Jay added.[17]

Being a celebrity coach has carried a price—loss of family privacy. Beginning in about 1968 Joe realized that he would have serious difficulty relating to his own children in public, that his fame would prevent him from doing many things that a father ordinarily did. He had become the victim of too many photos and sports stories. "One day, I realized I couldn't show my face without attracting a crowd," he recalled. "My kids had to push and shove just to get near me. Some days, they felt like they'd lost their father." When he took the family to an amusement park in Hershey, Pennsylvania, autograph hounds and well-wishers suddenly surrounded him. Little Jay Paterno pouted to his mother, "We brought Daddy. They didn't." Joe sent the family off to enjoy the rides and the chocolate treats, while he slipped through the parking lot and hid in the car for the rest of the day, playing with X's and O's on a yellow pad. "It would get to the point where it wasn't worth taking Dad anywhere," David recalled.[18]

Activities other families took for granted, the Paterno family couldn't do. They seldom dined out in State College because hordes of autograph seekers would ruin the event. Twice Joe tried to sneak into Jay's State College High School football games, but so much attention was focused on him that he left. "He never made it through the whole game," said Jay. Scott was a hockey player, Mary Kay a gymnast, and Diana a cheerleader, but Joe seldom watched their events either, because autograph seekers would mob him. "It was tough on him because he wanted to [attend]," Scott said. "It was also tough on us because he couldn't."

Once a group of students ran across the Paternos' lawn, stood on the porch, and had themselves photographed next to a Joe Paterno cardboard look-alike. Sue Paterno wanted to shout at them, "This isn't a circus!" Unhappy about the way people treated Joe and the family, she mused, "You're no longer a person. You're a thing. . . . What people don't see is that we're private people." Sue continued: "People gawking interferes with our privacy. They're not very subtle, and it makes Joe uncomfortable."

Joe and Sue scrupulously tried to keep the children out of the public eye, insisting that they take pride in their own identities and achievements. Joe didn't allow a photo of his family to appear in the football program. The Paternos had steadfast rules for the media—no photographs or interviews with the children. "They shouldn't have their picture in the paper because their dad is the coach," Sue insisted. "If they have their pictures in the paper, it should be for something they've done."

When a sportswriter inquired about doing a story on Jay while he was a freshman quarterback at Penn State, Joe intervened and turned down the request. "I don't want my family involved in interviews," he insisted. "I don't want my family involved in my business. My personal life is my personal life and I don't want you probing."[19]

Still, Joe's celebrity status complicated the life of the children. While in college at Penn State, Mary Kay quietly wondered if a young man was asking her for a date mainly because her father was a famous coach. "You start to doubt yourself," she reflected.

When Jay played on the high school football team in State College, he observed that some of the parents of players interfered with and disagreed with the head coach. Consequently, players then echoed their parents' complaints, damaging team morale. But Joe wouldn't undermine the coach to assist his own son. His advice to Jay was to listen to the coach. "Do whatever the coach tells you."

In the late 1980s Jay was a backup quarterback on the Penn State team, and playing for the Nittany Lions brought him and his father closer together. When Jay was younger, his father hadn't had time for Little League or Boy Scouts. Penn State's football fortunes, though, were something both could share. After every home game the pair walked home from the stadium together, sharing their thoughts. "I was always glad to walk home with him," Jay recalled, "especially after a tough loss, because he and I had just been through it together. It made me happy to know that maybe my company on the walk home helped cheer him up if we lost."[20]

After graduation from college, Jay followed his father into the college coaching profession. After stints as an assistant at Virginia, Connecticut, and James Madison, he joined the Penn State staff in February 1995. He and his father have exchanged game tapes and watched football films together. "I think he gets a real kick out of the fact that I'm so involved in what he does and really like it so much," Jay said. "I think he's proud."

"There was never a feeling of discontinuity within the family," Scott observed. "There was always a certain order to things." Joe and Sue insisted that their children be clean-cut and well mannered, honest and moral, disciplined and dedicated, self-reliant and self-effacing. Lying and swearing were major offenses in the Paterno household. "If you ever wanted to get in big trouble, all you had to do was lie and get caught," said Mary Kay. No one was allowed to swear or tell a dirty joke. "The word f-a-r-t was not even said around my father," David said. ("You don't need that in your vocabulary," Joe advised the offender.) The Paterno children had to be punctual and must not attend underaged beer parties or R-rated movies. "My parents . . . were both pretty strict," said Mary Kay.

On trips to bowl games, the girls had to dress up and each boy wore a coat and tie. Scott was never allowed to grow his hair long or wear ripped jeans or trashy T-shirts, because his father thought such fashion trends looked "scummy." "I usually wore button-downs," Scott said, and jeans that were "nice and clean." The children were seldom allowed to watch television, especially during the school year. If they were not doing homework, they were expected to be outside playing.

Although strict, Joe and Sue were usually reasonable. If Diana called from a party and said she wanted to stay a little later and had a solid explanation to back up her request, the permission was granted. "If you violated that trust," observed Diana, "and they found out you were lying, then you had to regain that trust."

Education was the key to the future. Working taught self-reliance and responsibility. Joe insisted his children work to help pay their way through college. "If I were very rich, I'd still expect them to work and earn through their college years. It's an essential part of their education," he said.[21]

Both parents encouraged the children to live up to their potential, to be risk takers and leaders. It was better to do the right thing than to be popular. If you believed strongly in something, be committed to it, Joe taught. Don't change your mind. "Don't go with the flow." When Mary Kay wanted a new pair of shoes, Joe asked why the shoes were important. "Everyone else has them," she said. That was the wrong response, resulting in the rejection of her request. "You don't have to have them because everyone else has them," Joe declared. "Be different. Don't be so concerned with what everyone else is doing."

He encouraged his children to strive for excellence in everything they did. "You had to have a certain air about you," said Scott. "You had to strive to do better. Otherwise, you weren't trying. He stressed that throughout my life." Sometimes Joe's personal example was enough to motivate his children. "A lot of the things I learned from my father, he didn't come out and say," Scott observed.

After David received a mediocre report card from school, Joe asked, "If you tell me you did the best you could, then I'm happy with what you got. Is this the best you could do?" David knew it wasn't the best he could do, that he could have worked harder. Then Joe encouraged him to rededicate himself to his academic work. If David made a serious mistake, Joe advised, "It's happened. Everybody makes a mistake. . . . A lot of people will judge your character by how you handle it, what you do about it. Do you do the responsible thing?"

Unlike David, young Jay Paterno tried to convince his father that a B-plus *was* as good as he could do.

"But, Dad, I really worked hard," Jay said.

"Now, wait a minute," Joe responded. "I've seen you in your room drawing up football plays or playing video games. I know full well you didn't dedicate as much time as you could."

Then Joe lectured Jay about the need for commitment: "There are two things that will always follow you in your life: one is your reputation and the other is your transcript." Jay concluded that he couldn't fool his father. "He knew full well I could have gotten an A-minus."

"Material possessions have not been important to either him or my mother," Mary Kay observed. "What is important is you, not what you have." The Paternos didn't need a new car every year; the house didn't need frequent redecorating.

Because of his traditional view of the family, Joe's two daughters teased him about being a male chauvinist. "He has never really been chauvinist," commented Mary Kay. "He has always been open to anyone who can work hard or prove themselves." He encouraged his daughters to pursue careers.

"He's been a great father," Mary Kay concluded at age twenty-seven, especially in terms of teaching values. "I still have those values that he's given me and not everyone has been that fortunate." Diana wrote Joe a letter during her first year at college, thanking her father for imparting values to her. "When he read it, [Joe] cried," said Sue.

Like many football players who labored under Joe's tutelage, Jay agreed, "The older we get, the smarter he looks. . . . He tries to instill in you the values of hard work, ethics, morality, discipline—things that pay off for you when you're forty-five years old and you have a family. . . . He is not [just] preparing you to win football games. He is preparing you to become productive people and the right kind of people.

"Coming from me, his own son, it may sound boastful or less than modest when I am talking about my own dad, but I am really speaking about him now as an ex-player and not as my own father. And I am quoting what other players have told me. That, in and of itself, will be the reason he will probably be a timeless figure in college coaching."

Several close observers thought Joe and Sue had succeeded in raising fine children. "They are the most unassuming, self-effacing kids you've ever met," said George Paterno. Overall, Joe did not focus on his role as father because he was too preoccupied with his work. He was fatherly, though, in a different sense, regarding his football team as a large, extended family. "Some days I feel like I've got a hundred sons to worry about," he said. "If any squad member gets into a jam, it's like my own kid getting into a jam."[22]

"Leisure? He doesn't have any leisure!" laughed assistant coach Tom Bradley. "That doesn't exist." Outside of his work and family, Joe hasn't had many diversions. He never took up bridge, golf, tennis, fishing, hunting, or bowling. He is not mechanically inclined. "He couldn't fix the car if he had a manual," said Scott. Joe's lifestyle hasn't left time for much recreation. He has preferred using his free time doing something for the university, such as fund-raising. "For me to be out playing golf is a waste of time when I could be out doing something constructive."

Although State College was quite an adjustment from Brooklyn, Joe came to enjoy the slower pace of life and particularly the academic atmosphere. "I can go to an Elizabethan festival or a Milton festival, or a great lecture," he said in 1982. For over two decades during the football season, all the coaches and their wives went out to dinner on Thursday evening at the Tavern in State College. "Great times," said former assistant coach Jim Weaver.

Sue and Joe took several trips to Europe. In 1974 they went to Italy; ten years later they toured England and France. Then in May 1994, they took a two-week vacation in Germany and Austria. "The best part was we were alone with each other," Sue said.

One of Joe's favorite pastimes has been a long walk alone. In the woods north of his home on McKee Street, he has walked about four days a week, about five miles each time. He has looked at houses and thought about his wife and children, financial matters, politics, Penn State University, and, of course, football plays and problems with specific players. He has taken a pencil and paper with him. On walks, "I get some of my better ideas."[23]

In the mid-1980s the Paternos purchased a vacation home on the South New Jersey shore, where they spent several weeks each year, renting it out much of the rest of the year. There Joe rose early, walked the empty beach, and returned to read and listen to music. If he felt like working on plays, he worked on plays. Then, about 5:00 P.M., when the beach was empty again, he took another walk. The second home was a place where he could hide away. Only certain people who needed to talk to him could get in touch with him.

Joe has seemed perfectly happy and content with his simple lifestyle. He has enjoyed his work, and he has liked the way he spent his leisure. "It isn't as if I'm forcing myself to do something I don't like." (He has "worked" during his "leisure" because he has enjoyed looking at football films or fiddling with plays.) He debunked his brother George's suggestion that he take time to "smell the roses," which Joe likened to nostalgia. "Nostalgia is nothing but a form of melancholia as far as I'm concerned," Joe said. "I'm not interested in nostalgia. I want to get *on* with something!"

"We have a lot of things we want to do," Sue said. "We would like to travel. We enjoy each other. We both enjoy reading. We both enjoy sitting on the beach. . . . We like a lot of the same things."

"People don't understand the kind of lifestyle we have," said Joe. "When we are home, [Sue] will watch television and sew. I will do some football or read. We are perfectly content doing that."[24]

～9～

RECENT YEARS

THE YEARS HAVE RUN TOGETHER, BUT EACH SEASON HAS REMAINED A FRESH CHALLENGE FOR JOE. "I think this is going to be a fun year," he said about the 1987 season. "You get a bunch of kids for x number of years, then they go and now you've got a new group to work with." It was an endless cycle, and he loved it.

Joe has been head coach during the administrations of three athletic directors and four Penn State presidents. The dimensions of the ball had changed, the width of the uprights had been reduced, and scholarship numbers had shrunk, but Joe was still coaching.

In recent years elaborate athletic facilities had sprouted at Penn State, providing new football locker rooms, training facilities, a mirror-lined weight area, and an academic support center. An indoor practice facility—cavernous Holuba Hall—was so massive that players and coaches sometimes practiced golf in it. The Greenberg Indoor Sports Complex housed the coaches' offices, meeting and film rooms, lounge, and the Penn State Football Hall of Fame.

Coaching used to be much simpler. In 1966 the staff worked out of one room in Recreation Hall, assisted by one secretary. Serving the needs of the coaches three decades later was a battery of secretaries, computers, videotapes of future opponents, and a satellite dish to tape games. Piles of mail, pictures to sign, public relations, and scores of media interviews all consumed Joe's time.

During thirty years of change, Joe has enjoyed remarkable success and staying power, flourishing in the 1960s, 1970s, 1980s, and the 1990s. "That takes some incredible flexibility and adaptability and a great deal of foresight, patience, and political savvy," said former assistant coach Craig Cirbus.[1]

In 1966 Beaver Stadium had a seating capacity of 46,284; after several expansions, in 1995 the stadium accommodated 93,967, becoming the second-largest campus stadium in the country and third-largest overall. Only the Rose Bowl (104,091) and Michigan Stadium (101,701) served larger audiences.

Penn State's success on the field and its huge stadium translated into substantial leverage. When Syracuse balked at playing two games in Beaver Stadium in exchange for one in the Carrier Dome, Penn State broke off a sixty-eight-game relationship. The financial benefit of the extra home contest, worth $1.5 million in gross income, was more valuable than tradition, but the decision riled fans and the media, who supported continuation of the long-standing rivalry.

When Penn State defeated Bowling Green, 45-19, on September 5, 1987, Joe entered a fraternity that has admitted only eight other Division I-A college football coaches. The victory was his two-hundredth as skipper of the Nittany Lions. "Sure it has a lot of meaning to me," Joe told a crowded media room following the game. "But I just don't have time to sit back. I'd like to see us get 201." When the season ended, Joe's victory total stood at 207, his team having finished with an 8-4 record.[2]

The 1988 season, though, was disappointing and—worse— unprecedented. As Penn State headed for its nationally televised final game against undefeated Notre Dame, it seemed most important that the contest would determine whether Penn State had a winning season (6-5) or its first losing season (5-6) in fifty years and the first in Joe's coaching career.

It didn't bother him that a loss would end Penn State's nonlosing streak, Joe kept stating. "To me, 6-5 isn't any different than 5-6. I haven't thought about the [nonlosing] streak before and I'm not thinking about it now. The streak was going to be broken somewhere down the line."

Notre Dame won, 21-3, and subsequently Joe admitted that the prospect of a losing season had, indeed, bothered him. "I kept saying to writers, to callers on my weekly radio show, to TV interviewers, that the losing-season prospect was an overblown issue. . . . [Only] Sue knows that late at night in the privacy of my own kitchen, the prospect of a losing season irritated the hell out of me."[3]

Paterno's teams have consistently won much more than they lost, as evidenced by this plaque given Paterno in 1987 and acknowledging his 200 victories, achieved in only 21-plus seasons. (AP/Wide World Photo)

Usually, the weeks before Christmas had been a bustling time for fans and players as Penn State prepared for a year-end bowl game. But in 1988 the Lions stayed home, licking their wounds. Penn State was clearly in a down cycle again, the lowest point since the late-season collapse in 1984.

Predictably, some fans and pundits criticized Joe for his first losing season. They thought Joe needed everything from a new offensive coordinator to a new offense. "The Lions played without much confidence, with little or no leadership and without much of the character that has been a hallmark of Paterno teams," Ron Christ said in the *Patriot-News.* "While Paterno teams have always made the majority of key offensive and defensive plays, this one didn't," Neil Rudel contended. "While Paterno teams have always specialized in excellent special teams, this one could not field kickoffs consistently well, had no punt-return game, and provided an adventure every time it lined up to attempt a field goal." Paterno teams usually dominated teams physically, but his 1988 team was often manhandled up front.

Several obvious factors explained the bleak season—inexperience, key injuries, bad luck. Exaggerating his own responsibility, Joe thought his outside commitments prevented him from devoting enough time to his assistants and players. He left too many coaching meetings with problems still unresolved, hadn't followed through on details, and sometimes confused his assistants. "I think that [inattention] probably filtered down to the football team. . . . I deserved the kind of season we had."[4]

In 1989 Random House published Joe's autobiography, *Paterno: By the Book.* Co-authored by Penn State English professor Bernard Asbell, who had earlier written books about politics and government, the book described Joe's childhood in Brooklyn and his formative years at Brooklyn Prep and Brown, bringing his story up to the end of the 1988 season. Joe commented on his family, fame, race relations, and presented his thoughts on management, loyalty, teamwork, motivation, discipline, practice, recruiting, and football reforms.

The book contained few shocking revelations or deep, dark secrets. The most controversial portions expressed displeasure with the media for bringing a negative tone to sports reporting, criticized players on his 1988 team for bullying athletes from other sports, and included his admission that his losing season in 1988 bothered him tremendously. The closest the book came to scathing commentary about contemporaries was Joe's revelation that his dislike of Jackie Sherrill stemmed partly from an incident in 1978. When both Joe and Sherrill were recruiting the same high school player, friction developed. Sherrill angrily phoned Joe's home and, according to Sue Paterno, called Joe a derogatory name and threatened to injure him. Sue added that Sherrill also called her several names before hanging up.

One reason Joe wrote the book was to clarify misconceptions. His deified reputation was making him squirm. He wasn't comfortable with the unrealistic image people had of him. "People were writing 'Joe, you're so great.'" he said. "Half of the time, I don't even know what I'm doing. People say we graduate everybody. We don't. All our kids are not great kids. Our program has problems and jerks, just like everybody else's."

The reviewer for the *New York Times Book Review* described Joe as the nation's "most-revered college football coach" and found the book "refreshing." Joe was "sentimental, sanctimonious, and old-fashioned, but he is no phony." Joe told an interviewer that the book was "as honest as I can make it." Then he paused, his conscience tugging. "When you talk about yourself, I don't know if you're ever completely honest."[5]

The philosophy of the Grand Experiment still permeated the football program at Penn State, but Joe had stopped using the label because it had struck some people over the years as holier-than-thou. He didn't want to appear overbearing and pompous; he thought his zealousness may have offended. "I felt I've alienated some people. After a while, people get tired of me preaching," he said. "There are people trying to do it the right way plenty of other places, and I never meant to imply there weren't."

"People are always looking for chinks in the Paterno armor, the Penn State armor," said Jim Tarman. "Maybe it's envy, maybe it's resentment, maybe it's just human nature. In all frankness, we have probably brought on a lot of it ourselves, by our attitude. You should never say you're perfect, and we're not."

Although downplaying the Grand Experiment motto, Joe has continued to implement its philosophy. He refused to take five players—

three of them regulars—to the Fiesta Bowl in 1991 because of their sub-par academic performances. The players were eligible to play according to NCAA regulations but did not live up to Joe's academic regulations. He wanted to send a message that no one was indispensable. "I feel bad about it, but it was drastic action I had to take," he said. "Yes, they are eligible, but they have got to understand that academics come first regardless of what year they are in or what aspirations they have for pro football."[6]

In early April 1987, Joe and Sue attended a White House dinner in honor of French prime minister Jacques Chirac. Joe talked with President Ronald Reagan—"The president had me at his own table," Joe gushed to a reporter. Thrilled by the invitation, he told Julie Nixon Eisenhower, "It's hard for me to believe I'm here, in the White House, sitting under a picture of Abraham Lincoln, having dinner with the president of the United States—me, a football coach."

After a few initial forays into state and local elections, appearing on behalf of various candidates, Joe cut back his involvement to avoid partisan state and local races. But national politics was another matter.

Joe struck up a friendship with George Bush when he supported Bush over Reagan in the Pennsylvania primary in 1980. Eight years later Joe became an early supporter of Vice President Bush's presidential bid, trekking to New Hampshire to boost Bush's campaign, which had faltered after a poor showing in the Iowa caucuses.[7]

As the 1988 Republican National Convention approached, Bush asked Joe to give one of the seconding speeches for his nomination at the convention in New Orleans on August 17, 1988, and Joe agreed. The *Philadelphia Inquirer* thought Bush selected Joe because Penn State's coach "stands above politics" and was "a leading advocate of the pursuit of excellence through honest sweat and teamwork."

Pennsylvania Democrats and Republicans sharply disagreed on the wisdom of Joe's speaking to the GOP convention. House majority leader James Manderino (Democrat, Westmoreland) objected to his decision. "I think he represents Penn State and Penn State is a state-aided university. I think he should have used better judgment." Democratic governor Robert Casey agreed, stating that the head coach at a university subsidized by state funds could threaten the funding by engaging in partisan politics.

Joe's defenders countered that he was speaking as a private citizen, enjoyed the same constitutional rights as any other citizen, and that Democrats were just envious. "Joe Paterno speaks for himself," said Republican Robert C. Jubelirer, the state senate president pro tem. "Joe Paterno says what he means and means what he says, and nobody is going to muzzle Joe Paterno." The Bill of Rights also applied to "football coaches," continued Jubelirer. "I'm sure if the shoe was on the other foot the Democrats would welcome the chance to have an individual with the popularity, the charisma, and the credibility of Joe Paterno." To endorse Bush was Joe's "right," editorialized the *Philadelphia Inquirer*. "The university will survive any resulting discomfort, so long as Mr. Paterno keeps inspiring young athletes and winning football games." Joe scoffed at the criticism: "Being a football coach doesn't make me a noncitizen."

Some wondered if Joe intended to abandon coaching after the 1988 election to enter politics. "If Bush wins the presidential sweepstakes, will Paterno become a member of the Bush team?" speculated Ron Christ. "Maybe secretary of defense, ambassador to Italy, or chairman of the Republican Party?" If Joe gave a spellbinding speech, others speculated, Pennsylvania Republicans could find themselves with a ready-made candidate for governor in 1992. But Joe dismissed suggestions that his speech might serve as a springboard into the political arena and again reiterated that he had no political aspirations.

Some experts doubted that Joe's speech for Bush would have *any* effect. "Joe Paterno can't hurt you," said a political consultant. "But I can't imagine there are too many people in the state who are going to go into the voting booth and vote for George Bush because Joe Paterno is for him."[8]

Republican senator John Heinz chaired Pennsylvania's delegation to the Republican convention, but Joe was its star. At a news conference in New Orleans, Joe said he doubted he could do much else for Bush during the fall campaign because of the demands of the football season. But he wasn't in New Orleans to give a "lukewarm endorsement. . . . I think [Bush] is a great man." He wanted to appear on national television to endorse Bush because "It is a vehicle for a private citizen to have an impact in a political campaign. I want to have an impact on something I think is important. My dad always had a feeling that he owed something to this country, that he wanted to give something back."

Joe's two-minute nominating speech turned out to be mundane. He said, "A lot of you are wondering what an Italian-American football coach from Brooklyn is doing here. So am I. But after forty years of trying to help young men and women reach their potential as human beings, I'm here as an educator." He compared Bush's "quiet, dignified confidence" to that of New York Yankees great Joe DiMaggio and retired Chicago Bears running back Walter Payton. Recalling the spirited defense of Bush from former president Gerald Ford earlier in the week, Joe shouted, "I'll be damned if I'll sit still while people who can't carry George Bush's shoes ridicule him."[9]

During Bush's four-year presidency, Joe was a "little disappointed" that Bush hadn't been a stronger leader on some problems. "I always thought Bush was going to be a more liberal Republican," he said. Particularly bothersome was the failure of the nation to focus on the problems of the inner cities, "a massive group of people who are not contributing to this society in any way, [who] have absolutely no hope." The problems of the inner cities were a "cancer that we are not addressing. I don't know the answer, but it seems to me we have not directed enough energy to [solving the problems]."

Still, Joe endorsed President Bush's reelection bid. On Wednesday, September 23, 1992, Bush made a stop at Penn State during his campaign against Bill Clinton. The Bush campaign selected Joe to introduce the president at a large rally scheduled on campus. "He's a person I've enjoyed being around and [whom] I admire very, very much," Joe said the day before Bush's arrival. "I consider it an honor to introduce the president of the United States."

About twenty thousand people filled the Old Main Lawn and lined sidewalks to listen to Bush's twenty-minute speech. While Joe stood at the podium waiting to start his introduction, the crowd chanted, "Joepa, Joepa, Joepa."

"Number one," Joe began, "I think it's absolutely phenomenal the president would come here for our Beat Maryland rally." (Penn State played Maryland the following Saturday.) Joe then linked Bush with traditional values. "[Let's] not speak of poorer days ahead, but of sterner, and more disciplined days, . . . days of individual responsibility, for our own good, our family's good, and our own people's good." Joe challenged listeners to get involved in the political process. "If you don't vote, don't

gripe." (One comment Joe made while introducing Bush had some people scratching their heads. "The impact George Bush has had on history
will not be understood for generations to come," he said. A wag in the
press commented, "They better understand by November 3 or there'll
be trouble.")

Bush also held a brief, closed meeting with the football team in
the squad room. After Joe's flattering introduction, Bush said, "Discount
about 90 percent of what Joe said." Interrupting, Joe snapped, "They do
that anyway." Joe seemed bemused that President Bush would take an
interest in a college football coach. "On the other hand," Joe said imp-
ishly, "I think, 'Isn't it marvelous that the president of the United States
is interested in what I'm doing?'"

In 1994 various candidates asked for Joe's assistance, but he
refused to grant his public support. "He has to have a strong conviction
about the particular individual," said Sue Paterno. However, Joe did
attend a few functions for Republican senatorial candidate Rick Santorium, who subsequently defeated incumbent Pennsylvania senator Harris
Wofford. After the Republican victory in the congressional elections in
1994, the new Speaker of the House, Newt Gingrich, telephoned Joe asking his advice about how to handle freshmen Republicans who were often
more qualified for leadership than senior Republicans.

In midsummer 1997, after a plot to topple him as Speaker, Gingrich again phoned Joe for advice. "I'm clearly not doing a good job of
explaining to my assistant coaches what I'm going to do," Gingrich
recalled telling Paterno. The coach's response: "Slow down, listen, focus."

From Harry Truman to Bill Clinton, Paterno's tenure at Penn
State has spanned ten presidential administrations. Although he has
avidly followed political events, he has been less informed about popular
culture. In the winter of 1996 he was invited to a White House dinner
honoring the Italian ambassador. Although he recognized Sophia Loren,
he had never heard of his table guest, whose name was on a place card.
When Paterno returned home, his son quizzed him about the dinner.

"I sat beside this guy, Nick Cage," Joe said.

"Who?" his son asked.

"Nick Cage," Joe repeated.

"You mean Nicholas Cage, the Academy Award-winning actor?"

"I don't know. He said his name was Nick Cage."[10]

Occasionally, Joe's actions have met criticism, but the various incidents have sparked little attention outside central Pennsylvania. In November 1989, during a nationally televised game against West Virginia, a delay-of-game penalty against Penn State ignited an outburst by Joe directed against an assistant coach. The sideline incident, seen by millions of viewers, sparked a flurry of objecting letters to the *Centre Daily Times*. "If Coach Paterno wants to chew out an assistant for a mistake, let him do it after the game, in the locker room, so that an entire television audience will not be embarrassed by such an outburst."

In two instances players left Penn State and blasted Joe and his program, partly because he delayed releasing them from their commitment to Penn State. Fullback J. T. Morris had personal conflicts with Joe; cornerback Ricky Rowe objected to the "conformity" demanded at Penn State. "I felt like a robot," Rowe told the *Daily Collegian*. "I wasn't comfortable at all."

In 1992 Joe used poor judgment in publicly venting his frustration with the academic deficiency of a player. When a reporter questioned him about disciplinary action taken against cornerback Bobby Samuels, Joe responded quickly and his rash public statement probably violated the Buckley Amendment, the federal law that protects student records from public disclosure. "Someone ought to take a look at Bobby Samuels's transcript," he said. "Bobby Samuels got a 0.75 [grade-point average on a 4.0 scale] for twelve credits in his last semester. I'm not supposed to say that, that's a Buckley Amendment [stipulation] and I probably should keep my mouth shut about that. . . . I leaned over backward for Bobby Samuels. I gave him every chance. Maybe I should have kicked him in the rear end earlier."

Perennial critic John Swinton latched on to Joe's statement about Samuels, writing university administrators demanding that action be taken against Joe for his "inhumane outburst," and for violating the Buckley Amendment. In a public letter to the *Centre Daily Times*, Swinton urged the newspaper to follow up on Joe's "most disturbing behavior" of "intentionally holding [Samuels] up to ridicule and possibly warning off potential employers." But no action was taken against Joe.[11]

Joe's every move has come under close scrutiny by fans and the media. Luncheon quarterbacks, sportswriting quarterbacks, radio call-in quarterbacks, and second-guessing fans who have written him letters all questioned the previous Saturday's decisions until Penn State played the next game. At one gathering the questions came rapidly.

"Why didn't you use your receivers more? Why did you play so conservatively?"

"In a game like that you try to control the ball," Joe responded. "Ball control comes from your running game. In sixty-seven plays we gained over four hundred yards."

"Why didn't you adjust and do something about stopping their option play at halftime? Don't tell me you did!"

Joe said no, they didn't handle the option very well. But the defense had been working hard on it all week. He hoped they'll be able to stop it on Saturday.

"Why didn't you think of using more screen passes?"

Joe laughed. "You guys out there must be betting on the score of the game. We won, didn't we?"

Every Wednesday noon since 1966, Joe has attended Penn State's Quarterback Club, a gathering of State College boosters at the Nittany Lion Inn. The audience asks a variety of questions about the team, but in 1993 a fan had a unique one.

"Joe, why do you roll up the cuffs on your pants so high?"

Everyone giggled.

Paterno scratched his head and said, "I was getting paid twenty thousand dollars my first year, had a house I couldn't afford, a young family, and I only had a couple of pairs of pants. I started rolling them up so I wouldn't get mud on them during games. Now I have four pairs of pants and out of habit I still roll them up."

His relationship with the media, once warm, became more distant and tense after 1979. As Penn State's teams succeeded year after year, the size of the media vastly increased, disrupting Joe's informal, friendly relations with reporters. In the 1980s about 150 media representatives covered the team's home games. Penn State was big news because the team went to a major bowl contest almost every year, sometimes contended for the national championship, and sent scores of players to the pros. The press box at Beaver Stadium, once cozy, was expanded "to a three-tier monolith stretching between the twenty-yard lines." The intimate press parties outgrew homes and a series of meeting rooms at inns and hotels. Sportswriter Bill Conlin observed the change: "Nobody believes me when I tell them that after games, I would run down the stadium steps with the spotters-booth coaches and ride over to the locker room on the third bus. Most interviews with Paterno, his assistant coaches, and players were one-on-one. Those were the days."[12]

Writers and broadcasters had come to resent closed practices, carefully monitored interviews with players, secretiveness about injuries, and Joe's inaccessibility. "Joe Paterno's image as college football's saintliest coach is unraveling," a sportswriter for the *Pittsburgh Post-Gazette* charged. "It was constructed to a large degree by sportswriters who enjoyed his wit and off-the-record candor, and ironically, it is being altered by the same writers who no longer can contact him."

Sometimes reporters wanted an immediate comment from Joe but couldn't secure it. It was difficult to get him to return a phone call on the same day. State College was still so remote, a reporter joked, that "Paterno could suddenly decide to turn Penn State into State Pen and nobody would notice for four or five years."

In the mid-1980s Joe canceled the traditional Wednesday media conference, irritating the sports media. He was available after Saturday's game and at a Tuesday teleconference. Normally, he was unavailable for on-the-record questions on Sunday and Monday and, more importantly, from Wednesday through Friday. If injuries or other developments occurred during the heavy practice days after Tuesday, the media didn't learn about them until Saturday's game. Joe did meet with the Penn State booster club at noon on Wednesday, but his remarks were off-the-record. On Thursday he informatively fielded questions from fans for an hour on a local radio call-in program.

He has taken a firm stance with the media. If a reporter asks him a question he does not want to answer, he just doesn't answer. After 1979 he usually did his interviews en masse via teleconferences. The Tuesday news conference did not satisfy some in the media because of the impersonal telephone hookup, the large number of participants, and because questioners could ask only one question with no follow-up. "They are not terribly informative, to be honest," said Ray Parrillo.[13]

On the Friday evening of home games, Joe has made a thirty-minute appearance at a social gathering with the media, but his remarks have been off-the-record. "It is very impersonal," said Ralph Bernstein of the Friday night sessions with the media. "Joe comes in, spends a half hour, tries to spread himself around to everybody, and then runs out. It is not what it used to be. I guess it cannot be."

A ritual for games on the road has included an informal gathering of the media on Friday evening in the suite of Penn State's sports information director. Joe arrives about 9:30 P.M., after a final meeting with his players, and circulates among the media for an hour.

Penn State's secretiveness, especially about reporting injuries, has irritated those who have covered Penn State. They have argued that Joe had an obligation to fans. Those people who shelled out the money to go to the stadium on Saturday had a right to know who was going to play that day. "My analogy," said Ron Bracken, "is that you don't go to a Broadway play to see the stand-in. You go there to see the star. If the star isn't there, you may not want to go."

Some have thought Joe was acting petty by not listing freshmen in the Lions' media guide and for making freshmen inaccessible to reporters. Some of the freshmen have played. Why shouldn't they be in the media guide? Ron Christ thought he knew why Joe didn't want the media at practice. "He doesn't want us to see Joe Paterno yelling and screaming because that might alter our image of him." But all coaches yell and scream, Christ thought. "If he's trying to make me believe he doesn't, he's only fooling himself."

Penn State has controlled access and information. When quarterback Tom Bill spent time in an alcohol rehabilitation center, there was no attempt to cover up, but there was also no effort to elaborate. "Tom has recovered from his illness," said Joe, making clear that the media should address another subject.[14]

"They have pretty much [created] a closed society," said Christ. "[They] try to hide information on an athlete who flunks out, or is in jail, or on drugs, or injured. They have become so image conscious that . . . they become protective. When they do that, they sometimes hurt themselves a lot more than if they'd be honest in the very beginning. What's wrong with announcing that a player has flunked out of school? It happens everywhere."

Bill Zimpfer was the play-by-play announcer for Penn State's football games until he assumed the same job announcing games for the professional Miami Dolphins. The Dolphins opened their doors, allowing him easy access to players and coaches. By contrast, Zimpfer observed, "If you would try to do that with Penn State, it would almost be like you were trying to breach the Pentagon. It was quite a difference."

"For years some have claimed that Joe Paterno has had the media in his pocket, controlling every word they say or write," observed Ron Bracken in August 1992. "The truth is that Paterno has had them blindfolded, allowing them to see only what he wants them to see and hear what he wants them to hear."

A sportswriter, who started covering Penn State's football teams when he was twenty-four, complained that Joe was rude to young reporters. "When he deals with a young reporter, such as myself, he is very antagonistic. . . . He favors people closer to his age." In 1985, after Penn State narrowly defeated East Carolina, 17-10, the sportswriter asked Joe, "Did East Carolina surprise you?" According to the reporter, Joe slammed his fist on the table and said, "You guys drive me absolutely up a wall! I tell you all the time. These are great football teams!" Observed the resentful reporter: "He just screamed at me for about . . . two and a half minutes."

Critics have charged that Penn State's athletic program has become overbearing about its image. "They take exception to an awful lot of little things—they become very thin-skinned about their image," said Christ. "No one is supposed to say anything uncomplimentary about Penn State." Christ concluded sardonically that Penn State's athletic program could stand a "lesson in public relations."[15]

Most likely the media have magnified and exaggerated their problems with Joe. They all have sat together in the press box, exchanging the same complaints. "It becomes easy to keep complaining about the same thing," observed Bill Lyon. "I'm sure there is some exaggeration, some magnification involved."

Joe has respected the professionalism, sincerity, and honesty of most reporters, but others he has found irritating. Some have been inexperienced, artless, and have wasted his time. "They don't do their homework," he said. "Some of them are lazy. They'll call me up and ask me things they could have gotten out of the press guide. They haven't done any research." They inquire about his attitude toward freshmen eligibility. "I've been on record for a thousand years that freshmen shouldn't be [eligible]!"

"A lot of people [in the media] made a pest out of themselves," conceded Christ. "[They] just wanted to talk to Joe Paterno to say they had talked to Joe Paterno. That created a lot of inconvenience for him."

"[The media] like to find something bad about you," said George Paterno. "So [Joe] is very careful." Quotations attributed to Joe that had come out of the off-the-record Friday night sessions particularly bothered him. "Things which were said at those sessions got repeated, gossiped around, distorted, and it's to the point now where I don't feel comfortable around sportswriters," Joe said. "I guess I will just have to always understand that a sportswriter is always looking for a story and I can't be friends with him. And that has me concerned because it sets up an immediate adversarial situation."

With respect to a reporter who has wanted a personal interview, Joe admitted he has been less accessible. Unfortunately, he hasn't been able to give each reporter what each wanted because there have been far too many who wanted personal access to him. Every time a national issue has arisen about football, Joe has received scores of calls—not just from Pennsylvania reporters, but from New York, Chicago, Dallas. If the calls arrive in the off-season, he can usually handle them, but during the season he hasn't had time. "It's impossible for me to handle the media the way they would want me to handle them," he declared.[16]

Joe and his defenders have argued that the players couldn't concentrate at practice with the distractions of the media. If a player was admonished, that should be between the coach and the player. "That's strictly family," John Bove said. "That is what goes on in our house. The reporter may not understand what is going on." The media cramped the coach's style. "I'd feel very uncomfortable if I had to ream somebody out in front of reporters," said assistant coach Dick Anderson. "You have to do that sometimes on the practice field."

Also, an upcoming opponent might learn through media reports the innovations Penn State was planning. "You never know how far those stories go," said assistant coach Robert Phillips. Joe thought it was crucial to maintain confidentiality about discussions at team meetings, as well. "This has got to be like the family," he advised the team. "What we talk about here has to stay here."

Injuries have been no one's business but the team's. "Most coaches would rather the opposing coach didn't know [about an injury]," said Phillips. "If you let them know, you're really giving them an advantage." If a Penn State halfback had a sprained ankle, making uncertain whether he could play on Saturday, the coaches would just as soon keep the opponent guessing.

Some reporters have been "inconsiderate" and bothered young players. "I get concerned when you've got a kid in his first year of college and all of a sudden people are hassling him," said Joe. An eighteen-year-old player was too young to handle the sophisticated media, Joe's defenders argued. Freshman players were vulnerable. "Half the time you don't know what is going to come out of their mouth," said Dick Anderson. When quarterback John Shaffer and fellow players were freshmen, they were reluctant to talk to the media for fear of creating controversy. "It's difficult for a freshman . . . to be able to know the impact that every word and every sentence . . . may have," said Shaffer. "[The reporters] put words in the kids' minds and the next thing you know it is in the papers," Ron Dickerson contended; "I think it is unfair."[17]

That sports pages have seemed to stress the negative aspects of sports and competition also has irritated Joe. He has wearied of reading about salary disputes and labor lawyers on the sports pages. "I don't want to read where some kid is saying, 'Play me or trade me!' or 'Coach isn't treating me right.'" Reporters have always preferred to go behind the scenes "where the gossip is—and the playing isn't."

"Some media people are preoccupied with taunting, bad-mouthing, and emphasizing mistakes and slip-ups instead of achievements," Joe charged in his autobiography. "I wish they'd pay—and educate fans to pay—more respectful attention to the strains these young kids endure in a hard-fought game. I wish sports reporters wouldn't try to make themselves look good by putting words into the mouths of stressed and inexperienced nineteen-year-olds, leading them to say something about their teammates, or their opponents, or their coach, so that the reporter can get a headline and byline by making a kid look bad." Some sportswriters agreed with Joe's accusations, including Bill Conlin, who thought Joe's charges were "difficult to refute."

Covering the Nittany Lions and their "eloquent, driven, and driving taskmaster" has been a "career highlight" for the veteran Conlin. Unfortunately, Conlin realized, the small intimate gatherings with Joe had vanished. "I have long since stopped trying to explain Joe Paterno to younger colleagues who find that Penn State football assignments are increasingly unrewarding ventures into a late twentieth-century fiefdom, a football Xanadu, moats and all," Conlin sadly reflected in 1989. "Many younger writers, their assignments created by Penn State's emergence as a yearly national power, have developed deep and abiding animosities toward Paterno. The feeling is mutual."[18]

Joe's relationship with a young quarterback provided an illustration of a controversy played out in the media. In 1988 Joe was forced to start a freshman, Tony Sacca, at quarterback because three quarterbacks ahead of him in the depth chart went down with injuries. In his first year Sacca completed only 37 percent of his passes; as a sophomore the following year, he again often misfired, completing 41 percent. The team suffered because of his inexperience and ineffectiveness. He slowly improved his game and as a junior in 1990 coolly led a 24-21 upset over top-ranked Notre Dame in South Bend. In 1991, as a senior, his game came together, and he enjoyed an outstanding season, completing 169 of 292 passes (57.9 percent), throwing for twenty-one touchdowns, while being intercepted only five times.

Strong-willed, independent, surly, and not inclined to attend his classes, the six-foot-five, 225-pound Sacca had stormy encounters with Joe. The media knew that their relationship was often tense, so when Joe referred to "my buddy, Tony" at a press conference, everyone laughed. At the end of his successful senior season, Sacca gave his version of his experience at Penn State to Ray Parrillo of the *Philadelphia Inquirer*. The article appeared on December 29, 1991, just before Sacca's fortieth and final start for Penn State against Tennessee in the Fiesta Bowl on New Year's Day. Sacca charged that during a spring practice in 1990, after he had nonchalantly thrown another poor pass in practice, the quarterback heard Joe's shrill voice yelling at him, "Sacca, you're the biggest quarterback flop in Penn State history!"

(In private Joe spoke harshly of Sacca. "I'm about fed up with him," Paterno told Denlinger after the outburst. "He's gonna drive me up the wall. I had a real tough meeting with him yesterday. He's one of the toughest kids I've ever had to coach at that position. Very immature. Silly. I got my message across, that he's not doing anywhere near well enough.")

According to Sacca, he and Joe bickered for three years. The young quarterback said he resented being yelled at. "I felt like I was playing against my coach as well as against the other team," Sacca said. "I'm kind of relieved it's almost over. It's time to move on."

When Sacca had complained publicly about Penn State's run-oriented and allegedly unimaginative passing offense, he said Joe told him to shut up and stop complaining. "I can remember going into his office and he would say some outrageous things to me. He once told me I was the worst quarterback that ever came here. . . . I'd tell him it's tough to complete passes when you only throw on third and long, when you only have two receivers to go to."

Did Sacca ever see himself returning to State College to visit Paterno some day? the article concluded. "Right now, no," Sacca responded. "I can't envision myself doing that. I just can't."[19]

For his part Joe was quoted as saying, "I was hard on Tony because I knew how great he could be. . . . But I really like Tony. He's a tough, tough kid." Joe continued: "I'd tell Sacca to keep his mouth shut, and he'd give me this look. I'd look back and say, 'What's that supposed to mean?' He just shrugs and says, 'I still think we should throw the ball more.' Tony and I are two Italians who like to shoot off our mouths."

A few months later Sacca modified his view and spoke affectionately about Joe, indicating that his feud with his coach may have been more smoke than fire. "I went in and talked to Joe about [the article]," Sacca subsequently said. "He hadn't even seen it. But when you level with him he's a pretty reasonable guy. It didn't affect our relationship at all." Sacca stated that he had many "fond memories" and was going to miss Penn State. "I had my ups and downs, but that happens a lot when you go to college. . . . I'm happy with the way things went and my relationship with Joe couldn't be better."

"I do believe [Sacca] was right" in his original criticism, one sportswriter concluded. Others thought the controversy was a tempest in a teapot, overblown by the media.[20]

Joe has wanted to maintain good relations with the media. When both the *New York Times* and *Sports Illustrated* requested his attention, he sighed and said to a friend, "It seems the reporters get younger every year. They ask the same questions every year, and I try to answer them because they are trying to do their job. I think it is my obligation [to do the interviews]."

Despite their criticism, most of the media have continued to enjoy and respect Joe. "Almost everyone admired him for the [Grand

Experiment]," said Christ. "He is always friendly [and] very congenial," commented Parrillo of Joe at social functions. "He is a terrific conversationalist. He is an interesting guy. He is likable. Just inaccessible."

"I like him a lot," said Bill Carroll of the Lancaster *New Era*, who covered Penn State football for over two decades. "I think he is an exemplary person."

Some continued to regard him as an excellent interview, as well. Said a reporter for the *Boston Globe*, "He has opinions and answers. He knows when to be serious. When to be cute. When to joke. When to gently chastise and deflect. It all looks so easy, so natural."

After Ralph Bernstein and Ray Parrillo combined for a delightful interview with Joe, one lasting three times longer than originally scheduled, Joe said, "Fellas, I enjoyed that. That takes me back to the old days when we were much closer. I wish I could do more of this, but I just can't."[21]

For the most part, Joe's life has remained remarkably consistent. "Same employer for forty-one years," noted Bill Lyon in 1990. "Same wife for twenty-eight. Same house for twenty-three. Same values. Same idealism. Same frailties. Same shortcomings."

"I know so many men his age that have lost their [zest]," said Fr. Thomas Bermingham in 1994. "Life has become lackluster. They are just coping, getting along. [But] Joe is just as full of enthusiasm and happiness because he is doing the things he loves."

"He's still the same person," added Jerry Sandusky. "The foremost quality that comes to mind when I think of him is that competitiveness, that drive to succeed. I don't think he's changed in that way. He's still anxious to get better."

Fran Ganter agreed that the electricity that flowed through Joe was still direct current, high voltage. "The thing that still amazes me, the thing that has not changed about him is that fierce desire to win, to be the best," he said. "He is constantly thinking, every day, about how to make us better, how we can win the national championship. That never changes."

In one respect, though, Ganter thought Joe had changed. He was more understanding. "[His] understanding of what the players have to go through has changed; he's more concerned with their well-being off the field. He understands the price they have to pay now." Ganter continued: "I see a Kenny Jackson or a Todd Blackledge throw their arm around him, hug him, tease him, and there is no way that would have happened when I played [in the late 1960s]. Back then you almost wanted to go down the other side of the street if you saw him coming because he was always on you, telling you to get a haircut, asking where your socks were. So I think the players now are probably closer to him than those in the past."[22]

In the fall of 1992, Joe's assistant-coaching staff averaged an extraordinary thirteen years of service at Penn State. Defensive coordinator Sandusky was entering his twenty-fourth year and offensive coordinator Ganter was starting his twenty-second. When a member of his Penn State football family suffered a misfortune, Joe remained intensely loyal. After former Penn State player and assistant coach Dick Anderson was fired by Rutgers University for not winning enough, Joe took him back as his offensive line coach. When former Penn State quarterback Galen Hall did too much to win at Florida, causing a scandal by breaking NCAA rules, he was fired, and Joe gave him a job as a graduate assistant coach at Penn State in 1990. "He is my friend," Joe said of Hall. "I don't necessarily condone what he did, but he didn't commit murder, either."[23]

For the most part, Joe's popularity has remained high, and he has continued to win honors and praise. In 1988, when Harrisburg's *Patriot-News* asked readers to name Pennsylvania's most popular personality, six hundred people responded and named Joe by more than a two-to-one margin over any other person. (Among those receiving far fewer votes than Joe were the governor, the state's two U.S. senators, and golfing great Arnold Palmer.)

Joe became the first active college football coach to win the National Football Foundation and Hall of Fame's Distinguished American award. The award was presented at the annual Hall of Fame dinner at the Waldorf-Astoria Hotel in New York on December 10, 1991. It honored a person "who over a long period of time has made significant contributions to the betterment of amateur football in America." A letter of praise from President Bush was read to the sold-out gathering.

"Paterno cares," praised Paul Attner, senior writer for *The Sporting News*. "He cares about Penn State, about the NCAA, about the future of

Paterno's loyalty to his former players and assistants is one of his many trademarks. Here he shakes hands with former assistant Dick Anderson, about to coach his first game as Rutgers's new head coach against his old boss. Paterno later hired Anderson back after Anderson was fired from his position. (AP/Wide World Photo)

college sports. In a profession littered with too many cheaters and fast-talkers, he has always been a welcomed breath of fresh air."[24]

In 1992 major preseason polls ranked Penn State eighth, and Joe uncharacteristically expressed optimism about the upcoming season. Then disaster struck. Only one other season, 1979, compared to the turbulence that buffeted Penn State's team in 1992.

That summer several Nittany Lions players were involved in a string of arrests, reminiscent of the problems Joe had faced in 1979. At a community arts festival, police arrested O. J. McDuffie, Ricky Sayles, and Mark Graham for a scuffle outside a bar. That was followed by the arrest of incoming freshman Brian Miller on charges of selling cocaine in his hometown. Then the police charged Sayles and Bobby Engram with burglary, theft, and receiving stolen property after catching them stealing stereo equipment and other household goods from an occupied apartment.

Three years earlier Joe had expressed his concern about the kind of problems that erupted in the summer of 1992:

> I worry so much more about things like drinking. Kids drink so much more these days. I know some kids have a couple of beers on a Saturday night, but I've had a couple that I know of who had serious problems.
>
> I worry all the time about drugs. I hear rumors all the time and I keep running them down. . . .
>
> I worry about the poor kids we have. I worry that some kid who is dirt poor and can't get some thing is going to steal.[25]

The arrests gave the impression that Joe was losing control of his program. On August 30, 1992, a critical editorial in the *Centre Daily Times* added to the humiliation. "The unflattering preseason show put on by a number of Penn State football players casts shame on the individuals and tarnishes the reputation of the team and the university."

Over the years Penn State players had been involved in their share of trouble—public drunkenness, fights at downtown bars. Despite those instances, when people thought of Penn State, they thought of a clean program. Freshmen players were lectured about avoiding situations that drew them into trouble. "They're supposed to walk away from it," John Coyle said. "They're not supposed to be drawn into it." Although the spate of problems in 1992 was not unprecedented, they were uncommon at Penn State. "For the most part, Penn State has been fortunate," said Ron Bracken. "The huge majority of athletes in its programs have been solid citizens."[26]

On October 10, 1992, Penn State faced Miami in the biggest game since the Lions' victory over the Hurricanes in the 1987 Fiesta Bowl. Both teams entered the game undefeated—Penn State 5-0 and ranked seventh, and Miami 4-0 and ranked second. A beyond-capacity crowd of 96,704 at Beaver Stadium watched the nationally televised game.

To rattle Miami, conservative Joe Paterno concocted a radical plan. He attempted to intimidate the Hurricanes and make as much noise as possible by using a three-thousand-dollar sound system to blare out "Takin' Care of Business." With the Beaver Stadium fans rocking, he hoped to unnerve the Hurricanes. "Usually, Paterno intimidated through silence," Denlinger noted. "Let the other guys prance and talk trash, wear little doodads on their helmets and emotions on their sleeves. We are Penn State. Stoic in public." But on this occasion, "Joe Pa had gone out of his everlovin' mind."

In the tense contest the Lions outgained Miami, 370-218, but hurt themselves with poor kicking and penalties. The crucial play came with Miami ahead, 10-7, late in the third quarter, when Penn State's quarterback, John Sacca (Tony Sacca's brother), threw an ill-advised screen pass right into the hands of Miami's defensive end Darren Krein, who returned it twenty-eight yards for a Miami touchdown. Miami's 17-14 victory torpedoed Penn State's chances for a national championship. It was one of the most disappointing losses in memory and commenced a dizzying descent into one of the worst seasons of Joe's career.

(As for the high-decibel music, Joe was later flooded with complaints. "You may have heard the last of it," he said afterward. It had been "an honest mistake," not well choreographed.)[27]

After the wrenching loss to Miami, Joe still assumed that pride and tradition would carry his team forward and everything would take care of itself. But the following week Penn State played poorly in losing to Boston College. In only two weeks the Nittany Lions moved from serious national championship contender to also-ran. Neil Rudel thought the team was "confused, angry, and maybe coming apart at the seams."

Although vague about details, some players publicly suggested dissension. "What was said was said [behind] closed doors," commented one player, referring to a locker-room scene before the loss to Boston College. "Obviously, some dreams had gone down the drain after Miami. There were some people who needed to be talked to."

Following the loss to Boston College, critics started debating whether Joe Paterno should be forced out of coaching. The Lions seemed to have more talent than their performance indicated, which hung a question mark on the coaching staff. "One more listless, sloppy effort Saturday [at West Virginia] and the critics might be on the verge of calling for Paterno's scalp," said Rudel.

As expected, Penn State defeated West Virginia, but on October 31 unheralded Brigham Young passed over and ran through Penn State, defeating the Lions, 30-17, giving Penn State its third loss in four weeks. "Confusion reigns in the Penn State camp," Rudel reported. Discouraged after the loss to Brigham Young, instead of riding the team bus back to the hotel in Provo, Utah, Joe walked the three miles by himself. ("He got lost," reported Ray Parrillo.)

What had gone wrong? "Let's start at the top," Rudel said after the Brigham Young game. "This club is poorly coached. Joe Paterno would be hard-pressed to come up with a season in which he and his staff have done a worse job."

The final two games of the season—a spirited effort in losing to Notre Dame (17-16) and a slaughter of Pittsburgh (57-13)—gave encouragement for the contest against Stanford in the Blockbuster Bowl on January 1, 1993. After all, Joe had repeatedly proven in the past that given a month to prepare for an opponent, he seldom lost.[28]

Bowl officials hyped the game as a matchup of great coaches: the "Genius" vs. the "Legend." Joe was the legend, one of college football's all-time-winningest coaches. The genius was Bill Walsh, who as coach of the San Francisco 49ers had won three Super Bowl titles. After a stint in the NBC broadcast booth, in 1992 Walsh led Stanford to the co-championship of the Pac-10.

CBS went overboard in hyping the coaching matchup. "Imagine Vince Lombardi and George Halas facing off," announcer Jim Nantz said. "Well, that's kind of what we have today." When one bowl official explained why they had pushed the slogan in advertisements, Joe showed

"The Genius" meets "the Legend" prior to the kickoff of the 1993 Blockbuster Bowl between Stanford and Penn State. Bill Walsh's Stanford team prevailed over Paterno's Nittany Lions, 24-3. (AP/Wide World Photo)

good humor. "The Genius vs. the Legend," he said with a smile. "I didn't know which one I was."

"We're going at this football game like we were going to a national championship," Joe said. "It's important to us." But Stanford easily prevailed, winning, 24-3. The Lions managed only four first downs in the second half and had a season low of twelve overall. They gained only 107 yards rushing and 263 total yards.

Joe was bitterly disappointed. It was obvious that Walsh had gotten the better of the coaching matchup—that the Genius had bested the Legend. Penn State's season, which began with aspirations for a national title, ended 7-5, including five losses in its last seven games and no victories over a ranked opponent.

Following the embarrassing defeat, Joe spent a long night soul-searching. He said he was up every couple of hours. When he met the media the next morning at 8:00 A.M., he admitted his motivation had been waning, and he called the football program complacent. But he also said he was going to recommit himself and stay the course. "I'm going to make it happen one more time," he said. "I'm going to do it. Or I'll kill myself."[29]

Several factors explained the disappointing season. On the field the team displayed numerous weaknesses: poor tackling, mindless penalties, flimsy pass defense, no pass rush, dropped passes, offensive inconsistency. Before the season Penn State had committed itself to the Blockbuster Bowl (if it won at least six games). After the crushing loss to Miami, Penn State dropped out of the running for the national championship, and since the bowl game had already been locked up, there was little to motivate the players except pride.

The team's chemistry—its personality, work ethic, leadership, unity, and ability to overcome adversity—was deficient. "In 1992 I don't think we had a great chemistry," reflected Dick Anderson. Some players were not good leaders, Anderson said, yet they were "influential on the squad."

Factions developed behind the two contenders for starting quarterback, John Sacca and Kerry Collins. Moreover, center Bucky Greeley judged a few veteran players insufficiently dedicated and committed; needing only a few credits to graduate, they drank and partied. Their lethargy was "hurting us at practice," Greeley said.

An apparent double standard or inconsistency in discipline disturbed some players. When a reserve player violated a rule, he was severely punished; when star player O. J. McDuffie committed a more serious offense, he was leniently treated. Assistant coach Tom Bradley observed: "[Paterno] would discipline a player and the kids [thought] the discipline was unfair. 'Why did you do that to him, and you didn't do that to the other guy who did a similar thing.'"

Some players thought Joe didn't care about them. "I felt the players weren't talking to him [about] our problems," fullback Brian O'Neal said. "Instead, everything just kind of stayed in the locker room. That developed resentment. There was a lot of finger-pointing. To me, it was a lack of communication with the coaches."

Joe thought he and the coaching staff became too complacent. "We certainly took some things for granted. We got careless and sloppy.

You go onto the practice field and a kid makes a mistake. You say, 'Oh well,' and go on. Or you look at a game plan and you say, 'Supposing they do this?' You say, 'Well, they're not going to do that because it's going to take another ten minutes [of the coaches' meeting].' It's easy to overlook the little things."[30]

Joe foolishly blamed the media for some of the misfortune in 1992. "You guys are part of the problem and you may not want to admit it," he said after the loss to Stanford. The media argued that Penn State didn't pass effectively. "I have got to sell our guys that you guys are wrong. I tell them that hard-nosed football is going to win. The key is hard-nosed football, defensive football, and knocking the crap out of people on the line of scrimmage. . . ."

Ron Bracken effectively countered Joe's whining. "If it's true that we do wield that much influence on a team when it loses, doesn't it follow that we should also receive some of the credit when it wins? In which case, I guess my national championship rings must have gotten lost or overlooked somewhere in all of the celebration."[31]

For six seasons, from 1987 through 1992, Penn State's record had been 48-23-1, unremarkable by Joe's previous standards. Could Penn State return to the elite of college football? Could the Lions ever win another national championship?

Several times Joe has made a thorough reevaluation of his program following a painful season: in 1979 after a disappointing 8-4 record; in 1984 when the team went 6-5; and in 1988, his only losing season. After the Blockbuster Bowl he held private meetings with small groups of his returning players, trying to find out what had gone wrong. Some players were brutally honest, telling him he was too concerned with outside activities, distant, arrogant, unapproachable, uninterested in their input.

Center Bucky Greeley and two other returning linemen met with Joe in January 1993. "I want to know what you feel the problem was and why we didn't get things done," Joe asked them. "Do you feel the coaches and the players weren't communicating? What do you think we can do to make it better?" Greeley, who thought Joe had become "too authoritarian," told his coach that practices were too long and too businesslike, taking the fun out of the game. Consequently, players "were just going through the motions." He also said that a barrier seemed to exist between players and coaches, preventing effective communications.

Joe didn't realize his team had been in disarray. "I didn't really know what was going on with the squad," he said. "I assumed some guys were leaders when they weren't. I didn't spend enough time with the players, one-on-one. . . . I was amazed to find out some of the things the kids thought."[32]

Jay Paterno thought his father was irritated by postseason grumbling that he was over the hill. "It was almost a catalyst for him to go at it again," Jay said. "There is something inside him that won't let him step back from a challenge," said Scott Paterno, "especially when other people say you can't do it. That's what motivates him. He always wants to . . . do a little better."

"I'm losing touch with the kids," Joe told his brother George after the season. "I'm going to get it straightened out. I'm going to have another great team even if they carry me out on my shield."[33]

To improve communications and trust with his players, Joe set up a breakfast council. Two players from each class, selected by their classmates, met with Joe at 7:15 A.M. on Wednesday mornings in a campus dining room during the 1993 season. He asked about their problems and welcomed their suggestions. The breakfast sessions clarified disciplinary actions, assuring players there was no double standard. Small disagreements were discussed before they festered. "How is everything doing?" Joe inquired. "What did you think about last week's practices? Is there something you want me to address with the coaches? This is what we have to get done this week. . . ."

"It's a great time for the kids," Joe said. "This week we talked about the Phillies." The players enjoyed the informal sessions and understood Joe better. As a consequence of the meetings, Bucky Greeley believed practices were more efficient in 1993, but, he added, "the truth is we didn't do that much different in practice." Nonetheless, the meetings improved trust between coaches and players. "The players felt they could talk to the coaches," said Greeley; "it worked out a lot better." "To a man," Ron Bracken observed, "the players . . . have pointed back to [the breakfast meetings] and said how helpful [they've] been."[34]

After a long secret courtship, in 1990 Penn State accepted an invitation from the Big Ten presidents to join the conference, surprising the conference's athletic directors and coaches, who were kept in the dark. After 106 years as an independent, Penn State began its first conference football schedule in the fall of 1993.

Since 1966 Joe had been a cheerleader for the respectability of eastern football, but then he went out and consistently whipped eastern teams, proving there was little substance to his claim. Through 1992 his record against Maryland was 23-0-1, against West Virginia 25-2. Even against Pittsburgh, which became a national power under Johnny Majors and Jackie Sherrill, Joe compiled a record of 20-6-1. Boston College defeated Penn State only twice, Rutgers once, and Temple never beat Joe's teams. Joe admitted that the great games involving Penn State were against Nebraska, Notre Dame, Alabama, and Miami. "To be brutally frank," he said, "many of our eastern rivalries just weren't competitive. I think our fans were getting tired of coming up here and seeing . . . lopsided games."

"If you take away the logistics of travel, there is nothing negative about having Penn State in our league," said McKinley Boston, Minnesota's men's athletic director. "Athletics are a people business, and they are excellent people." Penn State brought to the Big Ten the conference's second-largest stadium and an eastern television market of 5.3 million. "They also bring tradition, class, and quality to what was already a good league," said Boston.[35]

Joe repeatedly sang the praises of the Big Ten: One in every seven college graduates had graduated from a Big Ten school; the Big Ten awarded half the Ph.D.'s in the country. In football, the Big Ten had produced more Heisman Trophy winners than any other conference, had three of the largest stadiums in college football, and the first four finishers in the conference went to bowl games.

Actually, in recent years the Big Ten had been less than formidable. No Big Ten team won more than eight games in 1992, the league compiled a shaky 14-19-1 record against nonconference opponents, and was 1-2 in bowl games. "I know it's had a couple of down years in football," Joe conceded, "but I think by far, traditionally, it's a great conference in football."

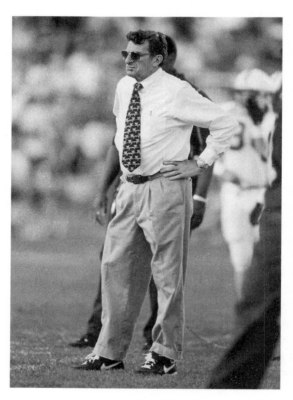

By joining the Big Ten Conference in 1993, Penn State ended 106 years as an independent. With the new affiliation came new headaches, as suggested here by Joe, watching on as his Nittany Lions fall, 38-7, to Big Ten powerhouse Ohio State in 1996. (Allsport USA photo by Jonathan Daniel)

Two years before Penn State played its first game in the Big Ten, Joe started watching scores of tapes of Big Ten games. "Every time there's been a game televised with the Big Ten, I've looked at it. I go to sleep watching those tapes, trying to get a feel for it." Joe admitted he harbored ambition to play in the Rose Bowl, especially "when I'm alone, walking in the woods in back of my house."

To prepare for the rigors of the Big Ten schedule in 1993, Joe lifted weights, walked six miles a day, did sit-ups, watched his diet, and made sure he had enough sleep. "I'm probably in better shape now than I've been maybe in twenty years," he claimed. At spring practice in 1993, he acted like it was his rookie season, not his twenty-eighth. Players marveled at his energy and appreciated his efforts to communicate more effectively with them. "He's like a kid now," said Brian O'Neal. "He's running around screaming, he's hollering, he's joking around with us. He's also letting us know what we're in for."

"Exceptional people do exceptional things, and at age sixty-six, when most men of his stature are playing golf and organizing their memoirs, Paterno is hell-bent for the Rose Bowl," wrote Bill Conlin in the *Philadelphia Daily News* in August 1993. "Most startling—to this longtime Paterno-watcher, at least—the coach who held forth for a sweltering, standing-room-only media mob on Picture Day was kinder, gentler, humbler and less confrontational than I have ever seen him."[36]

In the 1993 season Penn State again started 5-0 and prepared for its first Big Ten showdown at Beaver Stadium against Michigan. In the most telling series, at the end of the third quarter Penn State threatened on Michigan's one-yard line. After four running plays into the stomach of Michigan's defense, Penn State finished outside the one. Michigan's goal-line stand preserved a 14-10 lead, and the Wolverines won, 21-13. The series reminded pundits of the 1979 Sugar Bowl when Penn State failed in two drives up the middle, allowing Alabama to win and claim the national championship.

This time, though, Penn State didn't collapse. Its record of 6-2 tied for third place in the Big Ten Conference behind Ohio State and Wisconsin. The Lions led the Big Ten in scoring (32.5 points per game) and were second in rushing (236.1 yards per game) and total offense (416.6 yards per game). Then in the Florida Citrus Bowl, the Lions clubbed Tennessee, 31-13. With its impressive victory over the Volunteers, a 10-2 overall record, a five-game winning streak, and forty-one returning lettermen, Penn State looked confidently and optimistically to the 1994 season.[37]

In August 1994, Ken Denlinger, a sportswriter for the *Washington Post* and a Penn State graduate, published his book *For the Glory*, an inside look at the rigors of the Penn State football program covering 1988–1992. By focusing on one group of players, Denlinger hoped to shed light on the larger world of big-time college football.

He followed Penn State's recruiting class of 1988 for five years. After first meeting them as high school seniors, he elicited extraordinary frankness by promising not to quote them until after they left Penn State. The group included O. J. McDuffie, a highly touted tailback from Ohio, and Tony Sacca, the cocky quarterback from New Jersey.

Joe boldly provided the author almost complete access to the players. (The only aspects of the program off-limits to Denlinger were the coaches' meetings.) "The access that Paterno gave me was virtually unlimited," said Denlinger. Joe gave the author only one mandate: "I want it honest. I don't want it one way or the other." He wanted it to be a book that someone could pick up and understand what the players endured with the "stress and strain of big-time college football."[38]

The book's prevailing theme is pain: physical injury, lack of success on the field, academic pressure. Some players wanted to escape the sweaty, frenetic rat race, "where any result less than the national championship was deemed a failure."

The book showed Joe as a recruiter; disciplinarian; mentor; and ranting, stubborn coach. Some of the views were less than flattering. "Joe could do better with communications with the players," lineman Eric Renkey said. "A lot of guys don't know where they stand. That leads to a lot of frustration. He talks about this being a family. I sometimes think it's a dysfunctional family, because there's not much communication."

The book depicted Joe as caring and sensitive as well. Suffering from injuries and family problems, Leonard Humphries packed his bags in the spring of his freshman year and prepared to quit. Word soon reached Paterno, and he and Humphries met in the equipment area of the main locker room. "He understood," Humphries said. "He told me I was a decent player and definitely had a future here. He told me to take a week or so off. Then he hugged me."

For Eric Renkey football went far better than school during his first year. Because Renkey's grades were poor, Joe excused him from spring practice. "Joe would write notes to me about how he expects more of Eric," Eric's mother, Marilyn Renkey, said. "If anybody ever says [Paterno] doesn't care about his players academically, I can give him a personal endorsement."[39]

After five years inside the Penn State program, Denlinger concluded that Joe demanded excellence from his players and became loudly personal when he didn't get it: "Throw out the most positive virtues—passion, loyalty, wit, warmth, tenacity, a brilliant mind, and a

Upon Penn State's joining of the bruising Big Ten in 1993, Paterno, at age sixty-six, recommitted himself to a physical-fitness regimen taxing to men half as age. No sweat for this pre-game run onto the field at Giants Stadium in 1996 prior to the Nittany Lion's 41-0 trampling of Temple. (Allsport USA photo by Al Bello)

work ethic second to none—and they all fit Paterno. Yet he also can be abrasive, sarcastic, judgmental, unbending. Not to mention a hair-trigger temper that frequently erupts on the sideline and sometimes gets captured on television."

Did the positive virtues outweigh the negative? "I think that they do," Denlinger wrote, and he thought the players, on reflection, thought so as well.

Underscoring the problems Joe encountered with his 1992 team, Denlinger judged that Joe failed in one specific regard—not giving himself enough to his players. Extended up-close glimpses of Paterno were rare. The class saw him often but almost always in the same ways: as the loud taskmaster at practice, as the father-figure being stern about discipline and academics during team meetings and one-on-one sessions in his office, and as the author of he-can-do-better notes to parents. They wanted the man they called Joe to act like an ordinary Joe now and then.

Joe was too overworked to develop a relatively close relationship with his players. Paterno knew about his players, often more than they wanted him to, but he frequently would breeze past them in an otherwise empty locker room. He wasn't cold or impolite, simply an unimaginably busy man in a hurry.

Unfortunately for Joe and his program, the recruiting class of 1988 was one of his worst and most unfortunate. Of the twenty-eight scholarship recipients, few became starters or effective team leaders, and twelve suffered injuries that required surgery. He privately told his brother of his disappointment with the quality of the class Denlinger happened to select. "That [class] is not the norm at Penn State," he said. (The class fared well academically, though; only six had not gotten their degrees at Penn State or somewhere else by the winter of 1993.)

"I didn't know this class would be as interesting as some of the others I've had," Joe said publicly about the book. "Ken has written an honest book. I don't like some of it because it happened, not because Ken wrote it."

"I think if you look at [the book] objectively," Denlinger said after publication, "you're going to see Joe in a lot of different ways. I've got a tremendous amount of respect for him."[40]

In the 1994 season the Nittany Lions gave Joe little reason to go to the whip. In the early portion of the season Penn State's trail of carnage included victories over Minnesota (56-3), Iowa (61-21), and Temple (48-21). "They're a spectacular offensive football team," said Rutgers coach Doug Graber after Penn State's 55-27 victory. When thinking of classic Paterno teams, seldom did anyone mention the words *spectacular* and *offense* in the same sentence. "Conservative, methodical, maybe," observed *Football News*. "But spectacular?"

Through five spectacular offensive performances, Penn State averaged 51.6 points in outscoring the opposition, 258-86, even with most of the starters on the bench by midway through the third quarter. (Their average halftime lead was 35-8.) Striking with extraordinary speed, of the Lions' thirty-eight scoring drives, twenty-eight consumed three minutes or less—including thirteen that required no more than one minute.

After fattening up on the early portion of the schedule, the Nittany Lions again stood at 5-0 as it awaited another crucial contest with fifth-ranked Michigan (4-1). During the week before the game, *Sports Illustrated* and ESPN stopped by Penn State, and Joe's Tuesday press conference was speckled with midwestern sportswriters. Anticipation was in the air, and Joe had more bounce to his step. "He's running around and stretching before practice," linebacker Brian Gelzheiser said. "You can tell he's excited, and when he gets excited, we get excited."

"If we haven't been working for this game, we're in the wrong business," Joe said. "This is what you talk about when you recruit kids, playing in big games, in big stadiums. I'm excited to be part of it."

Questions still remained about whether or not Penn State could win the crucial game. A loss at Michigan on October 15 would mark the third consecutive season that Penn State started 5-0 but could not clear the big hurdle. "We're looking at this game as a possible way to get back into the elite teams in the country," quarterback Kerry Collins said. "We haven't gotten there in the past few years, or we've laid an egg in the big games."[41]

In a magnificent contest at Ann Arbor, Penn State defeated Michigan, 31-24. Afterward, ten thousand Penn State students back in State College streamed out of dormitories and apartment buildings, swarmed Beaver Stadium, carried goalposts across campus, and jammed traffic in celebration. The players were relieved. "It takes a big monkey off our backs," tight end Kyle Brady said. "You start to get a reputation for not being able to win the big one, of blowing it. We blew it against Michigan last year."

Victory over Michigan landed Penn State on the cover of *Sports Illustrated* for the first time in four years, and also earned the Lions the number-one ranking in the AP and CNN/*USA Today* polls. At press conferences for the remainder of the season, Joe squirmed at the mere mention of football polls. Questions about rankings in the polls irritated him. "I don't even pay attention," he said, his voice rising. "I always sound a little bit exasperated because I don't know how to answer these questions. I don't even think about the darn things. I come to these [press conferences] and all I hear is this nonsense."[42]

Because of all the national acclaim for his team and for individual players, Joe constantly warned against complacency. "He had to make us modest," said Bucky Greeley. On October 29, Penn State (6-0 overall, 3-0 in Big Ten) hosted Ohio State (5-2, 2-1) in what was expected to be a tense contest. (The Buckeyes had defeated the Lions, 24-6, in Columbus the previous year.) But Penn State buried the Buckeyes, 63-14. "I'm as surprised as anybody," Joe said. "It was just one of those days. We had a great week of practice and played a great game. We're not that good and they're not that bad."

Against Illinois, Penn State turned in a sterling comeback performance. Down 21-0, the Lions rallied and pulled out a 35-31 victory. The comeback, Neil Rudel wrote, "proved no team this season combines more ability, character, heart, and poise." In the last regular-season game, Penn State put an exclamation point on its perfect regular season (11-0), smashing Michigan State, 59-31. Early in the fourth quarter fans in the west stands of Beaver Stadium turned to the press box and chanted, "We're number one." "We played a great game when we had to," Joe said after being doused with Gatorade and presented with the game ball. "I don't know if you can play much better."[43]

The Big Ten champion and the champion of the Pac-10 Conference meet each year in Pasadena in the Rose Bowl, a bowl contest Joe had never coached in. Fifteen thousand Penn State fans jammed a parking lot for a pep rally the day before the game. "This is overwhelming! In all my years of coaching, this is the most thrilling moment I've ever had. I've got goose bumps," Joe yelled at the crowd. On January 2, 1995, Penn State defeated Oregon, 38-20, to end the season 12-0, and extended its winning streak to seventeen games.

Many sports reporters and coaches believed Penn State's offense in 1994 was among the best in college football's history. In various surveys five offensive players earned first-team All-America honors. Penn State led the nation in total offense (520.2 yards per game) and scoring offense (47.8 points per game).

As Joe spoke to the media after the game, Penn State's three captains—Kerry Collins, Brian Gelzheiser, and Bucky Greeley—interrupted to present the game ball to their coach. "To the winningest bowl coach in the history of college football. He's won all four major bowls and been an inspiration to myself and the rest of the team and is the national championship coach this year," stated Collins as he presented the ball to Joe.

The presentation by the three captains surprised and almost overwhelmed Joe. "I didn't want you guys [in the media] to think I was soft,"

Joe said the following day, "otherwise I might have choked up. That was a moving moment for me."[44]

Joe's entire season had been gratifying. Unlike some of his teams in the past, he didn't have to drive and push the squad, and there were few problems and no internal dissent. With its fine work habits and excellent leadership, the players "made it easier for all of us," said Dick Anderson. "He loves these kids," Tom Bradley said. "They've given us everything they've got. There's been no complaining from them. There's been no hollering and no screaming from us." The Breakfast Club had no longer met regularly during the 1994 season. "We didn't do it as much," said Greeley. "He got away from it a little more." Because the team was so dedicated and unified, though, Joe probably didn't think the meetings were necessary.

Once a week during the season Jay Paterno talked to his father on the phone. After the Lions defeated Southern California in the second game, Joe told his son, "This is just so exciting. We are really on the threshold of being a great football team. If we coaches can just keep them going." Sue Paterno observed that her husband was excited all year. "It has been magical. They're just good kids [and] fun to be around. He has loved every minute of it."[45]

Joe was miffed after the polls selected Nebraska as the college national champion, but he didn't whine. Why should he respect the judgment of sixty newspaper writers, he said, "half of whom I don't really have much regard for their writing." He congratulated Tom Osborne, Nebraska's coach. Other coaches would have complained much more than Paterno, reasoned sportswriter Jim Litke. "It's hard enough finding one coach who had one team go unbeaten without winning a national title—let alone someone like Paterno, who has had four teams suffer that mean fate."

The media repeatedly asked Joe to restate his twenty-five-year position on polls and a play-off. "I think a play-off is the only way to do it," he said. "I think it's a disgrace to college football that football [is] the only Division I-A sport that isn't decided on the field."

Consequently, Paterno prodded Big Ten coaches to push for inclusion of the Rose Bowl in the new bowl alliance. In 1996 the Rose Bowl agreed to join the alliance beginning in 1998, thus ending a fifty-two-year tradition of exclusively matching the Big Ten champion and the winner of the Pac-10, and almost assuring a national championship game. "He has great vision of how things should be," said Sue Paterno.

Paterno's 1995 team, stung by consecutive defeats to Wisconsin (snapping Penn State's twenty-game winning streak) and Ohio State, finished 9-3. The following year they improved to 11-2 and ranked seventh in final polls. In 1997 they were 9-3 again.[46]

Because Joe seemed to be in the twilight of his career, he was repeatedly asked about his retirement plans. Twilight, though, turned out to be midafternoon. As Ron Bracken noted, Joe kept "hitting the reset button on his retirement clock." In the mid-1980s, recruiters for other major universities began using age against Joe, planting in the minds of young recruiting prospects that Joe probably wouldn't be at Penn State throughout the prospect's entire football career, leaving the player in the lurch.

Periodically, Joe fretted about overstaying in coaching. "I don't want to stay too long," he had said in 1973—and again in 1978, 1982, 1986, and 1990. "I don't want to linger. I sometimes wonder if Bear Bryant didn't stay too long."

In 1986 Joe indicated that he planned to coach four or five more years. He said then: "The thing I want to do most now is make sure when I get out of it I turn it over in good shape. I want to give a young guy a chance to come in and do better. If I go more than four or five [years], what I'm concerned about is that you get a little bit like Coach [Bear] Bryant. You can't do anything else. And then you're trapped." He didn't expect to pick his own successor, he said. "I'm not going to hire him because I'm not going to work with him. For me to say I want so-and-so to be the coach wouldn't be fair to the coach or the athletic director."[47]

He hinted at retirement when he suggested that his long crusade to clean up college football was nearing an end. Asked in 1989 if he would serve on a commission to investigate the workings of the NCAA, he said he didn't know if he would be around long enough to serve. "I have to back away from telling people what to do," he said. "I think the younger [coaches] have to sit down and see where they want this game to go in the next fifteen years. I used to preach all the time. I thought that I could change the game in my lifetime, but I think that's up to somebody else."

Some have wondered why Joe would want to keep coaching after he had already accomplished so much. What milestones remained?

Another national championship? Another undefeated season? What was left to prove? "How much more fame is to be had?" Bill Lyon asked. "How much more gilding can a reputation take? How much bigger does the legend need to grow?" Being revered could become addictive. "It can make retirement seem a tepid, anticlimactic alternative," Lyon said. On the other hand, if Joe wanted to continue coaching, who was going to tell him he couldn't?

Remarkably, Joe has showed few signs of aging. In 1992 his hair was still thick and wavy and had only a touch of gray. His walk was still strong and quick, his energy level still high. "Joe Paterno is sixty-five going on forty-five," Jim Tarman said. "I've never been around anyone who has aged as reluctantly as Joe. He won't give in to growing old."

Stop coaching? Not after a moment like this, as Joe celebrates his team's 1990 victory over Notre Dame in South Bend, Indiana, knocking the Fighting Irish off their No. 1 perch. (AP/Wide World Photo)

What would Joe do after he retired? "I cannot see myself doing nothing," he said. "I do not think I will want to wake up every morning to see how many holes of golf I can play." Penn State officials would love to have him concentrate more on fund-raising. Another possibility would be to step up his public service. He and Sue thought about financially adopting an inner-city elementary school class, perhaps in Philadelphia, "and take them to the museum, give them incentives to go on to college—put a little scholarship money away for them."[48]

"For him to say 'I'm done working' is going to be very hard," said Scott Paterno. "He really does love fall Saturdays. He *lives* for that. It is part of his makeup, part of who he is." For a long time, George Paterno hoped that his brother would "smell the roses" and retire. "Then I got to thinking," George said in 1995, "he is at the top of his game again. So why should be retire? He is not a grandfather yet. If he gets to be a grandfather, he'll go over to the other side of the mountain. Then maybe he'll relax." (By 1997 Joe had three grandchildren.)

Joe confided to Ken Denlinger in the spring of 1990, "I'm scared to death to retire, to be frank with you. I don't know what I'd do. . . . I have absolutely no hobbies." Yes, Bear Bryant had stayed too long, but Joe had also seen some coaches and noncoaches who retired too soon. "They get old fast," Joe said.[49]

Antsy, itching for a new challenge, he changed his thoughts about retirement in 1990 when the Big Ten announced it was accepting Penn State as a member of its conference—with football starting in 1993. Before Joe retired, he wanted to coach in a Rose Bowl championship. "Absolutely," he said. "No question about it."

After the announcement Joe declared that he would continue to coach for seven more years, until he was seventy.

"The number-one thing is, I still really enjoy coaching," he said. "There aren't many other things I like. I kept telling my staff, I'll go another year or two. Yes, I'm going to retire. No, I'm not going to retire. It wasn't fair to the staff. It wasn't fair to the kids. And it wasn't fair to the university." The bottom line was that he didn't want to retire. "I'm in good health. God's been good to me. So I thought I'd stick with it and the time to make the next decision will be when I'm seventy."[50]

He had also changed his mind about picking his own successor. He was going to do what Rip Engle had done for him when Engle was close to retirement. "When I get a year or two away," Joe said, "I'm just going to say: so-and-so's going to be assistant head coach. This guy's going to have to recruit, and I'm going to get out."

Who would succeed Joe when he put away his whistle and clipboard was a subject of speculation. In 1992 most guessed it would be defensive coordinator Jerry Sandusky, forty-eight; offensive coordinator Fran Ganter, forty-three; or perhaps offensive line coach Dick Anderson, fifty-one.

In August 1994 Joe again changed his timetable, saying he would coach at least five more years. "I don't know what I'm going to do. I may stay until I'm eighty," he said. If there was one potential drawback to his decision to stay five more years, it was the impact it could have on members of his staff who might be entertaining dreams of succeeding him. Earlier Joe had said he would retire at seventy to remove the uncertainty from his staff, allowing them to make plans for their own futures. "Now, for all intents and purposes, there is no timetable," said Ron Bracken. "Basically, Paterno will coach as long as he wants and as long as his health permits."[51]

Once again, in July 1997, Joe revised his thoughts on retirement. "I feel great," he said. "I think I'm a better coach at seventy because I don't make the dumb mistakes I used to. I don't want to retire." In an interview with the *Philadelphia Inquirer*, he added, "It's been a joyride. . . . If I can go to seventy-five, that'd be great."

"I don't know what it is about him," standout defensive lineman Brandon Noble of the 1996 Nittany Lions said. "It seems like he gets younger and younger every year. We get older. He's not aging. He just keeps going. And he still gets excited about every team."

Joe may be harboring thoughts of seeking the all-time Division I-A record for victories, 323, set by Bryant. Neil Rudel observed: "It will be interesting to see if Paterno will be in a position, physically, and whether he'd be interested in carving his name atop the all-time-win list, because he would probably break the record in the year 2000."

How would people eventually judge him? Joe wondered. What would be his legacy? He could only hope. "I hope they're not going to judge me on how many games I won or lost. . . . I hope they judge me on some other things, the impact we've had on people's lives. Some have been good and, obviously, some have not been so good. But I hope the overall picture is that we have done some good for people."[52]

∾ ENDNOTES ∾

Introduction

1 *Centre Daily Times*, August 13, 1994; *Philadelphia Inquirer*, January 5, 1983; Benjamin Rader, *American Sports: From the Age of Folk Games to the Age of Spectators* (Englewood Cliffs: Prentice-Hall, Inc., 1983), pp. 266-273; Ken Denlinger, *For the Glory* (New York: St. Martin's Press, 1994), p. 296.

2 John Underwood, *Death of an American Game: Crisis in Football* (Boston: Little, Brown, and Company, 1979), p. 244.

3 Interview, Steve Smear.

4 *Dallas Morning News*, December 27, 1986; *Philadelphia Inquirer*, January 4, 1983; *Philadelphia Inquirer Magazine*, August 30, 1987.

5 *Philadelphia Inquirer*, December 28, 1986; *Philadelphia Inquirer Magazine*, August 30, 1987; *Sports Illustrated*, March 17, 1980.

6 *Boston Globe*, August 22, 1986; Joseph Hurley to author, August 3, 1992.

Chapter 1

1 Michael O'Brien, *Vince: A Personal Biography of Vince Lombardi* (New York: William Morrow and Company, Inc., 1987), pp. 19-20.

2 "Paterno family tree," unpublished typescript, Marie Giffone Papers, Milton, Wisconsin.

3 *Pittsburgh Press*, August 4, 1974; Joe Paterno (with Bernard Asbell), *Paterno: By the Book* (New York: Random House, 1989), pp. 24-31; interviews, Florence Mittleman, George Paterno.

4 *Philadelphia Inquirer*, May 20, 1970; Mervin Hyman and Gordon White, *Joe Paterno: "Football My Way"* (New York: MacMillan, 1971), p. 62; Paterno, *By the Book*, pp. 25-28; interviews, George Arkwright, Joe Cassidy, Nicholas Mangracina, Frank Mastoloni, Rosemary McGinn, Florence Mittleman, Jim O'Hora, George Paterno.

5 Dennis Booher, "Joseph Vincent Paterno, Football Coach: His Involvement with the Pennsylvania State University and American Intercollegiate Football" (Ph.D. dissertation, Pennsylvania State University, 1985), pp. 2-3; Hyman and White, *Joe Paterno*, p. 62; Paterno, *By the Book*, pp. 26-29; interviews, Thomas Bermingham, Florence Mittleman, George Paterno.

6 *Washington Post*, November 3, 1987; Paterno, *By the Book*, pp. 24-30; interviews, Thomas Bermingham, Marty Gresh, Nicholas Mangracina, Frank Mastoloni, Rosemary McGinn, Florence Mittleman, Joseph Murphy, George Paterno.

7 Paterno, *By the Book*, pp. 29, 94.

8 *Vim and Vigor*, Fall 1987; Booher, "Joseph Paterno," p. 2; O'Brien, *Vince Lombardi*, p. 24; Paterno, *By the Book*, pp. 24, 155; interview, Rosemary McGinn.

9 Joe Paterno Clipping File, Sports Information Office Papers, Pennsylvania State University; *Town and Gown*, September 1972; *Vim and Vigor*, Fall 1987; Booher, "Joseph Paterno," pp. 3, 4, 17-18; Hyman and White, *Joe Paterno*, p. 64; interviews, Nicholas Dambra, Nicholas Mangracina, Florence Mittleman.

10 *Philadelphia Inquirer*, May 20, 1970; *Washington Post*, November 3, 1987; Paterno, *By the Book*, p. 32; interview, George Paterno.

11 Joe Paterno to Barbara Costigan, February 15, 1993, unprocessed Rosemary McGinn Papers, Staten Island, New York; clipping, Joe Paterno Clipping File; *New York Daily News*, November 23, 1978; *Philadelphia Daily News*, November 8, 1982; *Town and Gown*, September 1972; Booher, "Joseph Paterno," p. 1; Paterno, *By the Book*, pp. 27, 32; interviews, Joe Cassidy, Nicholas Dambra, Nicholas Mangracina, Rosemary McGinn.

12 *Miami Herald*, December 31, 1986; *Washington Post*, January 1, 1987; Hyman and White, *Joe Paterno*, p. 64; Paterno, *By the Book*, p. 60; interviews, George Arkwright, Rita Buckhorn, Joe Cassidy, Nicholas Dambra, Nicholas Mangracina, Frank Mastoloni, Rosemary McGinn, Giro Scotti.

13 *Town and Gown*, September 1972; interviews, Thomas Bermingham, Joe Cassidy, Florence Mittleman, George Paterno.

14 *Philadelphia Inquirer*, January 5, 1983; *Washington Post*, November 3, 1987; *Sports Illustrated*, December 22-29, 1986; Hyman and White, *Joe Paterno*, p. 65; interviews, Frank Mastoloni, Florence Mittleman, George Paterno.

15 *Blue Book 1945*; *Blue Jug*, September 29, 1942, and October 6, 1944; interviews, Walter McCurdy, Joseph Murphy.

16 *Blue Jug*, October 29, 1943; Booher, "Joseph Paterno," pp. 5-6; Hyman and White, *Joe Paterno*, pp. 66-67; Paterno, *By the Book*, p. 35; interviews, Joseph Murphy, Charles O'Connor, John Plunkett, Charles Weis.

17 *Blue Jug*, October 29, 1943; *Pittsburgh Press*, August 4, 1974; Hyman and White, *Joe Paterno*, p. 66; interviews, Joe Hurley, Joseph Murphy, George Paterno.

18 Paterno, *By the Book*, p. 36; interview, John Plunkett.

19 Interviews, Joe Hurley, George Paterno, John Plunkett, John Scott.

20 *Blue Jug*, November 22, 1944; Paterno, *By the Book*, p. 36; interviews, Joseph Murphy, George Paterno.

21 Joe Hurley Papers, Breezy Point, New York; *Blue Jug*, October 27 and November 22, 1944.

22 Joe Hurley Papers; *Blue Book 1945*; *Blue Jug*, November 22, 1944; Paterno, *By the Book*, p. 36; interviews, John Plunkett, Charles Weis.

23 *Blue Jug*, January 28, March 4, April 2, and June 4, 1943, and March 8, 1944; also *Blue Jug* anniversary supplement issue, April 1944; interviews, Walter McCurdy, John Plunkett.

24 *Blue Jug*, January 25, 1945; interviews, Thomas Bermingham, Frank Mastoloni, Walter McCurdy.

25 *Blue Jug*, November 22, 1944; interviews, William Hundley, Joe Hurley, Rosemary McGinn, Joseph Murphy, John Plunkett, James Reilly.

26 One confidential interview.

27 Clipping, unprocessed, G. David Gearhart Papers, University Park, Pennsylvania; *Blue Book 1945*; *Blue Jug*, January 27, October 6 and 27, 1944; interviews, Thomas Bermingham, Charles O'Connor.

28 Charles Manz and Henry Sims, *Super-Leadership: Leading Others to Lead Themselves* (New York: Prentice-Hall Press, 1989), p. 61; Paterno, *By the Book*, pp. 37, 40; interview, Joseph Murphy.

29 Paterno, *By the Book*, pp. 37, 40; interviews, Thomas Bermingham, Charles O'Connor.

30 *Washington Post*, January 1, 1979; *America*, April 2, 1994; Paterno, *By the Book*, pp. 41-42; interview, Thomas Bermingham.

31 George Duckworth, "Aeneid," *Encyclopedia Americana*, International Edition, Volume 1 (Danbury, Connecticut: Grolier Incorporated, 1984), pp. 215-216; Paterno, *By the Book*, p. 43; interview, Thomas Bermingham.

32 *America*, April 2, 1994; Paterno, *By the Book*, pp. 42-46; interview, Thomas Bermingham.

33 *Blue Book 1945*; *Blue Jug*, January 25, 1945; *Town and Gown*, September 1972; interviews, Joseph Murphy, Charles O'Connor, Charles Weis.

34 Hyman and White, *Joe Paterno*, pp. 69-70; interviews, Thomas Bermingham, John Hanlon, Paul Mackesey, George Paterno.

35 Paterno, *By the Book*, p. 49; interview, Joe Paterno.

36 *Philadelphia Inquirer Magazine*, August 30, 1987; interviews, Joseph Murphy, Gerard Walters.

37 *Brown Daily Herald*, November 27, 1946; Michael Bezilla, *Penn State: An Illustrated History* (University Park: the Pennsylvania State University, 1985),

pp. 278-279; Paterno, *By the Book*, p. 54; interviews, Bill Doolittle, John Hanlon, Fred Kozak, Paul Mackesey, Walter Paster, George Paterno, Gerard Walters, Joe Yukica.

[38] Joe Paterno Clipping File; *Brown Daily Herald*, October 14 and 28, 1947; *Pawtucket Times*, October 11, 1948; *Philadelphia Daily News*, November 8, 1982; *Providence Evening Bulletin*, October 21, 1948; Booher, "Joseph Paterno," p. 8; interviews, Walter Paster, Gerard Walters.

[39] Clipping, Football Scrapbook 1949, Brown University Papers, Brown University Library, Providence, Rhode Island; *Brown Daily Herald*, December 7, 1948; *Quest*, September/October 1978; Hyman and White, *Joe Paterno*, pp. 71-73; interviews, Robert Priestley, and one confidential interview.

[40] *Beaver Stadium Pictorial*, December 7, 1968; *Brown Daily Herald*, December 3, 1948, and June 17, 1949; Booher, "Joseph Paterno," p. 10; interviews, Bill Doolittle, John Hanlon, Paul Mackesey, Walter Paster, George Paterno, John Scott, Gerard Walters.

[41] *Brown Daily Herald*, October 27, 1947; *Beaver Stadium Pictorial*, December 7, 1968; *Collegian Magazine*, October 23, 1981; *Providence Sunday Journal*, October 16, 1949; Paul Beers, *Profiles in Pennsylvania Sports* (Harrisburg: Stackpole Books, 1975), p. 76; Hyman and White, *Joe Paterno*, p. 74; interviews, Bill Doolittle, Walter Paster, George Paterno.

[42] *Beaver Stadium Pictorial*, December 7, 1968; *Philadelphia Inquirer*, January 5, 1983; Booher, "Joseph Paterno," p. 14; Hyman and White, *Joe Paterno*, p. 74; interviews, Bill Doolittle, Arnie Green, Fred Kozak, Walter Paster, George Paterno, Robert Priestley, John Scott, Gerard Walters.

[43] *Beaver Stadium Pictorial*, December 7, 1968; *Brown Daily Herald*, November 28, 1949; *Pawtucket Times*, November 25, 1949; *Providence Journal*, November 25, 1949; Hyman and White, *Joe Paterno*, pp. 75-76; interviews, Arnie

Green, John Hanlon, Ed Kiely, Robert Priestley, John Scott.

[44] *Brown Daily Herald*, December 6 and 7, 1949; *Providence Evening Bulletin*, November 22, 1949; Booher, "Joseph Paterno," p. 13.

[45] *Brown Daily Herald*, December 10, 1946, February 26, 1947, March 2, 3, and 16, 1948, December 9, 1948, and February 17, 1949; *Philadelphia Inquirer*, May 20, 1970; Booher, "Joseph Paterno," p. 10; Hyman and White, *Joe Paterno*, p. 72; interview, Weeb Ewbank.

[46] Paterno, *By the Book*, p. 16; interviews, Florence Mittleman, George Paterno, Gerard Walters.

[47] Clipping, G. David Gearhart Papers, University Park, Pennsylvania; Joe Paterno Clipping File; *Brown Daily Herald*, October 28 and November 4, 1948; *Town and Gown*, September 1972; Paterno, *By the Book*, pp. 49-50; interview, John Scott.

[48] Joe Paterno Clipping File; *Town and Gown*, September 1972; Booher, "Joseph Paterno," p. 12; interviews, Arnie Green, Ed Kiely, George Paterno, Robert Priestley, John Scott, Gerard Walters.

[49] Paterno, *By the Book*, pp. 50-53; interview, Gerard Walters.

[50] *Brown Daily Herald*, March 1 and October 7, 1948, and March 14, 1949; interviews, Pat Flynn, Ed Kiely, Gerard Walters.

[51] *Brown Daily Herald*, April 24, 1950; *Pittsburgh Press*, August 4, 1974; Hyman and White, *Joe Paterno*, p. 77; Paterno, *By the Book*, p. 55.

[52] Joe Paterno Clipping File; *Centre Daily Times*, July 22, 1986; *Daily Collegian*, May 27, 1950; Hyman and White, *Joe Paterno*, p. 77; Paterno, *By the Book*, p. 56; interview, Florence Mittleman.

Chapter 2

[1] Bezilla, *Penn State*, pp. 176, 228-229, 234-235, 292-293.

[2] *Ibid.*, p. 279; Booher, "Joseph Paterno," pp. 63, 114; interview, Robert Scannell.

3 *Spectator*, November 9, 1987; Bezilla, *Penn State*, p. 280.

4 Joe Paterno Clipping File; *Philadelphia Daily News*, November 8, 1982; Booher, "Joseph Paterno," pp. 19-20; Paterno, *By the Book*, p. 68; interview, Jim O'Hora.

5 Hyman and White, *Joe Paterno*, p. 81; O'Brien, *Vince Lombardi*, p. 66; Paterno, *By the Book*, p. 68; interviews, Vince O'Bara, Joe Yukica.

6 Paterno, *By the Book*, p. 71; Ridge Riley, *Road to Number One: A Personal Chronicle of Penn State Football* (Garden City: Doubleday and Company, Inc., 1977), p. 46; interviews, Don Bailey, Ed Sulkowski.

7 Booher, "Joseph Paterno," p. 21; Paterno, *By the Book*, p. 69.

8 Hyman and White, *Joe Paterno*, p. 84.

9 *Washington Post*, January 1, 1979; Booher, "Joseph Paterno," p. 22; Paterno, *By the Book*, p. 74; interviews, Bets O'Hora, Jim O'Hora.

10 *Pittsburgh Press*, August 4, 1974; Booher, "Joseph Paterno," pp. 23-24; Hyman and White, *Joe Paterno*, pp. 88-89; interviews, Bets O'Hora, Jim O'Hora.

11 Booher, "Joseph Paterno," pp. 27-29; Hyman and White, *Joe Paterno*, p. 82; Paterno, *By the Book*, pp. 72, 85; interviews, Mike Irwin, Al Jacks, Pete Liske, Bets O'Hora, Jim O'Hora, Frank Patrick. One confidential interview.

12 Hyman and White, *Joe Paterno*, p. 114; interviews, Bets O'Hora, Jim O'Hora, Sever Toretti, J. T. White.

13 *Philadelphia Inquirer Magazine*, August 30, 1987; Booher, "Joseph Paterno," pp. 29-33; Hyman and White, *Joe Paterno*, p. 114; interviews, Bets O'Hora, Jim O'Hora.

14 *Philadelphia Inquirer*, December 30, 1986; *Pittsburgh Press*, February 20, 1966; Hyman and White, *Joe Paterno*, p. 82; Joe Paterno, *Coaching Winning Football* (Phoenix: Universal Dimensions, Inc., 1983), p. 10; interviews, Don Bailey, Steve Garban, Warren Hartenstine, Edward Hintz, Al Jacks, Florence Mittleman, George Paterno.

15 Paterno, *By the Book*, p. 62; interview, Joe Yukica.

16 *Pittsburgh Press*, August 4, 1974; Booher, "Joseph Paterno," pp. 24, 31; Hyman and White, *Joe Paterno*, p. 33; interviews, Warren Hartenstine, Bets O'Hora, Jim O'Hora, Frank Patrick.

17 Joe Paterno Clipping File; *Pittsburgh Press*, August 4, 1974; Booher, "Joseph Paterno," p. 38; interviews, Jesse Arnelle, Chuck Medlar, Frank Patrick, Sever Toretti.

18 *Life*, October 9, 1970; Paterno, *By the Book*, pp. 73-76; interviews, Bets O'Hora, Jim O'Hora.

19 *Daily Collegian*, September 23, 1959; Booher, "Joseph Paterno," pp. 34-35; interviews, Jesse Arnelle, Don Bailey, Milton Bergstein, Earl Bruce, Edward Hintz, Al Jacks, Pete Liske, Vince O'Bara, Jim O'Hora, Jack White.

20 *Pittsburgh Press*, August 4, 1974; Booher, "Joseph Paterno," p. 30; Paterno, *By the Book*, pp. 82-83; interviews, Jesse Arnelle, Warren Hartenstine, Mike Irwin, Jack White.

21 Joe Paterno Clipping File; Hyman and White, *Joe Paterno*, p. 97; interview, Richie Lucas.

22 Paterno, *By the Book*, p. 70; interviews, Jesse Arnelle, Don Bailey, Pete Liske.

23 *Philadelphia Inquirer*, December 24 and 30, 1986; *Quest*, September/October 1978; Bezilla, *Penn State*, p. 279; Hyman and White, *Joe Paterno*, p. 100; interviews, Earl Bruce, Warren Hartenstine, Al Jacks, Frank Patrick, Sever Toretti, Jack White.

24 *Philadelphia Inquirer*, December 20, 1986; Booher, "Joseph Paterno," pp. 33-34, 84-85, 99; Hyman and White, *Joe Paterno*, p. 99; Paterno, *By the Book*, p. 176.

25 Hyman and White, *Joe Paterno*, p. 101.

26 *Washington Post*, January 1, 1979; Hyman and White, *Joe Paterno*, pp. 89-90; Paterno, *By the Book*, p. 77; interview, Jim O'Hora.

27 *Washington Post*, January 1, 1979; Booher, "Joseph Paterno," p. 20; Hyman and White, *Joe Paterno*, p. 114; interviews, Bets O'Hora, J. T. White.

28 Joe Paterno Clipping File; Booher, "Joseph Paterno," p. 26; Denlinger, *For the Glory*, p. 62; Hyman and White, *Joe Paterno*, p. 115; Paterno, *By the Book*, pp. 78-80; interview, J. T. White.

29 Joe Paterno Clipping File; *Philadelphia Daily News*, November 8, 1982; *Pittsburgh Press*, August 5, 1979; *Quest*, September/October 1978; Booher, "Joseph Paterno," p. 31; Hyman and White, *Joe Paterno*, pp. 94, 113; interviews, Jim O'Hora, J. T. White.

30 Joe Paterno Clipping File; *Pittsburgh Press*, August 5, 1974; Hyman and White, *Joe Paterno*, pp. 110-111; interview, Weeb Ewbank.

31 *Centre Daily Times*, July 22, 1986; *Daily Collegian*, July 2, 1964; Hyman and White, *Joe Paterno*, pp. 111-112.

32 *Centre Daily Times*, August 12, 1990; Paterno, *By the Book*, p. 91.

Chapter 3

1 *Beaver Stadium Pictorial*, November 5, 1966; *Centre Daily Times*, February 21, 1966, and July 21, 1986; *Sunday Patriot-News*, February 20 and 21, 1966.

2 Hyman and White, *Joe Paterno*, pp. 118-119, 131; Paterno, *By the Book*, pp. 72, 92-93, 131; interviews, Warren Hartenstine, Mike Irwin, Jack White.

3 Hyman and White, *Joe Paterno*, pp. 29, 125-128; Paterno, *By the Book*, p. 95.

4 Hyman and White, *Joe Paterno*, p. 124; interviews, Jim O'Hora, Frank Patrick, Dan Radakovich.

5 Hyman and White, *Joe Paterno*, pp. 188-189; Paterno, *By the Book*, p. 98.

6 Hyman and White, *Joe Paterno*, p. 33; Paterno, *By the Book*, pp. 98-101.

7 Paterno, *By the Book*, pp. 105, 114; interview, Robert Phillips.

8 *Centre Daily Times*, July 21, 1986; Hyman and White, *Joe Paterno*, p. 192; Paterno, *By the Book*, pp. 110-111; interview, Jim O'Hora.

9 *Centre Daily Times*, July 21, 1986; Hyman and White, *Joe Paterno*, pp. 194, 200; Riley, *Road to Number One*, pp. 421-424.

10 Hyman and White, *Joe Paterno*, p. 36; Riley, *Road to Number One*, p. 425.

11 *Pittsburgh Post-Gazette*, January 13, 1969; *Life*, October 9, 1970; Hyman and White, *Joe Paterno*, p. 211; Riley, *Road to Number One*, p. 439; Loran Smith, *Fifty Years on the Fifty: the Orange Bowl Story* (Charlotte, North Carolina: East Woods Press, 1983), p. 124.

12 Booher, "Joseph Paterno," pp. 61, 147; Paterno, *By the Book*, pp. 117-118.

13 *Centre Daily Times*, July 28, 1966.

14 Joe Paterno Clipping File.

15 *Philadelphia Daily News*, October 19, 1967.

16 *Centre Daily Times*, December 23, 1968; *Los Angeles Times*, August 31, 1973; *Saturday Evening Post*, October 1983; Hyman and White, *Joe Paterno*, pp. 141-142.

17 *Centre Daily Times*, August 17, 1989; interviews, Ernie Accorsi, Dave Baker, Ralph Bernstein, Bill Lyon, John Morris.

18 *Centre Daily Times*, August 17, 1989; *Chicago Tribune*, September 15, 1978; *Philadelphia Evening Bulletin*, December 28, 1972; Hyman and White, *Joe Paterno*, p. 13; Riley, *Road to Number One*, p. 427; interviews, Ernie Accorsi, Dave Baker, Ralph Bernstein, Bill Lyon, John Morris.

19 Joe Paterno Clipping File; *Beaver Stadium Pictorial*, December 7, 1968; *Life*, October 9, 1970.

20 *Centre Daily Times*, December 28, 1967; *Cleveland Plain Dealer*, February 18, 1969; *New York Times*, January 9, 1969; *Philadelphia Daily News*, August 31, 1993; *Pittsburgh Post-Gazette*, January 13, 1969, January 8, 1973, and August 29, 1993; Hyman and White, *Joe Paterno*, pp. 204-207; Riley, *Road to Number One*, pp. 429, 439; interview, Steve Smear.

21 *Cleveland Plain Dealer*, February 18, 1969; Hyman and White, *Joe Paterno*, p. 208.

22 Paterno, *By the Book*, pp. 136-139.

23 *Philadelphia Inquirer*, May 20, 1970; *New York Times*, January 2, 1983; Hyman and White, *Joe Paterno*, pp. 4-

6; Riley, *Road to Number One*, pp. 440-447; Smith, *Orange Bowl*, p. 206.

24 *New York Times*, October 15, 1968 and January 2, 1983; *Philadelphia Inquirer*, January 2, 1970; Hyman and White, *Joe Paterno*, p. 8; Paterno, *By the Book*, pp. 134, 146; Riley, *Road to Number One*, pp. 449-450.

25 *New York Times*, September 18, 1994; Booher, "Joseph Paterno," pp. 53-54; Smith, *Orange Bowl*, p. 124; interviews, Charlie Pittman, Steve Smear.

26 *Pittsburgh Press*, August 6, 1974; Hyman and White, *Joe Paterno*, pp. 227, 250-251.

27 *Daily Collegian*, September 29, 1970; *Life*, October 9, 1970; Hyman and White, *Joe Paterno*, p. 27; Riley, *Road to Number One*, p. 454; Paterno, *By the Book*, p. 157.

28 Joe Paterno Clipping File; *Centre Daily Times*, November 24, 1970; *New York Times Book Review*, December 5, 1971; *Pittsburgh Post-Gazette*, March 25, 1972; *Library Journal*, January 15, 1972; *New Republic*, December 18, 1971; *Saturday Review*, January 1, 1972; Beers, *Profiles*, p. 73.

29 *Philadelphia Evening Bulletin*, December 28, 1972; *Pittsburgh Post-Gazette*, January 8, 1973; Hyman and White, *Joe Paterno*, pp. 253-255.

30 *Pittsburgh Post-Gazette*, January 8, 1973; *Quest*, September/October 1978; *Sports Illustrated*, November 19, 1973; Paterno, *By the Book*, pp. 3-7; Riley, *Road to Number One*, pp. 486-487; interview, Greg Buttle.

31 *Boston Globe*, August 22, 1986; *Sports Illustrated*, November 19, 1973; Paterno, *By the Book*, pp. 8-10; interview, George Paterno.

32 *Los Angeles Times*, August 31, 1973; *Quest*, September/October 1978; *Sports Illustrated*, November 19, 1973; Paterno, *By the Book*, pp. 10-14; Riley, *Road to Number One*, p. 486; interview, Robert Patterson.

33 *Centre Daily Times*, February 15, 1973; *Pittsburgh Post-Gazette*, January 8, 1973; *Quest*, September/October 1978.

34 *Pittsburgh Post-Gazette*, January 8, 1973; *Sports Illustrated*, November 19,

1973; Booher, "Joseph Paterno," p. 42; Jim Benagh, *Making It to #1* (New York: Dodd, Mead and Company, 1976), p. 50; Ken Rappoport, *Nittany Lions: A Story of Penn State Football* (The Strode Publishers, 1973), p. 255.

35 *Centre Daily Times*, February 28 and March 24, 1973; *Sunday Patriot-News*, April 1, 1973.

36 *Los Angeles Times*, August 31, 1973; Booher, "Joseph Paterno," pp. 43, 194-196.

37 *Dallas Morning News*, September 17, 1977; Booher, "Joseph Paterno," pp. 195-198.

38 *Pittsburgh Press*, August 5, 1974; *Sports Illustrated*, November 19, 1973; Beers, *Profiles*, p. 77; interview, Greg Buttle.

39 *Philadelphia Daily News*, October 24, 1977; *Philadelphia Inquirer*, October 18, 1977; Paterno, *By the Book*, pp. 201-202; interview, Thomas Bermingham.

40 *New York Times*, July 10, 1978; *Philadelphia Daily News*, October 24, 1977; *Quest*, September/October 1978; Paterno, *By the Book*, p. 203.

41 *Boston Globe*, August 26, 1986; *New York Times*, November 26, 1978; *Washington Post*, January 1, 1979; *Reader's Digest*, November 1979.

42 *Washington Post*, January 1, 1979; Riley, *Road to Number One*, p. 538.

Chapter 4

1 *New York Daily News*, November 24, 1978; *New York Times*, January 2, 1983; *Washington Post*, January 1, 1979; *Sports Illustrated*, September 25, 1978; interview, Ernie Accorsi.

2 *Centre Daily Times*, January 2, 1979; *Philadelphia Daily News*, November 10, 1982; *Philadelphia Inquirer*, January 2, 1979, January 6, 1983, and December 26, 1986; Paterno, *By the Book*, p. 215; interview, Ernie Accorsi.

3 *New York Times*, January 2, 1983; *Philadelphia Daily News*, November 10, 1982; *Philadelphia Inquirer*, January 6, 1983; *Newsweek*, January 15, 1979.

4 *New York Times*, December 17, 1979; *Philadelphia Inquirer*, August 30, 1982;

Sports Illustrated, March 17, 1980; *Street and Smith's College Football, 1987*; Paterno, *By the Book*, p. 216; interview, John Morris.

5 *Philadelphia Bulletin*, August 23, 1979; *Philadelphia Daily News*, November 9, 1982; *Sports Illustrated*, March 17, 1980.

6 *Philadelphia Daily News*, November 9, 1982; *Sports Illustrated*, March 17, 1980. One confidential interview.

7 *Daily Collegian*, September 28, 1979; *Philadelphia Daily News*, November 9, 1982; *Sunday Patriot-News*, November 4, 1979; *Washington Post*, September 27, 1980; *Sports Illustrated*, March 17, 1980; Paterno, *By the Book*, p. 217.

8 *New York Times*, December 17, 1979; *Philadelphia Daily News*, November 9, 1982; *Washington Post*, September 27, 1980; *Sports Illustrated*, March 17, 1980.

9 *Philadelphia Daily News*, November 9, 1982; *Sports Illustrated*, March 17, 1980; *Street and Smith's College Football, 1987*.

10 *New York Times*, December 17, 1979; *Sports Illustrated*, March 17, 1980, and December 26, 1988/January 2, 1989; interview, George Paterno.

11 *Philadelphia Daily News*, November 12, 1982, and August 27, 1986; *Sports Illustrated*, March 17, 1980, December 26, 1988/January 2, 1989, and December 24, 1990; Barry Switzer (with Bud Shrake), *Bootlegger's Boy* (New York: William Morrow and Co., 1990), pp. 200-201; interview, George Paterno.

12 Booher, "Joseph Paterno," pp. 121-122; Riley, *Road to Number One*, p. 458.

13 *Centre Daily Times*, January 15, 1980; *Pittsburgh Post-Gazette*, January 15, 1980; *Pittsburgh Press*, February 3 and 7, 1980.

14 *Ibid*.

15 Joe Paterno Clipping File; Booher, "Joseph Paterno," pp. 116-126; interviews, Dennis Booher, Steve Garban, Robert Patterson.

16 Joe Paterno Clipping File; *Centre Daily Times*, January 15 and 16, 1980; *Washington Post*, September 27, 1980; Booher, "Joseph Paterno," p. 126.

17 Joe Paterno Clipping File; *Centre Daily Times*, June 13, 1980, and January 25, 1982; *Pittsburgh Press*, January 20, 1982; Booher, "Joseph Paterno," p. 133.

18 *Centre Daily Times*, January 19 and 25, 1982; *Pittsburgh Press*, January 20 and February 1, 1982; interview, Richie Lucas.

19 *Philadelphia Inquirer*, January 3 and 6, 1983, and January 2, 1987; *Saturday Evening Post*, October 1983; interview, Neil Rudel.

20 *Dallas Times Herald*, January 3, 1983; *Philadelphia Inquirer*, January 3, 1983, and January 2, 1987; *Sports Illustrated*, January 10, 1983; Paterno, *By the Book*, pp. 230-232.

21 *Centre Daily Times*, January 3, 1983; *Philadelphia Inquirer*, January 4, 1983; *Sports Illustrated*, January 10, 1983; interview, George Paterno.

22 *Dallas Times Herald*, January 3, 1983; *Philadelphia Inquirer*, January 3, 1983.

23 *Centre Daily Times*, January 3 and 9, 1983; *Philadelphia Inquirer*, January 3, 1983; Paterno, *By the Book*, p. 232.

24 *Centre Daily Times*, January 24, 1983; *Daily Collegian*, April 25, 1984; Charles Moritz (ed.), *Current Biography Yearbook 1984* (New York: The H. W. Wilson Co., 1984), s.v. "Paterno, Joe," p. 315; Paterno, *By the Book*, pp. 233, 238.

25 *Centre Daily Times*, January 24 and 30, 1983; Booher, "Joseph Paterno," pp. 208-211.

26 *Centre Daily Times*, January 24, 1983; *Daily Collegian*, January 24 and April 6, 1983; *Los Angeles Times*, May 17, 1987; *Philadelphia Inquirer*, December 28, 1986; *Sports Illustrated*, December 22-29, 1986.

27 *Milwaukee Sentinel*, January 11, 1989; *New York Times*, January 16 and February 28, 1983; *Pittsburgh Press*, February 13, 1983; Booher, "Joseph Paterno," p. 101; Rader, *American Sports*, pp. 289-290.

28 *Centre Daily Times*, January 12, 1983; *New York Times*, February 28, 1983.

29 *Centre Daily Times*, January 12, 1983; *New York Times*, January 13, 16 and

February 28, 1983; *Pittsburgh Press,* February 13, 1983.

[30] *Milwaukee Sentinel,* January 24, 1989; *New York Times,* February 28, 1983; Booher, "Joseph Paterno," p. 105; interview, Donald Sheffield.

[31] *Centre Daily Times,* January 12, 1983; Booher, "Joseph Paterno," pp. 105-107.

[32] *New York Times,* February 28, 1983; Booher, "Joseph Paterno," p. 108; interviews, John Coyle, Ron Dickerson, Donald Ferrell, Jerry Sandusky, Donald Sheffield.

[33] *Daily Collegian,* February 8, 1983; *New York Times,* January 28, 1983; *Pittsburgh Post-Gazette,* January 28, 1983; *Pittsburgh Press,* February 13, 1983; Booher, "Joseph Paterno," pp. 55-56.

[34] *Centre Daily Times,* March 13 and 14, 1983; interviews, Ron Dickerson, Donald Ferrell.

[35] *Pittsburgh Post-Gazette,* November 26 and December 14, 1984, and July 15, 1985; *USA Today,* November 1, 1985; Moritz (ed.), "Joe Paterno," *Current Biography,* p. 315.

[36] *Patriot,* November 26 and 30, 1984; *Pittsburgh Post-Gazette,* July 15, 1985.

[37] *Boston Globe,* August 22, 1986; *Centre Daily Times,* January 2, 1986; *Philadelphia Inquirer,* December 29, 1986; *Pittsburgh Post-Gazette,* October 23, 1985; Paterno, *By the Book,* p. 243; interview, Jerry Sandusky.

[38] Joe Paterno Clipping File; *Centre Daily Times,* January 2 and March 21, 1986; *Philadelphia Inquirer,* January 4, 1987.

[39] Joe Paterno Clipping File; *Arizona Republic,* December 28, 1986; *Philadelphia Inquirer,* December 27, 1986.

[40] Joe Paterno Clipping File.

[41] Joe Paterno Clipping File; *Beaver Stadium Pictorial,* September 12, 1987.

[42] Joe Paterno Clipping File; *Miami News,* January 3, 1987; *Philadelphia Inquirer,* December 27 and 30, 1986, and January 2 and 4, 1987.

[43] Joe Paterno Clipping File; *Chicago Sun-Times,* December 29, 1986; *Patriot-News,* January 9, 1987; *Philadelphia Inquirer,* December 29 and 30, 1986, and January 4, 1987.

[44] *Dallas Morning News,* January 2, 1987; *Patriot-News,* January 9, 1987; *Philadelphia Inquirer,* December 29, 1986; Paterno, *By the Book,* pp. 17-18, 247.

[45] Joe Paterno Clipping File; *Altoona Mirror,* January 2, 1987; *Centre Daily Times,* December 17, 1986; *Los Angeles Herald Examiner,* January 1, 1987; *Philadelphia Inquirer,* January 2, 1987; *Sharon Herald,* January 2, 1987; interview, Matt Knizner.

[46] Joe Paterno Clipping File; *Altoona Mirror,* January 2 and 5, 1987; *Los Angeles Herald Examiner,* January 1, 1987; *Philadelphia Inquirer,* January 2 and 4, 1987; *Pittsburgh Press,* January 4, 1987; Paterno, *By the Book,* p. 245.

[47] Joe Paterno Clipping File; *Altoona Mirror,* January 5, 1987; *Marietta Daily Journal,* January 4, 1987; *Miami News,* January 3, 1987; *Philadelphia Inquirer,* January 3 and 4, 1987.

[48] Joe Paterno Clipping File; *Altoona Mirror,* January 3, 1987.

[49] Joe Paterno Clipping File; *Altoona Mirror,* January 5, 1987; *Marietta Daily Journal,* January 4, 1987; *Patriot,* March 11, 1987; *Philadelphia Inquirer,* January 7, 1987.

Chapter 5

[1] Rader, *American Sports,* p. 263; Hyman and White, *Joe Paterno,* pp. 39-40.

[2] *Philadelphia Inquirer,* December 28, 1986; Booher, "Joseph Paterno," p. 52; Hyman and White, *Joe Paterno,* p. 44; Paterno, *By the Book,* p. 81; interview, George Paterno.

[3] *Los Angeles Times,* August 31, 1973; Manz and Sims, *SuperLeadership,* p. 64; Paterno, *By the Book,* p. 124.

[4] Joe Paterno Clipping File; interviews, Dick Anderson, John Bove, Tom Bradley, Fran Ganter, Joe Paterno.

[5] *Blue-White Illustrated,* October 17, 1987; *Philadelphia Inquirer,* January 5, 1983; *Pittsburgh Press,* August 6, 1974; *Washington Post,* January 1, 1979; interviews, John Bove, Tom Bradley, George Paterno, Mary Kay Paterno, Sue Paterno, Robert Scannell.

[6] *Blue-White Illustrated*, October 17, 1987; *Philadelphia Inquirer*, January 5, 1983; Hyman and White, *Joe Paterno*, pp. 58, 60; Paterno, *Coaching Winning Football*, p. 19; interviews, Ron Bracken, Tom Bradley, Booker Brooks, Ron Dickerson, Jim O'Hora, Ray Parrillo, Sue Paterno, Frank Patrick, William Schreyer.

[7] *Sports Illustrated*, September 25, 1978; Jack Clary, *Great College Football Coaches* (New York: Gallery Books, 1990), p. 119; Paterno, *Coaching Winning Football*, p. 4; interviews, Dick Anderson, John Bove, Tom Bradley, Craig Cirbus, Steve Garban, Nick Gasparato, Robert Phillips, Jerry Sandusky, Jim Weaver, Joe Yukica.

[8] Interview, Gregg Ducatte.

[9] Interviews, Tom Bradley, Fran Ganter, George Paterno, Frank Patrick, Dan Radakovich, Jerry Sandusky, Donald Sheffield.

[10] Interviews, Booker Brooks, Gregg Ducatte, Fran Ganter, Jerry Sandusky.

[11] Joe Paterno Clipping File; *Daily Collegian*, December 12, 1986; interviews, Booker Brooks, Gregg Ducatte, Nick Gasparato, Robert Phillips.

[12] Joe Paterno Clipping File; Manz and Sims, *SuperLeadership*, p. 66; interview, Jerry Sandusky.

[13] Interview, Fran Ganter.

[14] *Blue-White Illustrated*, October 17, 1987; *Centre Daily Times*, March 21, 1986; Hyman and White, *Joe Paterno*, p. 52; Paterno, *Coaching Winning Football*, pp. 11-12; interviews, Ron Bracken, Chuck Burkhart, Bill Lyon, Dennis Onkotz, Robert Phillips.

[15] *Philadelphia Inquirer*, August 30, 1987; Paterno, *By the Book*, pp. 51, 96; interviews, Booker Brooks, Gregg Ducatte, Robert Phillips, Neil Rudel.

[16] Joe Paterno Clipping File; *Centre Daily Times*, July 22, 1986; interviews, Ron Christ, Gregg Ducatte, Bill Lyon, Charlie Pittman.

[17] *Spectator*, November 9, 1987; interviews, Chuck Medlar, Harry Weller, James Whiteside.

[18] Booher, "Joseph Paterno," p. 45; *Reader's Digest*, November 1979; Denlinger, *For the Glory*, p. 71; Hyman and White, *Joe Paterno*, p. 22; Jack Newcombe, *Six Days to Saturday* (New York: Farrar, Straus, and Giroux, 1974), p. 15; Paterno, *Coaching Winning Football*, p. 69; Paterno, *By the Book*, p. 84; interviews, Gregg Ducatte, Dave Joyner, Dennis Onkotz, Robert Phillips.

[19] *Reader's Digest*, November 1979; Paterno, *Coaching Winning Football*, pp. 115-116; Paterno, *By the Book*, p. 83; interviews, John Bove, Jim Weaver.

[20] *Newsday*, October 15; 1993; *Reader's Digest*, November 1979; Denlinger, *For the Glory*, pp. 70-71; Newcombe, *Six Days*, pp. 25-27; interviews, Tom Bradley, Mike Irwin, Tom Jackson, Dave Joyner, Matt Knizner.

[21] Joe Paterno Clipping File; *Philadelphia Inquirer*, December 28, 1986; *Sports Illustrated*, December 22-29, 1986; Denlinger, *For the Glory*, p. 69; Paterno, *By the Book*, p. 70; interviews, Mike Irwin, Matt Knizner, Bill Zimpfer.

[22] Newcombe, *Six Days*, pp. 6, 21, 22, 39, 67, 72.

[23] *Ibid.*, pp. 17-21, 36-37.

[24] *Ibid.*, p. 59; interviews, Bill Lenkaitis, Dennis Onkotz.

[25] Denlinger, *For the Glory*, pp. 10, 24, 32; Newcombe, *Six Days*, pp. 6-7.

[26] *New York Times*, July 9, 1978; *Philadelphia Daily News*, November 8, 1982.

[27] Joe Paterno Clipping File; *Philadelphia Inquirer*, December 21, 1986, and January 2, 1987; Paterno, *By the Book*, p. 180; interviews, Ron Bracken, Tom Bradley, Robert Phillips, Jerry Sandusky.

[28] Paterno, *By the Book*, pp. 22, 182; interviews, John Bove, Fran Ganter, Robert Phillips.

[29] Denlinger, *For the Glory*, p. 35; Paterno, *By the Book*, pp. 180, 182; interviews, Bernard Asbell, Ron Dickerson, Robert Phillips, Charlie Pittman, J. T. White.

[30] Joe Paterno Clipping File; *Lehighton Times News*, January 29, 1987; *Sports Illustrated*, March 15, 1976.

[31] "Penn State Football, Player Clippings, 1991 Season" (pamphlet), Sports Information Office Papers, Pennsylvania

State University; *Quest,*
September/October 1978; Denlinger,
For the Glory, p. 41; interviews, Todd
Blackledge, Booker Brooks, Frank
Patrick, Robert Phillips, Dan
Radakovich, Sever Toretti.
32 *Philadelphia Inquirer Magazine*, August
30, 1987.
33 *Quest*, September/October 1978;
Booher, "Joseph Paterno," pp. 86, 90;
Paterno, *By the Book*, p. 176; inter-
views, Jerry Sandusky, Sever Toretti.
34 *Centre Daily Times*, February 28, 1985;
Chicago Tribune, September 15, 1978;
Philadelphia Inquirer, January 6, 1983;
Pittsburgh Press, February 1, 1982; Den-
linger, *For the Glory*, pp. 15, 68, 304.
35 *Chicago Tribune*, September 15, 1978;
Philadelphia Inquirer, January 6, 1983;
Pittsburgh Press, February 1, 1982;
interview, Ron Bracken.
36 *Quest*, September/October 1978; *Sports
Illustrated*, September 25, 1978;
Paterno, *By the Book*, pp. 130, 151;
interviews, Ron Bracken, Joe Paterno.
37 *Washington Post*, January 1, 1979;
Quest, September/October 1978.

Chapter 6

1 *New York Daily News*, November 23,
1978; *New York Times*, July 10, 1978;
Philadelphia Inquirer, December 29,
1986, and January 2, 1987; *USA Today*,
November 17, 1986; interviews, Mil-
ton Bergstein, Dan Radakovich.
2 *Success*, October 1983; *Town and Gown*,
September 1972; Denlinger, *For the
Glory*, pp. 57, 214; interviews, Fran
Ganter, Bucky Greeley, John Shaffer.
3 Joe Paterno Clipping File; *Los Angeles
Times*, May 17, 1987; *Philadelphia
Inquirer Magazine*, August 30, 1987;
Denlinger, *For the Glory*, pp. 66, 194;
Hyman and White, *Joe Paterno*, p. 139;
interviews, Milton Bergstein, Todd
Blackledge, Tom Bradley, Fran Ganter,
Matt Knizner, James Whiteside.
4 *Sunday Patriot-News*, August 30, 1987;
Philadelphia Inquirer Magazine, August
30, 1987; *Success*, October 1983; *Wash-
ington Post*, January 1, 1979; Booher,

"Joseph Paterno," p. 45; Clary, *College
Football Coaches*, p. 119; Don Kowet,
Franco Harris (New York: Coward,
McCann and Geoghegan, Inc., 1977),
pp. 30, 35; Paterno, *Coaching Winning
Football*, pp. 6-8; interviews, Todd
Blackledge, Warren Hartenstine, John
Shaffer.
5 *Philadelphia Daily News*, November 12,
1982; interviews, Todd Blackledge,
Dennis Onkotz, Dan Radakovich.
6 *Philadelphia Daily News*, November 9,
1982; *Sports Illustrated*, March 15,
1976; Hyman and White, *Joe Paterno*,
p. 37; interviews, John Bove, Steve
Smear.
7 *Sports Illustrated*, September 25, 1978;
Hyman and White, *Joe Paterno*, pp. 50,
238; Paterno, *Coaching Winning Football*, p. 20; Paterno, *By the Book*, p. 95;
interviews, John Bove, Greg Buttle,
John Hufnagel, Robert Phillips, Dan
Radakovich, John Shaffer.
8 Interviews, Todd Blackledge, Greg Buttle.
9 Denlinger, *For the Glory*, p. 187; interviews, Todd Blackledge, Greg Buttle.
10 Newcombe, *Six Days*, p. 51.
11 *Sports Illustrated*, September 25, 1978;
Manz and Sims, *SuperLeadership*, p. 62;
Riley, *Road to Number One*, p. 481;
Paterno, *By the Book*, p. 121.
12 Joe Paterno Clipping File; *Philadelphia
Inquirer Magazine*, August 30, 1987;
Manz and Sims, *SuperLeadership*, p. 63;
interview, Robert Phillips.
13 Joe Paterno Clipping File; *Philadelphia
Daily News*, November 8, 1982;
Booher, "Joseph Paterno," p. 53; Denlinger, *For the Glory*, pp. 72, 303-304;
interviews, Ray Didinger, Charlie
Pittman.
14 *Philadelphia Daily News*, November 8
and 9, 1982; Booher, "Joseph Paterno,"
pp. 46-47; Hyman and White, *Joe
Paterno*, p. 59; Rappoport, *Nittany
Lions*, p. 254.
15 Joe Paterno Clipping File; *Philadelphia
Daily News*, November 8, 1982; interviews, Greg Buttle, Dave Joyner.
16 *Los Angeles Times*, May 17, 1987; *Penn
State Basketball and Football: 1991*, Volume 9, No. 2, p. 9.

[17] *Philadelphia Inquirer*, January 1, 1987.

[18] *Los Angeles Times*, May 17, 1987; Booher, "Joseph Paterno," pp. 47-48; Paterno, *By the Book*, pp. 86-87.

[19] *Philadelphia Daily News*, August 27, 1986; *Philadelphia Inquirer*, December 25 and 28, 1986; interviews, Charlie Pittman, John Shaffer.

[20] *Lancaster New Era*, December 18, 1986.

[21] *Philadelphia Inquirer*, December 23, 1986; Hyman and White, *Joe Paterno*, p. 14; interview, Charlie Pittman.

[22] Paterno, *By the Book*, p. 153.

[23] Denlinger, *For the Glory*, p. 59; Kowet, *Franco Harris*, p. 28; interview, Jesse Arnelle.

[24] *Philadelphia Inquirer*, December 31, 1986; Hyman and White, *Joe Paterno*, p. 161.

[25] Hyman and White, *Joe Paterno*, pp. 153-160; Paterno, *By the Book*, p. 52.

[26] Hyman and White, *Joe Paterno*, p. 162; interviews, Charlie Pittman, John Swinton.

[27] Paterno, *By the Book*, pp. 154-160.

[28] *Centre Daily Times*, March 13 and 15, 1983; *Philadelphia Daily News*, November 11, 1982; *Pittsburgh Press*, February 13, 1983; Booher, "Joseph Paterno," p. 54.

[29] Interview, Jesse Arnelle.

[30] *Philadelphia Daily News*, November 11, 1982; *Pittsburgh Press*, February 13, 1983; Bezilla, *Penn State*, p. 354; interview, Charlie Pittman.

[31] *Centre Daily Times*, March 15, 1983; *Philadelphia Daily News*, November 11, 1982; *Pittsburgh Press*, February 13, 1983; Booher, "Joseph Paterno," pp. 58-59.

[32] *Philadelphia Daily News*, November 11, 1982; Booher, "Joseph Paterno," p. 57; interviews, Bernard Asbell, Booker Brooks, Ron Dickerson, Bill Lyon, Dan Radakovich.

[33] Joe Paterno Clipping File; *Reader's Digest*, November 1979; Bezilla, *Penn State*, p. 379; Denlinger, *For the Glory*, p. 302; Hyman and White, *Joe Paterno*, p. 16; Paterno, *By the Book*, p. 16; Riley, *Road to Number One*, p. 488; interviews, John Coyle, Don Ferrell, Dave Joyner.

[34] *Dallas Morning News*, September 17, 1977; *Philadelphia Daily News*, November 12, 1982; Paterno, *By the Book*, pp. 17, 270; Riley, *Road to Number One*, p. 488.

[35] Joe Paterno Clipping File; "Penn State Football, Player Clippings, 1991 Season"; *Los Angeles Times*, May 17, 1987; *Philadelphia Inquirer*, December 25, 1986; *Saturday Evening Post*, October 1983; interviews, Chuck Burkhart, Ron Dickerson, Gregg Ducatte.

[36] Denlinger, *For the Glory*, pp. 111, 131.

[37] *Sports Illustrated*, December 22-29, 1986; Paterno, *By the Book*, pp. 19-20.

[38] Interview, Ron Dickerson.

[39] *Philadelphia Inquirer*, December 25, 1986; interviews, Chuck Burkhart, Ron Dickerson, Gregg Ducatte, Don Ferrell, Nick Gasparato, Bucky Greeley, James Whiteside.

[40] Interviews, Milton Bergstein, Booker Brooks, Phil Grosz, Robert Phillips.

[41] Joe Paterno Clipping File; *New York Times*, December 23, 1986; *Sunday Patriot-News*, November 4, 1979; *Philadelphia Inquirer*, January 4, 1983; *Sharon Herald*, January 2, 1987; Paterno, *By the Book*, p. 20; interviews, Robert Phillips, Ronald Smith.

[42] Interview, Milton Bergstein.

[43] Joe Paterno Clipping File, *Centre Daily Times*, November 2, 1979; Booher, "Joseph Paterno," pp. 75-77; interviews, John Coyle, Steve Garban, Robert Phillips, Ronald Smith.

[44] *Philadelphia Inquirer*, January 4, 1983.

[45] Joe Paterno Clipping File; *Altoona Mirror*, May 1, 1988; *New York Times*, February 21, 1975; *Sharon Herald*, January 2, 1987; Hyman and White, *Joe Paterno*, p. 176.

[46] *Philadelphia Inquirer*, May 20, 1970; Hyman and White, *Joe Paterno*, p. 170.

[47] Hyman and White, *Joe Paterno*, pp. 184-185.

[48] Joe Paterno Clipping File; *Los Angeles Times*, May 17, 1987; *Philadelphia Daily News*, November 12, 1982; *Sports Illustrated*, November 19, 1973; Hyman and White, *Joe Paterno*, pp. 167-174; Paterno, *By the Book*, p. 191.

49 *Dallas Morning News*, September 17, 1977; *Philadelphia Bulletin*, November 5, 1980; Paterno, *By the Book*, pp. 194-196.

50 *Dallas Morning News*, September 17, 1977; *Philadelphia Bulletin*, November 5, 1980; Paterno, *By the Book*, p. 219; Riley, *Road to Number One*, p. 483.

51 Joe Paterno Clipping File; *Philadelphia Inquirer*, December 30, 1986; *Patriot*, January 10, 1978; *Quest*, September/October 1978; Paterno, *By the Book*, pp. 148-150; Rader, *American Sports*, p. 271.

52 *Centre Daily Times*, August 21, 1983; Paterno, *By the Book*, p. 187.

53 Booher, "Joseph Paterno," pp. 93-97; Paterno, *By the Book*, p. 193; Rader, *American Sports*, p. 275.

54 "Academic Achievement Award Winners" (memo), College Football Marketing Corporation Papers, Boulder, Colorado; *Sidelines*, June 1992; *Football News*, January 8, 1973; *Centre Daily Times*, February 2, 1990; *New York Times*, February 28, 1983; *Pittsburgh Press*, August 6, 1974; *Washington Post*, November 3, 1987; *Saturday Evening Post*, October 1983; Booher, "Joseph Paterno," pp. 67-68, 80; Riley, *Road to Number One*, p. 506; interviews, Dave Baker, Vito Stellino.

Chapter 7

1 *Centre Daily Times*, July 22, 1986; Booher, "Joseph Paterno," p. 140; interviews, John Morris, Ronald Smith.

2 *Philadelphia Inquirer*, January 5, 1983; Booher, "Joseph Paterno," pp. 138-139; Beers, *Profiles*, p. 74; interview, John Morris.

3 *Philadelphia Daily News*, November 8, 1982; *Philadelphia Inquirer*, January 5, 1983; interviews, Don Ferrell, George Paterno.

4 Joe Paterno Clipping File; *Philadelphia Inquirer*, January 5, 1983; Booher, "Joseph Paterno," p. 141; interviews, George Paterno, Jim Tarman.

5 *Philadelphia Evening Bulletin*, December 28, 1972; *Philadelphia Inquirer*, January

5, 1983; *Washington Post*, January 1, 1979; *Quest*, September/October 1978; interviews, Ralph Bernstein, Ron Bracken, Jim Tarman.

6 Joe Paterno Clipping File; *Philadelphia Inquirer*, January 5, 1983; *Washington Post*, October 12, 1969; *Saturday Evening Post*, October 1983; Paterno, *By the Book*, p. 139; interviews, Bernard Asbell, David Gearhart, Bill Lyon, John Morris.

7 Joe Paterno to Barbara Savignano, July 12, 1994, unprocessed Barbara Savignano Papers, Seekonk, Massachusetts; *Washington Post*, January 1, 1979; *Penn State Basketball and Football: 1991*, vol. 9, no. 2; interviews, Tom Bradley, Chuck Burkhart, Gregg Ducatte, Marty Gresh, Donald Sheffield, Joe Yukica.

8 Joe Paterno Clipping File; *Philadelphia Inquirer*, January 5, 1983; *Washington Post*, January 1, 1979; Hyman and White, *Joe Paterno*, p. 48; interview, Joe Paterno.

9 *Chicago Tribune*, November 24, 1981; *Philadelphia Inquirer*, January 5, 1983; *Washington Post*, January 1, 1979; Hyman and White, *Joe Paterno*, p. 48; interview, Bill Lyon.

10 *Centre Daily Times*, May 20, 1984; *Philadelphia Inquirer*, January 5, 1983; *Washington Post*, January 1, 1979; Booher, "Joseph Paterno," p. 140; Hyman and White, *Joe Paterno*, p. 47; interviews, Bernard Asbell, Ron Bracken, Gregg Ducatte, Steve Garban, George Paterno, Scott Paterno, Sue Paterno, Jim Weaver, Harry Weller.

11 *Philadelphia Inquirer*, January 5, 1983; *Washington Post*, January 1, 1979; *Sports Illustrated*, December 22-29, 1986; interviews, Bill Lyon, Jerry Sandusky.

12 *Sports Illustrated*, December 22-29, 1986.

13 Joe Paterno Clipping File; *Northeast Magazine*, Fall 1987; *Reader's Digest*, November 1979; Paterno, *By the Book*, p. 121; interview, Jerry Sandusky.

14 Joe Paterno Clipping File; *Cincinnati Post*, September 3, 1991; Paterno, *By the Book*, p. 94; interview, John Morris.

15 Paterno, *By the Book*, p. 210; interviews, Sue Paterno, Harry Weller.
16 Booher, "Joseph Paterno," pp. 90-91; William Baker and John Carroll, *Sports in Modern America* (Saint Louis: River City Publishers Limited, 1981), pp. 121-122; Hyman and White, *Joe Paterno*, p. 147; Rader, *American Sports*, pp. 340-341.
17 *Centre Daily Times*, June 26, 1975; *Chicago Tribune*, August 2, 1975.
18 *Chicago Tribune*, August 2, 1975; Booher, "Joseph Paterno," pp. 91-93; interviews, Ron Bracken, Ronald Smith.
19 Bezilla, *Penn State*, p. 375; Paterno, *By the Book*, pp. 62-63.
20 *Family*, June 1987; *Philadelphia Inquirer*, May 20, 1970, and January 3, 1987; Paterno, *By the Book*, pp. 50, 132; interviews, Jay Paterno, Scott Paterno.
21 Joe Paterno to William Schreyer, August 3, 1986, unprocessed William Schreyer Papers, Plainsboro, New Jersey. Schreyer read the letter to the author over the telephone. *Family*, June 1987; *Philadelphia Inquirer*, May 20, 1979; Paterno, *By the Book*, pp. 211-212; interviews, Joe Paterno, William Schreyer.
22 *Dallas Morning News*, September 17, 1977; *Philadelphia Inquirer*, January 5, 1983, and December 25, 1986; *Washington Post*, November 3, 1987; *Sports Illustrated*, September 25, 1987; Hyman and White, *Joe Paterno*, p. 15.
23 "Speech by Joe Paterno, Gettysburg College Commencement, June 3, 1979," Joe Paterno Clipping File; *Sports Illustrated*, December 22-29, 1986; interview, Bill Lyon.
24 *Sports Illustrated*, December 22-29, 1986; *Success*, October 1983; interviews, Sue Paterno, Robert Scannell.
25 *Philadelphia Inquirer Magazine*, August 30, 1987; interviews, Bernard Asbell, Thomas Bermingham, Ron Christ, John Coyle, Gregg Ducatte, Bill Lyon, Sue Paterno.
26 Joe Paterno Clipping File; *Patriot News*, December 1, 1988; *Newsweek*, January 15, 1979; *Sports Illustrated*, March 17,

1980; Booher, "Joseph Paterno," pp. 41, 143; interviews, Jesse Arnelle, David Yukelson.
27 *Philadelphia Inquirer*, January 5, 1983; *Washington Post*, November 3, 1987; interview, Charlie Pittman.
28 Joe Paterno Clipping File; *San Diego Union*, January 1, 1987; *Quest*, September/October 1978.
29 Joe Paterno Clipping File; *Boston Globe*, August 22, 1986; *Quest*, September/October 1978; interviews, John Bove, Steve Garban, David Gearhart, Sue Paterno, William Schreyer.
30 Interview, Joe Paterno.
31 *Philadelphia Inquirer*, January 5, 1983; *Sports Illustrated*, March 15, 1976; interviews, Ray Parrillo, Joe Paterno.
32 *Philadelphia Inquirer*, January 6, 1983; *Washington Post*, January 1, 1979; *Sports Illustrated*, March 15, 1976; Paterno, *By the Book*, pp. 156-157, 260.
33 Joe Paterno Clipping File; *Centre Daily Times*, May 20, 1984; *Daily Collegian*, April 28, 1989; *Patriot*, April 20, 1983; interviews, Bill Lyon, Florence Mittleman.
34 *Philadelphia Inquirer*, August 14, 1988; *Penn State 1988 Football Annual*, vol. 7, no. 1, 1988; interviews, Milton Bergstein, Bill Lyon, George Paterno, Jay Paterno, Joe Paterno, Scott Paterno, Sue Paterno.
35 Joe Paterno Clipping File; *Washington Post*, October 12, 1969; Hyman and White, *Joe Paterno*, pp. 256-257; interviews, Ralph Bernstein, Bill Lyon, Joe Paterno.
36 Joe Paterno Clipping File; *Dallas Morning News*, December 8, 1971; *Philadelphia Inquirer*, January 4, 1983; *Reader's Digest*, November 1979; *Sports Illustrated*, March 15, 1976, and December 22-29, 1986; Hyman and White, *Joe Paterno*, p. 12; Beers, *Profiles*, p. 74.
37 *Los Angeles Times*, September 19, 1991; "Penn State, 1990 Season, Paterno/Player Features," Sports Information Office Papers, Pennsylvania State University; *Sports Illustrated*, March 15, 1976

38 *Centre Daily Times*, June 4, 1982; *Cincinnati Post*, September 3, 1991; *Miami Herald*, December 31, 1986; *Philadelphia Inquirer Magazine*, August 30, 1987; *Pittsburgh Post-Gazette*, January 8, 1973; Booher, "Joseph Paterno," p. 74; interview, George Paterno.

39 *Fund Raising Management*, April 1995; *Northeast Magazine*, Fall 1987; *Pittsburgh Post-Gazette*, November 13, 1987; interview, Steve Garban.

40 Joe Paterno Clipping File; *Asbury Park Press*, December 29, 1985; *Philadelphia Inquirer*, December 28, 1986; *USA Today*, September 6, 1989; *Sports Illustrated*, March 17, 1980; interview, Beano Cook.

41 *New York Times*, November 26, 1979; *Sports Illustrated*, March 17, 1980.

42 *Altoona Mirror*, December 30, 1990; *Philadelphia Inquirer Magazine*, August 30, 1987; *Sports Illustrated*, December 22-29, 1986.

43 Joe Paterno Clipping File; *Philadelphia Daily News*, November 8, 1982; *Philadelphia Inquirer*, January 4, 1983; *Philadelphia Inquirer Magazine*, August 30, 1987; *Saturday Evening Post*, October 1983.

44 *Asbury Park Press*, December 29, 1985; *Centre Daily News*, March 28, 1986; *Los Angeles Times*, May 17, 1987; *Miami Herald*, December 31, 1986; *New York Times*, February 28, 1983; *USA Today*, November 1, 1985; Rick Telander, *Hundred Yard Lie* (New York: Simon and Schuster, 1989), p. 51; interviews, Dennis Booher, John Swinton.

45 *Centre Daily News*, July 27, 1978.

46 *Philadelphia Daily News*, November 8 and 9, 1982; *USA Today*, September 6, 1989.

47 *Philadelphia Daily News*, November 8 and 12, 1982; interview, Ray Didinger.

48 Joe Paterno Clipping File; *Philadelphia Inquirer*, January 6, 1983; *Sports Illustrated*, March 17, 1980.

49 *Philadelphia Inquirer*, January 5, 1983; interview, Booker Brooks.

50 Joe Paterno Clipping File; interviews, Ralph Bernstein, Bill Lyon.

Chapter 8

1 *Town and Gown*, September 1972; Bezilla, *Penn State*, pp. 355, 359-360.

2 *Ibid.*; *Dallas Morning News*, December 8, 1971; Paterno, *By the Book*, p. 117.

3 Clipping, Gearhart Papers, University Park, Pennsylvania; *Fund Raising Management*, April 1995.

4 *Ibid.*; *Beaver Stadium Pictorial*, November 2, 1985, and September 12, 1987; *Northeast Magazine*, Fall 1987; *Philadelphia Inquirer Magazine*, August 30, 1987; *Washington Post*, November 3, 1987; interview, Nancy Cline.

5 Joe Paterno Clipping File; *Los Angeles Times*, May 17, 1987; *Philadelphia Daily News*, August 27, 1986; *Philadelphia Inquirer*, December 28, 1986; *Fund Raising Management*, April 1995; interview, David Gearhart.

6 Joe Paterno Clipping File; *Fund Raising Management*, April 1995; interview, Bryce Jordan.

7 *Fund Raising Management*, April 1995; interviews, David Gearhart, Edward Hintz, William Schreyer.

8 Interviews, David Gearhart, William Schreyer.

9 *Fund Raising Management*, April 1995; interviews, David Gearhart, Sue Paterno.

10 *Centre Daily Times*, April 23, 1992; *Chronicle of Higher Education*, January 13, 1993; *Fund Raising Management*, April 1995; *Penn State News*, July 15, 1994; interviews, Nancy Cline, David Gearhart.

11 *Fund Raising Management*, April 1995; interview, David Gearhart.

12 Interview, Edward Hintz.

13 *Fund Raising Management*, April 1995; *Penn State News*, July 15, 1994; *USA Today*, January 19, 1998; interview, Sue Paterno.

14 *Centre Daily Times*, January 18, 1987; interview, Ron Christ.

15 *Asbury Park Press*, December 29, 1985; *Centre Daily Times*, January 18, 1987; *Sports Illustrated*, December 22-29, 1986; interviews, Bernard Asbell, David Gearhart, George Paterno, Scott Paterno, Sue Paterno.

[16] *Asbury Park Press*, December 29, 1985; *Boston Globe*, August 22, 1986; *Centre Daily Times*, January 19, 1982; *Philadelphia Daily News*, November 8, 1982; *Penn State Basketball and Football: 1991*, vol. 9, no. 2; Hyman and White, *Joe Paterno*, p. 117; interviews, David Paterno, Jay Paterno. Mary Kay Paterno, Scott Paterno, Sue Paterno.

[17] *Town and Gown*, September 1972; interviews, Diana Giegerich, David Paterno, Jay Paterno, Mary Kay Paterno, Scott Paterno, Sue Paterno.

[18] *Boston Globe*, August 22, 1986; *Centre Daily Times*, January 18, 1987; Paterno, *By the Book*, p. 197; interviews, Bernard Asbell, David Paterno, Sue Paterno.

[19] *Boston Globe*, August 22, 1986; *Centre Daily Times*, January 18, 1987; *Success*, October 1983; interviews, Ralph Bernstein, Jay Paterno, Scott Paterno, Sue Paterno.

[20] *Penn State Basketball and Football: 1991*, vol. 8, no. 2; interviews, Jay Paterno, Mary Kay Paterno.

[21] *Ibid.*; Paterno, *By the Book*, p. 197; interviews, Diana Giegerich, David Paterno, Scott Paterno.

[22] *Philadelphia Inquirer*, January 15, 1983; Paterno, *By the Book*, p. 197; interviews, David Paterno, George Paterno, Jay Paterno, Mary Kay Paterno, Scott Paterno.

[23] *Philadelphia Daily News*, November 8, 1982; *Pittsburgh Press*, August 6, 1974; interviews, Ralph Bernstein, Tom Bradley, John Morris, Joe Paterno, Scott Paterno, Sue Paterno, Dan Radakovich, Jim Weaver.

[24] Interviews, Bernard Asbell, Thomas Bermingham, Jay Paterno, Joe Paterno, Sue Paterno.

Chapter 9

[1] Joe Paterno Clipping File; "Penn State Player Clippings, 1994 Season" (pamphlet), Sports Information Office Papers, Pennsylvania State University; *Centre Daily Times*, September 7, 1992; *Detroit Free Press*, October 14, 1993;

Denlinger, *For the Glory*, p. 36; interview, Craig Cirbus.

[2] Joe Paterno Clipping File; *Centre Daily Times*, October 12, 1988; *Philadelphia Inquirer*, September 6, 1990; *The Sporting News*, September 21, 1992.

[3] *Pittsburgh Post-Gazette*, November 16, 1988; Paterno, *By the Book*, p. 261.

[4] Joe Paterno Clipping File; *Altoona Mirror*, November 25 and December 9, 1988; *Patriot-News*, November 25, 1988; *Washington Post*, September 6, 1989; Paterno, *By the Book*, p. 262.

[5] *Centre Daily Times*, August 3 and August 8, 1989; *New York Times Book Review*, October 1, 1989; *USA Today*, September 6, 1989.

[6] Joe Paterno Clipping File; *Altoona Mirror*, January 3, 1992; *Philadelphia Inquirer*, January 4, 1983; interview, Bill Lyon.

[7] *Los Angeles Times*, May 17, 1987; *Patriot-News*, August 18, 1988; *Philadelphia Inquirer*, August 14, 1988; interview, Steve Garban.

[8] *Altoona Mirror*, August 18, 1988; *Patriot-News*, August 14, 1988; *Philadelphia Inquirer*, August 9, 10, and 14, 1988.

[9] *Altoona Mirror*, August 18, 1988; *Patriot-News*, August 14, 1988; *Philadelphia Inquirer*, August 14, 1988.

[10] *Centre Daily Times*, September 23 and 24, 1992; *Courier Journal*, September 6, 1996; *Washington Post*, September 25, 1992; *Washington Post National Weekly*, November 24, 1997; Denlinger, *For the Glory*, p. 278; interviews, Joe Paterno, Sue Paterno.

[11] John Swinton to John Brighton, August 26, 1992, unprocessed John Swinton Papers, State College, Pennsylvania; *Centre Daily Times*, November 15 and 24, 1989, August 25 and October 9, 1992, and April 15, 1994.

[12] *Centre Daily Times*, August 17, 1989; *Detroit Free Press*, October 14, 1993; Newcombe, *Six Days*, p. 63; interviews, Milton Bergstein, Ralph Bernstein, Bill Lyon, Neil Rudel.

[13] Joe Paterno Clipping File; *Centre Daily Times*, August 17, 1989; *Pittsburgh Post-Gazette*, February 8, 1980; *Sports*

Illustrated, December 22-29, 1986; interviews, Ron Bracken, Ray Parrillo, Neil Rudel.

14 *Altoona Mirror*, November 7, 1994; *Boston Globe*, September 7, 1990; *Philadelphia Daily News*, August 27, 1986; interviews, Ralph Bernstein, Ron Bracken, Ron Christ, Neil Rudel.

15 *Centre Daily Times*, August 26, 1992; interviews, Ron Christ, Bill Zimpfer. One confidential interview.

16 *Centre Daily Times*, June 23, 1980; interviews, Ron Christ, John Morris, Bill Lyon, George Paterno, Joe Paterno.

17 *Centre Daily Times*, May 20, 1984; interviews, Dick Anderson, John Bove, Ron Dickerson, Sue Paterno, Robert Phillips, John Shaffer.

18 *Centre Daily Times*, August 17, 1989; *Saturday Evening Post*, October 1983; Paterno, *By the Book*, p. 226.

19 *Centre Daily Times*, December 31, 1991, and March 1, 1992; *Philadelphia Inquirer*, December 29, 1991; Denlinger, *For the Glory*, pp. 93, 94, 143, 206, 219.

20 *Ibid.*; interviews, Ron Bracken, George Paterno. One confidential interview.

21 *Boston Globe*, September 7, 1990; interviews, Milton Bergstein, Ralph Bernstein, Ron Bracken, Bill Carroll, Ron Christ, Ray Parrillo, Ron Smith.

22 "Penn State, 1990 Season, Paterno/Player Features" (pamphlet), Sports Information Office Papers, Pennsylvania State University; *Philadelphia Inquirer*, September 6, 1990; *The Sporting News*, September 21, 1992; interview, Thomas Bermingham.

23 "Penn State, 1990 Season, Paterno/Player Features," *Boston Globe*, September 7, 1990; *Washington Post*, September 25, 1992.

24 Joe Paterno Clipping File; *Patriot-News*, August 28 and December 1, 1988; *The Sporting News*, September 21, 1992.

25 *Centre Daily Times*, August 27, 28, and 30, 1992.

26 *Centre Daily Times*, August 22, 28, and 20, 1992; *Newsday*, October 15, 1993.

27 *Altoona Mirror*, October 11 and 14, 1992; *Centre Daily Times*, October 5, 1992; *Philadelphia Daily News*, August

31, 1993; *Philadelphia Inquirer*, October 11, 1992; Denlinger, *For the Glory*, pp. 267, 271.

28 *Altoona Mirror*, October 18, 22, and November 1, 1992; *Centre Daily Times*, December 30, 1992; *New York Times*, October 10, 1994; *Philadelphia Inquirer*, January 3, 1993.

29 *Altoona Mirror*, January 2 and 3, 1993; *Centre Daily Times*, December 8, 1992, and January 2, 1993; *Philadelphia Inquirer*, January 2, 1993.

30 "Penn State Player Clippings: 1993 Season" (pamphlet), Sports Information Office Papers, Pennsylvania State University; *Altoona Mirror*, October 18 and November 2, 1992; *Philadelphia Inquirer*, November 1, 1992; Denlinger, *For the Glory*, pp. 256, 306; interviews, Dick Anderson, Tom Bradley, Ron Christ, Bucky Greeley.

31 *Centre Daily Times*, January 3 and 5, 1993.

32 *Centre Daily Times*, January 3, 1993; *Los Angeles Times*, August 27, 1993; *Patriot*, October 20, 1994; interviews, Ron Christ, Bucky Greeley.

33 Interviews, George Paterno, Jay Paterno, Scott Paterno, William Schreyer.

34 "Penn State Player Clippings: 1993 Season" (pamphlet), *Newsday*, October 15, 1993; *New York Times*, October 10, 1994; interviews, Ron Bracken, Tom Bradley, Bucky Greeley, Sue Paterno.

35 *New York Times*, September 4, 1993; *Patriot*, October 20, 1994; *Philadelphia Daily News*, August 31, 1993; *Pittsburgh Post-Gazette*, August 29, 1993.

36 "Penn State Player Clippings: 1993 Season" (pamphlet), *Los Angeles Times*, August 27, 1993; *Philadelphia Daily News*, August 31, 1993; *Pittsburgh Post-Gazette*, May 23 and August 29, 1993; *The Sporting News*, October 25, 1993.

37 "Penn State Player Clippings: 1993 Season" (pamphlet), *The Sporting News*, October 25, 1993.

38 *Altoona Mirror*, October 30, 1994; *Centre Daily Times*, August 21, 1994; *Daily Collegian*, August 25, 1994; Denlinger, *For the Glory*, p. 5.

[39] *Centre Daily Times*, August 21, 1994; *Daily Collegian*, August 25, 1994; Denlinger, *For the Glory*, pp. 2, 110, 198, 304.

[40] *Altoona Mirror*, October 30, 1994; *Centre Daily Times*, August 21, 1994; *Daily Collegian*, August 25, 1994; Denlinger, *For the Glory*, p. 5.

[41] *Altoona Mirror*, October 12 and 13, 1994; *Football News*, October 15, 1994.

[42] *Altoona Mirror*, October 16, 17, 19, and 22, 1994.

[43] *Altoona Mirror*, October 19, 30, and November 13 and 27, 1994; interview, Bucky Greeley.

[44] *Penn State Football Yearbook: 1995* (University Park: Sports Information Office, Penn State University, 1995), pp. 44, 162-163.

[45] "Penn State Player Clippings: 1993 Season" (pamphlet); interviews, Dick Anderson, Ron Christ, Bucky Greeley, Jay Paterno, Sue Paterno.

[46] *Altoona Mirror*, November 2, 1994; *Appleton Post-Crescent*, January 4, 1995; *Sunday Record*, August 25, 1996; *1997 Penn State Football Yearbook*, p. 135.

[47] *Altoona Mirror*, October 2, 1992; *Centre Daily Times*, August 13, 1994; Denlinger, *For the Glory*, pp. 11, 33.

[48] Joe Paterno Clipping File; *Philadelphia Inquirer*, September 6, 1990; *Washington Post*, September 25, 1992.

[49] Denlinger, *For the Glory*, p. 305; interviews, George Paterno, Scott Paterno.

[50] *Centre Daily Times*, August 12, 1990; *Milwaukee Sentinel*, July 27, 1990; *Patriot-News*, August 9, 1992; *The Sporting News*, September 21, 1992.

[51] *Altoona Mirror*, October 2, 1992; *Centre Daily Times*, August 13, 1994.

[52] *Altoona Mirror*, October 2, 1992; *Centre Daily Times*, September 7, 1992; *New York Times*, July 10, 1997; *1997 Penn State Football Yearbook*, p. 125.

∾ SOURCES ∾

This essay does not include a complete list of all the sources used for this study. Readers should consult endnote citations for specific sources.

Manuscripts

The personal papers of Joe Paterno are not currently open for research and probably will not be for many years. The most significant source presently available is the voluminous Joe Paterno clipping file in the Sports Information Office Papers (Pennsylvania State University, University Park, Pennsylvania). Other helpful collections were the Brown University football scrapbooks in the Brown University Papers (Brown University Archives, Providence, Rhode Island); Charles A. Engle Papers (Pennsylvania State University Archives, University Park, Pennsylvania); G. David Gearhart Papers (University Park, Pennsylvania); Joseph Hurley Papers (Breezy Point, New York); the clipping file in the Joseph Paterno Papers (Pennsylvania State University Archives, University Park, Pennsylvania); Barbara Savignano Papers (Seekonk, Massachusetts); and the John Swinton Papers (State College, Pennsylvania). Several individuals and institutions sent me their collections for photocopying.

Books and Articles

Mervin Hyman and Gordon White, *Joe Paterno: "Football My Way"* (New York: Macmillan, 1971), sometimes insightfully describes Joe's early life and the beginning of his coaching career, but often borders on hagiography. More interesting and more modestly written, but not comprehensive, is Paterno's recent autobiography, Joe Paterno (with Bernard Asbell), *Paterno: By the Book* (New York: Random House, 1989). Three other books provide important insights into his coaching. Ken Denlinger, *For the Glory* (New York: St. Martin's Press, 1994), followed a recruiting class from the beginning of their football careers at Penn State to the end.

Jack Newcombe, *Six Days to Saturday: Joe Paterno and Penn State* (New York: Farrar, Straus and Giroux, 1974), studied Joe and his coaching staff for one week as they prepared for a game in 1973. Paterno described his coaching philosophy and techniques in *Joe Paterno, Coaching Winning Football* (Phoenix: Universal Dimensions, Inc., 1983).

Several other books provide information about Paterno and football at Penn State, including Paul Beers, *Profiles in Pennsylvania Sports* (Harrisburg: Stackpole Books, 1975); Frank Bilovsky, *Lion Country: Inside Penn State Football* (West Point, New York: Leisure Press, 1982); Ken Rappoport, *Nittany Lions: A Story of Penn State Football* (The Strode Publishers, 1973); and Ridge Riley, *Road to Number One: A Personal Chronicle of Penn State Football* (Garden City, New York: Doubleday and Company, Inc., 1977).

Former football players at Penn State have written autobiographies which shed light on Paterno. The most noteworthy are Roosevelt Grier, *Rosey: An Autobiography* (Tulsa: Honor Books, 1986); Jeff Hostetler, *One Giant Leap* (New York: G. P. Putnam's Sons, 1991); and Don Kowet, *Franco Harris* (New York: Coward, McCann and Geoghegan, Inc., 1977). Paterno's coaching rival, Barry Switzer, comments on Joe in his autobiography, *Barry Switzer, Bootlegger's Boy* (with Bud Shrake) (New York: William Morrow and Co., 1990). Paterno wrote the introduction for Switzer's book. Other books with information on Paterno are Jack Clary, *Great College Football Coaches* (New York: Gallery Books, 1990); Charles Manz and Henry Sims, *SuperLeadership: Leading Others to Lead Themselves* (New York: Prentice-Hall, 1989); and Loran Smith, *Fifty Years on the Fifty: Orange Bowl Story* (Charlotte, North Carolina: Eastwoods Press, 1983).

Dennis Booher, "Joseph Vincent Paterno, Football Coach: His Involvement with the Pennsylvania State University and American Intercollegiate Football" (Ph.D. dissertation, Pennsylvania State University, 1985), is flawed in its composition but provides a wealth of information and an excellent bibliography. Michael Bezilla, *Penn State: An Illustrated History* (University Park: The Pennsylvania State University, 1985), furnished helpful background about the history of Penn State.

Important articles about Joe include Michael Bezilla, "Penn State's Paterno: The Coach as Fund Raiser," *Fund Raising Management* (April 1995); Kevin Cash, "Joe Paterno: Professor of the Gridiron," *Reader's Digest* (November 1979); Thomas Granger, "Joe Paterno: The Lion in

Autumn," *Saturday Evening Post* (October 1983); William Johnson, "Not Such An Ordinary Joe," *Sports Illustrated* (November 19, 1973); Douglas Looney, " 'There Are a Lot of People Who Think I'm a Phony and Now They Think They Have the Proof,'" *Sports Illustrated* (March 17, 1980); Keith Mano, "Say 'Cheese,' Mom and Pop," *Sports Illustrated* (March 15, 1976); Jack Newcombe, "The Devoutly Unorthodox Ways of Joe Paterno," *Sport* (November 1970); Jack Newcombe, "The Winningest Coach Takes His Lumps," *Life* (October 9, 1970); Pat Putnam, "Saved by the Itch to Switch," *Sports Illustrated* (October 25, 1971); and Rick Reilly, "Not an Ordinary Joe," *Sports Illustrated* (December 22-29, 1986).

Newspapers and Periodicals

Research into newspapers and periodicals proved exceptionally time-consuming, but the results were indispensable. I studied ninety-eight different newspapers and magazines. Those used most comprehensively were the *Altoona Mirror* (1987–1995); *Beaver Stadium Pictorial* (1966–1968, 1987, 1990); *Blue Jug* (Brooklyn Preparatory School, student newspaper, 1942–1946); *Brown Daily Herald* (Brown University, student newspaper, 1946–1950); *Centre Daily Times* (1956–1995); *Daily Collegian* (Pennsylvania State University, student newspaper, 1950, 1959–1989); *Los Angeles Times* (1973, 1987–1991); *New York Times* (1966–1990); *Patriot* (Harrisburg, Pennsylvania, 1966–1988); *Pawtucket Times* (1948–1949); *Pennsylvania Mirror* (1968–1973); *Philadelphia Bulletin* (1966–1980); *Philadelphia Daily News* (1967–1986); *Philadelphia Inquirer* (1968–1994); *Pittsburgh Post-Gazette* (1966–1988); *Pittsburgh Press* (1966–1987); *Providence Journal* (1948–1949); *USA Today* (1982–1989); and the *Washington Post* (1969–1987). In addition, the Sports Information Office at Penn State compiles an annual booklet of football clippings. I used the booklets for the years 1989–1994.

Interviews

Valuable intimate material was gathered in interviews with 137 persons. One-fifth of them were personal interviews; four-fifths were telephone interviews. The "live" interview is most desired, of course, but the telephone approach had one compelling, practical benefit: Since the persons I needed to interview were scattered throughout the country, the travel costs would have been prohibitive. I found the telephone interview to be almost as effective as the live one. A few interviews were brief; some persons were interviewed at length or more than once. Almost all the interviews were tape-recorded. All the taped interviews are in my possession, and, at some future date, I intend to donate them to a historical depository. (See next page.)

~ INTERVIEWS ~

Accorsi, Ernie
Anderson, Dick
Arkwright, George
Arnelle, Jesse
Asbell, Bernard
Bailey, Don
Baker, Dave
Barrett, Richard
Bergstein, Milton
Bermingham, Thomas
Bernstein, Ralph
Bezilla, Mike
Bill, Tom
Blackledge, Todd
Booher, Dennis
Bove, John
Bracken, Ron
Bradley, Tom
Brooks, Booker
Bruce, Earl
Buckhorn, Rita
Burkhart, Chuck
Buttle, Greg
Campbell, Bobby
Carroll, Bill
Cassidy, Joe
Christ, Ron
Cirbus, Craig
Cline, Nancy
Cook, Beano
Coyle, John
Dambra, Nicholas
DeCourcy, Mike
Dickerson, Ron
Didinger, Ray
Doolittle, Bill
Ducatte, Gregg
Ewbank, Weeb
Ferrell, Don
Flynn, Pat
Ganter, Fran
Garban, Steve
Gasparato, Nick
Gearhart, David G.
Giegerich, Diana
(Paterno)
Giffone, Marie

Greeley, Paul ("Bucky")
Green, Arnie
Gresh, Marty
Grosz, Phil
Guido, Joseph
Hall, Galen
Hanlon, John
Hartenstine, Warren
Hintz, Edward
Hufnagel, John
Hundley, William
Hurley, Joseph
Irwin, Mike
Jacks, Al
Jackson, Tom
Jordan, Bryce
Joyner, Dave
Kenepp, Diana
Kiely, Edward
Knizner, Matt
Kozak, Fred
Lenkaitis, Bill
Liske, Pete
Lucas, Richard
Lyon, Bill
Mackesey, Paul
Mangracina, Nicholas
Mastoloni, Frank
McCurdy, Walter
McGinn, Rosemary
McGovern, Tom
Medlar, Chuck
Mittleman, Florence
Moore, John
Morris, John
Murnane, Ed
Murphy, Joseph
O'Bara, Vince
O'Connor, Charles
O'Hora, Elizabeth
("Bets")
O'Hora, Jim
Onkotz, Dennis
Parrillo, Ray
Paster (formerly
Pastuszak), Walter
Paterno, David

Paterno, George
Paterno, Jay
Paterno, Joe
Paterno, Mary Kathryn
Paterno, Scott
Paterno, Sue
Patterson, Robert
Patrick, Frank
Phillips, Robert
Pittman, Charlie
Plunkett, John
Powell, John
Priestley, Robert
Radakovich, Dan
Reilly, James
Rudel, Neil
Sandusky, Jerry
Savignano, Barbara
Scannell, Robert
Schreyer, William
Scott, John
Scotti, Giro
Shaffer, John
Sheffield, Donald
Shiebler, Catherine
Shiebler, George
Smear, Steve
Smith, Ron
Stellino, Vito
Sulkowski, Edward
Swinton, John
Tarman, Jim
Thomas, Joab
Toretti, Sever
Walker, Eric
Walters, Gerard
Weaver, Jim
Weis, Charles
Weller, Harry
White, Jack
White, J. T.
White, Verna
Whiteside, James
Yukelson, David
Yukica, Joe
Zimpfer, Bill

∾ INDEX ∾

A

Aaron, Hank, 163
Abbey, Don, 86
Accorsi, Ernie, assistant sports information
    director at Penn State, 77, 104
ACT *see* American College Testing
Advertisements, 237
Aeneas, 221
    see also Aeneid
Aeneid (Virgil), influence of, 22-25, 228
Allen, Doug, 100
Allocco, Rich, 94
Alston, Debra, 225
Alumni clubs, x, 202
American Cancer Society, 244
American College Football Coaches'
    Association, named Coach of the
    Year by, 72
American College Testing (ACT), 124
American Council on Education, 124
American Football Coaches Association,
    224
    named Coach of the Year by, ix, 133
American Football League, 79
American Legion, 59
Amory, Cleveland, 89
Anderson, Dave, 101
Anderson, Dick, 277, 278, 282, 288, 299,
    303
    fired from Rutgers, 282
Arnelle, Jesse, 51, 54, 57, 128, 191, 192,
    194, 195
Arnold, Everett M. "Busy," college tuition
    paid by, 26, 27
Asbell, Bernard (writer), 165, 229, 254, 266
Asbury, Bill, 128
Ashley, Walker Lee, 117
Associated Press (AP), weekly press poll
    conducted by, 209

Athletics
    exploitation in, 123
    intercollegiate, corruption in, 72
    not an end in itself, 74
    women's, 223-225
Attner, Paul (sportswriter), 282, 284
Auden, W. H. (poet), 96, 97
Axthelm, Pete, 105, 230

B

Bach, Johnny, 86
Bahr, Matt, 188
Bailey, Don, 45, 54, 56
Baker, Dave, sports information director at
    Penn State, 76
Baltimore Colts, 61, 112, 128
Bannon, Bruce, 100, 199
Bauer, Trey, 157
Beaver Stadium, 52, 264, 285, 293, 297
    press box, 273
Bedenk, Joe, 43, 47
Bergen, Candice, 237
Bergstein, Milton, 108, 178, 203
Berkow, Ira, 123
Bermingham, Fr. Thomas, 5, 100, 229,
    281
    encouraged young Joe in intellectual
    endeavors, 21-26
Bernstein, Ralph (sportswriter), 77, 140,
    243, 274, 281
Bezilla, Michael, 41, 250
Bias, Len, death from cocaine, 132
Bicknell, Jack, 152, 164
Big Ten conference, 291-293, 298, 302
Bill, Tom, 275
Bilovsky, Frank (sportswriter), 76-77
Bishop Loughlin (high school), 18
Bishop McDonnel Memorial High School,
    graduation from, 25

Black
  activists, 85
  athletes
    academic programs and, 123
    exploitation of, 193
    graduation rates, 123
    "raped" by system, 124
  coaches, 127-128
  college presidents, threat to leave NCAA,
    126
  high school students, SAT scores, 126, 127
  Penn State football players, 191-197
  special admittance, 196
Black Scholars Program, 195
Blackledge, Todd, 116, 167, 178, 181, 282
Bloom, Allan, 229
Booher, Dennis, 85, 114, 211
Booster clubs, x, 202, 206, 273
  members, Milton Bergstein, 178, 179
Boston, McKinley, 291
Bove, John, 143, 277
Bowl games
  Aloha Bowl, 129
  Blockbuster Bowl, 286, 287, 288
  Cotton Bowl, 82, 180
  Fiesta Bowl, 135, 136, 137, 237, 268, 285
  Florida Citrus Bowl, 293
  Gator Bowl, 70-71, 192, 216
  Liberty Bowl, 108, 113
  on New Year's Day, 209
  Orange Bowl, 71, 77, 82, 83, 84, 85, 131,
    132, 175, 209, 216
  Rose Bowl, 251, 292, 298, 299, 302
  Sugar Bowl, 91, 103, 116, 120, 134, 195,
    230, 293
  Sunkist Fiesta Bowl, 132
  Super Bowl, 286
Bracken, Ron (sportswriter), ix, 171, 194,
    215, 225, 275, 276, 285, 289, 303
Braddock High, 57
Bradley, Bill, 234
Bradley, Tom, 142, 146, 147, 158, 164, 171,
    217, 260, 288, 299
Brady, Kyle, 297
Bratton, Melvin, 134
Brooklyn Preparatory School, 12, 95, 218
  basketball at, 18-19
  Blue Jug (school paper), 15, 17, 18, 20

  football at, 13-15, 17-19
  graduation from, 26, 27
  values of Catholicism and patriotism in,
    12-13
Brooks, Booker, 128, 144, 149, 196, 202,
  243
Brown, Jerome, 134, 135
Brown University *see* Colleges and
  Universities
Brown v. Board of Education, case striking
  down separate but equal doctrine,
  192
Browning, Robert, 96, 228, 229, 240
  quote of, 218
Bruce, Earl, 57, 60, 61, 64, 164
Bruno, John, 137
Bryant, Bear, 66, 80, 81, 103, 104, 110, 117,
  133, 198, 300, 302
Bryce Jordan Center, new athletic arena,
  247, 251
Buckley Amendment, protects student
  records, 272
Burkhart, Chuck, 71, 86, 151, 217
Bush, George, 269, 270, 271, 282
  friendship with, 268
Buttle, Greg, 91, 98, 181, 182, 183, 186,
  189, 201
Butts, Wally, 52

C
Cafiero, Florence *see* Paterno, Florence
Cage, Nicholas, 271
Campaign for Penn State, six-year
  development plan, 246, 247
Campana, Baron, 2
Campbell, Bobby, 71, 72
Cappelletti, John, 94, 100
  Heisman Trophy winner, 98, 162
Caprara, Emil, 57, 58
Cardinal Hayes (high school), 17
Carlson, Jim, 213
Carroll, Bill, 281
Case, Frank, 106
Casey, Robert, 268
Cassidy, Joe, 9
Catholic Church
  Italian family life and, 2
  Paterno family's values and, 6, 26

Catholicism, 12-13, 225-227
Cayette, Carl, 196, 197
Cefalo, Jimmy, 163, 197
CFA *see* College Football Association
Chamberlain, Wilt, 237
Charles, Ray, 237
Chicago Bears, 130, 270
Chirac, Jacques (French prime minister), 268
Christ, Ron (sportswriter), 130, 135, 136, 152, 188, 229, 243, 252, 266, 269, 275, 276
Churchill, Winston, quote on success, 215
Cirbus, Craig, 264
Citizen's Committee on Basic Education (PA), 244
Clark, Bruce, 167
Claster, Jay B., 122
Cline, Nancy (dean of university libraries), 246, 249, 250
Clinger, William F., Jr., 234
Clinton, Bill, 270, 271
The Closing of the American Mind (Bloom), 229
Coaches
  academic rank and, 42
  analogies between General Patton and, 218-219
  Big Ten, 299
  obligations of, 142
  Penn State assistant, 64, 145, 148, 149
  secrecy about player injuries, 277-278
  studied Penn State's defensive schemes, 69
  successful, 141
Coaching
  changed nature of, 263
  Paterno system of, 141-174
Coaching Winning Football (Paterno), 156, 157, 180
Cobbs, Duffy, 131
Coles, Joel, 172
College Football Association (CFA), 210
  leadership in, 211
Colleges and Universities
  Alabama, 61, 80, 103, 104, 105, 110, 116, 131, 133, 183, 195, 198, 209, 291

Allegheny College, honorary doctor of laws degree from, 101
Arkansas, 82
Boston College, 78, 79, 89, 115, 129, 130, 152, 285, 286, 291
Boston University Law School, 39
Bowling Green, 264
Brigham Young, 286
Brown University, 28-32, 34-40, 61, 72, 159, 191
  about, 27
  honorary doctor of laws degree from, 101
  Joe and George's alma mater, 26
Colgate, 29, 34
Colorado, 86
Connecticut, 258
Duke, 211
East Carolina, 276
Fayetteville State University, 126
Florida, 282
Florida State, 70, 71, 192, 216
Fordham University, 13, 25
Georgia, 52
Georgia Tech, 61, 65
Gettysburg College, honorary doctor of humane letters from, 101
Grambling State, 126
Hamline College, 72-73
Harvard, 31, 32, 230
Holy Cross, 31, 35
Houston, 243
Illinois, 42, 298
Indiana University, 62
Iowa, 296
James Madison, 258
Kansas, 71, 72, 84
Kent State, 98
Maryland, 58, 131, 132, 166, 270, 291
Miami, 38, 70, 107, 133, 135, 136, 137, 236, 285, 288, 291
  reputation as outlaw team, 134
Michigan, 42, 85, 239, 293, 297
Michigan State, 65, 298
Minnesota, 291, 296
Missouri, 42, 82, 83, 84
Navy, 70, 197
Nebraska, 100, 129, 183, 291

North Carolina State, 42, 103, 123, 160
Notre Dame, 28, 52, 85, 100, 108, 129,
  131, 182, 183, 209, 211, 264, 286,
  291
Ohio State, 41, 50, 103, 172, 183, 184,
  209, 293, 297, 298
Ohio University, 70, 162
Oklahoma, 52, 91, 131, 132, 209, 212,
  243
Oregon, 61, 298
Pennsylvania, 78
Penn State *see* Penn State
Pittsburgh, 39, 57, 65, 70, 78, 79, 89,
  108, 110, 115, 129, 131, 142, 162,
  183, 185, 238, 291
Princeton, 29, 216
Rutgers, 79, 103, 183, 282, 291, 296
Sorbonne, 230
Southern California, 61, 100, 124, 299
Southern Methodist University, 117,
  119, 206, 243
Stanford, 286, 287, 289
Syracuse, 41, 78, 79, 100, 115, 130, 142,
  154, 172, 185, 264
Temple, 78, 79, 103, 183, 291, 296
Tennessee, 134, 168, 169, 293
Texas, 82, 84, 111, 133, 209
Texas A&M, 111
Tulane, 113
UC-Berkeley, 127
UCLA, 66, 70, 126, 133
Virginia, 211, 258
Washington, 129
West Virginia, 78, 79, 129, 130, 286, 291
Wisconsin, 39, 42, 293
Yale, 39, 61, 62
Collier, Gene, 78
Collins, Kerry, 288, 297, 298
Competition, related to compassion, 222
Condon, Joe, 30
Conference
  attempts to organize, 115
  Big Ten, 292-293
    invitation to join, 291
  Southeastern, 116
Conlan, Shane, 132, 199
Conlin, Bill (sportswriter), 75, 77, 273, 278,
  293

Cook, Beano, 238
Cooper, Mike, 193, 194
Corrigan, Gene, 211
Costas, Bob (television commentator),
  137
Cousy, Bob, 35
Coyle, John, 128, 203, 229, 284
  faculty representative to NCAA, 197, 198
Cuomo, Mario, 234
Czekaj, Edward, 111, 112, 113, 144

D
Dambra, Nicholas (cousin to Joe), 8, 9, 10
Davis, Don, 29
Degrees
  honorary awards, 101
  percentage earned by athletes, 123
Delta Kappa Epsilon, Joe became vice-
  president of, 38
Denlinger, Ken, author of book about Penn
  State's harsh regimen, 154, 156,
  162, 171, 198, 199, 285, 293, 294,
  295, 296, 302
Denver Broncos, 130
Devine, Dan, 83, 89, 108
Dickerson, Ron, 127, 128, 129, 137, 144,
  165, 278
  Grand Experiment and, 201
Didinger, Ray (sportswriter), wrote critical
  series, 241, 242
DiMaggio, Joe, 270
Doolittle, Bill, 32
Downing, Dr. Frank, 203, 204
Drug testing, 179
Ducatte, Gregg, 146, 147, 149, 152
Duckworth, George, Princeton University
  scholar, 23

E
Ebersole, John, 86, 100
Educational Amendment Act (1972), Title
  IX, 223, 224
Edwards, Earl, 43
Edwards, Harry, 127
Eisenhower, Dwight D., 42
Eisenhower, Milton (brother of Dwight),
  42
Empire (Vidal), 229

Engle, Charles A. "Rip," 26, 30, 34, 39, 40,
  43, 48, 52, 53, 57, 59, 60, 62, 64,
  66, 99, 145, 302
  about, 27-29
  accepted coaching position at Penn
    State, 39
  advice on coaching, 50
  believed that academics and athletics
    could coexist, 72
  let Joe direct team at Brown, 32
  as mentor, 49
  offered coaching position at USC, 61
  race relations and, 192
  wing-T formation of, 44, 51, 64
Engle, Sunny (wife of Rip), 48
Engram, Bobby, 284
Ewbank, Weeb, 35, 61, 79

F
Fairbanks, Douglas, Jr., 10, 218
Ferrell, Donald, 127, 129, 194, 201, 214
Fielder, Leslie, 59
Finn, Ed, 30
Flynn, Errol, 10, 218
Football
  bowl games *see* Bowl games
  corruption pervading, 72
  costs of fielding teams, 114
  difficulty combining with academic
    excellence, 198
  drug testing of players, 179
  Engle's concerns about, 50
  many colleges dropped programs in, 112
  new defensive system in, 67-69
  Paterno way, 64-102
  practice, 154, 156-163, 290
    no media at, 275
  professional, Penn Staters on teams of,
    100, 107, 217
  profitable at Penn State, 43, 114, 224
  scholarships, 208
  temptations to cheat in, x
Football Writers Association of America,
    224
  Bear Bryant Award presented by, 133
For the Glory (Denlinger), 154, 293
  about, 294
Ford, Gerald, 270

Freshmen eligibility, 208
Freud, Sigmund, 97
Fund-raising, 120
  needed by Penn State, 121
  the Paternos and, 244-252
Fusina, Chuck, 105, 167

G
Gabel, Paul, 189
Galiffa, Arnold, 31
Ganter, Fran, 143, 147, 148, 149, 150, 151,
  166, 170, 177, 281, 303
Garban, Steve, 179
Garrity, Gregg, 190
Gattuso, Greg, 217
Gearhart, David, 216, 231, 246, 247, 248,
  249, 250, 251
Gelzheiser, Brian, 297, 298
Giftopoulos, Pete, 138, 154
Gingrich, Newt, 271
Gooden, Dwight, 132
Graber, Doug, 296
Grades
  concern over players,' 55-56, 74, 202
    see also Grand Experiment
  Paterno children's, 259
Graduation rates, 211
Graham, Earl "Zev," 13, 14, 17, 18, 26, 95
Graham, Mark, 284
Grand Experiment
  philosophy of football and academic
    excellence, x-xi, 72-75, 105, 110,
    117, 230, 237, 239, 240, 267
  player relations and, 175-212
Greeley, Bucky, 288, 289, 290, 297, 298
Green, Arnie, 34, 37
Green Bay Packers, 89, 132, 192
Gresh, Marty, 31, 217
Grier, Rosey, 191
Griess, Dr. Al, 47
Guman, Mike, 105

H
Halas, George, 286
"Half coverage," system of, 68
Hall, Galen, 53, 282
Hall, Tracy, 186
Ham, Jack, 82, 100, 188

Hanlon, John (sportswriter), 26
Hannameyer, Jack, 58
Harris, Franco, 82, 100, 106
    demoted for tardiness, 180
Harris, Pete (brother of Franco), 106
Hartenstine, Warren, 50, 54, 55, 65
Harter, Dick, 108
Hayes, Woody, 51, 77, 103, 172, 244
Heinz, John, 269
Heisman Trophy, 75, 98, 117, 133, 291
Hemingway, Ernest, 228, 229
Higgins, Bob, retired as Penn State head
    coach, 43
Hintz, Ed, 251
Hoak, Dick, 53
Hodne, Todd, former Penn State player
    arrested on rape charges, 106
Holderman, Kenneth L., 122
Homo Ludens (Huizinga), 232
Hood, Dr. Henry, 100
Hooper, Fr. John, 12, 13, 21
Hostetler, Ron, 213
Hufnagel, John, 88, 194
Huizinga, Johan (Dutch historian), 232
Humphries, Leonard, 294
Hurley, Joe, 19
Hyman, Mervin (sportswriter), 29, 59, 60,
    77, 88, 206, 227

I
Immigration Restriction Act (1924), 2
Irvin, Michael, 134
Irwin, Mike, 65, 159
Isom, Ray, 175
Italians
    immigration patterns of, 1
    virtues of, 2
Ivy League, feelings of castigation by, 206

J
Jacks, Al, 47, 52, 53, 54
Jackson, Kenny, 190, 282
Jackson, Tom, 86
Jenkins, Dan (writer), 209
Jesuits, 12, 219
Joe Paterno: Football My Way (Hyman and
    White), 29, 206, 227
    about, 88-89

"Joe Paterno Day," 95
John (uncle), 8
Johnson, Dr. Joseph, 126
Johnson, Jimmy, 134, 136
Johnson, Magic, 124
Johnson, Mark, 230
Johnson, Paul, 86
Johnson, Pete, 70
Johnson, William, 94
Jordan, Dr. Bryce, 246
    new athletic facility named for, 247
Joyner, Dave, 158, 186
Jubelirer, Robert C., 269

K
Kates, Jim, 70, 85, 86, 193
Keating, Ed, handled Joe's endorsements,
    237
Keating Management Agency, 237
Kennedy, John F., 234, 235
Kennedy, Robert, 245
Kickoff Classic, 129
King, Martin Luther, Jr., 98, 245
Kline, Ernest, (lieutenant governor of
    Pennsylvania), 95
Knizner, Matt, 136, 159, 178
Kozak, Fred, 32, 35
Krein, Darren, 285
Kwalick, Ted, 100, 190

L
Lambert Trophy, 82, 110
Laslavic, Jim, 100
Lauritto, Joseph (father of Nucenza), 2
Lauritto, Nucenza *see* Paterno, Nucenza
Law school
    acceptance into, 39
    thoughts about, 56
Leaders (Nixon), 229
Leahy, Frank, 52
LeBlanc, William, 108
Lenkaitis, Bill, 162
Lewis, Drew, urged Joe to run for
    lieutenant governor, 234-235
Library
    fund-raising for, 245-252
    named after Paternos, 252
Lippincott, Lincoln III, 216

Lippmann, Walter, 96
Liske, Pete, 47, 53, 56
Litke, Jim (sportswriter), 299
Little League, criticism of, 223
Lofton, James, 132
Lombardi, Vince, 17, 66, 286
Looney, Douglas, 107, 108
Loren, Sophia, 271
Los Angeles Raiders, 107
Lucas, Richie, 53, 55, 115
Lyon, Bill (sportswriter), ix, 77, 105, 117,
        196, 214, 218, 220, 230, 232, 235,
        239, 243, 301
    on sameness in Paterno life, 281
Lyons, Charles Jr., 126

M
McClelland, Leo, 107
McCloskey, Mike, 80
McCoy, Ernest, 42, 48, 57, 62, 64, 80
    believed that academics and athletics
            could coexist, 72
    offered head coach position to Joe, 63
    retirement, 111
    time needed to find replacement for,
            113
McCoy, Karl, 106
McCurdy, Walter, 18, 19
McDonald, Quintus, 170, 171
    mother of, 170
McDuffie, O. J., 284, 288, 294
McGinn, Rosemary Smith, 9, 19
McHugh, Roy (sportswriter), 76
Mackesey, Paul, 26, 30
McMillan, Terry, 83
McMullen, Joe, 64
McPherson, Dick, 172
Madden, Barney, 40
Mahoney, Frank, 30, 31, 32
Majors, Johnny, 168, 169
Manderino, James, 268
Mangracina, Nicholas (cousin to Joe), 9, 10
Mann, Charles, 59
Markowitz, Ron, 57, 58
Mascaro, Rose see Paterno, Rose
Mastolini, Frank, 4, 11, 12, 19
Media
    firm stance with, 273-281

    obligation to maintain good relations
            with, 280
    plan to cultivate, 76
    steadfast rules for, 257
    see also Sportswriters
Medlar, Chuck, 51
Miami Dolphins, 275
Michigan Stadium, 264
Millen, Matt, 203
    removed from co-captain position, 106-
            107
Miller, Brian, 284
Mira, George Jr., 134
Mitchell, Lydell, 82, 100
Mitinger, Robert, 57
Montour High School, 64
Moore, Booker, 107
Moore, Lenny, 128, 129, 191
Morale
    bolstering, 184
    maintaining, 183
Morris, Bob, 35
Morris, John, 106, 223
    Penn State sports information director,
            101
Morris, J. T., 272
Mount Nittany, 43
Mount Saint Michael (high school), 17
Multiple Sclerosis Foundation, 244
Murnane, Ed, 9, 11
Murphy, Joseph, 20
Musick, Phil (sportswriter), 76
Myrdal, Gunnar, 96

N
Nantz, Jim, 286
National Basketball Association see NBA
National Collegiate Athletic Association see
        NCAA
National Development Council, 246, 248,
        249, 251, 252
National Football Foundation and Hall of
        Fame, award, 282
National Football League see NFL
NBA, college degrees of players in,
        percentages, 123
NCAA
    black presidents threatened to leave, 126

declined to serve in, 300
Football Rules Committee, attack on, 78
headquarters, 207
image of Penn State compared to other
    members of, 239
John Coyle faculty representative to, 197
penalty given to SMU, 206
petitioned for overtime, 136
Postgraduate Scholarship, 204
Presidents Commission, 123
probation given to Texas A&M, 111
Proposition 48, 123, 124, 126, 127, 128,
    129
Proposition 49B, 124
rules and guidelines, 26, 42, 72, 202,
    204, 207, 210, 282
    recruiting, 165, 169-170, 171, 207
schools on probation, 243
Neinas, Charles, 211
New England Patriots, 89-94, 96, 101, 230
New Jersey Generals, 101
New York, Italian immigrants to, 1-3
New York Giants, 101
New York Jets, 35, 79
New York Yankees, 270
Newcombe, Jack, 86, 159, 160
NFL
    college degrees of players in,
        percentages, 123, 211
    pro scout for observed practice, 162
Nittany Lion Club, 203
Nittany Lion Inn, 165, 273
Nittany Lion Shrine, 42
Nixon, Richard, 82, 83, 84, 96, 229
    proclaimed Texas number-one team, 209
Noble, Brandon, 303

O
Oakland Raiders, 61
O'Bara, Vince, 53, 55, 56
O'Connor, Charles, 13
O'Hora, Bets (wife of Jim), 46, 47, 48, 49,
    50, 51, 52, 57, 58, 59
O'Hora, Jim, 46, 47, 48, 49, 52, 53, 58, 59,
    60, 64, 66, 99
O'Neal, Brian, 288, 293
O'Neil, Ed, 100
O'Neill, Tip, 237

Onkotz, Dennis, 70, 86, 151, 162, 181
Order of Malta, Joe rejected nomination
    into, 226-227
Osborne, Tom, 299
Oswald, John, 95, 113, 115, 121, 195, 204
    named Joe athletic director of Penn
        State, 111, 112
Our Lady of Victory School, 100
Outland Trophy, 134

P
Paffenroth, Dave, 107
Palmer, Arnold, 282
Parents, of recruits, 165-166
Parilli, Babe, 31
Parlavecchio, Chet, 163
Parrillo, Ray (sportswriter), 134, 274, 281,
    286
Parsons, Bob, 193, 194
Pastuszak, Walt, 29, 30
Paterno: By the Book (Paterno and Asbell), 4,
    50
    reviews of, 266-267
Paterno, Angelo (father of Joe), 3, 25, 26,
    36, 39
    admired FDR, 233
    backed athletic careers of sons, 19
    death of, 5, 46
    fought in WWI, 3
    influence of, 214
    passed bar exam, 3
    reaction to son's choice of career, 45
    values of, 4, 5, 6
Paterno, David (son of Joe), 256, 258, 259
    birth of, 254
    skull fracture in, 100-101
Paterno, Diana Lynn (daughter of Joe),
    256, 258
    birth of, 254
Paterno, Florence (sister of Joe), 3, 36
    taken to concerts by Joe, 12
Paterno, Florence Cafiero (mother of Joe),
    3, 4, 26, 40
    backed athletic careers of sons, 19
    influence of, 214
    insistence on family moves, 8
    pride for son, 95
    values of, 5-6

Paterno, Francisco (great-grandfather of Joe), 2
Paterno, Franklin (brother of Joe), death of as baby, 3
Paterno, George (brother of Joe), 3, 4, 5, 8, 14, 15, 31, 36, 49, 91, 100, 107, 110, 132, 143, 215, 236, 253, 260, 261, 302
    about, 11, 12
    attended Brown University, 26, 27
    brother's confidant, 214
    coaching activities, 214
    described brother as Byzantine humanist, 219
    football stats, 34
    high school football and, 17
    injured ribs during game, 32
    television analyst, 214
    thoughts
        on brother's loyalty to Penn State, 252
        on brother's success, 95, 141
        on critics, 242
        on media, 277
    understanding of brother's brusqueness, 186, 188
    watching football practice, 159
Paterno, George "Scott" (son of Joe), 226, 254, 256, 258, 259, 290, 302
    birth of, 254
Paterno, Joseph (Joe)
    abilities to analyze opponents, 151
    accepted by fraternity, 38
    accepted into law school, 39
    affection developed for players, 191
    ancestors of, 1-3
    appearance, 235
    assigned to be quarterback coach, 44
    attack on NCAA by, 78
    awards and honors
        American College Football Coaches' Association, 72
        American Football Coaches Association, ix, 133
        Bear Bryant Award, 133
        Coach of the Year, 80, 122, 133
        honorary degrees, 101
        "Joe Paterno Day," 95

        Kodak Division I-A Coach-of-the-Year, 133
        National Football Foundation and Hall of Fame Distinguished American award, 282
        Pennsylvania Award, 101
        Pennsylvania's most popular personality, 282
        Sports Illustrated, ix
        Sportsman of the Year, 133, 140
    basketball and, 18, 35
    became head football coach at Penn State, ix, 63
    began dating Sue, 59
    Big Ten conference association and, 291-299
    birth of, 3
    book
        about, 29, 88-89
        by, 156, 157
    Byzantine humanist, 219
    career spanned ten presidential administrations, 271
    Catholic Church and, 225-227
    celebrity status, 231
        negative aspects of, 232, 256, 257
    changes during coaching tenure of, 263
    childhood of, 3-11
    children of, 232, 255-260
        not allowed to be interviewed, 238, 257
    children's praise of, 260
    clash with Jackie Sherrill, 110-111
    coaching system of, 141-174
    as college football player, 29-35
    community service involvement, 244
    complex nature of, ix
    concerns, 284
    criticisms by of Miami, 136
    critics of, xi, 105, 108, 152, 185, 186, 188, 189, 237, 238, 239, 240, 241, 242, 243, 272, 295
    decision to make coaching his career, 45
    delegation abilities improved in, 150
    described as the "Voice of Ethics," xi
    devised new defensive system, 67
    distaste for female reporters in locker room, 225

early years, 1-40
earnings, 45, 63, 91, 236
endorsed play-off system, 209
endorsement of traditional moral values
    by, 223
endorsements and advertisements, 237
fans of, 231
father's death and, 46
favorite movie of, 218-219
few friends, 214
first athletic coach to deliver
    commencement address at Penn
    State, 95-98
fund-raising interests, 121, 244-252
game statistics, 17
gifts given to Penn State by, 245, 250
    largest, 252
good grades earned by, 10
graduation from high school, 25
Grand Experiment of, x-xi, 72-75, 105,
    110, 117, 175-212, 230, 237, 239,
    240, 267
grandchildren of, 302
health of, 235
high school football and, 13-15, 17-19
historic heroes of, 218
"I" formation of, 64
insistence on prayer before games, 172
intellectual endeavors of, 21-26, 228
kindness of, 217
leadership abilities in, 14, 20-21, 211
the "legend" in bowl match, 286, 287
leisure activities, 59
library fund-raiser, 245-246, 249, 250,
    251, 252
literature
    avid reader of, 11, 59, 227
    degree in, 227
    discussions with Sue, 60
    Greek classic, benefits of, 24, 27, 222,
        228
    majored in English, 36
    quotes from at commencement
        address, 96
    reading list, 229
lobbied for eastern conference, 78
losing, feelings about, 233
loyalty to assistant coaching staff, 148

loyalty of valued, 220
marriage to Sue, 60
matriculation at Brown University, 26
moved from O'Hora's home, 58
musical interests, 227, 228
named athletic director at Penn State,
    111
named to All-Metropolitan Prep School
    First Team, 18
note-writing obsession, 51, 144
opinionated, 76
opposition to freshmen eligibility, 208
other job offers, 101
    Baltimore Colts, 61, 112
    New England Patriots, 89-94, 230
    Oakland Raiders, 61
    Philadelphia Eagles, 61
    Pittsburgh Steelers, 79
personality, 213-243
politics and, 233-235
practice sample regimen, 156, 161
prejudice encountered, 13, 38
pride encouraged by, 175
private life of, 252-262
problems with assistant coaches, 66
products named after, ix
public image, 230
quest for the best, 102
race relations and, 191-197
racist accusations against, 122-123, 126,
    129, 194
recreation and leisure, 260-262
recruiting and, 49, 57, 88, 91, 162-172,
    202
rejected Patriots' offer, 93, 230
reputation damaged by practice
    incident, 189
retirement plans, 300-303
sameness of, 281
seconded nomination of U.S. president,
    ix
self-blame for problems with team, 109
speaker at Republican National
    Convention, 268
speech before games, 182
sportswriters and, 29, 76-78, 94, 103-
    104, 110, 112, 175, 273-281
successors to, 303

supervised academic progress of players,
    55
tenure granted as full professor, 80, 81,
    227, 235
tragedy in family, 100-101
travels, 261
two-hundredth victory, 264
unorthodox, 69
values, 213-243
views on women, 223
Paterno, Joseph Junior "Jay" (son of Joe),
    226, 256, 257, 259, 290
  birth of, 254
  joined coaching staff, 258
Paterno Libraries Endowment, 245
Paterno, Mary "Kay" Kathryn (daughter of
    Joe), 143, 256, 257, 258, 259, 260
  birth of, 254
Paterno, Nucenza Lauritto (great-
    grandmother of Joe), 2
Paterno, Rose Mascaro (grandmother of
    Joe), 2
Paterno, Sue (wife of Joe), 105, 256, 271,
    300
  about, 59, 253, 253-254
  children, 253-260
  devoted churchgoer, 226
  during David's coma, 100
  fending off annoying calls, 88, 193, 267
  fund-raising, 246, 249, 250
  hospitality of, 165
  marriage, 60
  member of Libraries Development
      Advisory Board, 249
  music interests, 228
  politics and, 234
  private life of, 252-262
  seats received for game, 238
  supported decision to become athletic
      director, 114
  thoughts
    on emotional intensity, 220-221
    on family values, 223
    on Joe's hard work, 144
    on loyalty to Penn State, 252
    on memory for details about past,
        229
    on Patriots' job offer, 92

  on Pittsburgh Steelers offer, 80
  travels, 261
  tutoring of players by, 200
  upset when Penn State charged with
      hypocrisy, 242
Paterno, Vincent (grandfather of Joe), 2
Patrick, Frank, 47, 51, 64, 66, 145, 203
Patterson, Robert, 111, 112, 113
Patton, General George, 218
Patton (motion picture), qualities gleaned
    from, 218, 219
Payton, Walter, 270
Penn State
  Campaign for the Library, 250
  charged with hypocrisy by critics, 242
  controlled access and information, 275
  on cover of Sports Illustrated, 297
  demographics, 194
  fans, 174
  financial ranking, 244-245
  first athletic coach to deliver
      commencement address at, 95-98
  Football Hall of Fame, 263
  football program
    attire of players, 134, 177
    awards
      Academic All-Americans, 204
      All-American team members, 186,
          188, 192, 199
      Hall of Fame Scholar-Athletes,
          204
      Lambert Trophy, 82
      NCAA Postgraduate Scholarships,
          204
    black activists and, 85
    celebrated one hundred years, 140
    early years, 41-63
    game records, 60-61, 65, 70, 71, 72,
        82, 83, 84, 85, 86, 88, 89, 103, 106,
        107, 113, 115, 116, 129, 130, 131,
        138, 160, 162, 183, 215, 236, 264,
        266, 276, 285, 286, 287, 289, 291,
        293, 296, 297, 298
    Grand Experiment, x-xi, 72-75, 105,
        110, 117, 175-212, 230, 237, 239,
        240, 267
    Jay Paterno joined coaching staff of,
        258

Jay Paterno quarterback for, 257
Joe became head coach of, ix, 63
Joe hired as assistant coach of, 39
Joe named as associate coach of, 62
loss of players, 86
mascot: Nittany Lion, 42-43
mediocre season in, 106-110
never cited for major violations, x
never on probation, 243
Paterno way, 64-102
poise and manners encouraged in,
    180
practice in, 154, 156-163
problems with the polls, 83, 84
profitable, 43, 114
quest for first place, 103-140
rankings, 72, 98, 101, 105, 117, 132,
    162, 284, 285, 297
"Team in the Plain Wrapper," 175
tradition of, 177
fund-raising at, 121, 244-252
graduation rates, 211
Greenberg Indoor Sports Complex, 115,
    119, 263
history of, 41-42
Holuba Hall, 263
Joe named athletic director of, 111
joined Big Ten conference, 291-293,
    302
loyalty to, 252
medical staff, 153-154
National Development Council, 246,
    248, 249, 251, 252
players arrested, 284
Quarterback Club, 273
race relations at, 191-197
recruiting territory, 163
summer football camps at, 163
women's athletics at, 224-225
Pennsylvania Library Association, 245
Pennsylvania State College *see* Penn State
Pershing, General John, 3
Phil Donahue (television program), 127
Philadelphia Eagles, 61, 190
Phillips, Robert (Bob), 64, 69, 159, 164,
    168, 185, 277
Pittman, Charlie, 85, 86, 166, 189, 190,
    191, 193, 230

parents of, 165-166
Pittsburgh Steelers, 81, 188
    job offered by, 79
Play-off system
    in baseball and basketball, 210
    publicly endorsed, 209
Plum, Milt, 53
Plunkett, John, 14, 15
Plutarch's Lives (Plutarch), 228
Pohland, Suzanne *see* Paterno, Sue
Polls, weekly press, 209
Pont, John, 61, 62
Pope John XXIII, 226
"Presidential Special," special admittance
    policy, 196
Priestley, Bob, 30, 32, 37
Pro Football Hall of Fame, 188

Q
Quarterbacks, coaching, 44, 53, 54, 157-
    158
Quixote, Don, comparison to, 218

R
Radakovich, Dan, 64, 66, 147, 175, 181,
    182
Rader, Benjamin (sports historian), x, 123
Rados, Tony, 53
Reagan, Ronald, 268
Recruiting, 49, 57, 91, 162-172, 202, 207
    black players, 193
    distress with evils of expressed, 88
    Grand Experiment as cliché, 197
    statistics, 166
Reid, Mike, 86, 100, 199
Reilly, Rick, 122, 228, 231, 235
Renkey, Eric, 294
Renkey, Marilyn (mother of Eric), 294
Reporters, female, 225
Republican National Convention, 268
Ressler, Glenn, 56
Rice, Grantland (sportswriter), 30
Richards, Rev. Elton P., 94, 95
Riley, Ridge
    death of, 99
    Penn State's football chronicler, 78
Robinson, Dave, 192
Robinson, Mark, 117

Robinson, Steve, 133
Rockne, Knute, 28, 182
Rodgers, Pepper, 216
Romano, John, 203
Rooney, Art, 79
Roosevelt, Franklin D., 233
Rose Bowl (stadium), 264
"Rotate coverage," system of, 68
Rowe, Dave, 65
Rowe, Ricky, 272
Royal, Darrell, 82, 111, 133
Rudel, Neil, 136, 138, 238, 266, 285, 303
Rules, value of, 223

S
Sacca, John (brother of Tony), 285, 288
Sacca, Tony, 280, 285, 294
Sadat, Anwar, 245
Sadler, Norm (sportswriter), 29
Saint Agnes High School, 19
Saint Cecilia High School, 17
Saint Edmonds, Catholic grade school
        attended by Joe and George, 9, 10,
        12
Samuels, Bobby, 167, 272
San Francisco 49ers, 286
Sandusky, Jerry, 130, 137, 145, 148, 150,
        160, 281, 282, 303
Santorium, Rick, 271
SAT see Scholastic Aptitude Test
Savignano, Barbara (wife of Ernie), 217
Savignano, Ernie, death of, 217
Sayles, Ricky, 284
Scannell, Dr. Robert, 42, 111, 112, 143,
        228
Schembechler, Bo, 239
Scholarships, 208, 224
Scholastic Aptitude Test (SAT), 123, 126,
        127
Schreyer, William, 144, 226, 227, 231, 246,
        247, 248
Scott, John, 34
Scotti, Giro, 10
Searcy, Jay (writer), 168, 238
Shaffer, John, 184, 190, 278
Shakespeare, William, 229
Shapp, Milton (Governor of Pennsylvania),
        235

offered condolences after loss to
        Alabama, 104
    proclaimed "Joe Paterno Day," 95
Shapp, Mrs. Milton, 95
Sheffield, Donald, 126, 127, 217, 218
Sherrill, Jackie, 108, 110, 111, 267
Shoemaker, Willie, 237
Sims, Henry P., 122, 150
Six Days to Saturday (Newcombe), 159
60 Minutes (television program), 230
Skorupan, John, 100
Smear, Steve, x-xi, 70, 86, 181
Smith, Neal, 86, 186
Smith, Ron, 213, 239
Smith, Willie, 134
Smizik, Bob, 112
Snyder, Bill, 20
Sodality, religious club, 20, 25
Sportswriters, 29, 76-78, 94, 103-104, 110,
        112, 175, 257
    criticism of by fellow Penn State
        instructor, 240
    weekly press poll conducted by, 209
State College High School, son's games for,
        256
State College (PA), 45
    autograph seekers in, 256
    comfort and fondness of, 92
    home of Penn State, 41
    initially disliked, 43
    predominately white, 194
    remote location of, 238, 274
    slower pace of, 261
Steinbeck, John, 96
Stoedefalke, Karl, 113
Stubbs, Daniel, 134
Success, reflections on, 222
Suhey, Ginger (wife of Steve), 43, 45
Suhey, Matt, 105
Suhey, Steve, 43, 45
Suicide, kids committing, 221
Sulkowski, Ed, 44, 47
Sullivan, William H., president of Patriots,
        job offer from, 89-93
SuperLeadership: Leading Others to Lead
        Themselves (Sims), 150
Swinton, John, 272
    persistent critic, 239, 240

Switzer, Barry, 212, 242
  remarks against, 110-111

T
Tarman, Jim, 83, 91, 115, 138, 204, 213,
    214, 215, 219, 267, 301
Testaverde, Vinny, Heisman Trophy
    winner, 133, 137
Thomas, Joab (president of Penn State),
    250
Thompson, Leroy, 168-169, 170, 238
  mother of, 168-169
Thornburgh, Richard (governor of
    Pennsylvania), 119, 245
Toretti, Sever, 47, 48, 51, 170
Truman, Harry, 271
Trump, Donald, 101
Twain, Mark, 229

U
Underwood, John (sportswriter), x, 103
Uniforms, represent tradition, 175
United Press International (UPI), weekly
    press poll conducted by, 209
U.S. Football League, 101

V
Vatican II, 226
Victor Emmanuel II (king of Italy), 2
Vidal, Gore, 229
Vietnam War, 85, 98
Villa, Pancho, 3

W
Waldman, Leo (journalist), 17
Walker, Eric, 42, 64, 80
  demanded strict adherence to NCAA
    rules, 72
  president of Penn State, 62
Walker, Herschel, 124
  Heisman Trophy winner, 117
Wallace, Allen, 167
Walsh, Bill, "genius" coach in bowl game
    match, 286, 287

Walters, Gerard, 30, 32, 35, 36, 37, 38
Warner, Curt, 116, 117, 179, 184
Washburn, Chris, 123
Washington Redskins, 217
Washington, Rocky, 186
Watergate, 96
Weaver, Jim, 145, 261
Weis, Charles, 17
Weller, Dr. Harry, 153, 154, 223
Welsh, George, 64
West Point, 25
White, Bob, success story for Grand
    Experiment, 200
White, Gordon S. (sportswriter), 29, 59, 60,
    77, 206, 227
  about, 88
White, Jack, 53, 55, 65
White, J. T., 59, 61, 64
Whiteside, Dr. James, 153, 178
Wilkinson, Bud, 52
Will, George, 123
Wing-T formation, 44, 51, 64
Winning, obsession with, 222
Witherspoon, Tim, 132
Wofford, Harris, 271
Women, in sports competition, 223
Wooden, John, 133
Woodward, Stanley (sportswriter), 31
World War I, Angelo Paterno's fighting in,
    3
Wriston, Henry Merritt, 27

Y
Young, Philip, expert on Hemingway,
    228
Young, Dr. Charles, 126
Yukelson, Dr. David, 229

Z
Zimpfer, Bill, television announcer for
    Penn State games, 159, 275
Zumberge, Dr. James, 124